D0763935

# JOHN HUS: A BIOGRAPHY

# John Hus

## A BIOGRAPHY

MATTHEW SPINKA

GREENWOOD PRESS, PUBLISHERS
WESTPORT, CONNECTICUT

Library of Congress Cataloging in Publication Data

Spinka, Matthew, 1890-1972.
  John Hus, a biography.

    Reprint of the ed. published by Princeton Uni-
versity Press, Princeton, N. J.
    Bibliography:  p.
    Includes index.
    1.  Hus, Jan, 1369-1415.  2.  Reformation--
Czechoslavakia--Biography.
[BX4917.S69  1978]    284'.3 [B]     78-14366
ISBN 0-313-21050-0

Reprinted with the permission of Princeton University Press

Publication of this book has been aided by the Whitney Darrow
Publication Reserve Fund of Princeton University Press

Reprinted in 1979 by Greenwood Press
A division of Congressional Information Service
88 Post Road West, Westport, Connecticut 06881

Library of Congress Catalog Card Number 78-14366

ISBN 0-313-21050-0

Printed in the United States of America

10 9 8 7 6 5 4 3 2

# Contents

JOHN HUS: A BIOGRAPHY

# Pronunciation of Czech Words

The accent is always on the first syllable.

An acute diacritical mark on a vowel (´) lengthens it; for instance, Tábor=Taabor; on a "u" within a word, the mark of (°) lengthens it; for instance vůz=vooz.

Individual vowels and consonants always possess the same sound, and all are pronounced, none is elided or slurred.

á=as in *bar*

c=as *ts* in *tsar*

ck=each letter pronounced separately=tsk, as in Palacký

č=as *ch* in *church*

dᵛ=as the French *diable*

ě=as if short *i* preceded *e*

g=always hard, as *get*

h=as a decided aspirant: Hus=short *Hoos,* not *Hŭss*

ch=as *ch* in *loch*

i and y=*y* differs from *i* as tending slightly toward the French *u* or German *ü*

j=as *y* in *boy*

ň=as *ni* in *onion,* or Spanish *ñ*

o=as in *or*

ou=as in *soul*

ř=approximately as a combination or *r* with *zh,* but pronounced simultaneously, not separately as two syllables: Dvořák=as Dvo/rzhaak, not Dvor/zhak.

š=as in *sure*

tᵛ=as *t* in *bastion*

v=as a final letter sounds slightly as *f*; there is no *w* in Czech

ž=as *z* in *azure*

## Chapter 1

## Hus' Environment and His
## Predecessors in Reform

𝕴t is generally assumed that the Protestant Reformation began the moment Martin Luther nailed the Ninety-Five Theses on the door of the Castle Church in Wittenberg, on October 31, 1517. In reality, the Reformation was the result, rather than the beginning, of the movement that lasted for some two centuries prior to that date. The demand for reform had begun early in the fourteenth century and was particularly effective during the Conciliar period.[1] Had this movement succeeded permanently instead of only for a few decades, it would have transformed the Roman Church into a constitutional, instead of an absolute, monarchy. The reformatory demands of John Hus should not be treated as a sporadic and isolated effort on the part of a single individual, but as an integral part of an organized movement of which his very judges at the Council of Constance were outstanding representatives. Hus' work, then, may be regarded as a transitional stage from the earlier medieval period to the Reformation, and thus provides a link between the old and the new reform movements.

Even more significant for our times is the fact that the reformatory spirit and accomplishments of the Second Vatican Council link up, largely unconsciously, the program of reform of the fourteenth and fifteenth centuries with our own. Hus' ideas, condemned as heretical by the Council of Constance, are recognizably formative in the reforms adopted by the Vatican Council, although not consciously under his name. Despite the demand that his judicial process be reopened and that he be rehabilitated, such a radical step

[1] For a description of the highlights of this reformatory movement see Matthew Spinka, ed. and transl., *John Hus at the Council of Constance* (New York and London, Columbia University Press, 1965), pp. 3-86.

could hardly be expected at the present time. Nevertheless, the outstanding Catholic scholar of the life and thought of Hus, the Belgian Benedictine Paul de Vooght,[2] has recently summarized his view of the matter by writing:

To a great extent the profound ideas of the Second Vatican Council resemble the great ideas of Hussite thought . . . Today, without reopening the trial, even without speaking of it, the Second Vatican Council entirely condemned Hus' judges, because following John XXIII (Encyclical *Pacem in Terris*) it maintains that nobody can be condemned or executed because of his beliefs and convictions. The martyr of Constance is therefore well avenged; and this took place within and through the Church itself, in which he had never ceased to believe.

Having thus suggested Hus' largely unacknowledged influence in the contemporary world, let us turn our consideration to the political and social conditions of the country of his birth. The ruler of the hereditary lands of Bohemia and Moravia at the time was the most outstanding personality of the age, Charles IV (1316-78). He governed these lands as the king of Bohemia and margrave of Moravia. Educated at the French court by Pierre Roger, who later became Pope Clement VI, Charles earned for his age the proud designation of the "Golden Age." His father was the knight-errant king of Bohemia, John of Luxemburg, who died as he had lived, fighting; his last exploit was his participation in the battle of Crécy (1348). John left the country on the verge of ruin. Charles, upon succeeding him in the royal dignity in 1346 at the age of thirty (although he had begun to administer the country during his father's absence since 1333), added to it the imperial crown in succession to Ludwig the Bavarian. He wrote in his autobiography:

We found that kingdom so abandoned that there was not

---

[2] Paul de Vooght wrote *L'hérésie de Jean Huss* and *Hussiana* (both published in the Publications universitaires de Louvain, 1960). The quotation is from his article, "Jean Huss à l'heure de Vatican II," in *Naše Hlasy*, Toronto, Canada, July 6, 1965.

4

a free castle which was not mortgaged with all the royal possessions. We had no place where to reside, with the exception of city houses, just like any burger. The Prague castle was also abandoned and ruined; for it had been leveled to the ground since the time of King Přemysl.[3]

Having been away from the country from the age of seven (with two exceptions when he administered it), Charles had largely forgotten even the Czech language. But he quickly recovered it, and henceforth identified himself with his people. He showed great sagacity in making Bohemia central to the whole Empire, for only a strong hereditary territorial base could insure him strength in the rest of his domain. His first task, then, was that of rebuilding and beautifying the city of Prague, which became the educational as well as the administrative center of the Empire. Although urged by Cola di Rienzo and Francesco Petrarch to restore to Rome its past glories by making it his residence, Charles gave precedence to Prague. In 1344, before he received the crown, Charles' former tutor, then Pope Clement VI, made Prague an independent archbishopric, separating it from Mainz and subordinating to Prague the bishoprics of Litomyšl in Bohemia and Olomouc in Moravia. The first archbishop was the learned Ernest of Pardubice (1344-64), who was succeeded by John Očko of Vlaším (1364-80). Two years after his accession, on April 7, 1348, Charles signed the charter for the *studium generale,* the Prague University, endowing it with all the privileges enjoyed by the universities of Paris and Bologna. The only university in central Europe, it served the needs of all the lands of the Empire. It ranked with the other three great universities: Paris, Oxford, and Bologna. The number of students in the four faculties was estimated in an old record at 7,000,[4] although this was almost certainly an exaggeration. After other universities had

[3] Císař Karel IV, *Vlastní životopis* (Praha, J. Otto, n.d.), pp. 38-39. See Bede Jarrett, *The Emperor Charles IV* (New York, Sheed & Ward, Inc., 1935), pp. 46-47.
[4] Kamil Krofta, *Čechy do válek husitských* (Praha, Vesmír, 1930), p. 87.

5

been founded in central Europe and students had been drawn to them from Prague, the number of students remaining at Prague University was estimated at 2,000.

Charles also began rebuilding the castle on the heights of the left bank of the river Vltava, Hradčany, modeling it after the Louvre. He then began reconstruction of the St. Vitus Cathedral, rebuilding it in Gothic style, and created there thirty-two fully endowed and two half-endowed prebends. He also erected several churches both in Prague and in the principal cities of the country, such as the splendid church of St. Barbara in Kutná Hora. Because of the great influx of foreigners, he added to the Old Town, which was bounded on the eastern and southern sides by a wall, the New Town just east of it. Prague then comprised three cities; besides the two on the right bank of the river Vltava, there stood on the left bank the Small Side, as well as Hradčany, which was not a self-governing community. Nor were they governed by the same laws: the Old Town was subject to the Nuremberg law, while the Small Side introduced the Magdeburg law. These two sections of Prague were settled mostly by Germans, while the New Town, which soon exceeded its older neighbor in size, was inhabited chiefly by Czechs, from a number of previously existing Czech villages. Gradually, the Old Town was likewise settled by the Czech population. Charles also spanned the two sides of the river by a new stone bridge in place of the old one that had been destroyed by a flood; it stands as strong as ever to this day.

Twenty miles out of Prague, on a high craggy hill, Charles built the strongly fortified Castle of Karlštejn, the depository of the royal and imperial regalia and archives. Finally, he established the Benedictine monastery of Emaus for the preservation and cultivation of the Slavic Glagolitic rite, to which he called monks from Croatia, Bosnia, and Dalmatia.

Charles also completed the extension of his hereditary territories of Bohemia-Moravia by securing Lower Lusatia, directly north of Bohemia (Upper Silesia was already in his possession). He also acquired the Mark of Brandenburg

6

(1375) for his younger son Sigismund, thus penetrating deeply into central Germany. It remained in Czech hands for forty years. On the eastern border he linked his territories, by marriage with Anna of Schweidnitz, with the duchy of Silesia. These acquired lands were predominantly German, although pockets of Slavic population have survived in them to this day. Just before his death, Charles aimed to secure the Polish throne for his son Sigismund. But it went to the Lithuanian Grand Duke Władysław Jagiello (1386). Sigismund married the Hungarian heiress Marie, thus becoming the king of Hungary.

Among Charles' signal accomplishments as emperor was the regulation of the imperial elections by the provisions of the Golden Bull, promulgated in 1356. This document terminated the long-drawn-out struggle with the papacy, which had claimed the right of confirming the choice of the electors. The bull left the election in the hands of seven electors, the three archbishops of the Rhine and four lay princes, without any explicit mention of the papal claims. The elections were to be held in Frankfurt and the coronations in Aachen. This act stabilized the German Holy Roman Empire for over four centuries.

Charles has often been caricatured as the *Pfaffenkaiser*, although this characterization is far from justified. He certainly desired to live in amity with the papacy, but not under its dictates. The power of the Church was great; in Prague alone there existed forty-four parochial churches, twenty-seven chapels, three cathedral chapters, sixteen monasteries, and seven cloisters.[5] Charles' sincere regard for the reformation of the deplorable religious conditions of his lands is seen in his calling to Prague the Augustinian canon Conrad Waldhauser, for many years the court preacher in Vienna. At first, Conrad had but meagre success. In time, however, his censure of loose morals produced a remarkable effect: many rich ladies attending his services in ever-increasing numbers left off wearing the splendid, gold-ornamented dresses and veils; usurers restored unjust and excessive prof-

[5] F. Šmahel, *Jeroným Pražský* (Praha, Svobodné Slovo, 1966), p. 27.

its; and the youth exchanged their frivolous manners for real piety. The attendance increased so greatly that Waldhauser was forced to repeat his sermons outside the sanctuary. The hearers now comprised not only Germans but also Czechs who understood the language.

The success of these reforms naturally produced a reaction among those who felt themselves attacked by the denunciation of their vices, particularly the Dominicans. They now sought to silence the intrepid preacher. They charged him with his non-residence at his parish at Litoměřice (to which he had been appointed, although he actually preached at the church of St. Gall in Prague). At this time such absentee church-holding was very common. The clamor ceased when in 1363 Waldhauser was offered the vacant parsonage at Týn, the principal church of the Old Town. Henceforth his influence reached even wider circles. Nevertheless, his enemies secured his citation to Rome. He was acquitted, but soon after his return died, in December 1369. Nevertheless, as a result of his reform activity, a native reform movement was inaugurated, culminating in the work of John Hus.

Charles' provision regarding the decisive right of the imperial electors to elect the Roman kings has already been mentioned as a part of his religious reform. He exerted himself to the utmost to induce the popes to return from their Avignonese "captivity" to Rome. Despite his Francophile inclinations, he did not want France to dominate the papacy, which should occupy a position above all merely national interests. He visited Rome the second time in 1368 to welcome Pope Urban V upon his return, but was deeply chagrined when the latter decided to go back to Avignon. Charles died on November 29, 1378, shortly before the Great Schism broke out.

He was succeeded by his eldest son, Wenceslas IV (1378-1419), then seventeen years old, as the German and Bohemian king. Although Wenceslas was recognized as such by Pope Urban VI (1378-89), he never managed to get to Rome to be crowned emperor, despite his lukewarm attempts to do so. Wenceslas was a charming, intelligent, and well-educated young prince. But differences in character between him and his father soon appeared. In Bartoš' words:

The son, into whose lap the crown had fallen too soon, had no time to grow into a moral personality. Having been showered with everything he had desired at so early an age, he quickly rid himself of the moral discipline by which his serious father had bound him. Finding himself at once in unrestrained freedom by his father's death, he abandoned himself to pleasures, particularly to hunting, wine, and undoubtedly to women.[6]

His habit of hard drinking may have been brought on by the attempt that was made to poison him in 1393. He surrounded himself with boon-companions, into whose hands fell the major portion of the administration. Wenceslas lacked his father's sagacity and was easily bored with his duties. Hence, he was often grossly negligent as a ruler and acted on momentary impulses and whims instead of on the basis of well-considered policy. The king's companions were chosen largely from the lower gentry and plebeian ranks— a state of affairs that was violently resented by the high nobility, who sought to regain their privileged positions in the conduct of affairs. Under such conditions Wenceslas' authority both at home and abroad in the Empire soon almost collapsed. In 1389 the situation assumed the proportions of an open revolt, followed, in 1393, by a new and even more determined conflict with Archbishop John of Jenštejn (1378-96).

The archbishop had excommunicated the king's chief administrator, Sigismund Huler. In reprisal, the king determined to cut off from the Prague archdiocese the whole western territory, which was to be erected into a new bishopric, endowed with the revenue of the monastery of Kladruby. For that reason the king did not wish the monastery chapter to elect a new abbot in succession to the dy-

---

[6] F. M. Bartoš, *Čechy v době Husově, 1378-1415* (Praha, Jan Laichter, 1947), p. 116.

ing one. The archbishop, however, had instructed the chapter to proceed with the election, and the vicar-general, John of Pomuk,[7] confirmed the new abbot even before the old one was dead. Enraged at this thwarting of his will, Wenceslas seized and tortured four principal officials of the archbishop, among them Nicholas Puchník, later archbishop, and the vicar-general, Pomuk. He suspected a widespread plot against his rule, and wanted to extract confessions to that effect from the four officials. Three of the unfortunate prelates survived the ordeal, but not John of Pomuk. He died under torture, and was afterward thrown into the river Vltava.[8] The story of John's cruel fate grew into a legend of "martyrdom" until in 1729 he was canonized as a saint under the name of John of Nepomuk; he was even proclaimed the patron-saint of the Bohemian nation. Since at the time the archbishop's account of the gruesome affair had not been discovered in the Vatican archives, John of Nepomuk was officially declared to have died in defense of the sacrament of confession, having refused to reveal to the king the supposed confession of Queen Sophia, whose confessor he was supposed to have been (an office he never held!). Moreover, it was declared officially that he had died in 1383, ten years earlier than the real flesh-and-blood John of Pomuk. In 1752 the *Acta* of Archbishop Jenštejn were found in the papal archives, and his description of the historical John of Pomuk became known, but no effort was made either then or since to annul the wholly mistaken canonization. The holy day of the spurious John of Nepomuk is still celebrated.

John of Jenštejn appealed the case to Pope Boniface IX (1389-1404) in his *Acta in curia Romana Iohannis a Genzenstein, Archiepiscopi Pragensis III.*[9] It consists of thirty-seven articles dealing with a long list of financial

---

[7] *Ibid.*, pp. 105-106; also F. M. Bartoš, "Nový dokument z životopisu Jana z Pomuka" in *Jihočeský sborník historický*, XIV (1941) pp. 73-76.

[8] F. M. Bartoš, "Husův král," in *Jihočeský sborník historický*, XIII (1940), p. 9.

[9] The text of this document is published in Paul de Vooght's *Hussiana*, pp. 422-41.

10

losses the archbishop had suffered during Wenceslas' reign. The Pomuk affair in this report is incidental; it is related in a single article. De Vooght, declaring that the *Vita* of Jenštejn, written by a contemporary hagiographer, is untrustworthy, and basing his estimate on the *Acta*, differs widely in his judgment from other writers who depict the archbishop as a saintly ascetic.[10] Although DeVooght's judgment is shared in a milder form and on different grounds by Novotný,[11] it is resolutely opposed by Bartoš, who credits the main assertions of the *Vita* (written by Peter Clarificator, a confidant of the archbishop) as historically trustworthy. Although Bartoš admits Jenštejn's faults, he regards him as a man more sinned against than sinning.[12] It may be added that Jenštejn's request for the king's trial was rejected by the pope, thus forcing the archbishop's resignation (1396).

More serious were Wenceslas' constant embroilments with his great lords and the German princes. Under the leadership of King Sigismund of Hungary and of Margrave Jost of Moravia, the Czech lords seized the king and imprisoned him for several months. Another member of the royal family, John, Duke of Zhořelec, helped to free him. But the struggle flared up again in 1399. During this time Wenceslas gradually changed very much for the worse. He abandoned himself to profligacy, which undermined his health. Moreover, the high nobility seized the principal offices in the land, which they never completely relinquished; they were, therefore, the real rulers of the land. Since the king had

---

[10] *Ibid.*, pp. 411-12: "D'un esprit étroit à la fois faible et obstiné, Jenštejn est sans courage lorsqu'il voit l'ennemi en face. Mais il est retors, je croirais même un peu sournois . . . Ce qui lui fend l'âme, c'est que, précisément, ces richesses n'appartiennent pas à l'Eglise. Ce sont les siennes propres; *propria mea!* Ces deux mots infirment sans rémission le sot bavardage de son biographe sur son soi-disant détachment ascétique. Et, par voie de conséquence, l'autorité de l'insipide *Vita* se trouve ruinée dans une très large mesure."

[11] V. Novotný, *M. Jan Hus, život a dílo*, 2 vols. (Praha, Jan Laichter, 1919-21), I, pp. 51-55.

[12] F. M. Bartoš, "Jan z Jenštejna," in *Světci a kacíři* (Praha, Husova ev. fakulta bohoslovecká, 1949), pp. 62-82.

systematically neglected his duties as the German king, he finally provoked against himself a revolt on the part of the three German archbishops-electors; after ineffectual protests, they deposed him and elected Ruprecht of the Palatinate in his place (1400-10). Since Wenceslas refused to acknowledge the deposition, the Empire now had two heads as the Church had two popes.

After Waldhauser's death, his work was continued by native preachers, the predecessors of Hus. As I have dealt with this subject fairly extensively elsewhere,[13] I shall treat it here only briefly. "The Father in Czech Reform" is John Milič of Kroměříž (c. 1325-1374). Of his earlier life we know practically nothing. He came into view in 1358 as protonotary in the royal chancery. From the documents which passed through his hands, Milič had ample opportunity to learn at first hand of the voracious exactions practiced by both the Church and the state. He thus knew from experience the truth of the popular proverb that the Church sheared its sheep while the state skinned their hides. Accordingly, Milič felt spiritually disturbed, perhaps by Waldhauser's preaching. His dissatisfaction was caused more directly by the avaricious strivings of his fellow-officials for ever more lucrative posts. Moreover, Archbishop Ernest of Pardubice became interested in him and diverted him to an ecclesiastical career.

After five and a half years spent in the chancery, Milič was ordained to priesthood and appointed canon of St. Vitus Cathedral—the highest position, short of prelacy, available to any of the Prague clergy. A year later (1363) he exchanged this post for that of the cathedral sacristan. Yet the inner dissatisfaction soon drove him to a decision which greatly astonished his confrères. That same year he gave up his lucrative prebend in order to live in voluntary poverty, and after a half-year of preparation he devoted himself to preaching and to the wholehearted following of Christ.

---

[13] Matthew Spinka, *John Hus' Concept of the Church* (Princeton, Princeton University Press, 1966), pp. 14-21. See also T. Č. Zelinka, *Husitskou Prahou* (Praha, Blahoslav, 1955), pp. 23-25.

He thus yielded to the exhortation of Jesus, "Whoever of you renounces not all that he has, cannot be my disciple," and to the words of Revelation: "Come out of her, my people, and have no fellowship with her sins. . . ."[14]

At first (1364) Milič preached in the church of St. Nicholas in the Small Side—an important sanctuary, and in its present rebuilt form the most imposing building on the left bank, with the exception only of the St. Vitus Cathedral. Soon, however, he transferred his ministrations to St. Giles in the Old Town. Milič had hitherto spoken in public only in Latin. In order to reach the masses, he had to acquire facility in Czech and German. At first his success was meagre, particularly because of his native Hanák dialect. However, he soon gained wide influence both for his burning zeal in denouncing all superficial religiosity and mere external conformity to the gospel precepts and for his own strictly moral life. At St. Nicholas he had preached in Czech; when he began preaching at St. Giles, he was invited to preach at the Týn church in German and at St. Nicholas of the Old Town in Latin. The crowds filled these churches to overflowing; from 1370 he preached in all these three churches daily. Little wonder that within ten years he created a powerful native movement of reform, with devoted adherents not only among the masses of the common people but also among those of education and power in society. He saw in all deviation from, not to say opposition to, the gospel of Christ, a manifestation of the power of the Antichrist. In 1367 he wrote his *Libellus de Antichristo,* in which, on the basis of Daniel 12:11-12, he asserted that the prince of this world would appear in that year. The nefarious practices of both the Church and the state, which he had come to know so well during his service in the royal chancery and the cathedral ministry, he regarded as the causes of the degeneracy of the times. At first, he had identified the emperor with the Antichrist; on one occasion, when preaching while the emperor was present, Milič

---

[14] Luke 14:33 and Rev. 18:4; also F. M. Bartoš, "Miličovo obrácení" in *Ze zápasů české reformace* (Praha, Kalich, 1959), pp. 7-17.

pointed him out as the Antichrist. Magnanimously, Charles requested the archbishop, Ernest of Pardubice, to pardon the intrepid visionary.

Milič was not content merely to condemn the vices of the day; he undertook the practical work of active reform. As in every large city, there existed in Prague a notorious red-light district called Venice. Inspired by the apocalyptic vision of the heavenly Jerusalem descending from heaven upon the earth,[15] and with the financial aid of many friends, Milič, in 1372, transformed the brothel into a hospice for some two hundred converted prostitutes who determined henceforth to live unsullied lives. Among these new houses he placed a small church, fittingly dedicated to Mary Magdalene. In its vicinity he built a priestly house, in which he intended to educate an "apostolic priesthood" —young men who would carry on the work of reform in his and the Master's spirit.

This was too much for the anti-reform party; Milič was accused by its members of building his Jerusalem on the site of the former brothel. This was, of course, correct, but constituted no crime. Further, he was charged with dressing the women inmates of Jerusalem in what resembled a conventual habit, and with declaring himself their superior. Both charges were undoubtedly true, but not blameworthy or punishable. Jerusalem was not a convent, for its inmates took no vows and were, therefore, free to leave whenever they wished. Milič indeed trained them in piety, but that was the avowed purpose of the institution. He was their "superior" in the sense of being the founder and administrator, as well as the spiritual counselor, of the establishment. Finally, he was accused of imposing penalties for misconduct, but as a priest that was his duty.[16]

In the emphasis on the inward piety, the work of Milič resembles to an astonishing degree the *devotio moderna* of the Netherlands. It must be remembered that the founders

[15] Rev. 21:1-14.
[16] De Vooght, *Jean Huss*, pp. 8-10.

14

of that movement, Gerard Groote and Florentius Radewijns, studied at Prague during Milič's time (Groote in 1360, Radewijns in 1374-78, just when the Jerusalem was destroyed). Bartoš calls Groote "a sort of Dutch counterpart of the Czech Milič."[17] Groote and Milič have in common the revolt against arid scholasticism and forcibly imposed religious uniformity; both stressed the third way—the way of spiritual renewal. Moreover, the women living in the houses of the two enterprises earned their living by sewing, spinning, and copying manuscripts. Thus there exists an obvious connection between the two movements. In Holland and the Rhine Valley, however, the movement assumed a mystical character, which it did not have in Bohemia.[18]

In 1367 Milič went to Rome to clear himself of a previous charge of heresy before the pope, Urban V, whose removal from Avignon he expected. At that time he believed that he could secure papal support for his reform. In this he was disappointed; but the pope cleared him of the charge of heresy. To answer the second charge described above, he went to Avignon. He was there received with honor by Cardinal Grimoaldi and was invited by him to preach at his residence. He wrote a letter to Urban in which he denounced the granting of benefices and provisions, and the imposing of financial exactions by the pope, as the source of all evil—the sign of the advent of the Antichrist. He died before the verdict was reached (August 1374). As already mentioned, his work then suffered swift destruction; under pressure from the prelates, Emperor Charles gave the Jerusalem to the Cistercian Order to be converted into their uni-

17 F. M. Bartoš, "Hus, Lollardism and Devotio moderna in the Fight for a National Bible," in *Communio viatorum* (Praha, Ecumenical Institute of the Comenius Faculty of Protestant Theology, 1960), p. 248. Also Johanna Schreiber, "Devotio moderna in Böhmen," in *Bohemia: Jahrbuch des Collegium Carolinum*, Band 6 (München, Verlag Robert Lerche, 1965), pp. 93-122.

18 Rufus M. Jones, *The Flowering of Mysticism* (New York, The Macmillan Co., 1940); Albert Hyma, *The Christian Renaissance* (New York, The Century Co., 1924); Edward Winter, *Frühumanismus* (Berlin, Akademie Verlag, 1964).

15

versity college. Milič's pupils and friends were subjected to trials and expelled from Prague. The reform movement suffered a temporary repression.

Milič's influence on the later development of the Czech reform movement, however, was permanent. His immediate successor in the work of reform was Matthew of Janov (c. 1355-93), born in the village of Janov in the vicinity of Tábor. His parents were poor. Of his youth we know nothing. After receiving his elementary education, perhaps from the village priest, he was sent to Prague. There he became an enthusiastic disciple of Milič, and this early experience continued to inspire him for life. In 1373 he went to study in Paris, where he spent nine years at the university. Within the usual three years he earned the degree of master of arts. He then devoted the rest of his stay to the study of theology, although he never completed the doctoral course. Henceforth, at home he was known as "the Parisian master." He appears to have gone to Paris in order to secure a rich benefice; in 1377 he actually petitioned for one. The next year he received from the pope a "letter of grace" promising him a lucrative appointment. However, when the Great Schism divided the Church into supporters of the Roman Urban VI and the Avignonese Clement VII, the University of Paris was torn between the two camps. Matthew, an Urbanist, returned home in 1381 when Paris University decided to adhere to Clement VII. With him left many other masters from lands acknowledging the Roman obedience. He made a detour to Rome, where he secured from Urban VI a reservation for a canonry in St. Vitus Cathedral.

Upon reaching Prague, he was actually received among the cathedral clergy as a titular canon, but never secured a prebend there; others with better connections were always preferred. He was befriended by his countryman, the highly esteemed scholastic Vojtěch Raňkův of Ježov (Adalbertus Ranconis de Erecinio), in whose house he lived. This gave him an opportunity for zealous study of the Scriptures and for preaching. Moreover, he received a small income from his post as cathedral preacher and penitentiary. After 1388 his income was augmented by the rent from a small parish in Velká Ves, to which he had been appointed. For a long time he tried in various ways to gain the prebend promised him by the pope, but failed. It was this humiliating disappointment of his career and the poverty—at first forced and later voluntary—that brought about a complete and fundamental change in his whole view of life. We may speak of it as his conversion; he now repented of his former ambition and voluntarily embraced the life of apostolic poverty.[19]

Moreover, he was so devoted to the reading of Scripture "from his youth" that he always carried a copy of it with him wherever he went. "In every uncertainty, in every doubt I found in the Bible and through it an adequate and clear explanation and consolation for my soul; and in every disquietude of mine, persecution or sorrow, I always took refuge in the Bible. . . ." It was this sense of duty to bear witness to the precept of Scripture which prompted him to devote himself wholeheartedly to the continuation of the reform begun by Milič. He preached in the church of St. Nicholas in the Old Town, and castigated the sins not only of the lay leaders high and low, but also of the clergy and the Church generally. As in the case of Milič, the Antichrist ceaselessly haunted Matthew's imagination. Everything opposed to Christ was Antichrist. When Clement VII was elected as a rival to Urban VI, Matthew denounced him as Antichrist. As a salutary means to reform, he advocated frequent, in fact daily, communion on the part of laymen. This was to be no external, superficial or superstitious ceremony, but a participation in the real spiritual presence of Christ. But in October 1388, the synod forbade the practice of daily communion and ordered it to be administered only once a month.

Janov's emphasis on the teaching of Christ and his apostles obviously required that the Bible be translated into the vernacular for the use of lay Christians unversed

19 Rudolf Schenk, transl., *M. Matěj z Janova, Výbor z pravidel starého a nového zákona* (Praha, Blahoslav, 1954) , pp. 40-41.

in Latin. The demand went hand in hand with reform movements elsewhere. Wyclif had inspired the translation of the Scriptures into English; Matthew also gave much time, undoubtedly along with others, to the translation of the Bible into the Czech version of the so-called first redaction. The German translation in a magnificently ornamented copy had been made by an unknown scholar for the Prague patrician Rotlev, who donated it to King Wenceslas on the occasion of the latter's marriage. It is also known that the king's sister, Anne, when she married the English king Richard II (1381), took along with her a Latin lectionary with a Czech and German translation.

As was to be expected, the reforms advocated by Janov and his adherents were resolutely opposed by the anti-reform clergy. Janov, Jacob of Kaplice, and the priest Adam had been cited before the inquisitor, and at a solemn assembly of the synod in October 1389 were forced to recant publicly. Janov had to withdraw his opposition to the near-idolatrous veneration of images, relics, and the saints, and particularly to cease his advocacy of frequent communion.[20] Even so, he was forbidden to preach for half a year, to hear confessions, and to administer the eucharist anywhere but in his church.

Under these conditions, he turned to his literary work with increased zeal. His greatest work, written in 1388-92, was the five-volume *Regulae veteris et novi testamenti*,[21] a collection of treatises, not all his own, dealing with a large variety of urgently needed reforms. The ideas are drawn from Augustine, Ambrose, Jerome, Bernard of Clairvaux,

[20] The text is in F. Palacký, ed., *Documenta Mag. Joannis Hus* (Praha, F. Tempsky, 1869), pp. 699-702.

[21] V. Kybal, ed., *Matthew of Janov's Regulae veteris et novi testamenti*, 4 vols. (Innsbruck, Wagner University Press, 1908-13); O. Odložilík, ed., *ibid.*, v (Praha, Česká akademie věd a umění, 1926); and Schenk, *Výbor z pravidel starého a nového zákona, passim*; V. Novotný, *Náboženské hnutí české v 14. a 15. století* (Praha, J. Otto, n.d.), pp. 146 ff. See also O. Odložilík, "The Chapel of Bethlehem in Prague," in *Studien zur ältesten Geschichte Osteuropas* (Graz-Köln, Hermann Böhlaus Nachf., 1956), I, pp. 125-41. Odložilík argues that Janov wrote the preamble to the charter of the Bethlehem Chapel (p. 141).

Thomas Aquinas, Hugo of St. Victor, Marsiglio of Padua, William of Ockham, Joachim de Fiore, Spiritual Franciscans, Henry Suso, and of course his beloved teacher, Milič of Kroměříž. Nevertheless, Matthew is essentially biblical; he himself asserts that he expresses his thought predominantly and preferably in biblical, rather than in his own, language.[22] He aims primarily at the exposition of Scriptural truths. He addresses himself chiefly to the correction of abuses existing in the contemporary Church. He bewails too great a devotion to images, verging on adoration, the overemphasis on external ritualism and ceremonialism of the church services, and the prominence accorded to the legal over the biblical and theological studies. Current religious life, he says, consists largely of an effort to gain indulgences, of pilgrimages, and of a belief in miracles. He denounces corruption in high ecclesiastical offices, especially simony and venality. He castigates and even rejects monasticism and demands its abolition. His reform program may be summarized by defining it as restitutionalism—the return by the Church to the teaching and practice of the gospel of Christ and His apostles as exhibited in the primitive Church. He contrasts the Church militant with the true spiritual Church—the body of Christ. The latter is composed exclusively of the predestinate of whom Christ alone is the head. The Church militant comprises both the predestinate and the foreknown [praesciti].[23]

Among the devoted disciples of both Milič and Matthew was a squire, Thomas of Štítné (1331-1409).[24] He studied at the University of Prague where he was among the earliest Czech students. During these early years he heard Waldhauser and became particularly attracted by Milič, whom he gratefully remembered in his later writings. When about forty years old, he began to write in Czech, thus becoming

22 Schenk, Výbor, p. 34.
23 For a much fuller treatment of Matthew's teaching, see Spinka, John Hus' Concept of the Church, pp. 16-21.
24 Count Francis Lützow, A History of Bohemian Literature (London, W. Heineman, 1909), pp. 63-79; also Bartoš, Čechy v době Husově, pp. 254-55.

19

the earliest writer in the vernacular. This placed him in a separate category; his works were intended not for the learned, but at first for the education of his own children and later for the wider circle of readers not versed in Latin. About 1381, when he became a widower, he moved to Prague. Toward the end of his life he shared the home of his daughter, Agnes, who had built herself a house in the immediate vicinity of the Bethlehem Chapel, which both of them actively supported. Thomas was thus in close touch with the preachers of the Chapel, particularly Hus, although neither of them mentions the fact. After Thomas' death, Agnes gathered in her home pious single women friends, who thus formed an unofficial devotional circle. The house has recently been renovated in keeping with the restored Bethlehem Chapel. It was for these devout women that Hus wrote one of his most beautiful devotional books, entitled *Dcerka* [*The Daughter*]. Thomas' chief contribution to the reform movement was the fact that he wrote in Czech. Not only did he prove thereby that the vernacular was capable of expressing all that a religious writer needs to say; he was also a pioneer in the further development of the language for literary purposes. Hus found in Štítný an inspiring predecessor when, in exile, he himself wrote numerous Czech works for the common people.

It was this native reform program that Hus inherited and successfully developed to maximum effectiveness. There is no evidence that he personally knew Matthew of Janov, who died when Hus was a student at the university. Nevertheless, he was well acquainted with the aims of the antecedent reform movement and was consciously committed to them. It would be unthinkable that those responsible for the appointment of the rector and preacher of the Bethlehem Chapel—the place especially dedicated to the continuation of the work and ideals of the native reform— would have elected Hus had he not been known to be a sincere adherent of it. Thus his knowledge of the native reform preceded his acquaintance with the teachings of Wyclif.

Chapter II

The Young Hus

When in about the year 1372 or 1373 a son was
born to a poor family in the hamlet of Husinec in southern
Bohemia, no one dreamed that the infant would become
the country's most famous son and that his renown would
be worldwide. How could anyone have anticipated the infant's remarkable career? Would it not have been more natural to ask skeptically, even jeeringly, "Can any good thing
come out of Husinec" (i.e., Goosetown)? Even the date of
his birth had not been recorded (for there existed then no
parish registers); it has been thought to have been between
1369 and 1373. It is dubious whether Hus himself knew the
date. F. M. Bartoš' latest hypothesis rests on the year of Hus'
ordination and the beginning of his preaching at the Bethlehem Chapel. A Prague preacher and Hus' contemporary,
Johlin of Vodňany, declared in his *Postil* of 1403-05, on the
basis of various biblical examples, that a preacher should
not undertake his office until he is thirty years old. Bartoš
surmises that Johlin aimed his remark at several young
preachers who then began their ministry, especially at Hus,
whose activity at Bethlehem jeopardized Johlin's own ministry at the nearby Zderaz church. Since Johlin's pronouncement was penned in 1403, Bartoš calculated that Hus had received ordination at the age of 28-29. Hence, he was born in c.
1372-73, most likely in 1372.[1] Bartoš warns, however, against
regarding this deduction as a documentarily ascertained
proof. For the year of Hus' ordination is not absolutely
certain, since his name appears in the matriculation book
only as receiving, in 1400, the deacon's orders. It is assumed
that he received the priestly ordination during the next

[1] F. M. Bartoš, "Kde se narodil M. J. Hus," *Kostnické Jiskry* (Praha,
1965), No. 2; also the same author's "O rok narození Husova," *Listy
filologické* (Praha, 1965), pp. 117-18.

term at the archiepiscopal castle of Roudnice; for that reason the Prague register does not contain his name.

Of his parents and family we know equally little. Of his father, Michael, aside from his name, we know nothing. Hus does, however, mention his mother in one of the treatises written in exile.[2] He gratefully recalls that she had taught him to say, "Amen, may God grant it." Perhaps, as in many families, it was the mother's influence which exerted the greatest and most beneficial power over his life; the father receded into the background. It was she who wanted her son to become a priest and thus obtain a respected and secure living. Thus she gave her son the initial impulse toward the priestly career. In her limited circumstances, she regarded priesthood as the highest calling in which her son could engage.

Besides his parents, we know definitely that Hus had a brother, whether older or younger does not appear. The brother predeceased him, for Hus became guardian of his two nephews. About three weeks before his death he wrote to his pupil, Martin of Volyně, asking him to place the nephews as apprentices to some artisan, for he feared that they might not be properly qualified for a spiritual office.[3]

Hus' birthplace, Husinec, was a hamlet on the river Blanice in southern Bohemia. The house (No. 36), traditionally recognized as the one where he was born, still stands, although only the room of his birth was saved from fire in 1859.[4] The most important building in the village was the stone-built church, to which a wooden bell-tower was attached. Husinec had no resident priest, for it belonged to the parish of Vlachovo Březí, whose priest, Oldřich of Březí, son of the local patrician, occasionally came to minis-

---

[2] K. J. Erben, ed., *Výklad modlitby Páně*, in *Mistra Jana Husi Sebrané spisy české*, 3 vols. (Praha, B. Tempský, 1865), I, p. 358.

[3] Václav Novotný, ed., *M. Jana Husi Korespondence a dokumenty* (Praha, Komise pro vydávání pramenů náboženského hnutí českého 1920), No. 132.

[4] Ferd. Hrejsa, *Rodný domek Mistra Jana Husi* (Praha, 1916), *passim*. For a recent description of Vlachovo Březí, Husinec, and Prachatice, see Ladislav Stehlík, *Země zamyšlená*, 2 vols. (Praha, Československý spisovatel), I, pp. 231-47.

ter in the filial church. It was undoubtedly he who christened John. One wonders if, along with the infant's mother, the priest did not have a part in encouraging John toward the priesthood. Another fortunate circumstance for young John was the fact that the hamlet was hardly an hour's distance from the important commercial center of Prachatice.

This was a walled town, the transfer-point for the goods brought by horse from Bavaria and transshipped from there to Prague and other cities. The chief import was salt, but many other products such as wines, spices, and fine cloth were traded in as well. In turn, the local products—wheat, butter, cheese, fish, and liquor—were exported abroad. Each week from one hundred to a thousand horse-drawn wagons brought these goods. Merchants, mostly Germans, came to town in large numbers, so that Prachatice became one of the wealthiest commercial centers in southern Bohemia.[5] The oldest church in Prachatice was consecrated to Sts. Peter and Paul; there was also St. Jacob's church, the seat of the dean, which is still standing.

When John was five or six years old, the Great Schism between the rival popes Urban VI and Clement VII rent the Church. Although it is highly questionable whether the small village of Husinec learned of the catastrophic event, it was later to exercise its baneful influence upon Hus as well as upon the whole Western world. At the time of its occurrence, however, the small boy remained undisturbed in tending the flock of his parents' geese or perhaps a goat or two.

The first step taken by young John in his life career was his entry, in 1385, when he was perhaps thirteen years old, into the Prachatice elementary school.[6] A tradition, recorded by a Hussite priest, George Heremita, more than a century later—but which might have been in circulation much earlier—recounts that John's mother, accompanying

[5] A. Jirásek, "Z mladých let Husových," *Kostnické Jiskry*, 1953, Nos. 26-27. It is a reprint from *Sebrané spisy Jiráskovy* (Praha, 1931), XXIV, pp. 356-61.

[6] F. M. Bartoš, "Hus jako student and profesor Karlovy university," *Vojtiškův sborník* (Praha, 1958), pp. 9-10.

her son to the Prachatice school, carried a loaf of bread as a present to the schoolmaster. She knelt down seven times on the way to pray for him.[7] Although the details sound hagiographical, this tradition at least affords a confirmation of the hypothesis that Hus gained the rudiments of learning at Prachatice, and that his mother's determination to see her son become a priest was the chief factor in the decisive step thus taken.

The elementary schools, sometimes called trivial for they dealt with the three basic subjects of grammar, rhetoric, and logic, aimed to acquaint the beginner mainly with the art of reading Latin. For this purpose the elementary textbook of the Roman grammarian Aelius Donatus was used. Young Hus probably learned his letters and the elementary Latin in the parochial school in Prachatice. The other two subjects of the trivium he probably studied, at least more fully, in Prague, where he then followed them with the quadrivium, which comprised arithmetic, music, geometry, and astronomy.

He supported himself during this period as a singer in one of the Prachatice churches. This was the usual way of earning a living resorted to by poor students everywhere. One later recollection of his youth most likely belongs to the Prachatice period, although Hus does not definitely localize it. He confesses that on the Day of the Innocents he took part in the customary mummery permitted at Christmas to the choir boys. One of them dressed up as a bishop. Seated backward on a she-ass, and accompanied by roistering companions, he entered a church. There the whole troop

---

[7] F. M. Bartoš, ed., *Jiří Heremita, Život, to jest šlechetné obcování ctného svatého kněze, Mistra Jana Husi, kazatele českého* (Praha, Ministerstvo informací, 1947). Almost identical with Heremita's is the account of a hymn of V. Vodňanský of Radkov (d. 1564) in honor of Hus. It recounts briefly his whole life, particularly his childhood. It appears as No. CX in the *Kancionál* published by priest John Soběslavský; the hymns in it were composed mostly from the year 1569 onward. The portrait of Hus inserted immediately before Vodňanský's hymn is dated 1541. My copy lacks the title-page, so that I cannot verify the provenience of the *Kancionál*.

performed a blasphemous imitation of the mass.[8] Bartoš argues that this scandalous play occurred while Hus was still in Prachatice, for the Prague Archbishop, John of Jenštejn, had in 1386 forbidden all such frivolities.[9] In the far-off provincial town such reprehensible practices survived longer.

It was either in Prachatice or in Prague that the young Hus learned German. That he knew the language was un-equivocally asserted when, during the last day of his life, he is said to have addressed in German the crowd which accompanied him to the place of execution.[10]

From Prachatice young John, when he was eighteen years old (1390), went to the University of Prague for further studies. Emperor Charles IV clearly stated in the founding charter that he was establishing the university "to the end that the loyal inhabitants of our land, incessantly hungering after the fruits of learning, may not be constrained to beg alms but may find set out in our realm a table of refreshment."[11] Since it was the only centrally located university, placed in the capital city of the Empire, it attracted foreigners as well as the natives. It thus became from the beginning the university of the Holy Roman Empire rather than strictly a school for Charles' hereditary lands. All members, masters and students alike, received the privilege of autonomy. In the end there were organized four "nations"—the Saxon, the Bavarian, the Polish and the Czech. The Saxon "nation" included students from northern Germany, Scandinavia, and Finland; the Bavarian,

---

[8] Erben, *Výklad modlitby Páně*, in *Mistra Jana Husi Sebrané spisy české*, I, p. 302.

[9] F. M. Bartoš, "Ze studentských let M. J. Husa," *Křesťanská Revue* (Praha, 1956), p. 25.

[10] Richental's *Chronicle*, in Louise R. Loomis, transl., *The Council of Constance; the Unification of the Church*, ed. by John H. Mundy and Kennerly M. Woody (New York and London, Columbia University Press, 1961), p. 134.

[11] Otakar Odložilík, *The Caroline University, 1348-1948* (Praha, 1948), p. 14. See also Kamil Krofta, *Listy z náboženských dějin českých* (Praha, Historický klub, 1936), pp. 48 ff.

25

from southern Germany, Austria, the Tyrol, Switzerland, the Rhine valley, and the Netherlands; the Polish from Poland, Prussia, Lithuania, Silesia, Lusatia, Meissen, and Thuringia; the Czech, from Bohemia, Moravia, Slovakia, Hungary, Croatia, Transylvania, and even Spain. This was patterned after the University of Paris, where members were divided into the four nations of Gaul, Picardy, Normandy, and England. But there the ratio of predominance was the reverse of that in Prague; three were native and only one was foreign. At Prague, the foreigners were granted three votes in the university decisions, while the Czechs had only one. Charles had granted this unequal advantage to the foreigners in order to attract them and to retain them in Prague when the Austrian Duke Rudolf, his ambitious son-in-law, opened his own university at Vienna in 1365. An influx of additional foreign masters and students occurred when, in 1381, many German adherents of the Roman pope, Urban VI, left Paris, because France had acknowledged the jurisdiction of the Avignonese pope Clement VII. Nevertheless, because new German universities had been established in Heidelberg, Erfurt and Cologne, while in 1364 a Polish university had been founded in Cracow, the German element at Prague was steadily declining (although they still retained the three votes in university decisions).

The students of the four nations enjoyed even a certain degree of university rule. Each nation elected two procurators from among their numbers, who represented them before the outside world and had a place on the rector's inner council. Furthermore, each nation appointed one of its representatives for the half-yearly election of the rector. Their influence was extended even to the appointment of professorial positions and of the examining committees.

Because of the decrease of the German element and the corresponding rise in the number of Czechs, who by that time had almost one-half of the membership, a conflict between the two groups broke out in 1381. The Czechs demanded a larger share of the professorships, which alone were endowed by some ecclesiastical benefice and thus provided a form of remuneration. The Czechs gained the arrangement that they were to be assigned every second, rather than fourth, professorship as these became vacant. In this manner they secured rough justice in view of their numbers; the university was on the way to becoming a national, rather than an international, institution. The Czechs naturally stressed the national, the other nations the international, character of the university.

With its masters, doctors, and students, the university was a world set apart from the city and the kingdom. Its members were distinguished from ordinary citizens by their academic dress. The university was an independent institution governed by its own laws adopted freely at its own meetings. Its members were thus subject to their own jurisdictional rules, which were usually milder than those prevailing among the citizens. This tended to result in conflicts between the "gown and town." The university was ruled by a rector elected for one of the two annual semesters. Each faculty also had its own dean, elected likewise for a half-yearly term. In 1372 the faculty of law separated from the other three faculties—of arts, medicine, and theology—and constituted itself an independent unit. Among the remaining three, the faculty of theology was regarded as the highest. Some of the law and theology students were older men, who already held a benefice or were in some occupation.

Such was the situation when Hus matriculated at the university. This step already made him one of the few of his contemporaries in Prachatice, not to speak of Husinec, who succeeded in reaching the university level in their educational careers. The other two who preceded him five years earlier were Christian and Nicholas of Prachatice. Perhaps it was Christian who took Hus to the capital city and helped him to find a livelihood there. But since he himself had just obtained the master's degree, he could do but little for his protégé; yet Hus considered and spoke of him for the rest of his life as his benefactor. In Prague John was matriculated, as was the custom, as John of Husinec, since the name John was borne by a great many students and

27

others. Later he shortened the name to John Hus. He continued to earn his bread as a choir-boy in a church. He speaks of this period of his life with good-natured humor, although as a time of hunger and want. "When I was a hungry young student, I used to make a spoon out of bread to eat peas with it until I consumed the spoon as well."[12] In another place he remarks, "When I was a student and sang vigils with others, we sang them rapidly just to get the job done quickly; for others took the pay for it and merely harrowed and plowed with us."[13] Probably the reference here is to some priest in charge of the choir-boys, who cheated them of their share of the earnings. From a later anonymous source we learn that Hus paid the supervisor of the student hospice where he resided a heller a day for the beer served him noon and evening. No wonder he still entertained his mother's and his own ardent wish to become a priest; for as he frankly owned: "When I was a young student, I confess to have entertained an evil desire, for I had thought to become a priest quickly in order to secure a good livelihood and dress well and to be held in esteem of man."[14] For a poor student, however, it was not easy to reach such a goal; had he been the son of rich parents, he would have had no particular difficulty in obtaining a benefice. But clerics were so numerous that many of them could secure no appointment at all, particularly when many prelates and beneficed priests were pluralists. It is estimated that there were some twelve hundred priests in Prague, not counting the monks and nuns; thus every twenty-fifth or thirtieth inhabitant of Prague belonged to the clerical order. Bishops often refused to ordain a candidate unless he was already assured of placement. For a poor aspirant who had neither money nor the favor of someone possessing an advowson, the one promising way remain-

---

[12] Erben, *Výklad desatera*, in *Sebrané spisy*, I, p. 278.

[13] Erben, *Výklad modlitby Páně*, in *ibid.*, I, p. 307.

[14] Hus "On Simony," in Matthew Spinka, transl., *Advocates of Reform, Library of Christian Classics* (Philadelphia, The Westminster Press, 1953), XIV, p. 239.

ing open to him was a higher academic degree. This was the way chosen by Hus.

John was a good student, driven by his ambition to zeal and diligence in his studies. Later in life he tells us: "From the earliest time of my studies I have set up for myself the rule that whenever I discern a sounder opinion in any matter whatsoever, I gladly and humbly abandon the earlier one. For I know that those things I have learned are but the least in comparison with what I do not know."[15]

As a student in the faculty of arts Hus was, first of all, introduced to "the Philosopher"—Aristotle. The works of Aristotle formed the basis of, and general preparation for, all higher learning, not only in philosophy, but in logic, psychology, cosmogony, dialectics, rhetoric, and poetics. These works were usually studied in handbooks and commentaries. The most favored of such surveys was that of Peter Hispanus. The student had to learn the subject matter by rote; his memory was usually aided by versified summaries. Since there was no paper, and parchment was too expensive, the method of memorizing the subject matter was the only one open to an average student. Moreover, the aim of medieval education was not to make the student think independently but to assimilate all the accumulated wisdom of the past. Besides the two lectures a day which the student was supposed to attend, he also availed himself of the private instruction given by his teacher in the latter's room. The learning process was thus largely, if not entirely, sponge-like. All striving for new knowledge was suspect, as possibly leading to heresy. Education aimed at training men's minds in dialectical sharpness and in making fine distinctions, although the subject matter remained static. The dogmatic substructure remained unchanged, no matter how keen the logical dissection of it. The process was characterized by astounding mental gymnastics, but was barren of intellectual or religious insight. It signified the last gasp

[15] John Hus, "De Trinitate," in *Historia et monumenta Joannis Hus atque Hieronymi Pragensis, confessorum Christi,* 2 vols. (Norimberg, 1715) , I, p. 131.

of scholasticism. After mastering Latin, the pupil read Virgil and Cato in order to acquire appropriate quotations with which to enrich, or at least to embroider, his own compositions. The more quotations he could cite in his public disputations, the better his performance.

This kind of training led to the practice of copying from unacknowledged sources without any sense of plagiarism as we moderns would dub the process. The names of prominent thinkers were sometimes mentioned by way of bolstering the writer's own thought, even though the works quoted were not specifically named.

After this educational regime had been sustained by him for three years, the pupil received the degree of bachelor. The majority of students reached this point between ages eighteen and twenty-two. The "promotions" for the degree took place four times a year under the supervision of the dean of the faculty. The ceremony was attended by at least four university masters, one from each of the faculties. The *baccalariandus* had to choose a master who would serve as his "promoter"—usually the master under whom he had taken the major part of his work. This master introduced him to the faculty and declared that the candidate had studied all the required books and was properly prepared for the examination. The dean then received from the candidate a promise that he would pay 20 *grossi* into the faculty treasury and at the determination—as the ceremony was called—he would give the presiding master and the promoter a pair of gloves each. He further promised to hear three times a week lectures in the prescribed gown and receive the tonsure of a cleric. Thereupon, the *baccalariandus* was given a *questio* which he had to "determine." Finally, the promoter delivered a *recommendatio* in which he granted the candidate the bachelor's degree.[16]

The promotion of masters was similar to that of bachelors. Their promotion ceremony was called "inception," and was

16 A. Schmidtová, ed., *Johannes Hus, Positiones, recommendationes, sermones* (Praha, Státní pedagogické nakladatelství, 1958), pp. 220-21.

conducted once a year, usually in February, under the presidency of the chancellor or his substitute. The candidate was presented to the faculty by some master and was requested to solve a *questio*. Upon a successful defense of his exposition of the question, the promoter delivered a *recommendatio*. Thereupon the *magisteriandus* received a silken master's biretta, a pair of gloves, a golden ring, an open book, and—for good measure—a kiss. After taking an oath that he would deliver lectures at the Prague University and no other for the next two years, that he would attend all regular disputations, observe all regulations, and work for the good of the university, he was declared a master of arts.[17]

This completed the academic part of the proceedings. They were followed by a banquet which the newly promoted bachelor or master had to hold at his own expense for those directly participating in the affair. If the candidate could not bear the financial cost, he could delay his promotion for a time. He then was known as a licentiate; he could deliver the required lectures, but had no voting privileges. Hus, despite his poverty, took his degrees of bachelor and master. Hence it would appear that he had scraped together enough money to defray the considerable expense.

If the master desired to continue his studies in some professional faculty, such as the highest, the theological, his principal studies consisted of a thorough instruction in two books—the Bible and Peter Lombard's *Four Books of Sentences*. This preparatory period was then followed by the study of systematic theology and other subjects. The chief interpreter of the Bible, acknowledged in all theological faculties, was the French Hebraist, Nicholas of Lyra. Peter Lombard, a twelfth-century Italian by birth, was archbishop of Paris.

The first definitely dated event in Hus' life occurs in the year 1393, when he received his bachelor of arts degree. At this ceremony Hus' promoter was John of Mýto. His

17 *Ibid.*, p. 221.

speech[18] was based on Aristotle's remark that "by suffering one gains health." He gave the term "suffering" the sense of "working," and as such applied it to Hus. The candidate "had at first a sickly mind," but later by strenuous work he secured "a healthy mind." This phrasing does not mean that Hus' mind was at first unhealthy, but uninstructed; by diligent study he gained knowledge. "Therefore our candidate for the bachelor's degree, avoiding laziness, gained health by work and exercise and thus improved his health by work." The promoter further pedantically remarks that Hus improved his mind's health by spurning, or at the expense of, the health of his body; this does not surprise us, knowing what a struggle he had to gain a precarious living. But it appears that Hus, prior to the promotion, was physically ill. The promoter specifically asserts that "our candidate for the bachelor's degree had no care for his body in preference for his mind; for the weakness of his body which he suffered, as it was evident during the examination, had been caused by his constant study." The promoter could not deny himself the pleasure of punning on the candidate's name, Hus [i.e., goose], by remarking that, like the bird, Hus possesses wings by which "he lifts himself to higher spheres." Furthermore, he even made reference to the fact that the feast of St. Martin, at which geese were traditionally eaten, was not far off, and that for the very evening of the examination Hus has prepared "a good feast" for the examiners, presumably a goose.

That same year, 1393, the "year of grace," which had been celebrated in Rome three years before, was held in Prague. Hus heard John Štěkna preach indulgences in an eloquent sermon at Vyšehrad. He was so moved by it that he undertook to make the required confession and pilgrimage to the other three designated churches. He gave the confessor his last four *grossi*—whereupon he was forced to add to his pious acts an involuntary, but very real, fast!

[18] B. Havránek et al., eds., *Výbor z české literatury husitské doby*, 2 vols. (Praha, Československá akademie věd, 1963), I, pp. 75-80.

Having received his bachelor of arts degree, Hus promptly matriculated for further study toward the master's degree. As witnessed by John of Mýto's speech, Hus was a gifted student, although not actually first among his fellow-graduates. Nevertheless, he ranked sixth among twenty-two. During this period his living conditions were immeasurably improved; he became a servant in the largest of the university colleges, the *Carolinum*. For this service he received the free use of a room and all his meals. The servants kept the professors' rooms in order, and occasionally helped in the kitchen. There were comfortable rooms for twelve professors with provision for their servants. Hus' room was still shown to visitors two centuries later. It bore the inscription: *Haec olim haereseos damnati falso-Hussi, dum vixit, parva taberna fuit.*[19] The college, founded by Charles IV in 1366, was transferred in 1383 by King Wenceslas to the commodious house located near the monastery of St. Gall, formerly owned by the mint-master, Martin Rotlev. He had been guilty of drawing a weapon upon his opponent during his trial and, as a penalty, had to surrender his house to the king. In the new quarters the *Carolinum* exceeded in size and splendid equipment the older colleges—the All Saints' and the Wenceslas College. All the more important functions, promotions, and general assemblies were held there. Its imposing aula and the Gothic bay-windows have been preserved to this day, and the whole building has been restored to its original form. Later, in 1405, the College of the Nation (*Collegium nationis*) was founded, to serve the Czech masters exclusively. They also received a mansion, "At the Black Rose" on the Moat, and a hospice for their poor students in the Chapel of *Corpus Christi* in New Town. All this clearly reflects the large growth of the Czech element at the university.

Professor Bartoš has raised the interesting question as to which of the five professors at the time chose Hus as his famulus. His "educated guess" at first fell on Christian of

19 Quoted in Bartoš, "Hus jako student . . . ," p. 12, n. 9.

Prachatice; but later he settled on Master Stephen of Kolín.[20] In support of this theory he cites the high honor in which Hus held Stephen, and particularly the fact that when Stephen resigned the pulpit in the Bethlehem Chapel, he strongly supported Hus' appointment to that very important post. The choice of Hus as famulus bore testimony to his high academic standing and the moral deportment expected of the servant. In the *Carolinum*, his living problems were adequately solved. He was also placed in the very center of the university life, which position afforded him an admirable opportunity to become personally acquainted with the Czech academic leaders, to listen to their intimate conversation at the table, and thus to secure knowledge of the current movements of thought which he could not have obtained in any other way. He was being trained for the important role he played later.

Among the other Czech masters teaching at the time in the university was Nicholas of Litomyšl, who as rector (1386) had made the *Carolinum* the principal college of the whole university. Along with him, Nicholas of Rakovník, Peter of Znojmo, Přibyslav of Jesenice, and perhaps John of Mýto, constituted the faculty. Stephen of Kolín and Stanislav of Znojmo soon joined this group. In January 1396, at the earliest "inception" after completing his studies, Hus passed his master's examinations under Stanislav of Znojmo and three others, and received his degree. After the two years of teaching required of all newly created masters, Hus became a full teaching member of the arts faculty [*magister regens*]. Ever after he remembered Stanislav most gratefully. His fellow-student and later member of the theological faculty, Stephen Páleč, wrote of Hus that he had regarded Stanislav as having no equal under the sun.[21] Hus himself testified, even at the time when Stanislav became his principal enemy, that he had learned from his

[20] For the first reference, see Bartoš, *Co víme o Husovi nového* (Praha, Pokrok, 1946), p. 26; the second, Bartoš, "Ze studentských let M. J. Husa," p. 28. Also an excellent monograph of O. Odložilík, *M. Štěpán z Kolína* (Praha, Společnost Husova musea, 1924).

[21] Jan Sedlák, ed., *Pálčův Antihus* in *Hlídka* (Brno, 1910).

lessons and school lectures many good things.[22] He particularly praised him as an excellent logician.

In a sermon commemorating Emperor Charles, which Hus delivered as rector of the university on November 29, 1409,[23] he also recalled eight renowned Czech members of the faculty of theology and others. He mentioned the Dominican Nicholas of Jevíčko, known as Biceps, whom he characterized as the keenest arguer; Vojtěch Raňkův of Ježov, who had been rector of the University of Paris in 1355, as a brilliant orator; Nicholas of Litomyšl as the most perspicacious counselor; Stephen of Kolín as the most ardent patriot; John Štěkna as an eloquent preacher; and Peter of Stupno as the most accomplished musician and most fervent preacher.[24] Even so, he omitted the first of them in point of time, Jenek of Prague, one of the original six members of the newly founded *Carolinum*, who in 1383-84 held the rectorate. He was comparatively rich and left his property to the *natio Bohemica*. It consisted of an excellent library and of a house he had bought in 1400 for the purpose of establishing a new college—that of the Czech nation.[25]

Among the most prominent German masters, Henry Totting of Oyta, Conrad Soltaw, Albert of Engelschalk, and Matthew of Cracow were preeminent. In fact, they enjoyed European fame. They were, for the most part, adherents of the late Occamist nominalism,[26] which was no longer decidedly anti-papal and theologically suspect, but verged toward conservatism; nevertheless, it generally bore a strong conciliarist character. At first sight, this conservatism is diffi-

---

22 John Hus, *Contra Stanislaum*, in *Historia et monumenta*, I, p. 331.
23 "Confirmate corda vestra," based on James 5:8, in *Historia et monumenta*, II, pp. 62-66.
24 *Ibid.*, p. 65. See also Evžen Stein, ed. and transl., *M. J. Hus jako universitní rektor a profesor* (Praha, Jan Laichter, 1948), p. 85.
25 F. M. Bartoš, "M. Jenek z Prahy, rektor university Karlovy," in *Jihočeský sborník historický*, IX (1936), pp. 41-43.
26 Jan Sedlák, "Filosofické spory v době Husově," in *Studie a texty k náboženským dějinám českým* (Olomouc, 1914-15), II, pp. 197-224. Also Spinka, *John Hus at the Council of Constance*, pp. 8-11; and F. M. Bartoš, "Hus' Commentary on the Sentences of Peter Lombard," in *Communio viatorum* (Praha, 1960), No. 2.

cult to harmonize with the undoubted progressive tendency which it manifested later in philosophy and cultural history. When we recall, however, that Ockham affirmed that the truths of religion could neither be rationally ascertained nor denied, but must be accepted by faith, it becomes clear that in its logical consequences the movement strongly tended toward emancipation of science on the one hand and submission to the Church's authority on the other. Science was released from subjection to theology by affirming the "two separate truths"—those of science and theology. As such, it led to the rise of the modern empirical scientific view.

Beside nominalism, moderate Thomism was represented by the Dominican masters who had left Paris in 1381, when the university there adhered to the Avignonese pope. They transferred the main center of their studies to Prague, where they henceforth exerted the strongest influence in the faculty of theology. Among them, Henry Bitterfeld was the most outstanding. Hus, however, does not seem to have been greatly influenced by them, although he held Thomas Aquinas in high honor, and did not hesitate to criticize some other of their representatives. He frequently criticized the Franciscan great lights such as Duns Scotus and even Bonaventura, but spoke approvingly—strange to say —of William of Ockham.

The Czech masters under whom Hus had studied were to a greater or less degree adherents of the philosophical realism of the English reformer John Wyclif (1330-84). To the fashionable nominalism which held that reality existed only in concrete objects and not in the preexistent idea, he opposed his Platonic realism derived largely from St. Augustine.[27] This view asserted the existence of divine ideas em-

[27] G. H. W. Parker, *The Morning Star, Wycliffe and the Dawn of the Reformation* (Grand Rapids, Mich., Wm. B. Eerdmans Publishing Company, 1965), pp. 19-57; also Matthew Spinka, *Hus' Concept of the Church* (Princeton, Princeton University Press, 1966), pp. 22-36. The terminology to a modern seems confusing and even unintelligible, because the terms in modern philosophy are the reverse of the medieval: realism is a form of modern idealism, while nominalism is modern phenomenalism-materialism. Thus we are actually dealing with the same problems the medieval thinkers wrestled with.

bodied in things, which were but their carriers. This abstract concept actually proved favorable to reform, both in doctrine and practice. In reality, it was the desire to reform the notorious vices of the Church which prompted the changes in doctrine. Stanislav of Znojmo and Stephen Páleč were preeminent among the Czech philosophical realists. Sedlák declares of Stanislav's *De universalibus* (c. 1396) that "no other philosophical work [of the period] can compare with it."[28] In fact, for a long time it was regarded as Wyclif's own work. At first, prior to 1401, only the philosophical works of Wyclif had been known at the university. This is clearly stated by Hus in his reply to the Englishman John Stokes, who, during his stay in Prague in 1411, declared that whoever read Wyclif's writings must necessarily become a heretic. Hus retorted that "I and the members of our university have had and have read those books for more than twenty years" without becoming heretics. This would indicate the year 1390, when Hus had entered the university as a student.[29] Likewise at the Council of Constance Hus declared that he had read and admired Wyclif "twelve years ago, before Wyclif's theological books had been [available] in Bohemia, and his books dealing with arts had pleased me much, and I had known nothing but what was good of his life."[30] He is here referring to the year 1403, when apparently he was not yet fully acquainted with Wyclif's theological works, although as a matter of fact some of them were already available in the country.

Hus thus acknowledges his high regard for Wyclif's philosophical realism, in which he was thoroughly grounded by Stanislav, his preeminent teacher. Nevertheless, he did not accept either the philosophy or theology of Wyclif in all particulars, but always tested critically how far they affected essential orthodoxy. This was his invariable practice throughout his life, even when he did not specifically state it to be. Others, for instance Procopius of Plzeň, were even

---

28 J. Sedlák, *Studie a texty k náboženským dějinám českým*, 2 vols. (Olomouc, Matice Cyrilomethodějská, 1913-19) , II, p. 202.

29 *Historia et monumenta*, I, p. 135.

30 Spinka, *John Hus at the Council of Constance*, p. 174.

more "conservative," and came close to defending the moderate realism of Aquinas.[31] Later, Hus was accused of being a thoroughgoing Wyclifite both in philosophy and in theology; in particular, it was alleged that he professed remanentism, i.e., the doctrine that the bread and wine in the eucharist remain unchanged. Hus, however, branded the charge as false, and wrote in 1411 to Pope John XXIII:

I faithfully, truthfully, and steadfastly assert that I have been wrongfully indicted at the Apostolic See by the enemies of the truth. They have without doubt falsely indicted me and are indicting me that I have taught the people that in the sacrament of the altar the material substance of the bread remains. Falsely, that when the host is elevated, it is the body of Christ, and when it is laid down, then it is not. . . .[32]

Hus began teaching at the faculty of arts in 1396; during the first two years he lectured on Aristotle, with whose writings he became thoroughly acquainted. Thereafter, he devoted his lectures to Wyclif's philosophical works. He copied for his own use four of Wyclif's treatises (1398), namely: *De individuatione temporis, De ideis, De materia et forma,* and *De universalibus*. The last manuscript was carried away by the invading and looting Swedish armies during the Thirty Years' War, and is still kept at Stockholm. In the margins Hus had penned approving remarks, such as "Wyclif, Wyclif, you will unsettle many a man's mind";[33] or "What you have now read is worth a gulden . . ."; and "May God grant Wyclif the kingdom of heaven."

Besides lecturing, Hus had the duty of regularly conducting disputations in order to train his pupils to use the matter learned theoretically in speeches and the art of speaking. During his long academic career he wrote many theses

[31] R. Říčan and M. Flegl, eds., *Husův sborník* (Praha, Komenského ev. fakulta bohoslovecká, 1966), p. 27.

[32] Spinka, *John Hus at the Council of Constance*, p. 147.

[33] Spinka, *John Hus' Concept of the Church*, p. 36. In Czech the passage reads: "O Viklef, Viklef, nejednomu ty hlavu zvykleš!" The word "zvykleš" is an obvious play on Wyclif's name.

for disputations conducted by his students, or in his own disputations with his colleagues.

After two years of teaching, Hus was chosen for the first time as promoter of his earliest students to the grade of bachelor. The first among them, John Černý of Řečice, presented himself for examination in the Spring of 1398. The next year Hus officiated in the same capacity in the promotion of Matthew Knín and Matthew of Újezd; in 1400 of Wenceslas of Sušice and Martin Kunšov of Prague; in 1401 of Nicholas of Jisterbnice and of Nicholas of Miličín; and in 1402 of Martin of Križovec in Croatia. There were other promotions later which need not be mentioned here. It may be assumed that they all, with the exception of Martin Kunšov, had lived with Hus, as was then the custom. Altogether, throughout his academic career, Hus served as promoter at eleven bachelors' determinations and two masters' inceptions.[34]

On March 14, 1402, Hus was named rector and preacher of the Bethlehem Chapel; the appointment was in the power of the three oldest Czech professors. He thereby obtained for the first time an adequate income. To be sure, it was lower than that of the *Carolinum* professors, not to speak of the canons of the All Saints. But he never sought any other appointment. In this respect he was the first among the rectors of the chapel who, by giving his full time (aside from his academic duties) to his preaching office, fulfilled the original intention of the founders. He continued the practice of gathering about himself and of teaching students whom he later promoted to the rank of bachelor or master. From these beginnings there developed later the student hospice called Nazareth, not only in the immediate vicinity of Bethlehem but likewise under Hus' direct supervision and instruction. The needs of the students were provided as to both their residence and their living. The num-

---

34 Schmidtová, *Positiones*, p. 221. These Latin promotion speeches were published in a critical edition by Dr. Schmidtová. Previously, they were published by B. Ryba, *Nový Hus* (Praha, Jednota českých filologů, 1948) ; some also in Czech translation in Stein, *Hus co universitní rektor*.

ber of students whom he promoted during his academic career totaled at least thirty-six.[35] Whenever Hus presented a student for examination, he undertook the additional work of preparing him for the ordeal. As a rule, such students remained his staunch friends. Only one, Nicholas of Stojčín, appeared at Constance among his enemies.

As has already been mentioned, we possess at present thirteen of Hus' promotional speeches. They reveal him in a very different light from that of the zealous reformer and strict, almost ascetic, moralist. In some of these speeches he reveals himself as a jovial and genial young master whose puckish, though harmless, humor on a few occasions borders on the facetious. We can quote only a few such examples of this sort (in fact, there are only a few such cases to be found) : the most notable such "determination" occurred in the case of Wenceslas of Sušice, delivered on the text "A humble man shines with virtues," and was held on January 22, 1400.[36] It bears witness to the obvious intimacy of the teacher with his pupil which allowed the promoter to allude to the student's handsome personal appearance, his fine apparel, and his short stature, apparently without giving offence. Twice Hus alludes to Wenceslas' *enamorata*, Grace. Nevertheless, the promoter continues, "the possession of the most noble figure indicates the full treasure of the most noble virtue and knowledge."[37] Thereupon, Hus exhorts Wenceslas to flee the bodily pleasures for the intellectual and spiritual attainments. In the promotion of Martin Kunšov of Prague Hus again exhibits the easy and pleasing demeanor indicative of his intimate relations with his pupils. His theme is—of all things!—"the cuckoo, the clearest-singing bird"; it is based perhaps on the pseudo-Ovid's poem on a similar theme.[38] He frankly brands Martin as a somnolent and sluggish youth [*libeter dormit et est piger*], for some strange reason thought to be like a

[35] Bartoš, "Hus jako student . . . ," p. 17.
[36] Ryba, *Nový Hus*, pp. 1-10.
[37] Schmidtová, *Positiones*, pp. 51-54.
[38] "Conflictus Veris et Hiemis," Migne, *Patrologia latina*, Car. I, 271.

cuckoo. Much of the speech likewise deals with Martin's physical appearance. Nevertheless, Hus adds that the candidate has studied the six years (perhaps that is the reason for calling him "sluggish") and has deported himself with virtue and honesty.[39]

In only one of the hitherto recognized promotions is Hus "incepting" a master of arts; the candidate is not, however, designated by name.[40] Hus' other promotion speeches delivered prior to 1402 were those made at the promotion of Wenceslas of Police (1402) and Martin of Križovec (1402). These speeches as a whole may be characterized as distinctly academic; as a rule, they are based on some classical theme and are replete with poetic quotations, apt popular proverbs, and exhortations to virtue as well as warnings against sloth. The danger of too much indulgence in sleep is particularly stressed and tells us something of Hus' own habits. These speeches came to light only gradually and recently, and give us a glimpse not only of Hus' intimate contact with his students, but of his distinctly humanistic culture—an aspect of his personality which otherwise would have remained unknown.

Particularly noteworthy is Professor Bartoš' discovery of Hus' lectures on the handbook, *Summa naturalium*, ascribed to Albertus Magnus.[41] This treatise comprises all that was then known of natural sciences, including anthropology. It was based on the Aristotelian concept of physical sciences, particularly the movement of cosmic matter, of the earthly and heavenly spheres with the ten-storied heaven, of the sun, moon and the stars, of meteors, the atmosphere, storms, rain and sea; of optics; and finally of the origin and decline of the life process of creatures, both animal and vegetable. He concludes with the human soul. None of this physico-scientific material of Hus' academic lectures is to be found in the extant corpus of his published works; it is,

---

[39] Schmidtová, *Positiones*, pp. 56-61; Ryba, *Nový Hus*, pp. 28-36.

[40] Ryba, *Nový Hus*, pp. 37-43.

[41] F. M. Bartoš, "Hus na filosofické fakultě Karlovy university," in *Kostnické Jiskry* (1950), Nos. 26-27.

for that reason, especially noteworthy. The very fact that Hus held and taught these views and subjects indicates his interest in humanistic studies of the period and forms a transition from the medieval to the "modern" age. Neverthless, Hus shared with his age such bizarre notions as that the "Jewish land is situated in the middle of the world."[42]

Another interesting glimpse of Hus' academic teaching is afforded in a *lusus pennae*—a letter purporting to be a communication of King Wenceslas to Pope Boniface IX (August 1402).[43] The king besought the pope to put an end to the disorders and spoliations the land had then suffered. He threatened that he was losing patience with the situation and would not bear opposition to his will much longer. If disorders did not stop, he would punish the offenders even by drowning them in the river. This is in reality an example of Hus' own lessons on rhetoric, which included the art of letter writing. No other example of such model writing from his pen has survived except this curious sample. It was certainly not written by Wenceslas, for he was at the time a prisoner of his foster-brother, Sigismund. In the passage stating that those opposing the king's will would be drowned in Vltava there is an obvious reference to John of Pomuk, whose corpse had been thrown into the river in 1393.

There exists a possibility, although a rather problematical one, that in 1398, when Hus became a full member of the faculty of arts, he was included in the brilliant entourage of King Wenceslas in the journey to Rheims for the purpose of visiting the French King Charles VI. The meeting of the two kings was intended for consultation about the ending of the papal schism. That such an honor should have been bestowed on the young master of arts of the university is indeed remarkable. Hus never explicitly mentions the journey, unless we are to understand his remarks about the Rhine women wearing wigs and the bishops encased

[42] J. B. Jeschke, ed., *Mistr Jan Hus, Postilla* (Praha, Komenského ev. fakulta bohoslovecká, 1952), p. 433.
[43] Published for the first time in Novotný, *Korespondence*, pp. 3-4.

in steel accoutrements of war as referring to this journey.[44] But there is no mention that Hus ever went all the way to Rheims; he must have returned along with others before the final goal was reached.

From 1398 to 1402 Hus lived in the King Wenceslas College. He was a frequent visitor to the parsonage of his friend, Christian of Prachatice, who was pastor of the Church of St. Michael near the Týn square. It was in this intimate circle of friends that many burning issues of the day, such as Wyclif's doctrine of remanence, were discussed. At Constance, charges of Hus' adherence to remanence, dredged afresh after so many years from these discussions, were brought against him. After he was ordained to priesthood, most likely early in June 1400, he often preached, during the first year thereafter, in the pulpit of St. Michael Church as well as in other churches.

One of the principal puzzles of this period of Hus' academic life is the radical and fundamental change which occurred in his religious life prior to his ordination. He himself confesses that he had lived the life of a gay master, proud of his position, sharing freely in the pastimes of his colleagues. Even when he later, like Augustine in his *Confessions*, bemoaned these "youthful follies," he could think of no worse peccadilloes than that of taking pride in his academic costume and his apparel generally. The costume, by the way, was prescribed by the university regulations. He also deeply regretted wasting his time in playing chess. For some reason, chess was regarded as not a fit game for students or faculty. At Oxford, it was forbidden as a "noxious, inordinate and unhonest game." In his "Last Will," left in the hands of Martin of Volyně upon his departure for Constance, he wrote: "You know that—alas!—before I became priest, I had often and gladly played chess, had wasted time, and by that play had frequently unhappily provoked to anger both myself and others."[45] Hus also con-

[44] Kamil Krofta, *Francie a české hnutí náboženské* (Praha, Melantrich, n.d.) , pp. 29-30; F. M. Bartoš, *Po stopách pozůstalosti Husově* (Praha, Společnost Husova musea, 1939) , pp. 20-22.
[45] Spinka, *John Hus at the Council of Constance*, pp. 95-96.

fesses penitently: "Alas! I, too, had gowns and robes with wings, and hood with white fur; for they [the university authorities] had so hemmed in the master's degree with their regulations that no one could obtain the degree unless he possessed such apparel."[46]

More serious is his reference to the theological and other university masters, himself included, when he wrote in his treatise on *Simony* that the doctors of the Holy Scriptures

out of fear run away from the truth and have not courage to defend it. I myself—alas—had been one of them, for I did not dare to preach the truth plainly and openly. Why are we like that? Solely because some of us are timid, fearing the loss of worldly favor and praise, and others of us fear the loss of benefices; for we fear to be held in contempt by the people for the truth's sake, and to suffer bodily pain.[47]

Furthermore, he bewails his former lack of courage in denouncing an obvious evil.

And I, alas, had been afraid to speak out against a manifest evil, unwisely fearing legal proceedings, excommunication, condemnation and death. But the gracious Savior, Who admitted me to His office, now gives me courage not to fear, but to speak the truth against everyone who opposes the law of Jesus Christ.[48]

And, writing about the feasts held by the masters, he confesses:

Among them, alas! the goose [i.e., Hus] was plucked of virtue by the devil; for it also often fed excessively at those feasts and thus devoured the labor of the poor.[49]

Commenting on James' exhortation not to prefer the rich to the poor,[50] he writes:

[46] John Hus, *On Simony*, in Matthew Spinka, transl. *Advocates of Reform, Library of Christian Classics* (Philadelphia, The Westminster Press, 1953), XIV, p. 262.
[47] *Ibid.*, p. 263.
[48] Erben, *Výklad desatera*, in *Sebrané spisy*, I, p. 246.
[49] *Ibid.*, I, p. 124.
[50] James 2:1-9.

Woe is me! How many times I have transgressed this Holy Word, rising and doffing my hood, or bowing to a rich man but not a poor one, and rather sending a *gross* to the rich man for drinking than giving a heller to the poor! I trust, however, our merciful Jesus, our Savior, that He will forgive me and preserve me henceforth from such conduct.[51]

He repents also of the opinions formerly held contrary to the Word of God: "I confess that before I had known better, I grieved for the death of a good man or grumbled about bad weather, as if I could do better than the Almighty God."[52] And finally, he bewails conscious or unconscious hypocrisy prevalent among the university masters. "I myself have intently listened to their lectures in schools when they discoursed about humility, patience, poverty, courage, and other virtues. They praised them so persuasively and eloquently that no one could do it better, as if they themselves practiced them all. But later I found none of those virtues actually among them, for they were full of pride, avarice, impatience, and cowardice."[53]

What, then, changed this fun-loving, genial, and ambitious young man, who sought a life of ease and plenty in the priestly career which alone could provide him with these good things in life? What made him an earnest reformer, whose devotion to truth finally led him to the stake? What caused him to change so radically that toward the end of his life he exclaimed, "Cursed be he who abandons truth for a slice of bread"? What induced this man to demand that all priests and prelates live in apostolic poverty by being satisfied with the food and clothing provided by their priestly office and give the rest to the poor? One seeks in vain for an explicit statement of the cause. The only time he gave a hint of what happened was when he confessed, shortly before his death, in one of the Czech treatises: "When I was young in years and reason, I too belonged to that foolish sect. But when the Lord gave me knowledge of

[51] *Postilla*, p. 420.
[52] *Výklad desatera*, I, p. 227.
[53] *On Simony*, p. 262.

the Scriptures, I discarded from my foolish mind that kind of stupid fun-making."[54] It was the profound study of Scripture, therefore, which, by ruling his life and thought, transformed him into the earnest Reformer he became during the rest of his life. "Search the Scriptures!"[55] was then forever on his lips. It is worth noting that in all the instances of his former life cited above, it was the knowledge of Scripture which produced the radical change in his conduct. In attempting to solve the mystery of his "conversion" we can only suggest that just as the lives of his predecessors —Milič of Kroměříž and Matthew of Janov—from whom he had learned the principle of biblical primacy, were transformed by the study of the Scriptures, so too was Hus' life changed.

[54] Erben, *Výklad modlitby Páně*, in *Sebrané spisy*, I, p. 302.
[55] John 5:39.

## Chapter III

# The Early Years of
# Hus' Ministry

The Bethlehem Chapel, of which Hus became rector and preacher on March 14, 1402, was founded in 1391 by two followers of Milič of Kroměříž: Wenceslas Kříž, usually referred to as "the Merchant," and John of Milheim, one of the royal councilors and brother-in-law of the future archbishop of Prague, Zbyněk. Kříž, a member of the wealthy mercantile class, donated for this purpose the garden behind his house. In fact, one of the walls was built on what remained of Kříž's malt-house, while a corner of the building encroached on the cemetery of the adjoining parish church of Sts. Philip and James. The cellar of the malt-house was reserved by the owner for his further use and formed part of the chapel structure. Because all available space was thus used, the ground plan of the building formed an irregular quadrangle, divided by a massive pillar. In fact, even the well which was located within this space continued to serve the needs of the neighborhood. The chapel was a large, extremely plain structure, capable of accommodating some 3,000 hearers.[1] The upper structure of the malt-house was converted into the living quarters of the rector and his assistant. Because the chapel encroached on the property of the adjoining church and the services held therein presumably decreased the revenues of the parish pastor, John of Milheim promised to pay him 90 *grossi* annually. When Nicholas Zeiselmeister became pastor of Sts. Philip and James, he demanded and received 50 *kopy*, "propter bonum pacis et concordie."[2]

[1] Alois Kubíček, *Betlemská kaple* (Praha, 1953), p. 48. Also O. Odložilík, "The Chapel of Bethlehem in Prague," in *Studien zur ältesten Geschichte Osteuropas* (Graz-Köln, Hermann Böhlaus Nachf., 1956), I, pp. 126-41.

[2] V. Novotný, ed., *M. Jana Husi Korespondence a dokumenty* (Praha,

The chief feature of the interior was the square pulpit elevated on a stout pillar, placed against the priestly residence. Indeed, the entrance to it was not from the ground floor, but from the residential quarters. There was even an altar at which masses were offered by a special chancery priest. Although the chapel was consecrated in honor of the Holy Innocents, it was usually known as Bethlehem (the house of bread), because its chief function was to feed the hearers with the bread of life, the Word of God. As noted previously, there were also residential quarters for poor students; these were later expanded behind the chapel into a fairly extensive hospice called the Nazareth college. The chapel was decorated by several pictures always arranged in pairs: one of them portrayed the pope astride a large horse, resplendent in all papal pomp; its counterpart portrayed Christ in all his poverty, carrying the cross. "From this contrast," observed Bartoš "the people concluded that the pope is the Antichrist and the whole Roman Church is Antichrist's heretical sect."[3] The second pair of pictures depicted emperors Constantine and Ludwig in the act of donating to the pope the city of Rome, a palace, the state with all its glory and power; Constantine places a golden crown on the pope's head, clothes him in a purple mantle, and both emperors hold for him the stirrup, helping him into the saddle. The companion picture represented Christ before Pilate, submitting to all abuse, having a crown of thorns placed on his brow; he was also depicted as fleeing when the crowd wished to make him king. Further, Peter was painted hanging on the cross with his head down. In another picture, the pope was depicted sitting haughtily on the throne having his feet kissed; in contrast Christ was portrayed in a kneeling position washing his disciples' feet.

---

Komise pro vydávání pramenů náboženského hnutí českého, 1920), No. 4.

[3] F. M. Bartoš, "Po stopách obrazů v Betlemské kapli z doby Husovy," in *Jihočeský sborník historický*, xx (1951), pp. 121-22. In Constance, Hus once dreamed of these pictures and asked his friend the meaning of his dream. Novotný, *Korespondence*, p. 274.

Let it be noted that Hus approved of the use of pictures in the churches, provided they were not worshipped for themselves but venerated for the divine objects represented in them. He held that the use of pictures was introduced because the common people could not read; also because the mind has a surer grasp of a thing by seeing than by hearing; and lastly, because the mind retains an image longer than a sound.[4]

Even more remarkable was the discovery of the original text of Hus' *De sex erroribus*, which he had ordered to be inscribed on one of the walls. When the chapel was undergoing reconstruction in 1949, this fairly extensive inscription was found in a relatively good state of preservation under the protective covering of plaster. It was carefully copied by Professor B. Ryba, and the text with the description of the circumstances of its finding was published in 1951.[5] Of the earlier inscription of the Credo and the Decalogue not a syllable was preserved. Jakoubek of Stříbro, who succeeded Hus as the rector and preacher of the chapel, placed the text of his *Salvator noster* and *De communione parvulorum* on another wall.

As has already been noted, the Bethlehem Chapel was founded with the avowed purpose of providing preaching in the Czech language. It was consciously intended by its founders as the continuation of Milič's Jerusalem, particularly of that part of the former foundation which was to serve for the training of preachers imbued with the ideals and spirit of Milič. Except for the cathedral, where Peter of Stupno delivered sermons in Czech, there was no church in Prague where preaching was in the vernacular. As the foundation charter of Bethlehem stated:

There exist in the city of Prague many places devoted to divine services, but these are for the greatest part used exclusively for other sacred ministrations, so that there is not a single place primarily designed for the preaching of the

4 V. Flajšhans, ed., *Expositio decalogi*, in *Spisy M. Jana Husi* (Praha, Jaroslav Bursík, 1903), p. 110.
5 B. Ryba, *Betlemské texty* (Praha, Orbis, 1951).

Word of God; on the contrary . . . the preachers in Czech are, for the most part, forced to make use of houses and hiding places—which is unworthy.[6]

It was only with Waldhauser that preaching in German, prior to the reform movement, was begun. He also introduced singing into the Easter services, either "Crist ist erstanden" or the Czech hymn, "Buoh všemohúcí." Milič followed this practice by preaching in Czech and German as well as in Latin; furthermore, Matthew of Janov continued to have the gospels and the epistles read in Czech. About the same time the choral "Hospodine, pomiluj ny," found its way into the churches. Likewise the hymn in honor of St. Wenceslas was sung at his great pilgrimage in Prague. But these innovations were opposed by the ecclesiastical authorities as possibly endangering the Latin services.

Hus himself, although he continued the previous practice of hymn singing, was not an outstanding leader in this aspect of the reform movement, as were Jerome of Prague and Jakoubek of Stříbro. Nevertheless, he composed or reworked from the existing compositions, four hymns and translated one from the Latin. The four hymns of his authorship were "Jezu Kriste, štědrý kněže" [O Jesu Christ, bountiful priest]; "Navštiv nás, Kriste žádoucí" [Visit us, O Christ desired]; "Vstalť jest Buoh z mrtvých" [God had risen from the dead]; and "Králi slavný, Kriste dobrý" [Glorious king, good Christ]. He translated into Czech the Latin hymn "Jesus Christus, nostra salus." Later tradition ascribed to him the composition of other hymns, but these additional productions cannot be verified from the fragmentary available sources.[7]

[6] B. Havránek et al., eds., *Výbor z české literatury husitské doby* (Praha, Česká akademie věd a umění, 1964), II, p. 384.

[7] F. M. Bartoš, "Hus a česká bohoslužba," in *Jihočeský sborník historický*, XXI (1952), pp. 42-46; see also his *Literární činnost M. J. Husi* (Praha, Česká akademie věd a umění, 1948), pp. 119-20. Also Enrico C. S. Molnár, "The Liturgical Reforms of John Hus," in *Speculum*, April 1966, pp. 297-303. It is remarkable that the hymn "Jesus Christus, nostra salus" has recently been included in *The Catholic Hymnal and Service Book* (New York, Benziger Editions, 1946), No. 177. My friend the Rev. Dr. Holland F. Burr called my attention to it. He has also read the proof of this book, and suggested some improvements, for which I am grateful.

In a real sense Hus was the first rector of Bethlehem Chapel who fulfilled the intention of the founders. His predecessors were too much occupied with other interests to give themselves adequately, if not wholly, to the prescribed duties of their office. The earliest of them was John Protiva, at that time a determined defender of the reform movement, who later became Hus' inveterate enemy. He was succeeded by Stephen of Kolín, who in 1402 retired from that office in favor of Hus. Soon thereafter the co-founder, Kříž, established a second preaching office, which was first occupied by the then fervent reforming monk, John Štěkna. Although Hus continued to teach at the university and had enrolled, perhaps in 1400 or 1401, in the theological faculty as a candidate for the doctor's degree, Bethlehem was his first love and care. His Czech preaching constituted his preeminent service to the reform movement. He preached twice every Sunday and saint's day—morning and afternoon—although during the advent and fast days this duty was reduced to one sermon. Flajšhans estimates that during the twelve years of his ministry in Bethlehem Hus preached some 3,000 sermons, not counting the sermons he had preached during the year 1401 while he served the church of St. Michael and other churches.[8] His fame as preacher was soon firmly established and he was recognized as the unrivaled leader of the popular phase of the movement. The academic phase continued to be headed, until their craven defection, by Stanislav of Znojmo and Stephen Páleč. The Czech populace of Prague soon thronged the chapel—both the artisans and the lower classes and also the representatives of the educated and even noble classes from among the royal entourage, among them Queen Sophia herself.[9] The university masters and students also attended the services in large numbers.

Hus was not only an eloquent preacher but also a de-

[8] M. Svoboda and V. Flajšhans, eds., *Mistra Jana Husi Sebrané spisy*, 6 vols. (Praha, J. R. Vilímek, n.d.), VI, Postscript, p. iv.

[9] F. Palacký, ed., *Documenta Mag. Joannis Hus* (Praha, F. Tempsky, 1869), pp. 411 f, 413, 423. In these letters Queen Sophia pleaded with Pope Alexander V for the free preaching in Bethlehem Chapel, "in qua saepe audivimus verbum dei." She calls Hus "capellanum nostrum."

voted pastor. His genuine care for their spiritual welfare won him the hearts of his humble flock whom he called, in a letter from Constance, "doctors, my beloved brothers in Christ, cobblers, tailors, and scribes."[10] In another letter from Constance, written less than a month before his death, his solicitude for his parishioners is evident in this earnest appeal:

I beseech the lords that they deal mercifully with their poor and rule them justly. I beseech the burghers that they carry on their commerce justly. I beseech the craftsmen that they do their work faithfully and have their living from it. I beseech the masters that they, living worthily, teach their pupils faithfully: first of all to love God, and to study for the sake of His praise and the benefit of the community, as well as for the sake of their salvation—but not for the sake of avarice or of worldly prosperity. I beseech the students and other pupils that they obey and follow their masters in the good, and that they study diligently for the sake of God's praise and of their own and other people's salvation.[11]

Although most of Hus' sermons have been published, at present comprising fourteen volumes, some still await publication. The first of the published sermons covers the years 1401-03.[12] These are his oldest Czech sermons, preached both at St. Michael's and at the Bethlehem Chapel. They show Hus in the role of continuator of his predecessors in reform, Milič and Matthew. Like them, he addresses himself to the task of moral reform of his hearers, principally lay, although clerics and university masters are included. These sermons are unimpeachably orthodox. Even Jan Sedlák, usually very critical of Hus, states uninhibitedly "Hus shows himself in this postil an entirely orthodox cath-

[10] Novotný, *Korespondence*, p. 278.

[11] M. Spinka, ed. and transl., *John Hus at the Council of Constance* (New York and London, Columbia University Press, 1965), pp. 257-58.

[12] F. Šimek, ed., *Mistr Jan Hus, Česká kázání sváteční* (Praha, Blahoslav, n.d.). The content is dealt with extensively in my *John Hus' Concept of the Church* (Princeton, Princeton University Press, 1966), pp. 44-49.

olic priest. He simply presents catholic doctrine and explains it, expressing nowhere any doubts."[13]

The second collection of his sermons, preached during the years 1404-05, goes under the title of *Collecta*.[14] We have the Latin text of these sermons, written by Hus himself, although he preached them in Czech. This may appear a rather cumbersome way to go about the task of preaching in the vernacular; yet he continued to follow it throughout his Bethlehem ministry. He composed the Latin text carefully, perhaps to preserve in the preached sermon the unusual number of patristic and biblical quotations. In these scrupulously prepared sermons Hus denounces especially pride, luxury, fornication, and avarice. He stresses the familiar refrain that it is not enough to have faith: one must earn one's salvation by persevering in all good works in conformity with the precepts of Christ. The highest attainment man is capable of is to love God absolutely. Again the sermons are theologically unassailable, even though by that time Hus was acquainted with the theological treatises of Wyclif, which had been brought to Prague in 1401 by Jerome of Prague from his sojourn in Oxford. Nor is he as yet attacking the pope and the cardinals, although he does denounce various priestly sins.

During 1408 Hus preached a series of sermons on the Saints' Days entitled *Sermones de sanctis*,[15] replete with patristic quotations. A large number of them are devoted to the glorification of the Virgin Mary. He raises no objection, not even a warning, to the veneration of saints, as he does later. The collection also contains a sermon of Wyclif and one of Stephen of Kolín.[16]

[13] Jan Sedlák, "Husův vývoj dle jeho postil," *Studie a texty k náboženským dějinám českým*, 2 vols. (Olomouc, Matice Cyrilo-metodějská, 1913-19), II, p. 398.

[14] Anežka Schmidtová, ed., *Magistri Johannis Hus, Sermones de tempore qui Collecta dicuntur* (Praha, Academia scientiarum Bohemo-slovenica, 1959). For a more extended treatment, see *John Hus' Concept of the Church*, pp. 56-60.

[15] V. Flajšhans, ed., *Sermones de sanctis*, 2 vols. (Praha, 1907-08); see my *John Hus' Concept of the Church*, pp. 62-64.

[16] Bartoš, *Literární činnost M. Jana Husi*, p. 32.

To all this very full labor at the Bethlehem Chapel Hus not only added his accustomed academic work in the faculty of arts, where his prominence was attested by his being elected, for the winter semester of 1401-02, the dean of the faculty; he also busied himself with his theological studies. This course normally required about ten years for its completion[17] and, as in Hus' case, was pursued along with other professional work. Hus actually devoted twelve years to theological studies, and even then failed to receive the doctorate. It was not because he was deeply immersed in other work that he did not succeed in reaching his goal; the real reason was that he became so involved in controversies with the theological faculty that further effort to complete the course was impossible. Moreover, his exile effectively terminated the work. In 1404 he obtained his first degree in his B.D. course, and as a *baccalarius cursor* or *biblicus* began the exposition of the canonical epistles and some Psalms (1404-06). We possess the text of these lectures,[18] which comprise his comments on seven Pastoral Epistles and Psalms 109-18.

Considering, first of all, Hus' commentary on the Pastoral Epistles—James, I and II Peter, three letters of John, and Jude—one wonders why these rather minor writings had been assigned to him for elucidation at all. As if matching the undistinguished character of the Scriptural text, Hus' performance of his task falls below his usual standard. His comments are verbose; he often deals with every individual word or phrase, belaboring the obvious. Nevertheless, it is remarkable how mature his theological views are; on the whole, they are practically identical with those expressed by him in his later writings. He lauds the Scriptures as possessing the remedy for all ills.[19] It is astonishing how aptly he cites Scriptural passages in elucidating and confirming his comments. He explains Scripture by Scripture,

---

[17] In Paris, the minimum was eight years, and was later increased to fourteen; no one under the age of thirty-five could be made a doctor.

[18] *Historia et monumenta Joannis Hus atque Hieronymi Pragensis, confessorum Christi*, 2 vols. (Norimberg, 1715), II, pp. 165-511.

[19] *Ibid.*, II, pp. 172 ff.

utilizing the whole Bible for the explication of the text he is dealing with.[20] He admonishes the reader to follow James' command to look unto the "perfect law, the law of liberty, what manner of man he is."[21] There are practically no personal allusions in the work, nor does its nature afford an opportunity for them.

In commenting on I Peter 2:13-15, which deals with the duties of subjects to their superiors and governors, he asserts, in harmony with Wyclif, whom he does not name, that "All power comes from God."[22] To be sure, his text asserts the same, so that the supposition of Wyclifite provenience is entirely unnecessary. Commenting on I Peter 5:1, dealing with "seniores qui in vobis sunt," he places ecclesiastical rulers not above or over the subordinates, but among them as "those of them."[23] Passing on to II Peter, Hus comments in verse 1 on the phrase "in the justice of our God and Savior Jesus Christ," that our faith "saves without works" [*fide, quae sine operibus salvat*].[24] This assertion flatly contradicts his usual and persistently repeated view that only the faith formed in love [*fides caritate formata*] is the saving faith; in other words, that faith without works does not save. But the reference is so brief, and Hus' meaning by no means certain, that it does not warrant any doubt as to the validity of his settled and otherwise uniformly asserted conviction. In one of the rare instances where Hus refers to contemporary events, he comments on Chapter 1:16 regarding "fables artfully spun" that "in these last days" preachers concoct fables that spread like cancer and people delight in them.[25] Hus agreed with his age that "It is a greater and graver sin to deny the faith, as the heretics do, than to reject the faith, as the Jews and pagans do."[26] Hus remarks that Peter, doubtless "the immediate vicar of Christ," did not grant indulgences and thus free souls from purgatory;

---

[20] Paul de Vooght, *L'hérésie de Jean Huss* (Louvain, Publications universitaires de Louvain, 1960) , p. 49.

[21] James 1:25.

[22] *Historia et monumenta*, II, p. 253.

[23] *Ibid.*, II, p. 276.    [24] *Ibid.*, II, p. 280.

[25] *Ibid.*, II, pp. 288-89.    [26] *Ibid.*, II, p. 297.

instead, he demanded that Christians live good lives. Did he say this with tongue in cheek? It seems very probable; for later he altogether denied such indulgences as were granted by the popes. In Chapter 2:15, where a mention of Balaam's ass occurs, Hus drew the conclusion that a Christian could and should refuse to obey a prelate who ordered him to do something contrary to God's commands.

As for the exposition of Psalms 109-18, Hus' treatment of them is similar to that of the Epistles. It needs to be said that the numbering of these Psalms is one digit higher than that of our versions; they are thus comprised, with exceptions, in chapters 110-19, and I shall cite them in accordance with the latter numbering. About Psalm 110 Hus remarks, somewhat surprisingly, that it deals with "the two natures of Christ . . . His incarnation and His omnipotent deity."[27] It is indeed a messianic prophecy and from Hus' point of view, therefore, is applicable to Christ. Although less specifically, the text of all the Psalms dealt with by Hus is made to refer to Christ, and the New Testament interpretation is read into it. On the assumption that Scripture is a unit, this practice is understandable. Moreover, the text is considerably changed in its reading: in places, it is altogether missing; in others, additional verses are introduced into it. Psalm 111 is devoted, Hus writes, to the "miraculous work of God in the sacrament of the altar," because verse 4 reads that "He has caused his wonderful works to be remembered."[28] How the Psalmist could anticipate a solemn rite developed centuries later he does not say. Psalms 114-15 are combined in his exposition, so that Psalm 114 of Hus' text is 116 of ours, although only to verse 10. Thereafter, Hus begins his treatment of Psalm 115. The Psalm 119, the longest among them, contains 176 verses; he devotes 84 folio pages, almost two-thirds of his commentary, to its exposition.[29] In these commentaries, Hus "showed himself a disciple of Matthew of Janov, and even more of Milič."[30]

27 *Ibid.*, II, p. 375.      28 *Ibid.*, II, p. 384.
29 *Ibid.*, II, pp. 427-511.
30 De Vooght, *L'hérésie*, p. 54.

Having obtained the rank of *baccalarius sententiarius,*
Hus lectured for two years (1407-09) on Peter Lombard's
*Four Books of Sentences.*[31] Lombard, a pupil of Abelard,
was toward the end of his life professor at the Paris Cathedral School, which soon thereafter developed into the
University of Paris. His book became the most popular compendium of theology, required everywhere as the textbook
to be expounded by candidates for the doctorate in theology.
It was based on the views of various theological schools, although Augustine predominated. From Augustine "nine-
tenths of the book gets its material."[32] The editor of Hus'
lectures on Lombard's *Sentences,* V. Flajšhans, regards this
work as Hus' "best and longest."[33] It is indeed the best in
the sense that it represents the mature and systematic exposition of his theological views, while it is at the same time
his longest work. As such, it may be regarded as a standard
treatise.

It was customary when there were several doctoral candidates at this stage of their theological course to group
them in teams for the purpose of holding disputations with
which each book of the *Sentences* was introduced. During
the first year Hus disputed with Stephen Páleč, Nicholas
Stoer, and the friars John de Monte and Peter Mangold
(the latter probably identical with Peter of Uničov, later
lector in the Dominican monastery of St. Clement). During
the second year only John de Monte was left of the old team,
but he was joined by the Cistercian Matthew of Zbraslav
and John of Frankenstein.[34]

Since Hus was bound by the rules to restrict himself in
his comments to the recognized authorities in the field, he
cites such Fathers and outstanding theologians as Augustine,
Gregory, Chrysostom, Bonaventura, Thomas Aquinas, Peter
of Tarantasia (later Pope Innocent V) , John of Paris, Duns

[31] V. Flajšhans, ed., *M. Jan Hus, Super IV Sententiarum,* 3 vols.
(Praha, J. Bursík and J. R. Vilímek, 1904-06) .
[32] F. M. Bartoš, "Hus' Commentary on the Sentences of Peter Lombard," in *Communio viatorum* (Praha, 1962) , p. 148.
[33] Flajšhans, *Super IV Sententiarum,* I, p. xix.
[34] Bartoš, "Hus' Commentary," p. 146.

Scotus, William of Ockham, Thomas of Strasbourg, Hugo Repelin of Strasbourg, John Wyclif, and his own teacher, Stanislav of Znojmo. Repelin's *Compendium theologice veritatis*, which Hus regarded as the work of Aquinas, was a frequent source of Hus' own exposition, as was John of Paris. Besides, Hus made use of the commentaries on Lombard prepared previously by doctoral candidates at the university, of which twenty have been preserved. Thus he used the commentaries of Nicholas Biceps and Stanislav of Znojmo. Nevertheless, he shows himself to be independent of these authorities and demonstrates that they are sometimes inconsistent with each other. He particularly criticizes Duns Scotus and Bonavenutura, the Franciscans, but praises William of Ockham, the great heretic of that Order. Thus he displays a great degree of maturity and self-reliant judgment. Moreover, he is nonspeculative and practical in his choice of topics; he prefers the ethical, moral, and nonspeculative subjects. He avoids all merely curious and even fantastic theological speculation. This feature is of particular importance. To be sure, Hus is following a similar emphasis of his predecessors, Milič and Matthew, who also objected to the overwhelming stress on theological and legal studies to the detriment of biblical study and spiritual cultivation. His opposition to abstract scholastic speculation was more the effect of his practical emphasis on moral reform and spiritual transformation of life than on mysticism. Nevertheless, he does belong to those who realize the limitations of human reason—in this matter he agreed with Ockham—and eschewed attempts to penetrate into divine mysteries incapable of being rationally grasped. In this sense he may be classed with the rare spirits professing *docta ignorantia*—the conscious limitation of knowledge.

Hus was at the time entirely orthodox in his views,[35] despite the later charges that some of the opinions then expressed were heretical. As was his custom throughout his adult life, he accepts and defends the theologically unimpeachable views of Wyclif, but passes over in silence the

[35] De Vooght, *L'hérésie*, pp. 54, 58.

opinions of Wyclif which he regarded as objectionable. He drew upon Wyclif's *De benedicta incarnatione, De mandatis divinis,* and *De civili dominio.* He formulated his judgment of Wyclif in the following refusal to condemn him without a specific proven cause:

I, however, not wishing to pass a temerarious judgment, hope that he [Wyclif] is of the number of the saved. If he is in heaven, may the glorious Lord who placed him there be praised; if he is in purgatory, may the merciful Lord free him quickly; if he is in hell, may he, in accordance with God's judgment, remain there until its eternal fulfillment.[36]

Hus became better acquainted with Wyclif's theological works when Jerome of Prague, who had studied at Oxford during the years 1399-1401 and had there copied Wyclif's *Dialogus* and *Trialogus* and perhaps also *De eucharistia,* brought these works to Prague in 1401.[37] They contained Wyclif's mature thought in its final form. Jerome then became Hus' intimate companion and adherent—an attachment he preserved throughout his life.

As Hus' theological views have been discussed at considerable length in the companion volume to this book,[38] we need only mention here in brief Hus' teaching about the Church. Fundamentally, he defines the Church in Augustinian terms as "the congregation of the faithful to be saved, called catholic, i.e., universal, comprising the militant, dormient, and triumphant,"[39] churches, or "the totality of the predestinate." The Church militant comprises both the predestinate and the foreknown, but only the former constitute the true Church. This double membership will continue to exist until the Day of Judgment, when the Lord will separate the two groups as the sheep from the goats. The Church of the predestinate has Christ alone as its head,

[36] *Super IV Sententiarum,* I, p. 621.

[37] F. Šmahel, *Jeroným Pražský* (Praha, Svobodné Slovo, 1966), p. 60; also F. M. Bartoš, "M. Jeronym Pražský," in *Jihočeský sborník historický,* XIV (1941-45), pp. 41-52.

[38] *John Hus' Concept of the Church,* pp. 64-78.

[39] *Super IV Sententiarum,* I, p. 36.

while the Church of the reprobate is headed by the devil.
It is this view that Hus held consistently to the end. He was
accused by his enemies of thereby denying the very existence
of the Church militant. This basic subversion of his teaching was chiefly responsible, at the Council of Constance, for
condemning him as a heretic. He, however, never held it.

Having completed his two years of lecturing as *baccalarius
sententiarius*, he gained the degree of *baccalarius formatus*,
just preceding the doctorate. But he did not advance beyond
this degree to that of *doctor theologiae* for the reasons previously mentioned. Who was Hus' principal teacher during
his long theological course? In the first three of four years,
it was almost certainly Nicholas of Litomyšl, whom Hus
called *consiliarius perspicassimus*. But Nicholas appears to
have died c. 1403 when Hus became a member of the teaching staff. He therefore had to choose another professor
whose name we do not know. Without doubt he was one of
the Czechs. The professional staff was soon after increased
by four other Czech doctors—Stephen of Kolín, Stanislav
of Znojmo, Nicholas of Rakovník, and Peter of Stupno. Unfortunately, three of these men died soon afterward, leaving
only Stanislav of Znojmo, along with two older Czech members of the faculty—Peter of Znojmo and John Eliášův—
to carry on the task of instruction. Stanislav soon attained
the leading position in this faculty, but whether Hus chose
him as his mentor is not known.[40]

Bartoš counts among Hus' "teachers" even a simple
Prague priest, Matthew the Poor, who, according to contemporary sources, excelled all his confrères in humility and
voluntary poverty. He was also a zealous preacher and a
generous benefactor of the poor. It was his example which
inspired or confirmed Hus in his own emphasis on "apostolic poverty" and the proclamation and defense of the gospel.
Hus includes him among those whom he "especially" greets
from Constance.[41]

[40] F. M. Bartoš, "Hus a jeho učitelé a kolegové na bohoslovecké
fakultě Karlovy university," *Jihočeský sborník historický*, XIII (1940),
pp. 41-47.
[41] V. Novotný, *Korespondence*, p. 278.

During the time of Hus' study at the theological faculty, the life of the Church in Bohemia was undergoing important developments. The archiepiscopal see had been occupied by three different persons in quick succession. After the resignation of John of Jenštejn (1396), Olbram of Škvorec, Jenštejn's nephew, won the see as the candidate of the nobility and the hierarchy. But he died in May 1402. During the invasion of Bohemia by the Meissen soldiers of Prince William, Olbram had stood in the camp of the nobles revolting against King Wenceslas. The king was captured and kept prisoner of the nobles, while the land was administered by his half-brother, Sigismund of Hungary. With the latter's consent and by the election of the conservative faction of the St. Vitus chapter, the choice of the next archbishop fell on Nicholas Puchník, who had long served as Jenštejn's official. He was notorious as a highly successful pluralist; at the time of his death, he left behind him the rectorship of one church and four canonries, none of which he actually served. Pope Boniface IX, however, nullified the chapter's election on the ground that he had reserved the Prague archbishopric for himself. Thereupon, he appointed Puchník of his own choice, thus securing for himself a very high payment. Puchník had not only to pay the pope for his own appointment (3,300 gulden) but to assume the unpaid debts of his two predecessors (1,480 gulden).[42] He died, however, before he received the papal pallium of his office (September 19, 1402). Thereupon, the anti-royal party favored the bishop of Litomyšl, John surnamed the Iron. The royal party, however, together with some members of the St. Vitus chapter, petitioned the curia in behalf of Zbyněk Zajíc of Hasenburk. Since Zbyněk was willing not only to pay for his own appointment (2,800 gulden), but also to assume the accumulated arrears, he was quickly named to the post. Although appointed to office in November 1402, when he was only twenty-five years old, he was

---

[42] See my translation of Hus' *On Simony*, in *Advocates of Reform, Library of Christian Classics* (Philadelphia, The Westminster Press, 1953), XIV, p. 213, n. 56.

granted the papal dispensation to occupy the see. Nevertheless, he was not able to assume his full duties until August 1403.

Zbyněk was the youngest of the six sons of Lord William Zajíc of Hasenburk. He had been early destined for an ecclesiastical career, although his education was more military and courtly than theological. In c. 1389-90 he was made prior of the wealthy Mělník priory—a lucrative post coupled with Prague canonship. His military prowess gained him, in 1401, the royal appointment to the defense of several regions in Bohemia. He and his family had remained faithful to Wenceslas when a large party of lords joined a revolt against him, under the leadership of the king's half-brother, Sigismund. Zbyněk's soldiers opposed the invasion of troops from the Bavarian border. But the Meissen contingent succeeded in penetrating to the vicinity of Prague, and plundered and burned the villages and massacred their inhabitants. No wonder that when Wenceslas at last escaped from the imprisonment in Vienna, on November 11, 1403, he treated the young archbishop with great favor.

Before Zbyněk fully assumed the archiepiscopal office, an important event had occurred with which he had to deal throughout his administration. The Wyclifite realism espoused by the Czech university masters provoked the German masters, mostly nominalists, to an open attack in May 1403. This was not merely a struggle over rival philosophical systems; for the first time the German masters branded the Wyclifism of the Czechs a heresy. They had been instigated to this action by the cathedral canons, who had administered the archdiocese before Zbyněk took up his duties. A Silesian German, John Hübner, had sent a complaint to Rome about Stanislav's realism, using as the basis the twenty-four articles of Wyclif which had been condemned by the Blackfriar Synod held in London in 1382.[43] He added to them twenty-one articles he himself had chosen from Wy-

43 F. Palacký, ed., *Documenta Mag. Joannis Hus* (Praha, F. Tempsky, 1869), pp. 327-31. My translation of these articles in the 1412 version is found in *John Hus' Concept of the Church*, pp. 397-400.

clif's works, thus making a total of forty-five. Among the articles thus abstracted some stated that the bread and wine in the sacrament remained unchanged, and that a bishop or priest in mortal sin does not ordain, transubstantiate, consecrate, or baptize. Article six asserted that "God should obey the devil." Further, a foreknown pope does not have power over the faithful. For a priest to possess property is contrary to the Scriptures. It is permissible for deacon or priest to preach without authorization of the pope or bishop. No one is civil lord, bishop, or prelate while he is in mortal sin. Habitually delinquent clerics may be deprived by secular lords of their temporal possessions. Tithes are merely alms, and are not legally enforceable. Monks are not Christian. Pope Sylvester and Emperor Constantine erred in endowing the Church. The Roman Church is a synagogue of Satan, and the pope is not an immediate successor of Christ and of the apostles. It is not necessary for salvation to believe that the Roman Church is supreme over all other churches. To believe in papal or episcopal indulgences is vain.

Hübner then offered these forty-five articles to the archiepiscopal chapter, the Official John Kbel, and the Archdeacon Wenceslas Nos, for appraisal. They, in turn, requested the university faculty for an opinion. The rector at the time, Walter Harrasser, a Bavarian, called a meeting of the whole university to the *Carolinum* on May 28, 1403. He then read to the assembled masters the forty-five articles, asking that they be considered as to their orthodoxy. The meeting erupted into a violent dispute. The Czech masters, being acquainted principally with Wyclif's philosophical works, refused to believe that the forty-five articles had been correctly excerpted. Nicholas of Litomyšl accused Hübner of distorting their true meaning. Stanislav of Znojmo did not deny that some of the articles were erroneous, but refused to condemn all of them indiscriminately. Stephen Páleč, on his part, threw a copy of a treatise of Wyclif on the table—it was perhaps *De universalibus* —and challenged the whole assembly: "Let anyone who wishes rise and impugn one word of it, and I will defend it!"[44] But despite the opposition of the Czech masters, the Germans, having the majority vote, easily passed the verdict that the forty-five articles were theologically inadmissible, that in fact some of them were heretical. The articles, but not Wyclif's books, were forbidden to be held or taught. The university did not decide whether the articles had been correctly abstracted or whether they misrepresented Wyclif's authentic teaching. Nevertheless, they served henceforth as a touchstone of Wyclifite heresy. The Germans thereafter derisively formulated the Czech Wyclifite "genealogy," parodying Matthew's genealogy: "Stanislav begat Peter (of Znojmo), Peter begat Páleč, and Páleč begat Hus."[45]

Smarting under this defeat, the leader of the Czech philosophical realists, Stanislav, now responded by openly espousing the most denounced of Wyclif's articles—the doctrine of remanence. As the term indicates, this tenet asserts that the bread and wine in the sacrament remain unchanged after consecration, although the body and blood of Christ are "sacramentally" present in it. Stanislav explained it in the treatise *De corpore Christi*, written perhaps in 1403. He had quoted Wyclif in confirmation of his own views on the sacrament of the altar in his commentary on Lombard's *Sentences*:

A certain doctor, Master John Wyclif, among others an excellent theologian and philosopher, asserts the above-described opinion [concerning remanence]; he often publicly professed, as it stands in his writings, that he is ready, as a faithful son of the Church, to believe the opposite, if he were so instructed. Indeed, if it were necessary, that he is ready to correct it even by his death. Many less perspicuous call him a heretic on that and other accounts and befoul the memory of those who read his writings, ignoring the fact that the most beautiful roses are gathered among thorns.[46]

44 This is Hus' report in his polemic with Páleč in *Historia et monumenta*, I, p. 324.

45 V. Novotný, ed., *M. Jan Hus, život a dílo*, 2 vols. (Praha, Jan Laichter, 1919-21), I, pp. 112-13.

46 Hus, *Contra Stanislaum*, in *Historia et monumenta*, I, p. 334.

This declaration by Stanislav placed him, as well as Stephen Páleč and Jakoubek of Stříbro, who shared his espousal of remanence, in the forefront of the academic Wyclifite party. This movement now assumed a theological as well as philosophical aspect, and constituted the left wing of the movement. However, its membership consisted principally of the Czech university masters. Even among them, some of the older respected leaders, such as Stephen of Kolín, remained faithful to the orthodox dogma of transubstantiation. Indeed, it happened just then in June 1403 that Stephen, speaking to the clergy, took occasion to stress the official view. Neither did Hus follow his revered teacher, Stanislav, in this instance, but throughout his life adhered to and defended transubstantiation. In fact, this doctrine later became the bone of contention between him and his former friends. He remained a disciple of Wyclif in those doctrinal matters which did not infringe upon orthodoxy. On occasion, as De Vooght writes, he even "corrected" Wyclif "in the catholic sense."[47]

Stanislav's defiant attitude was promptly utilized for a further attack upon the "Wyclifites." At the *Quodlibet* held in January 1404, John Hübner again served as the spokesman for the German university masters. He denounced Wyclif as a heretic and as having called the Church "a synagogue of Satan." Soon after, Hus himself wrote a reply to Hübner and denied that Wyclif was a heretic just because he had written about heretics. So did Augustine, Lombard, and Aquinas "in dictis suis scolastice ponentes hereses"; why, then, not call them heretics as well? As to the Church being a "synagogue of Satan," Hus retorted that Hübner distorted Wyclif's meaning; it was the Roman curia, not the holy mother Church, which Wyclif had specified in his writing.[48] He furthermore repeated his opinion that the forty-five articles had been falsely abstracted from Wyclif's writings and did not, therefore, represent his true meaning. As De Vooght phrases it, Hus' "spirit was catholic, although his heart was with Wyclif."[49]

[47] *L'hérésie*, p. 214.
[48] Novotný, *Korespondence*, No. 6.     [49] *L'hérésie*, p. 85.

In the meantime Archbishop Zbyněk assumed his office in August 1403, at the age of twenty-six. He was still very much a soldier. Under such circumstances he could not, nor did he have the inclination to, acquire the education which would have fitted him adequately for the highest ecclesiastical office in the land. He was, however, a well-meaning young noble, favorably disposed toward the reform party. Had it been otherwise, it is questionable whether that party could have developed as freely and extensively as it did. He probably did not clearly understand the theological complexities involved in the movement; what appealed to him was the practical reform of the appalling conditions of his archdiocese. In 1408, when his attitude toward reform regrettably changed, the restraining effects were immediately felt by its leaders and resulted in the desertion of some of them. Nevertheless, during the five years of Zbyněk's favor, the party as a whole had gained sufficient strength to weather the storm. It was fortunate that among the reform leaders, Zbyněk singled out Hus in a special manner and made him almost his intimate adviser. He specifically requested Hus to point out and report to him either personally or by letter any failure or abuse that he had noticed.[50] Hus' rising reputation may also be gauged by the fact that he was chosen by the university to deliver in 1404, on the annual occasion of the commemoration of the founder, Charles IV, the sermon on the theme, "Let us cast away the works of darkness." He denounced the low level of priestly life and the clerical seeking after wealth.[51]

When King Wenceslas succeeded in escaping from his Viennese prison in November 1403, the new archbishop visited him at his court in Kutná Hora. The king immediately undertook to recover for the crown the lands, castles, and other property that had been alienated during his captivity. In this endeavor, the young archbishop was given the

[50] Hus himself reminded Zbyněk of these instructions in a letter in July 1408. Novotný, *Korespondence*, No. 11.

[51] "Abjicimus opera tenebrarum" in *Historia et monumenta*, II, pp. 57-62. The text is found in Rom. 13:12.

task of bringing to justice a robber lord, John Zúl of Ostředek. After a fierce struggle, he took Zúl prisoner along with his band of fifty retainers. All were hanged. On this occasion the close bond between Zbyněk and Hus is seen in the fact that the latter accompanied the hardened sinner to the gallows and brought him to repentance before his death. Zúl turned to the crowd gathered to witness the execution and implored it: "Holy congregation, I beg you that you beseech the Lord God for me."[52] Furthermore, Zbyněk instituted a number of reforms in the spirit of the national reform tradition: he forbade the demand for payment for sacramental functions, particularly confession; he denounced simony; he criticized clerical laxness in manners, their chess playing, and their roistering in public houses; and above all, he castigated their fornication and concubinage. He opposed pilgrimages to places of popular superstition, such as the sacred pine near Mnichovo Hradiště and the Blaník hill. As Novotný writes, he "identified himself with the efforts of the reform party."[53]

There were many cases of alleged appearance of the true blood of Christ on consecrated or unconsecrated hosts. Such cases were reported in Bologna in Italy, in Chrudim, Kutná Hora and Litomyšl in Bohemia, and Cracow in Poland. For the investigation of one outstanding case in Wilsnack in Brandenburg, near Wittenberg, Zbyněk appointed a commission of three. Hus and Stanislav were members of it, along with an unnamed master. The commission, by interrogating the returned Czech pilgrims, found the miracle to be a fraud perpetrated by the priest of the church in order to make up for the loss of the church, which had been burned along with the town. Pilgrims came from far and brought rich gifts to the church. As for the Litomyšl "miracle," Hus explains in his *Postil* written in exile that some priests dipped the wafer in blood and claimed it to have been miraculously transformed. Being subjected to a

---

[52] F. Šimek, ed., *Staré letopisy české* (Praha, Historický spolek a Společnost Husova musea, 1937), p. 5.

[53] Novotný, *Jan Hus*, I, p. 147.

rigorous examination, they confessed their fraud.[54] Upon the report of the Wilsnack commission of the fraudulent nature of the whole affair, Zbyněk, at the provisional synod held on June 15, 1405, forbade pilgrimages from Bohemia. Disregard of the prohibition was punishable by a ban.

Hus furthermore wrote a short treatise, *De omni sanguine Christi glorificato*,[55] which deals further with the Wilsnack and similar deceptions. This is one of his most "scholastic" as well as most "reformatory" works. In this small treatise he asserts that Christ at His resurrection "glorified" all the blood of His body, so that none remained on earth save that which exists sacramentally—but not materially— in the transubstantiated elements of the host. Therefore, "Christ's faithful today should not venerate the blood or the hair of Christ, no matter where on earth it is locally and visibly said to exist."[56] It was further commonly asserted at the time that there exist in various churches such relics as Jesus' tunic, the towel with which he wiped his sweat, the crown of thorns, the nails, the cross and the lance, as well as the robe of the Virgin Mary. The robe had been stained, reddened, and sprinkled by His blood, which could thus be seen. To this recital Hus replied that as in the sacrament of the altar the body and blood of Christ exist only sacramentally, not materially; the above-named objects exist in the same manner, but are not materially real. To the assertion that the foreskin of Jesus is shown in Rome and His blood, beard, and the Virgin's milk are exhibited in Prague,[57] Hus bluntly retorted that these "relics" were spurious. No one can prove them genuine even to the time of the Day of Judgment when the angel shall blow his trumpet. Instead of demands for a visible, miraculous proof, Hus stresses faith. He recalls the words of Jesus to Apostle Thomas, who refused to believe in the resurrected Christ until he placed his finger in His wound: "Blessed

---

[54] J. B. Jeschke, ed., *Mistr Jan Hus, Postilla* (Praha, Komenského ev. fakulta bohoslovecká, 1952), p. 207.

[55] *Historia et monumenta*, I, pp. 191-202.

[56] *Ibid.*, p. 193.

[57] *Ibid.*, pp. 193-94.

are they who believe without having seen."[58] He thus placed the chief emphasis on faith, not on visible proof. "Thence it is obvious that the true Christian should not seek proofs for his faith, but rather be firmly content with Scripture . . . ; those who need miracles are men of little faith."[59] De Vooght declares that in this treatise by Hus "all the elements of the catholic doctrine are found—the eucharistic symbolism, the efficacy of the sacrament, and the real presence."[60]

Archbishop Zbyněk further showed his favor toward Hus by inviting him to preach at the synodal meeting which he called as a means of clerical reform. At the synod held on October 19, 1405, in the archiepiscopal palace, which was then located on the left bank of the river near the Charles Bridge, Hus delivered a powerful sermon on the text, "Love the Lord thy God with all thy heart and with all thy soul and with all thy mind."[61] It was an all-out denunciation of the vices and degeneracy of the clergy. Zbyněk fully approved the strictures the ardent preacher had hurled at the clergy and prelates, and graciously received the text of the sermon from Hus' hand. The archbishop again appointed Hus as the preacher at the synodal meeting in the Fall of 1407, on which occasion he chose to deal with Paul's exhortation, "Stand, therefore, having girded your loins with truth . . ."[62]

Because of Zbyněk's lack of theological education, he undoubtedly was unaware of, or failed to be alarmed at, the firm hold which Wyclifism had on the Czech masters, particularly the academic leaders of the reform party. Hus, for instance, did not scruple to avow his admiration for Wyclif's earnest reformatory activity. He even declared in Zbyněk's presence that he wished his soul were where Wyclif's was.[63] The opposing camp, however, was more than

[58] John 20:27.
[59] *Historia et monumenta*, I, p. 197.
[60] De Vooght, *L'hérésie*, p. 62.
[61] Matt. 22:37; an extended account of the sermon is to be found in my *John Hus' Concept of the Church*, pp. 60-61.
[62] Eph. 6:14; for comments, see *John Hus' Concept of the Church*, p. 62.
[63] Palacký, *Documenta*, p. 154; Novotný, *Korespondence*, p. 49.

fully conscious of the inroads the movement had made upon their position. Among their leaders, Dr. John Štěkna, then professor of theology at the University of Cracow, but formerly one of the two earliest preachers at Bethlehem Chapel, took it upon himself to protest to the archbishop the already mentioned treatise of Stanislav of Znojmo, *De corpore Christi*. Štěkna's rather mild critique of the treatise in a sermon having failed of effect, he then denounced it as plainly heretical at the archiepiscopal court. Zbyněk could not ignore this open challenge; he entrusted the task of examination to a four-member commission. They, of course, found Stanislav guilty of holding remanence and advised that he be given a chance to be heard upon the matter.

Summoned to such a meeting, Stanislav declared that he had presented the remanence thesis as a subject of academic discussion [*per modum disputationis*], not as his personal conviction. He also claimed that the treatise in its present form was incomplete and promised to add the missing conclusion expressive of his own personal views. The commission accepted Stanislav's statement as made in good faith; nevertheless, it demanded that he repeat it before its own gathering attended by the archbishop and numerous masters. On these conditions, the archbishop allowed Stanislav, whom he still held in high honor, to "complete" his treatise. He even permitted him to read the radically amended treatise to a private audience in Stanislav's own room in the *Carolinum* (February 1406). The latter was thus spared the ignominy of a public recanting before the other masters and having it read from the pulpits.

Despite all these measures, however, the affair was not terminated. Zbyněk, therefore, issued a decree strictly forbidding the holding and teaching of Wyclif's errors, particularly remanence. These orders were read both at the meeting mentioned above and at the synodical meeting in June. He further ordered that the dogma of transubstantiation be declared from all pulpits, to the effect that after the consecration *nothing but* the body and blood of the Lord remained in the host. He even forbade any mention of bread and wine in this connection.[64]

Although Hus never shared Stanislav's remanentist position,[65] he felt that the unheroic conduct of Stanislav had damaged the prestige of the whole reforming party. In order to repair to some extent the harm done and to expound the true catholic doctrine of transubstantiation, which had been incorrectly stated in the archbishop's declaration, Hus undertook to write a treatise correctly explaining that doctrine. He did so because one of his fellow-students in the theological faculty, the *baccalarius formatus* Andrew of Brod, wrote a treatise warning Zbyněk of the rapid spread of the Wyclifite heresy, particularly of remanence.[66] Hus thereupon not only disobeyed Zbyněk's order that his pronouncement be read in every church and did not read it at Bethlehem, but also clarified the archbishop's position in his own *De corpore Christi* (1406),[67] which in effect corrected Zbyněk's definition. This treatise was in reality a reworked sermon which Hus had preached on June 14, the holy day of *Corpus Christi*, on the words, "My body is food indeed and my blood drink indeed."[68] Against Zbyněk's prohibition of the word "bread" in the sacrament of the altar, Hus posits a whole array of quotations from Christ Himself, Paul, and the Fathers to prove that they used the word; they meant thereby not the material, but the transubstantiated, bread. He points out that in the Gospel of John, chapter 6, Jesus used the word eleven times. He even quotes in Greek the word *epiousion* from the Lord's Prayer, defining it not as "daily" but as "supersubstantial," i.e., immaterial, bread.[69] The remainder of the treatise is devoted to the proof that since

---

[64] Palacký, *Documenta*, p. 335.

[65] Paul de Vooght, "Huss a-t-il enseigné la remanentia substantia panis post consecrationem," in *Hussiana* (Louvain, Publications universitaires de Louvain, 1960), pp. 263-91.

[66] Novotný, *Jan Hus*, I, p. 167; the title of Andrew's work is "Utrum in venerabili sacramento eucharistie post consecrationem manet panis." Novotný dates it 1406, Bartoš 1408.

[67] *Historia et monumenta*, I, pp. 202-07.

[68] John 6:55.

[69] *Historia et monumenta*, I, p. 203.

THE EARLY YEARS OF HUS' MINISTRY

the bread and wine after consecration are transubstantiated into the non-material body and blood of Christ, the host is not "broken into pieces, bitten into, crushed by the teeth, and materially masticated."[70] What is thus broken is the transubstantiated bread which appears to our senses, not the invisible and impalpable body of Christ. For the substance of the sacrament is not seen, only its accidents, which retain their natural appearance. This substance is apprehended by faith, not observed by sight. "To believe that in the sacrament of the altar exist the true body and blood of Christ is the faith by which the faithful adhere faithfully to the catholic truth; i.e., to believe that in the sacrament of the altar exist the true body and blood of Christ is faith in things non-apparent and invisible."[71]

The same argument applies to the false claim that the priest touches and handles the material elements of the sacrament, or that he and the communicants partake of them by eating. One should first communicate spiritually with Christ in the sacrament and then partake of it sacramentally. Hus goes so far as to suggest that the sacramental communion is not essential to salvation, for infants are saved without it; nevertheless, it ought to be partaken of, since it is an ecclesiastical ordinance.[72] Thus alone a man fulfills the command of Christ: "He who eats my body and drinks my blood has life eternal, and I will raise him up in the Last Day."[73]

Jakoubek of Stříbro, the outspoken adherent of Wyclif's remanence, deeply resented Stanislav's "flexibility of mind," to put it mildly. He regarded it as cowardice. He was not one of those who would betray the truth because it was dangerous to defend it. He wrote his own challenge to the archbishop in his treatise defending remanence.[74] He declared that the doctrine was the old faith of the Church, held prior to Pope Innocent's introduction of the dogma of tran-

[70] *Ibid.*
[71] *Ibid.*, p. 206.
[72] *Ibid.*, p. 207.
[73] John 6:40.
[74] Jakoubek of Stříbro, *Tractatus de remanentia panis*, in Jan Sedlák, ed., *Hlídka*, 1912.

substantiation in 1215. The latter was an innovation, not the former.

Mention has already been made in the previous chapter of the promotion speeches which Hus made for his graduates. Some of those delivered by him from 1405 to 1412 included the only member of the nobility among his students, Zdislav of Zvířetice (1405), who had spent several years in the Bethlehem hospice under Hus' immediate supervision. Hus chose for his text the words of Virgil: "Seek that which is virtuous and be an example of an honest man." He exhorts Zdislav to a life of probity on the ground that true nobility is not hereditary, but is of the mind and character. The intimate relation of the teacher and pupil is shown by Hus' playful reference to the student's laziness; Hus remarks that he himself often had to awaken Zdislav from sleep. Be it said in Zdislav's behalf that in latter life he proved himself a courageous and effective protector of Hus.

The foundations that provided living accommodations to students were also under Hus' care. In addition to the Nazareth College built by Kříž, the Polish Queen, Hedwiga, later established a similar dormitory in the vicinity of Bethlehem for the Lithuanian and other students from the Polish-Lithuanian territories, although it was not restricted to them. Thus, for instance, the Moravian student, Peter of Mladoňovice, who later wrote a detailed eyewitness account of Hus' trial at the Council of Constance,[75] lived there. The Nazareth College accommodated some forty students, while Queen Hedwiga's foundation provided room for twelve. Besides, two or three other students lived directly in the quarters of the Bethlehem Chapel, where they served Hus in various minor offices. We even know the names of two of them whom Hus mentioned in the "farewell letter" he had left behind prior to his journey to Constance. In it he designated gifts to these famuli, "who have served me

[75] My translation of it is found in *John Hus at the Council of Constance* (New York and London, Columbia University Press, 1965), pp. 89-234.

faithfully"; one of them bore the nickname of "the Pastor" and the other was named "Georgie."[76] To these famuli should be added Hus' former pupil, Martin of Volyně, to whom the letter was addressed and who was also included as a sharer of Hus' modest distribution of rewards. In that letter Hus again takes the occasion to speak intimately and with fatherly concern about Martin's conduct:

Remember, that ever since your youth I taught you to serve Christ Jesus and, if possible, would have liked to teach you in one day all I myself knew . . . I beg you also from my heart not to be greedy of benefices. Nevertheless, if you should be called to pastoral office, be motivated by the honor of God, the salvation of souls, and labor, instead of by ownership of sows or a plot of land . . . I also fear that, if you mind not your life by giving up splendid and super-fluous garments, you shall be severely rebuked by the Lord; as I, too, a miserable wretch, am being rebuked for having made use of such things, having been seduced by men's evil customs and praise. I beg you, however, for the sake of the mercies of Jesus Christ not to follow me in any levity that you may have seen in me. You know that—alas!—be-fore I became priest, I had gladly and often played chess, had wasted time, and by that play had frequently unhap-pily provoked to anger myself and others.[77]

Nothing illustrates better the close and intimate relation of Hus to his students than this letter!

We may notice in passing Hus' oft-repeated condemna-tion of splendid dress, which formerly he himself delighted in. This harping criticism may appear petty and harsh, re-minding one of the present-day Amish protest against "lux-ury" in dress. When, however, one remembers that from about 1350 to 1480 there prevailed the most extravagant fashion in foppish dress, both feminine and masculine, the matter assumes a different aspect. Men particularly indulged

[76] *Ibid.*, p. 96.
[77] *Ibid.*, pp. 95-96.

in extreme, even bizarre, attire; they laced their waists, and wore balloon sleeves, shoes that were pointed clumsily upward, and outlandish head gear. Moreover, their costume was often bespangled with glittering gewgaws and precious stones. It was against such ridiculous extravagance that many contemporaneous reformers and moralists, including Hus, protested.[78]

Some of the other candidates for degrees for whom Hus served as promoter were the aforementioned Peter of Mladoňovice and John of Příbram, both of whom received the bachelor's degree in 1409. In the next year Hus served as promoter at the inception of Nicholas of Stojčín and Sigismund of Brod.

In 1406 Hus had been preaching at the Bethlehem Chapel for four years; yet he had found it more convenient to write the concepts of his sermons, or even the whole carefully worked-out sermons, in Latin, although he delivered them in Czech. No wonder that he became increasingly aware of the need for improving the written Czech so as to make it more usable as a literary language. He now decided to take a hand in the needed reform of the Czech orthography, particularly for the guidance of the teachers in academies where his colleagues from the university taught and for the scribes who, from long usage, copied Czech treatises in an involved kind of transliteration. Thus motivated, Hus produced, *still in Latin*, his *Orthographia bohemica*.[79] The book opens with an alphabet in which he employs checks and points for the Czech letters not found in the Latin. These diacritical marks (to which acute accents were added indicative of the length of a vowel) were

[78] See J. Huizinga, *The Waning of the Middle Ages* (London, Edward Arnold & Co., 1924), pp. 228-29, 248. A similar, remarkably cogent denunciation of foppish dress is found in "The Parson's Tale" in Geoffrey Chaucer's *Canterbury Tales*, transl. by J. A. Nicholson (New York, Garden City Publishing Co., Inc. 1934), pp. 568 ff. The parson stingingly ridicules multicolored dress, and hose of contrasting colors, which accentuate the outlines of the cod-piece and buttocks.

[79] Al. V. Šembera, transl., *Ortografie česká* (1857). The Latin original is in Miklošić's *Slavische Bibliotek*, II, pp. 173 ff.

substituted for the clumsy conjunction of letters hitherto employed (such as ě instead of ie, the difference between i and y, and such consonants as č, dᵛ, h and ch, lᵛ, ň, ř, š, tᵛ, and ž).[80] Thus every syllable was to be expressed by one letter instead of a combination of letters. He then furnished examples of the use of these newly invented letters, and concluded with the transcription of Our Father, Ave Maria, and the Apostles' Creed. The innovations were not immediately adopted by the transcribers; but in the course of time Hus' rules, in their modernized form, came into common use and are so employed today; moreover, some other Slavic nations using the Latin alphabet (i.e., exclusive of those using the Cyrillic letters), such as the Polish, Slovene, Croatian, and Lusatian Sorbs, adopted them. Hus himself gave comparative examples from other Slavic languages, being aided therein by the students from the Nazareth College whose homes were in Moravia, Croatia, and Hungary.[81]

In this connection a few words may be said about Hus' "nationalism," of which he was accused. Thus, in 1401 the Bavarian and Meissen troops had invaded Bohemia and the latter had penetrated as far as the vicinity of Prague, burning the villages and plundering and killing the hapless inhabitants; Hus in a sermon indignantly castigated the nobles for their lack of resistance:

The Czechs are in this matter more wretched than dogs and snakes, for they do not defend their country, although their cause is just. Similarly I say that the Czechs in Bohemia, according to laws, both the divine law and the natural instinct, should be first in offices of the kingdom of Bohemia, as are the French in the kingdom of France and the Germans in their own lands; so that the Czechs should rule their subjects and the Germans theirs. To what advantage is it to anyone if a Czech ignorant of German becomes a priest or bishop in Germany? It is about as useful as a dumb dog,

[80] F. Jílek, "Mezinárodní význam Husovy pravopisné reformy," *Husův sborník* (Praha, 1966), pp. 57-60.
[81] F. M. Bartoš, "Husova reforma českého pravopisu a Betlemská kaple," in *Kostnické Jiskry*, July 2, 1959.

who cannot bark, is to a herd. A German is worth as much to us Czechs.[82]

That he was a good patriot is shown by the fact that he devoted his life to Czech preaching in the Bethlehem Chapel. He stated explicitly in one of his Czech treatises that it is the duty of princes to aid and support the use of the Czech language "that it may not perish." When a Czech marries a German woman, their children should immediately be taught to speak Czech and not mix the two languages. He cites the command of Emperor Charles IV given to Prague inhabitants "that they teach their children Czech and at the City Hall (which the Germans call Rathaus) that they speak and deal with their complaints in Czech . . . Also now the Praguers and other Czechs, who speak half Czech and half German, are worthy of being beaten . . . And thence come anger, envy, discord and contentions and the Czech disgrace."[83]

The increasing use of the vernacular went hand in hand with the rise of nationalism, the growth of cities, and the rise of the educated and wealthy burgher class. In Italy, it was Dante who introduced his native Tuscan dialect as the literary language of great power; in England, Chaucer did the same for English. Thus Hus' justification of the use of Czech kept pace with similar use of the vernacular elsewhere.

When in 1411 Hus learned that some priests in Plzeň forbade the reading of the Scriptures in Czech or German, he immediately remonstrated against it. He reminded the people that many of them know the truth and unless they defend it, they are betrayers of the truth in that

everyone may declare and confess the law of God, and if he can read, read it either in Latin as St. Mark wrote his gospel, or in Greek as St. John wrote his gospel and the

[82] Palacký, *Documenta*, p. 177; F. M. Bartoš, "Husův nacionalism," in *Jihočeský sborník historický*, VIII (1935), pp. 1-4.

[83] K. J. Erben, ed., *Výklad desatera*, in *Mistra Jana Husi Sebrané spisy české*, 3 vols. (Praha, B. Tempský, 1865), I, pp. 133-34.

canonicals or epistles, or in Persian, as St. Simon wrote and preached his gospel, or Judean, as St. Bartholomew, and in other languages; why then do you allow the priests to forbid that the people read the law of God either in Czech or in German?[84]

But that Hus was not a chauvinist-patriot is clearly stated in his declaration that "if I knew a virtuous foreigner, no matter from whence, who loves God and upholds the good more than my brother, I would like him better than my brother. Therefore, I like good English priests better than unworthy Czech priests; and I like a good German better than a bad brother."[85] Similarly he writes in his *Postil* that he loves "a virtuous and beneficent foreigner more than my own brother not so useful to the Holy Church; but on the other hand from natural inclination I love more my own brother when I observe that he is not manifestly a wicked man, than a foreigner who is more useful to the Church."[86]

Hus also revised and improved the existing texts of the Czech New Testament in 1406 (with minor omissions) and the Ecclesiastes (from Chapter 11:3), Song of Songs, Wisdom, Ecclesiasticus, and Psalms to 134. This he did probably at the request of his adherents, particularly the noble ladies living in the vicinity of the Bethlehem Chapel. One such lady was Archbishop Zbyněk's sister, then the widow of John Milheim. Hus' authorship of this improvement is testified to by the use of the orthographic rules set up by him in the previously mentioned work. Toward the end of his life, by the end of 1413 and the beginning of 1414, Hus under-

[84] Novotný, *Korespondence*, No. 35, pp. 106-07. Bartoš corrects the statement that St. Bartholomew's version was "Judean" to read "Indian." He follows therein Florentius Radewijn, who found the correction in the writings of fourth century Bishop Dorotheus. See F. M. Bartoš, *Ze zápasů české reformace* (Praha, Kalich, 1959), pp. 42-43.

[85] *Výklad desatera*, I, p. 156.

[86] *Postilla*, p. 406.

took a similar improvement of the so-called second redaction of the whole Czech Bible.[87]

The favor that Archbishop Zbyněk bestowed upon Hus and the reform party was naturally resented by those who felt themselves aggrieved by Hus' vehement strictures of evil clerical conduct. There is no doubt that the archbishop's benevolent attitude toward the "evangelical party" strengthened this resentment considerably. A number of its leaders continued to adhere to Wyclif's teaching, including his doctrine of remanence. Wyclif's books were still brought into Bohemia and were there diligently copied; when in the second half of the nineteenth century a group of scholars undertook to publish them, most of the manuscripts were found in Bohemia.

Moreover, Hus was rapidly forging his way to the forefront of the reform party. The older members of the party were gradually passing away, and Stanislav and Páleč were retreating from their advanced positions. Hus' revered teacher, Nicholas of Litomyšl, died c. 1403; his benefactor, Stephen of Kolín, and Peter of Stupno, in 1407. Because of his citation to the papal court, Stanislav of Znojmo was noticeably more reticent in his advocacy of Wyclifism until both he and Stephen Páleč joined the ranks of the extreme papalists. These circumstances forced Hus and Jakoubek of Stříbro to the forefront of the movement.

Jakoubek of Stříbro,[88] who thus became closely associated with Hus and was his successor, after Hus' death, at the Bethlehem Chapel and leader of the party, must be briefly mentioned here. He was about Hus' age. Receiving

---

[87] F. M. Bartoš, *Počátky české Bible* (Praha, Kalich, 1941). See also Bohuslav Souček, *Česká apokalypsa v husitství* (Praha, Českobratrská církev evangelická, 1967), esp. p. 35. The book was received too late for inclusion in the text.

[88] F. M. Bartoš, *Čechy v době Husově, 1378-1415* (Praha, Jan Laichter, 1947), pp. 274-77; also his *Literární činnost M. Jakoubka ze Stříbra* (Praha, Česká akademie věd a umění, 1925); also his "M. Jakoubek ze Stříbra, druhý zakladatel Husitství," in *Jihočeský sborník historický*, XII (1939), pp. 1-14; F. Borecký, *Mistr Jakoubek ze Stříbra* (Praha, Kalich, n.d.).

his B.A. degree in 1393 along with Hus, he gained the M.A. a year later than his friend (1397). Two years later he joined the philosophical faculty as *magister regens* but, like Hus, sought priestly ordination as a means to a more secure livelihood. Ordained in 1402, he gained, three years later, a rather meagre income as a chantry priest. Even so the place had been vacated in his favor by Christian of Prachatice, Hus' benefactor. Jakoubek was discriminated against by the archiepiscopal officers because he was known as a devoted adherent of Matthew of Janov. He had found in Matthew a spiritual guide, since he himself stressed humility as his ideal of following Christ in voluntary poverty. This, then, became the special message of Jakoubek, which was adopted by other members of the reform, including Hus. Avidly immersing himself in the reading of Matthew's *Regulae*, Jakoubek then subjected the teaching and the orders of the Church to the most searching scrutiny. Whatever did not agree with Christ's teaching or that of His apostles, he resolutely rejected. Thus he became the most consistent exponent of restorationism—the doctrine advocating the return to primitive Christianity. In this effort he even espoused Wyclif's remanence, declaring it, along with Wyclif, to be the ancient faith of the Church, while the dogma of transubstantiation was a fairly recent innovation. This position made him the leader of the left wing of the reform movement. His other radical tenet was his advocacy of the return of the clergy and the Church in general to the poverty of the primitive Church; he believed, however, that the clergy should be guaranteed a livelihood adequate to provide the necessities of life, i.e., sufficient food and clothing.

The crisis of the conflict between the reform party and its opponents was reached in December 1407 when Ludolf Meisterman, a Saxon bachelor of theology, was employed by the prelatical party for a direct attack upon Stanislav of Znojmo. He was commissioned by them to charge this most outstanding member of the reform party with the heresy of remanentism. Before Meisterman left for Rome, he had secured from the University of Heidelberg letters of recommendation. That university gladly joined in the action against the Czech leader, for it thus ingratiated itself into the favor of its ruler, Ruprecht, who was ever ready to do anything to damage the reputation of his rival, Wenceslas of Bohemia. Thus equipped, Ludolf laid charges of Wyclifism, both philosophical and theological, against Stanislav and others. He particularly charged Stanislav with espousing open heresy in his treatise *De corpore Christi* (1403), without mentioning the fact that the author had changed it into a wholly orthodox transubstantialist treatise. He demanded an investigation of his allegations, and the severest penalties for all who should be found guilty. The verdict was rendered within two months and published on April 20, 1408, at Lucca, where the new pope, Gregory XII, was at the time residing. The cardinal who handled the matter condemned the tenets of Wyclif and Stanislav's writings enumerated by Meisterman and declared that the owners of the treatises must surrender them to the curia on peril of a ban. Above all, Stanislav was cited to appear before the cardinal within two months. Thus the heresy charge had been carried to the Roman curia, where it was later to engulf Hus himself and lead to his death at Constance.

In the meantime, two young students, Nicholas Faulfiš[89] and George of Kněhnice, were sent to England (1407-08) to secure such works of Wyclif as were not yet obtainable in Bohemia. They found Oxford thoroughly "purged" of such works. Thereupon, they traveled to such out-of-the-way Lollard centers as Kemerton near Tewksbury and Braybroke in Northamptonshire. Faulfiš and George returned to Prague with a number of copies of Wyclif's works hitherto unknown there; they also brought a letter purporting to be an official recommendation by the University of Oxford

---

[89] Faulfiš was the son of a wealthy merchant of Budějovice. After his father's death, he inherited a considerable property which rendered him independent. He had traveled to England several times before the trip mentioned above. By 1411 he was already dead, apparently dying on a voyage to England. F. M. Bartoš, "Husův přítel z českých Budějovic," *Jihočeský sborník historický*, XIX (1950), pp. 43-44.

bearing testimony to Wyclif's orthodoxy and exemplary life. The letter was probably concocted and the university seal was appended by a Lollard, Peter Payne, who later sought refuge in Bohemia, where he spent the rest of his life. He and the two students thus concealed the fact that King Henry IV had secured the passage of the statute *De haeretico comburendo*, prohibiting Wyclifism, and that a number of Lollards had already been burned under its provisions. The University of Oxford had by this time been completely purged of all "heresy," and thus under no conceivable circumstances could have issued the letter. In addition, the two students brought a memento from Wyclif's grave at Lutterworth—a chip from his monument.

Jerome of Prague, who had returned late in 1406 from several years of study and teaching abroad, had brought some additional copies of Wyclif's books. He had acquired, during his stay abroad, three master of arts degrees—those of Paris, Cologne, and Heidelberg. At the last two institutions, however, he taught but a short time. In 1407 he was received among the masters of Prague University as one of its most brilliant members. But he remained a layman, never having sought a degree in theology.[90]

Another most serious complication aggravated the whole development of the ecclesiastical struggle in Bohemia as well as elsewhere. The two obstinate popes, Gregory XII and Benedict XIII, contrary to their repeated solemn promises, refused to meet each other in order to terminate the destructive Schism. Thereupon, thirteen cardinals of both obediences united in calling a general Council to meet at Pisa in order to depose both popes and elect a new one. Since the *via cessionis* for the ending of the Schism failed in the tragi-comic refusal of the popes to meet each other, although they were but a short distance from one another, the *via concilii* had to be resorted to. In May 1408, a strict prohibition of obedience to both popes was issued.

Stanislav of Znojmo postponed his compliance with the summons as long as he could. It was only after Meisterman

[90] Šmahel, *Jeroným Pražský*, pp. 59-77, particularly p. 69.

had sent his charges to the curia the second time, and on this occasion included Stephen Páleč in his accusation, that the two men obeyed. In the meantime other matters served to alienate the archbishop from Hus and his party. One of these was the arrest and imprisonment of young Matthew Knín, a master of the faculty of arts, on the charge that he had called Wyclif an "evangelical doctor" and that he held the tenet of remanence. His trial was held in Zbyněk's presence (May 14, 1408) at his court, with the attendance of many German masters. The Czech masters attended *en masse*, knowing that the attack was actually directed against them.

The examiner was the vicar general, John Kbel, who, without any preliminary proof of Knín's guilt, demanded that he recant remanence. The accused quite properly requested that his guilt be first proved by due legal process. This Kbel refused to do. Zbyněk supported the vicar by demanding: "Master, make an end to words and controversy; you will either take the oath and recant, or you will remain here!"[91] The Czech masters noisily supported Knín's position. In the end he appealed to Zbyněk: "Most reverend father, do not cause yourself and the kingdom and me the shame of my public recantation." This appeal seems to have induced the judges not to persist in the demand that Knín recant publicly; nevertheless, he had to do so in the presence of a few university masters, among whom the rector was included, after the assembly dispersed.

This defeat of the Czech masters was bitterly resented by them. Sixty masters met, on May 24, at their house "At the Black Rose," and in the presence of many bachelors and students took defensive measures. They declared that no one was to defend Wyclif's forty-five articles "in their heretical, erroneous, and objectionable sense," and they forbade the bachelors either to possess or to teach three of the most advanced books of Wyclif—the *Dialogus*, *Trialogus*, and *De corpore Christi*. This decision in reality allowed the possession and study of all Wyclif's works as far as the

91 Novotný, *Jan Hus*, I, p. 219.

83

masters were concerned. The three treatises mentioned above were prohibited to bachelors alone.[92] Obviously, this did not satisfy the archbishop; three weeks later at the synodical meeting he renewed his prohibition of remanence and ordered that all Wyclif's works be surrendered to him.

As a demonstration against Zbyněk's actions, the Czech masters chose, as the convener for the next *Quodlibet*, no less a person than Matthew Knín, who had recently been released from the archiepiscopal prison. No wonder that Zbyněk was more and more alienated from the cause of reform and particularly from Hus. He had ever been opposed to its extreme left, represented by such men as Jerome of Prague and Jakoubek of Stříbro. Nevertheless, the prelates and the higher clergy had been tireless in their efforts to divert the archbishop from favoring the reform party. The case of Matthew Knín showed clearly that they at last had succeeded. It was obvious that by their pressure on Zbyněk the two parties were inevitably thrown into an open conflict, which was nothing less than disastrous in its consequences. Without Zbyněk's and King Wenceslas' support, the cause of reform must either fail or result in an armed conflict. At this stage, no such extreme measure as an outbreak of military conflict was envisaged by either party, but the prelatical party was undoubtedly well aware that a struggle, aimed at a complete conquest over, and annihilation of, the opposite movement was beginning. Thus the religious conflict in Bohemia was soon to be brought into the all-European arena.

This changed atmosphere was palpably felt at the next meeting of the synod in June. The preacher on this occasion was very different from Hus, who had been the preacher at the previous synod. The prelatical party won an almost complete victory; the synod again adopted Zbyněk's previous prohibition of remanence, apparently even forbidding the use of the word "bread," with the addition that any transgressors of the prohibition be reported to the archiepiscopal court as heretics. All criticism of

[92] Bartoš, *Čechy v době Husově*, pp. 288-89.

prelates in Czech sermons was likewise forbidden; this was obviously aimed at Hus. The use of Czech hymns, with the exception of the traditional four, was prohibited under pain of dire punishment. This provision was likewise clearly aimed at Hus, Jerome, and Jakoubek.

Perhaps the possibility of such a radical outcome motivated Hus to write to the archbishop a letter which proved to be the last of such communications; he acted on the well-known behest of Zbyněk that Hus was to inform him whenever he perceived any disorder. In this instance Hus wrote on behalf of a priest Nicholas, called Abraham, who had been cited before the vicar general John Kbel for preaching without official approbation. Abraham declared that as a priest he was free to preach without any special permission. Kbel pronounced this sentiment to be heresy and turned the priest over to the inquisitor, Maurice Rvačka. Hus had been invited to the examination before the inquisitor, for apparently Abraham was known as his disciple or adherent. When the priest refused to take the prescribed oath on the gospel and the cross, although he was willing to swear by the living God, he was declared guilty of the Waldensian heresy. Hus defended him on the ground that, since Abraham was willing to swear by the living God, he was not guilty.[93]

Hus' intervention in fact proved effective. Abraham was not pronounced a heretic, but perhaps was merely banished from the diocese. There is no further mention of him. Nevertheless, Hus now wrote the archbishop (sometime after July 6, 1408), expostulating with him for "prohibiting the preaching of the gospel which Christ commanded his disciples as their principal task."[94] The responsibility for such acts of persecution, he said, falls upon the archbishop. This was the last such effort on Hus' part; henceforth, the rift between the two men steadily widened, although it was for the most part caused by external events over which Hus had no control.

[93] Novotný, *Jan Hus*, I, pp. 241-42.
[94] Palacký, *Documenta*, p. 4; Novotný, *Korespondence*, No. 11.

## Chapter IV

## Zbyněk's Opposition
## to Reform

The event which brought about a complete rupture between Hus and Zbyněk was the change of allegiance of papal obedience from Gregory XII to Alexander V. As mentioned in the preceding chapter, thirteen cardinals of the Roman and Avignonese obedience had repudiated their respective popes and had issued a call to the Council of Pisa. There the Schism was to be healed by the deposition of both reigning popes and the election of a new head of the Church, who would be recognized by all nations. This message was brought to King Wenceslas in May 1408 by the king's confessor, Bishop Nicholas of Nezero. It created a sensation. The king saw in this development an opportunity to play a decisive role in healing the Schism. But he realized that, first of all, he had to purge his own land of any aspersion of heresy, such as was occasioned by the citing of Stanislav and Páleč to the curia. Wenceslas therefore demanded of the archbishop that he declare the country free from any taint of heresy. The archbishop, who himself had been involved in the official complaint of heresy sent to the curia, was understandably reluctant to comply with the royal request. In this he was abetted by his chief official, John Kbel. In the end, he defied the king by taking refuge at his stronghold at Roudnice, where his officials joined him, bringing with them the cathedral treasures. The king's anger now was raised to white heat. Zbyněk, taking fright, quickly returned to Prague and on July 17, at the hurriedly summoned synod, issued the desired declaration. It stated that "he, through his vicars in spiritual matters and his prelates . . . had diligently made and held a strict examination in the city, diocese, and province of Prague and neither had found, nor could find, any error or heresy."[1] Wenceslas thereupon informed the cardinals that he was taking steps to cooperate with their efforts to terminate the Schism, without, however, as yet abandoning his obedience to Gregory XII.

Stanislav and Páleč in the meantime obeyed the citation to appear before the cardinal appointed as their judge. When they reached Bologna, however, they were arrested, robbed, and thrown into prison by Cardinal Baldassarre Cossa, who had joined the cardinals in revolt; he accused the Czech masters of continuing to acknowledge Gregory as pope. The news reached Prague in November and caused a sensation.

With heresy accusations being freely bandied about, it was inevitable that sooner or later Hus would be involved in them. A number of complaints had been levied against him by the Prague anti-reformist clergy, who submitted them to Archbishop Zbyněk some time in August or September.[2] He was not, however, charged with heresy, but with severe criticism of the morals and the simoniacal practices of the clergy. In the first place, he was accused of having declared that the payments for chrism, baptism, and funeral services were simony, and therefore heresy. Further, he was said to have defamed the memory of canon Peter of Všeruby, a notorious pluralist, by saying that he, Hus, would not wish to die with so many benefices in his possession. Next, he had expressed a wish that his soul would be where Wyclif's soul was. His enemies also charged that Hus had excessively criticized priestly vices contrary to the synodical prohibition of such preaching the preceding year. Finally, his adversaries complained—and this we learn from Hus' reply—that "remanence is still held by many in the city," although they did not assert that Hus was among them.

Hus easily defended himself against these charges.[3] He

---

[1] F. Palacký, ed., *Documenta Mag. Joannis Hus* (Praha, F. Tempsky, 1869) , p. 392.

[2] *Ibid.*, pp. 153-55; V. Novotný, ed., *M. Jana Husi Korespondence a dokumenty* (Praha, Komise pro vydávání pramenů náboženského hnutí českého, 1920) , No. 166.

[3] Novotný, *Korespondence*, No. 12; Palacký, *Documenta*, pp. 155-63;

pointed out that the Church itself forbade payments for sacraments as, for instance, had been done at the Council of Tribur. As for his statement about Peter of Všeruby, he had made it by way of personal determination not to follow his or other pluralists' example; this action was praiseworthy rather than reprehensible. He concluded his sermon by requesting his audience to pray for Peter and by declaring: "I hope that he is saved, although I fear lest he be damned." As for wishing to be where Wyclif's soul was, he pointed out that this expression only asserted that he hoped Wyclif would be among the saved, since he knew positively nothing to the contrary. As for his denouncing the clergy contrary to the synodical prohibition, Hus curtly replied that preaching the truth is not "excessive denunciation." Finally, he asserted that the charge of remanence needed to be factually proved, not loosely and irresponsibly tossed about.

Later, Hus expanded this defense into a treatise entitled *De arguendo clero pro concione.*[4] He deals therein with the question "whether in preaching the gospel before the clergy and the common people it is permissible to speak charitably against the vices of the clergy, to expose their hypocrisy, and to preach against manifest wickedness." He argues that both Christ and His apostles, as well as the prophets, upbraided evildoers. Moreover, it is proper to do so in the vernacular, for bad priesthood is odious both to the people and to God.

Hus' defense against the charges preferred to the archbishop did not satisfy all his friends. One such well-wisher was a former university master, but at the time a monk, John of Rakovník.[5] He approved of Hus' struggle against such clerical abuses as simony and pluralism, but was disquieted by what he regarded as Hus' inadequate or unsatisfactory reply to the charge concerning Wyclif and Peter of

---

see also Matthew Spinka, *John Hus' Concept of the Church* (Princeton, Princeton University Press, 1966), pp. 82-84.

[4] *Historia et monumenta Joannis Hus atque Hieronymi Pragensis, confessorum Christi,* 2 vols. (Norimberg, 1715), I, pp. 185-91.

[5] Novotný, *Korespondence,* No. 14.

Všeruby. He would have wished Hus to denounce Wyclif outright as a heretic. By renouncing Wyclif, Hus could have quieted the rising storm in the nation. "On you are fixed the hopes and desires of the nation," he cried. Hus, on his part, could not do it, for he understood clearly that Wyclif was being put forth only as a means of defeating all reforms. Evidently, John of Rakovník did not know Wyclif from his actual writings, but from such charges as were found in the forty-five articles. As has been remarked previously, this attitude toward Wyclif was all too common even among well-intentioned but ill-informed people.

Zbyněk continued to insist that all his clergy remain faithful to Gregory XII, despite the fact that Wenceslas, since the middle of the year 1408, had declared himself for "neutrality" between the two popes. Apparently Hus' opponents accused him of being "a disobedient son of the mother Church," because he too embraced neutrality. Sometime between October and December of that year he wrote a defense, which he sent to Archbishop Zbyněk. He professed that he was willing to obey both the pope and the archbishop as well as the civil authorities in whatever they "rightly" commanded. "But I cannot take part in the contention about the priority of honor . . . nor can I take sides with the apostolic lord in the fact that he does not keep his pledged oath which is evident to almost all Christendom . . . Therefore, in the matter of these two things—i.e., the contention of the pope with the antipope, and the non-fulfillment of his oath—I am neutral."[6]

The effort to gain King Wenceslas' active participation in ending the Schism was continued by the French court. It issued an invitation to the world to that effect in May. The defiant cardinals had requested the French King, Charles VI, to send a special delegation to Prague. He complied with the request toward the end of October. His delegation was joined by a Brabant embassy, which went to Prague to accompany the king's niece, Princess Agnes of Zhořelec, back to Brussels, where she was to wed the Brabant Duke

6 *Ibid.*, No. 13.

ınthony. The king's message was addressed not only to Wenceslas and the archbishop, but to the university as well. Among the French delegation was Jacob of Nouvion, a representative of the University of Paris. They reached Prague sometime in November, but had to await the return of the king from his visitation to Germany. Their stay was thus extended for some three months. This delay afforded them plenty of opportunity to explain to the university masters the French plans for the forthcoming Council of Pisa, including the newly adopted French ecclesiastical order, the so-called Gallican liberties. This plan, worked out by the Crown Council and the Sorbonne, was intended as a defiance of Benedict XIII. Basically, it was but an extension of the principle that the French king is master in his own country. The king's rule thus comprised the administrative part of the Church as well. The French Church was, therefore, ecclesiastically independent of the papacy and was governed through its councils by the king.

The Czech masters held a banquet for the French delegation, at which Jacob of Nouvion became involved in a rather stormy controversy about the question of "clerical voluntary poverty" in which no holds were barred.[7] On the Czech side the thesis was defended particularly by Jakoubek of Stříbro, who had shortly before claimed in a sermon that the reform of the Church was possible only by a radical return to the practices of the primitive Church. This, as will be remembered, was the favorite thesis of Matthew of Janov. In this stand Jakoubek was supported not only by Hus but by the whole reform party among the university masters. The Parisian theologian propounded the position that poverty was not required, but only counseled, by Christ. When driven to abandon this line of reasoning by the Scriptural evidence brought forth by the Czech masters, he changed his argument by asserting that "priests are not

<hr />

[7] V. Novotný, *M. Jan Hus, život a dílo*, 2 vols. (Praha, Jan Laichter, 1919-21), I, pp. 244-50; F. M. Bartoš, *Čechy v době Husově, 1378-1415* (Praha, Jan Laichter, 1947), pp. 296-97.

bound to observe all Christ's counsels."[8] This admission then led to the deeper and more important proposition as to whether the Church, by its own magisterial authority, can set aside and nullify Christ's plain teaching and command. There the Czech masters, denying that the Church had such power, were on solid ground. Nouvion later wrote a treatise about the disputation, in which he deftly implied that he had been victorious in the encounter; but the very fact that he wrote it in his own defense indicates that in his heart he was less than sure of his victory. At any rate, the disputation revealed, more clearly than anything else could do, the real cause of the controversy between the two parties: namely, whether Christ's teaching and practice were the supreme rule of the life of Christians or whether the Church's decision overrode even the plain command of Christ. This was not a conflict between the "heresy" of the Czech masters and the Church's rightful authority, nor did Nouvion treat it as such. It was a fundamental contradiction in the two concepts of the very essence of the Christian religion.

The tension between the reform party and its opponents was further augmented by an act of defiance on the part of the Czech masters directed against their German colleagues, the archbishop, and King Wenceslas, for the latter frowned upon all actions which might bring the country into disrepute. When the university masters considered the choice of the director for the January 1409 *Quodlibet*, young Matthew Knín voluntarily offered himself for the arduous task. His election was a foregone conclusion, for ever since 1391 there existed a regulation that a voluntary offer of directorship *must* be accepted. The *Quodlibet* proceedings, begun on January 3, were stormy; it was permissible to discuss any subject, for only the *conclusiones* could be forbidden by the chancellor-archbishop. Knín had chosen for the general

---

[8] Jan Sedlák, ed., "Jacobi de Noviano, magistri Parisiensis, Disputatio cum Hussitis," in *Tractatus causam Mg. Joannis Hus e parte catholica illustrantes* (Brno, 1914) , I, p. 21.

theme the proposition "whether the unchangeable highest good is the creator of the individual parts of the universe." The decidedly realistic character of this theme was obvious to all. There were 148 subjects distributed among the participants, although not all of them were actually presented. It was also the best attended of the recent *Quodlibets*; the great aula of the *Carolinum* was packed to the last inch of available space, and some could not even get in. The whole proceeding bore the character of an open conflict between the two warring factions of the university. For instance, John of Jesenice[9] dealt with a question based on Wyclif's treatise *De civili dominio*, formulated as "Whether a judge, knowing that the witnesses are falsely testifying and the accused is innocent, should condemn the latter"—a proposition with a transparent contemporary reference. The speaker, of course, answered his own question negatively.

Jerome of Prague,[10] who had recently returned from a prolonged stay abroad, had been entrusted with the honorable task of bringing to the *Quodlibet* the French and Brabant delegations. Among the latter were the bishop of Chalons-sur-Saône and Engelbert, the count of Nassau. On the last day of the tournament, Jerome himself held an eloquent defense of the universals—that ever lively subject of violent dispute between the Czech realists and the German nominalists. He declared that the earth, which is round, had been created by God in accordance with the ideal pattern, which is immanent in the physical world. The world is, therefore, governed by divine harmony. Whoever would deny this basic realist thesis is "a devilish heretic." He further shocked his audience by a definition of God's essence, which had led to his departure from the University of Cologne; he even repeated the graphic illustration of his concept—the so-called "shield of faith"—which he had then used. His view was contradicted by the elderly Blasius Vlk,

9 Jiří Kejř, *Husitský právník, M. Jan z Jesenice* (Praha, Československá akademie věd, 1965), p. 13.

10 F. Šmahel, *Jeroným Pražský* (Praha, Svobodné slovo, 1966), pp. 88-92.

who represented moderate realism and, therefore, repudiated Jerome's charge of "devilish heresy."

Jerome thereupon embarked on an eloquent praise of philosophy and its seven "resplendent virgins," the liberal arts. This was significant, because he thereby dethroned theology from its supreme position and replaced it by philosophy. It was likewise a reversal of the usual order of the university to ascribe hegemony to the faculty of arts. He did not, however, repudiate theology when it performed its rightful function.

From this purely philosophical theme he passed on to an impassioned avowal of Czech "sacrosanct" nationalism, excoriating the various attacks of the Germans upon it. He appealed to those who loved the dignity of the Bohemian king, his kingdom, and the city of Prague, "to strive to protect the good, in fact the best, reputation we have hitherto enjoyed in all lands. Do not believe the base and deceitful liars who endeavor to pollute that good reputation and to shame the representatives of our sacred Czech nation." This was again an obvious reference to the Germans who were slandering the good name of that city and its university.

Jerome then concluded with a qualified avowal of adherence to Wyclif, and exhorted the students to read his works. He declared that he himself read Wyclif the same way he read Aristotle: "I confess to you that I read and study the books of Wyclif as I do those of other doctors and that I have learned from them much good. . . . For that reason I appeal to you earnestly to read and study his writings, especially the philosophical. . . . If you meet there with something contrary to the faith, do not follow or hold it, but submit yourselves to the faith."[11] When the majority of the masters and the members of the foreign delegations had departed, Jerome read to the remaining audience the Oxford University letter recommending Wyclif and declaring him "an evangelical doctor." It asserted that

11 Quoted in Paul de Vooght, *L'hérésie de Jean Huss* (Louvain, Publications universitaires de Louvain, 1960) , p. 109; see Šmahel, *Jeroným Pražský*, p. 92.

he was not a heretic, nor was he condemned or burned as such. Like Hus, Jerome expressed a wish that his soul might be where Wyclif's was.

When finally King Wenceslas returned from his extended journey, the French delegation was at last able to present him, about the middle of January, their king's message at his residence in Kutná Hora. Their missive could be reduced to the request that Wenceslas publicly renounce his allegiance to the Roman pope, Gregory XII. Hitherto, despite the fact that Gregory had refused to annul his predecessor's approval of the election of Ruprecht of the Palatinate to the imperial dignity, Wenceslas hesitated to renounce his obedience to him. He had declared himself "neutral" as to the claims of both popes. Since Ruprecht also remained faithful to Gregory, the request of the French delegation seemed reasonable. The cardinals, moreover, promised that, if Wenceslas acceded to their urging, they would support his restoration to the crown of the king of the Romans. On this condition, Wenceslas was willing to accept the French proposal, although he did not immediately renounce his obedience to Gregory.

Naturally, the ambassadors also wished the express approval of their plans by Archbishop Zbyněk and by the university. It was extremely important for the restoration of the royal title to Wenceslas that the orthodoxy of the country be above question. To his surprise, the king met with rejection of his newly adopted policy; both the archbishop and the German masters at the university, who themselves had had the invitation to support the forthcoming Council for about three months, now openly refused to support the king. Zbyněk's reasons for the refusal are difficult to fathom. Bartoš credits him with a strong sense of loyalty to the Roman pope, whom hitherto all Bohemia acknowledged, such as befits the traditional soldier's code of honor.[12] However, the archbishop's conduct on many occasions actually contradicted this assumption. Kejř ascribes Zbyněk's attitude

---

[12] Bartoš, *Čechy v době Husově*, p. 314.

to "political conservatism."[13] One must not forget, however, that by this time the archbishop had been thoroughly committed to the anti-reformist policies of the high clergy, with the powerful Bishop John "the Iron" at their head. His attitude was also partly affected by his animus toward the Czech masters. The German masters, on the other hand, who came mostly from lands loyal to Ruprecht, feared the loss of the benefices which had been granted them by Gregory. The then rector, Henning of Baltenhagen, convoked the university masters (November 26 and December 5, 1408), at which meetings it was decided to remain loyal to Gregory.

King Wenceslas, as usual, was enraged at what he regarded as disloyalty and opposition to himself on the part of the Germans. He particularly resented their continued recognition of Ruprecht as emperor. He requested that the university send its delegation to his court at Kutná Hora. The university complied and sent an eight-member deputation, two from each nation. The Czechs were represented by two conservative theological professors, John Eliášův and Andrew of Brod. The deputation was received by the king at his court on January 18, 1409. As had been decided beforehand, the three German "nations" expressed their disapproval of the calling of the Council; only the Czechs approved. They perhaps hoped that the election of a new pope might bring about reforms. The stubbornness of the Germans sent the king into a paroxysm of rage; he dismissed the Germans with the threat of dire punishment, if they continued to defy his will. Thereupon, Wenceslas' crown Council, under the leadership of Nicholas called the Rich,[14] offered a solution which the king promptly accepted. It consisted of a radical subversion of the ratio of votes hitherto held by the university masters; the Czechs now received the three votes held by the foreign nations, and the

---

[13] Kejř, *Husitský právník*, p. 24.

[14] F. M. Bartoš, "Kdo vymohl Čechům dekret kutnohorský?" in *Jihočeský sborník historický*, XVIII (1939), pp. 66 ff. Bartoš credits Nicholas the Rich with the victory.

foreigners one. Thus by a mere scratch of the pen Wenceslas gained for his Pisa policy the majority of the university votes. This was the famous Decree of Kutná Hora, issued on January 18, 1409. It enabled the Czech element at the university to come into complete dominance of its affairs, to which it had been entitled numerically for some years past. Four days thereafter, the king informed the French delegation of his renunciation of obedience to Gregory XII.[15]

As might have been expected, however, the German masters refused to accept the royal decree and decided to take steps to have it repealed. The university rector, Henning of Baltenhagen, presented their protest to the king on February 6, 1409. In it, the German masters petitioned for the repeal of the Decree of Kutná Hora and offered a compromise: let the university be divided into German and Czech foundations and let both parties live side by side. They even offered to send one of their members to the Council of Pisa. The king was almost persuaded to withdraw his recent decree, but before coming to a final decision, he called the Czech masters to an audience. Among the delegates were also Hus and Jerome. Stanislav of Znojmo and Stephen Páleč were then in Italy, and the leadership of the party thus devolved upon Hus and Jerome. The scene which ensued was described, unfortunately, only by a hostile and biased eyewitness, the king's official, Dr. John Náz. He recounted it at the Council of Constance, testifying that the Germans had persuaded the king

to conserve their rights that they have held from ancient times. . . . Thereafter this Hus, having come with Jerome and others, persuaded him, the king, to another course. Nevertheless, moved by anger, the king exclaimed, "You are always making trouble for me with your associate, Jerome;

15 Spinka, *John Hus' Concept of the Church*, pp. 90-91; also Bartoš, *M. Jan Hus jako rektor Karlovy university* (Praha, Společnost Husova musea, 1936) .

and if those whose concern it is will not take care of it, I myself will burn you![16]

The Decree of Kutná Hora was now really in danger. The Czech masters were obviously deeply perturbed, even in panic; they prepared a new appeal, presented perhaps to Nicholas the Rich, in which they offered, by way of compromise, no less than seven suggestions, which sounded like counsels of despair. If all their other offers were rejected, they were willing to reduce their demands to the holding of the rectorate or at least to having the dean of the philosophical faculty chosen from the Czech nation.

The king seemed to have been inclined to revoke the decree altogether. In the end it was saved by the action of the German princes; Ruprecht recalled the masters and students who recognized him as their king to his own University of Heidelberg. The most important of these enticements was the promise of the Margrave of Meissen to found a university at Leipzig, for the Saxon masters and students constituted at Prague the most numerous contingent. The German masters now took a vow that if the decree remained in force, they would leave Prague University *en masse*. They bound themselves to this promise on pain of a heavy fine, the loss of honor, and expulsion from the university. Moreover, Pope Gregory ordered the Germans to leave the university, which he now placed under a ban.[17]

The decisive moment arrived toward the end of April when the election of the rector and the dean for the next semester was to take place. The conflict which then occurred made the choice of these officials impossible; both parties had to appeal to the crown Council for a decision. This body called representatives of the rival groups to the royal castle of Točník and there presented the foreigners with the

[16] Matthew Spinka, ed. and transl., *John Hus at the Council of Constance* (New York and London, Columbia University Press, 1965), p. 177.

[17] F. M. Bartoš, "Výročí Kutnohorského dekretu," in *Kostnické Jiskry*, January 15, 1959.

fourth alternative submitted by the Czechs earlier: namely, that the Czechs be divided into two nations, Czechs and Moravians, each of whom was to have a vote, while the foreigners be likewise divided into two, Polish and German contingents, each having a vote. The Germans, however, already determined to leave, rejected the compromise. It was this decision which saved the decree in its original form.[18]

Furthermore, John of Jesenice now wrote, apparently only for the guidance of the crown Council and particularly for Nicholas the Rich, a brilliant treatise entitled *Defensio mandati*,[19] which proved most helpful in defending the document legally. The *Defensio* is based on the principle that the king has the sovereign right and duty to rule his country and to protect the native population more than the foreigners. The Decree of Kutná Hora agreed with the legal and political requirements of the case, for the Czech element at the university had actually reached both numerical majority and intellectual superiority. Since the founding of the universities of Vienna, Heidelberg, Cologne, Erfurt, and Cracow, the number of Germans at Prague had been considerably reduced, while the Czech element kept steadily increasing. The decree, according to Jesenic, was in harmony with the intention of the founder of the university, Charles IV, who specifically stipulated that it was to provide an opportunity for higher learning to the native population. Jesenic furthermore drew on the inexhaustible material of the *Decretal*, the *Decretales*, and the Roman law, and skillfully refuted all the German arguments for the return of the *status quo ante*. This masterly piece of legal learning undoubtedly helped the crown Council, and particularly the powerful protector of the Czech interest, Nicholas the Rich, to defend the decree against all objections.

[18] Bartoš, *Čechy v době Husově*, pp. 311-12.
[19] Palacký, *Documenta*, pp. 355-63. There it is ascribed to Hus. But Kejř, in his *Husitský právník*, pp. 15-19, argues convincingly for Jesenic's authorship. See also Bartoš, "Kdo vymohl Čechům dekret Kutnohorský," pp. 67-70.

King Wenceslas actually was so influenced by his advisers that he again changed his mind, although the intransigent attitude of the Germans had already done much to influence him. On May 9 he convened all the university masters to hear his decision, announced to them by Nicholas the Rich, in the impasse of the election of the rector and dean. The king named for the summer semester Zdeněk of Labouň as rector and Simon of Tišnov as dean of the philosophical faculty, both members of the reform party. Moreover, since the previous rector, Henning of Baltenhagen, and the dean, Albert Varentrapp, had refused to surrender the insignia of office, these were forcibly taken from them by the police. Thereupon, in accordance with their vow, almost 1,500 German masters and students left Prague for their various destinations in Germany, mostly for Leipzig. Among them were seven or eight hundred masters. The faculty of law, however, which formed a separate institution, remained in Prague and was made up of both the Czech and the German masters and students.[20] The whole affair was completed by June 28, when the king declared the Germans to be expellees and deprived them of their university professorships. He then named Czech masters to the vacancies thus created. Thereafter, the Germans never missed an opportunity of vilifying the Czechs. Their hatred turned especially against Hus and Jesenic, particularly Jesenic, in whom they saw the principal literary and legal representative of the Czech cause. They invented a parody of Jesus' genealogy, in which Wyclif was designated as the ancestor of all Prague Czech masters: for the rest "Knín begat Jerome, the athlete of Antichrist; Jerome, before the migration of the three nations, begat Jesenic; and after the migration, Jesenic begat Zdislav the leper. . . ."[21] Kejř concludes: "With complete right it is possible to add Jesenic to Hus and Jerome, as the third principal creator of the program of the Czech party in the storms concerning the Decree [of Kutná Hora] and even perhaps as the leading actor."[22] This assumption does not

---

[20] De Vooght, *L'hérésie*, p. 112, n. 4.
[21] Kejř, *Husitský právník*, p. 22.　　　　　　　[22] *Ibid.*, p. 23.

necessarily contradict Bartoš' ascription of the victory to Nicholas the Rich.

In the middle of 1409 another accusation was leveled against Hus, mainly by the former preacher of Bethlehem Chapel, John Protiva. He had abandoned his reformist career and had become so fanatical a member of the opposing camp as to stoop to spying on Hus. Once Hus recognized him among the audience and called to him, "Write it down, you skulker, and carry it to that place!", pointing in the direction of the archiepiscopal palace. Zbyněk received Protiva's charges[23] and ordered Hus to respond to them before the inquisitor, Maurice Rvačka, who himself later spied on Hus at his preaching.[24] Protiva charged that Hus had declared in 1399 that "a priest in mortal sin cannot consecrate the venerable body of Christ in the sacrament or offer other sacraments of the Church." Hus answered that all who had heard him preach knew that he ever taught the very opposite, namely, that both good and bad priests consecrate the sacraments validly, although bad priests do not do so worthily; for it is the divine power which operates through them. Further, it was charged that at the same time he had asserted that Pope Gregory the Great was a rhymester (the word is given in Czech, *prlenec*). Hus willingly acknowledged having said that, but explained that he had used the word in the good sense of a "rhetor" and had found Gregory's poetry pleasing. In the third place, Protiva repeated the charge that Hus had declared that a priest not in grace does not consecrate the sacraments. Hus questioned Protiva as to where he had said it, and declared then that Protiva's reply was a lie. In the next charge Protiva stated that in talking about John of Pomuk and Nicholas Puchník, who had been tortured by the king in 1393, Hus had expressed himself slightingly of the two men. Hus replied that all he had said was that there was no reason why

---

[23] Palacký, *Documenta*, pp. 164-69. Hus recorded them, along with his remembered replies, only in 1414 when he was preparing to depart for Constance.

[24] Hus, *Replica contra occultum adversarium*, in *Historia et monumenta*, I, pp. 168-70.

the worship services should be stopped in the whole country on their account. Furthermore, Hus was charged with having said that the Antichrist had planted his foot in the Roman Church and that it would be difficult to remove it. He declared that even the saints taught that the Antichrist had fixed his foot in the Roman curia—which was quite a different matter from the Roman Church! De Vooght remarks that the Pisan cardinals obviously thought the same.[25] The next charge asserted that the archbishop had forbidden any "scandalous" preaching, and that Hus had not even after that prohibition ceased to preach sermons which incited the populace against the clergy to the defamation of their reputation. Hus replied that he had preached against the sins of the clergy in order to obtain their reformation, not to defame their reputation.

He was further accused of having declared that any priest charging a fee for the sacraments either by direct demand or by some indirect means is a heretic. Hus countered the charge by saying that according to Pope Innocent whoever secures an ecclesiastical office by a payment or takes pay for sacraments is a simoniac, and therefore a heretic. He was further charged with having called Wyclif "a catholic evangelical doctor," and having wished his soul were where Wyclif's was. Hus explained that if "catholic" meant "general," he hoped that Wyclif was a good Christian and that he is in the kingdom of heaven. He acknowledged that he had wished to be where Wyclif's soul was, although he did not assert "that Wyclif is among the saved, for I do not condemn anyone of whom I have no Scripture or revelation that he is damned." Being accused of having said that no one could be excommunicated by a prelate who had not first been excommunicated by God, Hus owned that he had said it and still asserted it. Charged with having said that Wyclif "would sway some heads" [*nejednomu hlavu zvykle*],[26] Hus replied that many hate Wyclif because he shows them

25 De Vooght, *L'hérésie*, p. 120.

26 Hus wrote this statement in the margin when he transcribed some of Wyclif's books for his own use in teaching at the beginning of his academic career.

the truth and insists that the clergy live in accordance with the law of Christ. The next charge stated that he had raised contentions between the Czechs and the Germans. Hus responded that "Christ knows that I love a good German more than a bad Czech, even if he were my brother." To the charge that his preaching incited the populace against the archbishop and the clergy, he commented that such had also been the charge against Jesus. Then the archbishop demanded that Hus show the letters of foundation of the Bethlehem Chapel to prove his right to preach to parishioners not of his own parish, but of another. Hus testified that the cornerstone of the chapel had been laid by Archbishop John of Jenštejn by the royal permission and the approbation of Pope Gregory. He himself preached by the authority of God and of the archbishop, having been confirmed as the preacher of the Word of God. As for his authority to conduct worship service with singing, he reaffirmed that he did so by divine authority and the terms of the chapel charter.

The examination of Hus before the inquisitor Maurice Rvačka must have satisfied that official. But the favorable result secured on that particular occasion by no means disposed of the charges permanently. We shall meet them again, and in full force, at Hus' trial conducted by the Council of Constance; there they were not dismissed as unfounded, but became a part of the final charges against him.

Since the university, by the terms of the Decree of Kutná Hora, passed wholly into the hands of the Czech masters, they were free now to choose one of their members as rector. Nevertheless, that office became singularly difficult to fill, for it exposed its holder to the incessant calumny of the Germans. On October 17, 1409, it was Hus who was chosen rector.[27] The difficulty of the office and of the life of the university in general was likewise the natural result of the loss

---

[27] It used to be asserted that Hus had been rector for the first time in 1402, and that this was his second rectorate. This assertion was based on a misreading of the pertinent document. Hus was rector only once, in the winter semester of 1409-10.

of the large number of Germans, which undoubtedly had weakened the whole institution. It did not, however, altogether ruin it, as the Germans had hoped their withdrawal would do.

Hus was inaugurated three days after his election by an unnamed master, perhaps the oldest among the electors, to whom Hus refers in his acceptance speech as "the venerable master." This dignitary introduced the new rector in a flowery oration replete with fulsome praise. Hus responded in an address based on the same text his introducer had chosen: "Many are called, but few are chosen."[28] He repeatedly disclaimed the exaggerated flattery of his introducer and professed himself inadequate for the great task ahead. He marveled that the electors, "out of so great a number have chosen exactly me," and in an excess of humility even suggested that they had allowed themselves to be duped. He asked the aid of the members of the faculty in the performance of the difficult tasks, and suggested that they choose men of wisdom who would help him to bear the heavy burden. He then exhorted his hearers to work faithfully for the liberties of the university and to "remain faithful to the most illustrious ruler Wenceslas . . . , his kingdom and the University of Prague." Hus delivered the second rectoral speech two weeks later, on the text; "And this I pray, that your love may abound yet more and more in knowledge and all discernment."[29] On that occasion it was customary to read the university statutes, now undoubtedly adjusted to the terms of the Decree, to the convocation of the whole body.

Hus thus succeeded to the leadership of the university, in addition to heading the popular movement. He took the place of Stanislav of Znojmo, who had returned from his imprisonment in Bologna of almost a year in a

---

[28] Matt. 22:14. The text of the address is found in B. Havránek et al., eds., *Výbor z české literatury husitské doby*, 2 vols. (Praha, Československá akademie věd, 1963-64) , I, pp. 105-10. See also Bartoš, *M. Jan Hus jako rektor Karlovy university*, pp. 11-14; also his "Dvě rektorské řeči Husovy" in *Jihočeský sborník historický*, X (1937) , pp. 1-15.

[29] Phil. 1:9.

chastened and broken spirit. Both he and Páleč had to renounce their adherence to Wyclif. In fact, from now on both masters gradually turned their backs upon their distinguished reforming past and became leaders of the camp of the reactionary papalist party. They became Hus' chief opponents; Páleč, after Stanislav's death, acted as Hus' principal enemy at the Council of Constance.

During his rectorate, Hus delivered the customary memorial oration on the anniversary of the death of Emperor Charles IV (November 29). On that occasion, as noted in Chapter II, he eloquently eulogized the memory of the outstanding Czech university masters.[30] He also completed at the theological faculty his lectures on Lombard's *Sentences*,[31] and published his Commentary on them. Shortly after assuming his office, he ordered that a new book of the university transactions be begun, the Decree of Kutná Hora forming its first entry. However, his martyrdom made his rectors' book "a relic," for it was no longer used. His successors in the office used the old book, and Hus' rectoral register was lost some time after the Battle of White Mountain (1620).[32] As rector, he presided over the university senate; therein he had the chief say in making the decisions.

Besides these rectoral labors, Hus prepared several of his students for promotion for the master's degree, such as that of John of Vlhlavy[33] and Nicholas of Pavlíkov.[34] On January 19, 1410, he preached before the university a powerful sermon on the text, "Go ye also into my vineyard."[35] He dealt with his concept of the Church, which consisted of

---

[30] Havránek, *Výbor*, I, pp. 110-13. Also in Evžen Stein, ed. and transl., *M. Jan Hus jako universitní rektor a profesor* (Praha, Jan Laichter, 1948), pp. 18-38.

[31] V. Flajšhans, ed., *Super IV Sententiarum*, 3 vols. (Praha, 1904-06).

[32] F. M. Bartoš, *Po stopách pozůstalosti M. J. Husi* (Praha, Společnost Husova musea, 1939), pp. 6-8.

[33] S. Harrison Thomson, "Four unpublished questiones of John Hus," in *Medievalia et Humanistica*, No. 7 (1952), pp. 86-88.

[34] F. M. Bartoš, *Literární činnost M. J. Husi* (Praha, Česká akademie věd a umění, 1948), pp. 59-60.

[35] Matt. 20:4. See A. Schmidtová, ed., *Johannes Hus, Positiones, recommendationes, sermones* (Praha, Státní pedagogické nakladatelství, 1958), pp. 131-39; also De Vooght, *L'hérésie*, pp. 125-27.

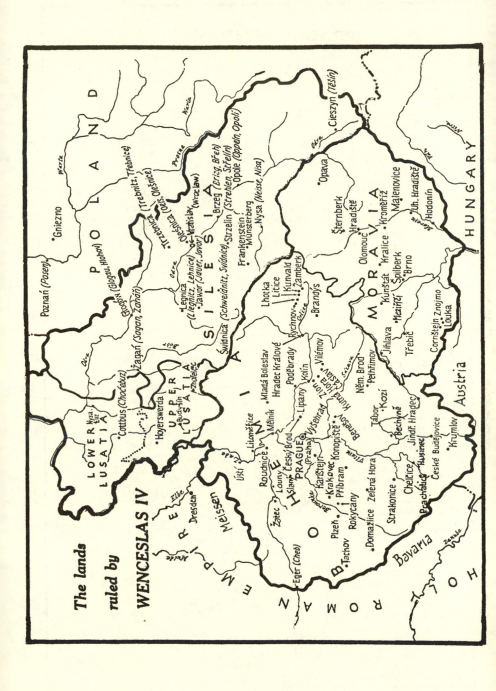

The lands ruled by WENCESLAS IV

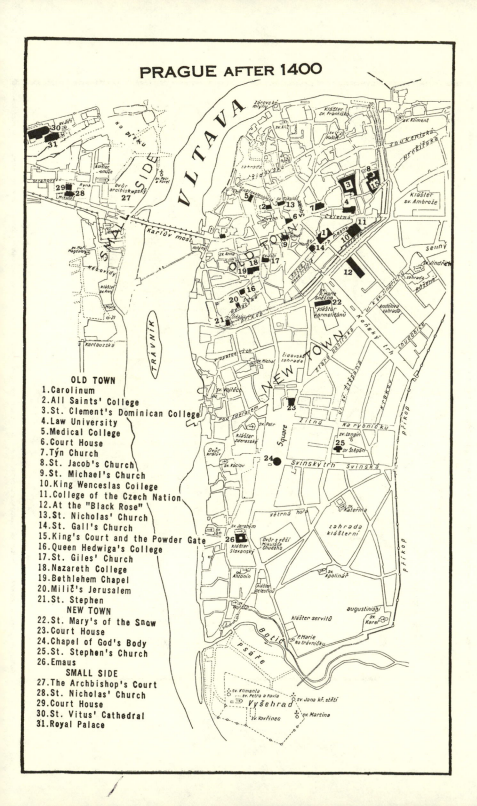

# PRAGUE AFTER 1400

**OLD TOWN**
1. Carolinum
2. All Saints' College
3. St. Clement's Dominican College
4. Law University
5. Medical College
6. Court House
7. Týn Church
8. St. Jacob's Church
9. St. Michael's Church
10. King Wenceslas College
11. College of the Czech Nation
12. At the "Black Rose"
13. St. Nicholas' Church
14. St. Gall's Church
15. King's Court and the Powder Gate
16. Queen Hedwiga's College
17. St. Giles' Church
18. Nazareth College
19. Bethlehem Chapel
20. Milič's Jerusalem
21. St. Stephen

**NEW TOWN**
22. St. Mary's of the Snow
23. Court House
24. Chapel of God's Body
25. St. Stephen's Church
26. Emaus

**SMALL SIDE**
27. The Archbishop's Court
28. St. Nicholas' Church
29. Court House
30. St. Vitus' Cathedral
31. Royal Palace

Hus at the stake

From the Litoměřice hymnbook (early sixteenth century)

Bethlehem Chapel, restored in 1949-54

three points, the first two of which are familiar and will be dealt with later. The third point refers to the pope and the cardinals as constituting the Church. This was actually inconsistent with the other two points, and Hus later abandoned it in that form. What he retained was only the assertion that if the pope and the cardinals were of the predestinate, they were members of the true Church.

In the meantime the Council of Pisa had held its sessions ever since March 25, 1409. Wenceslas sent to it numerous delegates; the university was represented by Andrew of Brod and Helmond of Soltwedel. The Council cited Gregory XII and Benedict XIII before its tribunal. The popes naturally refused on the ground that the Council had no jurisdiction over them. Thereupon, they were deposed on June 5 for non-appearance and excommunicated as "notorious schismatics, prompters of schism and notorious heretics, errant from the faith, and guilty of notorious and enormous crimes of perjury and violated oaths."[36] The populace burned the popes in effigy. John Gerson, chancellor of the University of Paris, justified this assumption of power over the popes in his treatise *De auferibilitate papae ab ecclesia*. However, against his advice not to proceed with the election of a new pope until a larger consensus as to the deposition of the two then reigning popes had been secured, the Council soon after undertook to elect a new pope. It chose the archbishop of Milan, Peter Philarghi, who assumed the name of Alexander V (June 26). He was favored because he was neither French nor Italian, but a Greek from Candia in Crete, a Franciscan, educated in Italy. If the French had expected that he would introduce reforms in the spirit of Gallican liberties, they were soon disappointed. He granted a few minor reforms, but deferred all the rest until the next Council, which he promised to call in three years. The Council was then dissolved on August 7.

The Czech delegation had for its principal task the secur-

[36] Quoted in James Westfall Thompson and Edgar N. Johnson, *An Introduction to Medieval Europe, 300-1500* (New York, W. W. Norton & Co., Inc., 1937), p. 975.

ing of recognition of King Wenceslas as the king of the Romans. Ruprecht had sent a delegation to the Council offering concessions, but it was too late. As long as he adhered to the deposed Gregory XII, his offer had no chance of being considered. Moreover, the cardinals had pledged their word to Wenceslas in order to induce him to support the call to Pisa, and felt themselves bound by it. One of the Czech representatives, Chancellor Wenceslas Králík, was even included in the delegation sent by the Council to Venice, to induce the republic to acknowledge Alexander as pope. The emissaries having succeeded in that mission, Pope Gregory, who was presiding at his own Council in the nearby Cividale, had to flee in disguise. But alas! the election of Alexander had for its consequence that the Schism was still further aggravated; since some nations refused to abandon the deposed popes, there now existed three popes! Alexander was acknowledged in France, England, Bohemia, Poland, and northern Italy. Germany was divided between him and Gregory. The entire Bohemian ecclesiastical province was now unified behind Alexander V with two most important exceptions: Archbishop Zbyněk and Bishop John of Litomyšl, who refused to recognize him. Indeed, both of them had sent their delegations to Gregory's Council at Cividale, and Zbyněk had placed Prague under an interdict —which was not, however, observed. He was furthermore appointed the papal legate for his archdiocese.

In the meantime, the appeal of the five university students who had refused to surrender their copies of Wyclif's books to the archbishop was being considered by the Pisan papal auditor, Henry Krumhart of Westerholz. Since Zbyněk had stubbornly refused to acknowledge the Pisan pope, the auditor started legal proceedings against him, which might have led to serious consequences for the archbishop. He took fright at the prospect, and sent two canonists to Pisa who, on September 2, announced Zbyněk's submission to the new pope.[37] The university, on its part, sent Mark of Hradec, the students' advocate, to Pisa. At first,

---

[37] Palacký, *Documenta*, pp. 372-73.

Zbyněk's belated action did not bring him an immediate release from the legal action. In fact, Henry Krumhart cited Zbyněk to the curia for December 8, and ordered him to take no steps against the student-appellants till then.

There occurred, however, a sudden change in Alexander's attitude toward Zbyněk. Whether the pope realized that he could bind Zbyněk to his cause by deciding in his favor, or whether the pope, "mendaciously misinformed," changed his mind upon receiving very generous gifts freely distributed by the archbishop's emissaries between the pope and the curia—as Hus always suggested and as Kejř asserts as an undoubted fact[38]—makes little difference. The fact remains that the pope issued, on December 20, a bull which completely approved Zbyněk's position.[39] He was authorized to appoint a six-member commission to examine Wyclif's books and, if they found them heretical, "to remove them from the eyes of the faithful." He was also to forbid the teaching of Wyclif's forty-five articles in his archdiocese. The most severe provision, obviously directed against Hus, although he was not named, was the prohibition of preaching in any but the cathedral, parochial, and monastic churches. Moreover, the pope rejected beforehand all appeals from the archbishop's actions. Although the Bethlehem Chapel was not a "private" place of worship, where alone preaching services were prohibited, yet it was assumed to be the very place against which the papal fulminations were directed. This is a clear proof that the reactionary party, regrettably now with the archbishop at its head, decided to stifle and silence the progressives at any cost. This was a grave blow at the reformers; they had zealously supported the Pisan Council, hoping that it would introduce reforms they had advocated. Now hardly had the Pisan pope been elected when he turned against them and joined Zbyněk's party.

Alexander's bull did not reach Prague until March 9,

[38] Kejř, *Husitský právník*, p. 29. The numerous instances where Hus mentions that the papal bull was acquired by the use of "suggestionem subdolam et informacionem vippeream ' are listed in Novotný, *Jan Hus*, I, p. 390, n. 2.
[39] Palacký, *Documenta*, pp. 374-76.

1410. The legal representative of the five students, Mark of Hradec, learned of its terms much sooner. As mentioned above, he had gone to the curia some time earlier and thus had learned that the students' case was, by the papal pronouncement, rendered utterly hopeless. He therefore declared in his and the students' names that he submitted to the archbishop's jurisdiction. Hus, who well knew that the action of the anti-reform party was aimed chiefly against him, appealed after the bull arrived in Prague, "from the pope ill-informed to a pope better-informed."[40]

Having been so strengthened by papal authority, Zbyněk now proceeded to act in accordance with its provisions. He appointed the commission for the examination of Wyclif's works, composed entirely of anti-Wyclifites. Under such circumstances the result could be safely anticipated. Without waiting for the verdict of the commission, Hus preached, on March 20, 1410, a sermon based on Paul's summary of the tradition he had received from the Lord about the Last Supper.[41] In it the Lord expressly stated: "This is my body . . ." Hus thus refuted the archbishop's repeated prohibition of the use of the word "bread" in the celebration of the sacrament of the altar. De Vooght calls Zbyněk's position "absurd" and Hus' doctrine "entirely catholic," although he thinks that the latter, by calling attention to the archbishop's theological error, intended to throw a suspicion of heresy on him.[42] But if Zbyněk's position was non-catholic, then De Vooght himself implies that the archbishop's prohibition tended toward heresy.

In the meantime, Pope Alexander V died on May 3, 1410, after a pontificate lasting less than a year. There was no great doubt about his successor. It was Cardinal Baldassarre

---

[40] The text of this appeal has not been preserved. It is mentioned by Hus in his *De ecclesia*, edited by S. Harrison Thomson (Boulder, Colorado, University of Colorado Press, 1956), p. 231; also in Novotný, *Korespondence*, p. 124: "A qua bulla appellavi ad informacionem meliorem ipsius Alexandri . . ."

[41] I. Cor. 11:26.

[42] De Vooght, *L'hérésie*, pp. 131-32.

Cossa, the archbishop of Bologna, who had refused the office when it had been offered to him at the Pisa Council. He came of a family which was engaged in piratical pursuits. Under Pope Boniface he quickly rose to high positions in the Church, despite his unfitness for any spiritual office; he was a "vir in temporalibus quidem magnus, in spiritualibus vero nullus omnino atque ineptus."[43] At the time of his elevation to the papacy, he possessed only the deacon's orders. He was ordained to priesthood on the same day, and within a week was consecrated bishop. For the highest spiritual office in the gift of the Church he, a soldier rather than a priest, was the worst possible choice. From a man of his character, no reforms of the abuses in the Church could be expected.

Before the result of the examination by Zbyněk's commission could be announced at the synodical meeting held on June 16, 1410, at Zbyněk's palace, the majority of the university masters, assembled by the rector, John Šindel, protested against the intended burning of Wyclif's books, if the archbishop should order such an action. Their decision was made public. At the synodical meeting the commission then declared fifteen of Wyclif's books to be heretical and condemned among them some purely nontheological works. Thereupon Zbyněk forbade holding or teaching any of the condemned tenets and ordered that, in accordance with the papal mandate, all Wyclif's books be surrendered to him. Furthermore, all preaching in "private" places was ordered stopped. As for the five students, they were bidden, along with their lawyer, Mark of Hradec, to surrender their books within six days on pain of excommunication. Furthermore, anyone disregarding all these orders was to be excommunicated.

Hus now openly opposed the archbishop's decision con-

---

[43] A. Franzen and W. Müller, eds., *Das Konzil von Konstanz* (Freiburg, Basel, Wien, Herder, 1964), p. 45; E. Delaruelle, E. R. Labande and Paul Ourliac, *L'Eglise au temps du Grand Schisme et de la crise conciliaire, 1338-1449*, 2 vols. (Bloud & Gay, 1962), I, p. 161.

cerning Wyclif's books by quickly composing *De libris hereticorum legendis* (June 21, 1410),[44] a short treatise in which he quotes a number of Fathers in support of the proposition that such books are to be read for the truth they contain, and not burned. This procedure does not imply the sharing of the heretics' opinions. Heresy, according to Augustine, "is an erroneous doctrine, contrary to the Holy Scriptures, stubbornly defended." Furthermore, on June 22 he preached a sermon[45] in which he declared that the judges of Wyclif's works were unjustified in their decision and particularly denounced the prohibition of preaching in chapels. Christ commanded that the gospel be preached everywhere. Hus asserted further that despite "our scribes' prohibition, I, wishing to obey God rather than men . . . appeal from this wrongful command first of all to God . . . and further to the apostolic see, which should radiate greater authority than that of the prelates."[46] This appeal was dated June 25 and was addressed to Pope John XXIII; it is a skillful legal document, most likely composed by Jesenic either in whole or in part. In this *Instrumentum*,[47] Hus protests against Zbyněk's order of surrender of Wyclif's books "which with great labor, money and expense we purchased and procured." He objects to Zbyněk's securing from Alexander the "pretended" bull of December 20 by dishonest means and adulation. He calls the bull false in its charge that there exists heresy in the land and that the hearts of many are polluted thereby. Zbyněk himself, as far back as July 17, 1408, had declared that he had found no heresy in his archdiocese. Moreover, Hus argues that with the death of Alexander his bull has lost its validity. Furthermore, Zbyněk proposed to burn some of Wyclif's books dealing with logic and philosophy, such as *De ideis*,

[44] *Historia et monumenta*, I, pp. 127-30; a new edition in Jaroslav Eršil, ed., *Magistri Johannis Hus, Polemica* (Praha, Academia scientiarum Bohemoslovaca, 1966), pp. 21-37.

[45] The full text has not been published; only a portion of it is to be found in Jan Sedlák, *M. Jan Hus* (Praha, Dědictví sv. Prokopa, 1915), supplement, pp. 168-70.

[46] Novotný, *Korespondence*, pp. 56-59.

[47] Palacký, *Documenta*, pp. 387-96.

*De hypotheticis, De universalibus realibus, De probationi-bus propositionum, De attributis, De individuatione temporis,* and others, which were taught and received everywhere in the universities and which were of great value in teaching. As well could the works of Aristotle and Averroès be burned! He also came to the defense of the Bethlehem Chapel, declaring that it had been founded and canonically consecrated for the preaching in the Czech language and, therefore, was not a "private" place. The prohibition of preaching there was, on that account, unjust.

Associated with Hus in this appeal were three of the five students who had formerly appealed to the Council of Pisa, and three others who now joined the group. In addition, the former noble student of Hus, Zdislav of Zvířetice, a member of a noble family held in high esteem, headed the list of Hus' associates, thus proving his loyalty to his teacher as well as to the reform party. At the service held on the same day at the Bethlehem Chapel, Hus, after preaching a stirring sermon,[48] read his appeal to an audience which thronged every inch of the spacious auditorium. He told the hearers that Pope Alexander had ordered Zbyněk to exterminate "the errors sown by Wyclif's books in Bohemia and Moravia; that there are many people who hold Wyclif's articles contrary to the faith and that the hearts of many are infected by heresy . . ." The people shouted, "They lie! they lie!" He then asked dramatically, "Behold! I appealed against the archbishop's mandate; . . . will you support me?" The congregation thunderingly burst forth, "We will and do support you!"

This was, for Zbyněk, the last straw; not awaiting, as he had promised the king, the arrival of Margrave Jost of Moravia, who was to mediate the dispute, the archbishop ordered the books gathered at his court to be burned (July 16, 1410) . One of the chief advisers of Zbyněk in this affair, Canon Zdeněk of Chrast, himself lighted the pyre. The gates of the courtyard were closed, but the ringing of the bells

[48] Extracts from this sermon were reported by Zbyněk to Cardinal Colonna on July 11. *Ibid.*, pp. 404-06.

111

in Prague and the chanting of the *Te Deum* heralded the fateful deed. Although the papal bull did not specifically state that Zbyněk was authorized to burn the books, but merely "to remove them from the eyes of the faithful," the archbishop, in his anger, was not deterred from acting by so fine a point. Thereupon, however, he felt unsafe in his Prague residence, or was so affrighted and cowed at the prospect of the consequences which were sure to follow, that he precipitously fled to his castle at Roudnice. Two days later (July 18), he excommunicated Hus and his fellow-protestors as disobedient impugners of the catholic faith.[49] This action was of doubtful legality, for the death of Pope Alexander had, as Hus claimed, rendered his order invalid. Moreover, the excommunication of Hus and his fellow-appellants was not observed, and Hus continued to preach.

This defiance of Zbyněk was aggravated when five members of the faculty of arts (later joined by a sixth), decided to protest against the burning of Wyclif's books by a public defense of some of them. Late in July, the disputation began and lasted for some two weeks. It was opened by Hus, who chose to discuss Wyclif's *De trinitate*.[50] He challenged the members of Zbyněk's commisson to prove wherein the book was heretical, and declared that he "does not consent nor has he consented to its burning." He further protested against the prohibition of preaching in chapels: Where is a Scripture or a reasonable proof that in a church consecrated by an archbishop and intended specifically for preaching, confirmed by the pope . . . should the gospel proclamation be so needlessly prohibited?" The next speaker was Jakoubek of Stříbro, who chose to defend Wyclif's *Dialogus* on the ground that truth should be defended even at the cost of one's life. Wyclif's *De probationibus propositionum* was chosen by the next disputant, Simon of

[49] *Ibid.*, pp. 397-99.

[50] *Ibid.*, pp. 399-400; Novotný, *Korespondence*, No. 19; Novotný, *Jan Hus*, I, pp. 418 ff. Hus' defense is published in *Historia et monumenta*, I, pp. 131 ff.; a new edition in Eršil, *Polemica*, pp. 41-56.

Tišnov. He employed wit and irony as his weapon, referring, for instance, to Pope Gregorius as "Errorius," to whom Zbyněk continued to adhere even though the Czech masters had long before abandoned his obedience. He also declared Alexander's bull regarding Wyclif's books as obtained by lies and surreptitious means. Thereupon John of Jičín undertook to defend *De materia et forma*. He was followed by Procopius of Plzeň, who undertook to prove that Wyclif's *De ideis* was free from all heresy (as indeed it was). The last of the disputants was Zdislav of Zvířetice, who challenged the archbishop to show what heresy was contained in *De universalibus*. He remarked that it was still read and commented on at Oxford. This disputation comprised the remarkably effective and brilliantly executed *Quodlibet* of July-August. On August 28 Hus himself concluded the lively intellectual tournament by preaching a sermon on the text, "Ye are the salt of the earth."[51] The first part, frankly drawn from Wyclif's sermons, was intended to show that this man, regarded as a heretic, could preach eloquently in genuine gospel terms. The concluding part is Hus' own application of the text to the situation confronting the contemporary Church. He particularly turned to the doctors in schools and those who "strive to stop the mouths of preachers, accusing the truth by lies, saying that the masters adhering to errors drove out foreign nations, and lying that they [the masters] think wrongly regarding the body of Christ . . ." Then Hus diplomatically turned to the prelates and the pope. He requested the people to pray for Alexander V and John XXIII that God may "preserve him from evil and he graciously pleased to grant that he be the salt of the earth."

The flames which had consumed an estimated 200 volumes of Wyclif's works also ignited a formidable tinderbox of popular protests. The university students composed derogatory ditties which were sung with great gusto by the common people, who demonstrated in large numbers in

---

[51] Matt. 5:13. The sermon, "Vos estis sal terre," is found in *Historia et monumenta*, II, pp. 85 ff.

churches and streets. The best-known doggerel among them asserted that

> Bishop Zbyněk ABC
> burned books although he
> knew not what they contained.

But the excitement did not spend itself in mere harmless lampoons; it broke out into violence in which church services were broken up and some priests were threatened with death. The prelatical party, however, remained not a whit behind their opponents, and beat and otherwise mistreated them. It was probably at this time that Hus was publicly called a heretic. At least there exist, probably from this period, two letters of Hus protesting against such an accusation. One is a reply to some nobleman,[52] in which he complains that many "call him a heretic before your nobility." The other[53] is addressed directly to the man who had called him a heretic; he was a notorious pluralist, Záviš of Zapy, pastor at Prachatice. He had held the post for the past thirty years without ever residing there. Hus calls him strictly to account for his conduct, charging that if he actually knew of Hus' heresy, he should have admonished him in accordance with the apostolic rule, rather than denounce him.

Hus' second appeal from the archbishop's ruling gave rise to a legal process at the curia, which was to prove fatal in the end. John XXIII committed the case into the hands of Cardinal Odo of Colonna, who later became Pope Martin V. Zbyněk tried to counteract whatever possible effect the complaint about the burning of the books might have by sending another accusation against Hus, in which he suggested that Hus be personally cited to the curia.[54] But before this missive reached the curia, the pope had ordered an investigation of the complaints concerning the burning of Wyclif's books.[55] The commission of four cardinals, to whom

[52] Novotný, *Korespondence*, No. 18.
[53] *Ibid.*, No. 20.
[54] Palacký, *Documenta*, pp. 404-06.
[55] Kejř, *Husitský právník*, p. 38.

the matter was entrusted, requested an opinion on the problem from the masters of the Bologna university—the famous center of legal studies. The dean of the Bologna theological faculty, Thomas of Utino, appealed to the three theologians of the universities of Bologna, Paris, and Oxford—the latter two happened to be visiting in the city—to join him in dealing with the problem. They met at the home of Cardinal Colonna sometime early in August. The debate brought out a variety of conflicting opinions, but the majority finally decided that under no circumstances should the books have been burned.[56] It was illogical, the masters held, that books on logic, philosophy, morals, and theology, in which much useful matter was found, be withdrawn from common use. Only some erroneous propositions, selected from the *Dialogus*, *Trialogus*, and *De corpore Christi* by the dean himself, should be prohibited in Bohemia from being held or taught.

The international scholars composing the Bologna committee thus in effect approved the position taken by Hus in *De libris hereticorum legendis*. De Vooght arrived at the same conclusion.[57] This almost unanimous decision of the scholars of the three most renowned universities should have exerted a decisive, or at least a meliorating, influence on Colonna. Moreover, at approximately the same time the Bohemian king, the queen, the nobles, the Prague councilors, and the university wrote to the pope and the cardinals (September 12-16), expressing regret at the stopping of preaching at the Bethlehem Chapel and urging the abrogation of the sentence consigning Wyclif's books to the flames.[58] Despite all that, Colonna completely ignored these opinions and pleas and issued his verdict fully approving Zbyněk's procedure in its entirety (August 25, 1410). He confirmed Hus' excommunication and commanded Zbyněk to continue the process against him "to

---

[56] *Ibid.*, pp. 38-39; also *Ordo procedendi*, in Palacký, *Documenta*, pp. 188 ff.; and Novotný, *Korespondence*, pp. 225-34. I follow Novotný's text.

[57] De Vooght, *L'hérésie*, p. 142.

[58] Palacký, *Documenta*, pp. 409-15.

aggravation, reaggravation, and the invocation of the secular arm."[59] Nothing was said as to Zbyněk's burning of the books. Perhaps later, Hus was cited to the curia at Bologna. The citation reached Prague on September 20,[60] and four days later the archbishop placed Hus under an aggravated excommunication [*in causa fidei*].[61]

The case now reached the proportions of an international affair, which the king and his court keenly resented. Hus himself wrote a humble petition to the pope, asking that he be permitted to preach at Bethlehem and that there be no further burning of Wyclif's books.[62] Kejř sees in this an organized action and supposes that it was again Nicholas the Rich who most likely urged such a campaign.[63] At any rate, the king and the queen again wrote to the pope and the cardinals supplicating them to absolve Hus, whom they twice called "our faithfully devoted chaplain," from personal appearance at Bologna. The king further suggested that "if anyone wishes to accuse him (Hus) of anything, let him do so in our kingdom before the university of Prague or another competent judge. For our kingdom does not see fit to expose so useful a preacher to the discrimination of his enemies and to the disturbance of the whole population."[64] Soon thereafter the king wrote directly to Cardinal Colonna, repeating the request and informing him that he was sending to Bologna two of his emissaries, Dr. John Náz and John Cardinal of Rejnštejn, for further "particular information."[65] Queen Sophia also wrote the cardinal the second time.

That the burning of Wyclif's books and the trial of Hus

[59] *Ibid.*, pp. 401-08.
[60] Kejř, *Husitský právník*, p. 40 f.
[61] Palacký, *Documenta*, p. 202; *Ordo procedendi*, p. 191.
[62] Novotný, *Korespondence*, No. 23.
[63] Kejř, *Husitský právník*, p. 41, n. 88.
[64] Palacký, *Documenta*, pp. 422-23; *Ordo procedendi*, in Novotný, *Korespondence*, p. 228, adds that the king suggested that the pope send legates to Bohemia and if they found Hus guilty, he himself would punish him. Either other letters were sent containing this message, or these were verbal instructions to the king's emissaries.
[65] Palacký, *Documenta*, p. 424.

had international repercussions is evident from the fact that the English Lollards now apparently dispatched to Bohemia a supply of Wyclif's books to replace those burned, although there is no specific mention of this in the letter they sent. The most outstanding of the Lollards was Sir John Oldcastle, Lord Cobham. He wrote (September 8, 1410) to King Wenceslas' favorite courtier, Voksa of Valdštejn (or in his absence to Zdislav of Zvířetice), exhorting him to steadfastness in the faith. He praises him "because he is not terrified by the pomp of anti-christians, but promotes as much as he can the Word of God and its true promulgators."[66] A similar letter, addressed directly to Hus and Jakoubek, was written the same day by a Wyclif disciple, priest Richard Wyche (or Whyche) of London. This certainly suggests cooperation between the two Lollard leaders, who knew the chief protagonists of the Czech reform movement. Wyche exhorts Hus to "labor like a good soldier of Jesus Christ; preach, stand firmly in the word and example, and call to the way of truth whoever you can."[67] He also mentions that in his country the hearts of many gladly suffer for the word of Christ, although imprisoned, exiled, and even put to death. This is, of course, a reference to King Henry's persecution of the Lollards in accordance with the decree *de haeretico comburendo.*

Hus replied to Wyche in March 1411. He informed the English Wyclifite that he had read his letter "in a public sermon at which were present, I estimate, about ten thousand people."[68] He wrote further that the Czech people would hear

---

[66] Novotný, *Korespondence*, p. 73.

[67] *Ibid.*, p. 78. Wyche was burned in 1440. See G. H. W. Parker, *The Morning Star, Wycliffe and the Dawn of the Reformation* (Grand Rapids, Michigan, Wm. B. Eerdmans Publishing Co., 1965), p. 176.

[68] Novotný, *Korespondence*, No. 24. Novotný remarks in a footnote that this number is perhaps exaggerated. But when one considers that the chapel could accommodate three thousand hearers at one time, it is conceivable that Hus could have read the letter to four audiences averaging 2,500 each.

nothing but the sacred Scriptures, particularly the gospels and the epistles; and whenever in city or village, town or castle, a preacher of saintly conversation appears, the people gather in crowds, spurning unready clergy. . . . Our lord king and his whole court, the queen, nobles, and the common people, stand up for the word of Jesus Christ.

In thanking the English Church for its gifts, he perhaps had in mind the Wyclif books presumably sent by it, although this is by no means certain.[69]

The news of the Czech reform reached even distant Scotland. There a Scots knight who went under the name of Quintin Folkhyrde sent to Bohemia in 1410 a treatise consisting of four "epistles."[70] He described the ecclesiastical conditions in Scotland, which did not differ much from those in England and elsewhere. The good knight asserted that he had declared war on the bishop of Glasgow and the clergy of the realm. He also appealed to the secular lords, exhorting them to bring about the needed reforms by force of arms. The letters were translated into Czech and exerted a considerable influence in the country.

The trial of Hus at the curia proceeded apace. Hus did not obey the citation of Cardinal Colonna to a personal appearance. Instead, he sent his legal representatives, who were to present the reasons for his non-appearance as well as defend his cause. The chief among them was the eminent lawyer and an ardent member of the reform party, John of Jesenice. With him were associated Mark of Hradec and the former pupil of Hus, Nicholas of Stojčín. Jesenic started for Italy about the beginning of October. The procedure is difficult to follow in detail, because a complete report of it, whether official or unofficial, is not extant. We have only an occasional reference to it in Hus' correspondence. Hus' friends collected a considerable sum of money for his defense at the curia, knowing that the living expenses for

---

[69] *Ibid.*, pp. 84-85.

[70] It is published in Sedlák, *Jan Hus*, supplement, pp. 182-88; see also Matthew Spinka, "Paul Kravař and the Lollard-Hussite Relations," in *Church History* (1956), pp. 16-26.

the three procurators, as well as the fees for the curial lawyers, would be excessively high. Jesenic had been given 1100
Florentine gulden for these purposes. He engaged in Bologna five other lawyers who enjoyed good standing at the
curia; chief among them were Peter of Ancorano, a famous
professor at the university, and John Scribani. Jesenic's principal aim was to secure the annulment of Hus' citation to
the curia. He, along with his fellow-procurators and advocates, had a hearing before Colonna and presented Hus'
own reasons for non-appearance as well as the king's and
queen's letters of appeal. All in vain. Jesenic also consulted Thomas of Utino and received from him an exact
report of the committee appointed to examine whether Wyclif's books should have been burned. He sent this report
to Prague to assist Hus and others in defense of their position against Zbyněk.[71] Similarly, he informed the royal coun-
cilor, Nicholas the Rich, of this, who, in turn, shared the
news with King Wenceslas.

Furthermore, Mark of Hradec now sent the pope an appeal against Colonna's irregular proceedings in Hus' case.
The pope referred this appeal to the papal auditor, John
de Thomariis, for adjudication. This act posed a danger
for Zbyněk's cause; he thereupon descended to plain bribery.
His representatives distributed rich gifts, consisting of horses,
precious cups, and rings, among the Cardinals Colonna,
Orsini, and even John XXIII. Money was also given to
papal procurators and advocates.[72] These means, quite usual
at the curia, yet on no account justifiable, brought about the
desired effect; as soon as the term for appearance given Hus
expired and despite the fact that another official was dealing
with the appeal against Colonna's handling of the case,
Colonna issued an excommunication for contumacy and

---

[71] Palacký, *Documenta*, pp. 426-28. In a letter to an unidentified
priest, Hus mentions that Colonna "was very angry that the letters
were brought to Bohemia which dealt with the agreement of the
masters, who were then in Bologna, that the books should not have
been burned." Novotný, *Korespondence*, No. 27.

[72] Hus himself describes this wholesale bribery in his treatise *Proti
knězi kuchmistrovi*. See Spinka, *Hus' Concept of the Church*, pp. 107-08.

119

non-appearance [*propter non-comparationem*]. This oc-curred in February 1411,[73] while the appeal was still pend-ing. It constituted a judicial error on Colonna's part. Let it be clearly understood, however, that the excommunica-tion was imposed not because Colonna had found Hus guilty of heresy, not even because he had properly exam-ined Hus' excuses and the royal pleading and found them wanting, but solely because of Hus' non-appearance.

It was now that the pope removed the case from the juris-diction of both Colonna and Thomariis and himself took charge of it for a time.[74] Nevertheless, the news of Colonna's action was received in Prague as a victory for Zbyněk's cause, and he had it announced as such in all churches on March 15, 1411. In only two churches—those of Chris-tian of Prachatice, pastor of St. Michael's and the German Knights' church of St. Benedict—was it not read.[75]

While these events were transpiring, Hus continued his work at the Bethlehem Chapel and the university quite un-disturbed. At this time he translated from Latin and slightly adapted a very beautiful little pamphlet entitled *Devět kusův zlatých* [*Nine Golden Theses*].[76] When Arch-bishop Zbyněk forbade the holding of the *Quodlibet* in Jan-uary 1410 (still during Hus' rectorate) , Hus was determined to hold it the next year. He wished thus to disprove the gibe of the Germans that their withdrawal from Prague had fatally crippled the university, although there was no doubt that it had seriously hurt it. But two of the elected managers of the *Quodlibet*—Stephen Páleč and Simon of Tišnov—declined to serve. Thereupon, he himself offered

[73] Palacký, *Documenta*, p. 202; *Ordo procedendi*, p. 228.

[74] *Ordo procedendi*, p. 228.

[75] In dealing with this whole matter of Colonna's and Thomariis' handling of the case, I have followed Kejř, *Husitský právník*, pp. 45-49. He corrects certain details of the reconstruction of Novotný and Sedlák.

[76] De Vooght, *L'hérésie*, pp. 124-25, where the whole text of the work is cited. Bartoš devoted to it a study in his *Ze zápasů české reformace* (Praha, Kalich, 1959) , pp. 29-36, where he concludes that this work was very likely written by Albertus Magnus, in German.

to assume the formidable task,[77] in order "that our life-giving university may not go stale in sciences for lack of practice, and that jealous men who bark at us would not be afforded a chance to defame us." This declaration well summarizes the importance of the public disputations in medieval universities. Hus prepared the program with the greatest care. The principal *questio* was formulated as follows: "Whether the best arrangement of the universe depends upon the prime being, rationally active and unchangeable, almighty and all-knowing"—an obviously Wyclifite realist thesis. Hus was able to recruit for the *Quodlibet* fifty-four disputants, mostly among the younger masters. Nevertheless, it became plainly evident that despite the absence of the German masters, the Czechs were not in complete accord. The fact was that now, when they could work together without hindrance, they were pulling apart and in a short time formed two mutually inimical camps—one, reactionary and pro-papal; the other, reformist and anti-papal.

Hus introduced the speakers, each of whom was given some classical name, with a short speech, serious or humorous. Of Ctibor of Velvary, for instance, he remarked that he likes to drink wine, displaying a touch of the young gay Hus, when he used to act as promoter of his students. Only Jakoubek of Stříbro sounded an aggressive note when he attacked the excessive ceremonialism of the church functions, the inappropriate music, and the over-zealous veneration of images. Hus then concluded the proceedings, which lasted several days, with a peroration extolling the beauties and glory of Prague, a speech obviously calculated to counter the calumnies spread about it by the Germans, and to encourage the Czech masters who now had to bear the burden of instruction alone.

[77] Full information regarding this recently discovered *Quodlibet* is reprinted from *Český časopis historický* (1938). But a more recent and complete text is given in B. Ryba, *Magistri Iohannis Hus, Quodlibet* (Praha, Orbis, 1948). Excerpts are found in Havránek, *Výbor*, I, pp. 114-19.

O most famous kingdom of Bohemia, O Prague, glorious city, arise, look about you and rejoice! All those gathered here . . . have sprung from thy loins; you have nurtured them, taught them, brought them up. They are yours; they seek your honor. Therefore be glad and rejoice! Do not fear the noise of your rivals who daily attempt to stifle your child, the university of Prague, by their unjust calumnies and sneers.[78]

The most curious of the letters written by Hus is the one addressed to the Polish king, Władysław Jagiello. In it he expressed his joy in the Polish victory over the Teutonic Order at the battle of Grünwald-Tannenberg (July 15, 1410). The success was to a large degree due to the Moravian lord in the service of the Polish king, John Sokol of Lamberk, who led the Czech-Moravian contingent. Among his officers was also John Žižka, who later gained fame as the leader of the Taborites. The war was concluded by the peace treaty of Toruń signed on February 1, 1411. Shortly thereafter Hus sent the king a letter of congratulation.[79] Nevertheless, he could not refrain from exhorting Władysław to remember that it is God who gives victory and to urge him to follow "the King of Peace, the Lord Jesus Christ." He promised to "pray, along with all the people, the grace of Almighty Lord" for peace. When one remembers the young Hus pasturing geese in the vicinity of his native village, and compares him with the recent university rector exhorting the Polish king, the contrast is indeed great!

Returning now to the process at the curia, we note, first of all, that toward the end of 1410 Zbyněk's faction had collected testimonies from a number of Prague priests hostile to Hus.[80] They bore witness to incidents going as far back

[78] Havránek, *Výbor*, I, p. 148.

[79] Novotný, *Korespondence*, No. 25; see also Frederick G. Heymann, *John Žižka and the Hussite Revolution* (Princeton, Princeton University Press, 1955), pp. 30-31.

[80] Novotný, *Jan Hus*, I, pp. 464-66, where their names are given; also Palacký, *Documenta*, pp. 174-85.

as Hus' student and early teaching days. They accused him of remanence and of his role in expelling the Germans from the university, and charged that he had taught that a sinful priest does not consecrate the host—all of which were groundless accusations. This is the first time that Hus was flatly accused of heresy, something the archbishop had not dared to do a few months previously. Furthermore, the archbishop's representatives in Rome secured for their ally priest Michael of Německý Brod, commonly called *de Causis*; he had formerly been pastor of a Prague church, but had fled the country because he had swindled the king. He now held a place at the curia as a procurator *in causa fidei*. Michael and Páleč became the principal accusers of Hus at the Council of Constance. In addition to Michael, the archiepiscopal procurators secured the services of a prominent curial official, Dietrich of Niem. He published on March 6, 1411, a treatise entitled *Contra damnatos Wiclifistas Prage*, in which he condemned as wrong the curial procedure in receiving Hus' appeals at all. He claimed that Zbyněk had the final jurisdiction in the matter. It was useless to examine the case any further; in case of heresy, mere suspicion sufficed for condemnation. He advised the pope to use the most drastic methods, even a crusade, to exterminate Wiclifism from Bohemia. He demanded: *incarcerare, degradare, tradere brachio seculari*.[81]

Michael de Causis did not remain behind his confrère in proceeding further against Hus; in March 1411, he presented accusatory articles against him, based on the testimonies of witnesses recently obtained in Prague.[82] He suggested that Hus be declared a heretic and as such either forced to recant or be turned over for punishment to the secular arm. It is not certain whether at this time Colonna still acted as judge or whether the pope had already taken the case into his own hands. But the latter was just

---

[81] Jan Sedlák, *Studie a texty k náboženským dějinám českým*, 3 vols. (Olomouc, 1914-16), I, pp. 45-55; also De Vooght, *L'hérésie*, p. 157.

[82] Palacký, *Documenta*, pp. 169-74.

then preoccupied with the transfer of his court from Bologna to Rome, and perhaps was too busy personally to take charge of it.

This uncertain situation lasted until June 1, when John XXIII named a four-member commission to examine the procedure at the Hus trial.[83] It consisted of four cardinals, among whom Francisco Zabarella, the archbishop of Florence, exercised predominant influence. He was a famous canonist and a highly educated humanist. This constituted a favorable turn of events for Hus' cause. At home the ensuing developments were likewise favorable and tended actually to a peaceable solution of the whole conflict between Zbyněk and Hus.

King Wenceslas was extremely angry at the curia that all his efforts in behalf of Hus had been so cavalierly ignored. He deeply resented the aspersion of heresy thus cast on his country by the cardinal and his own archbishop, even though Hus' excommunication was not for heresy but for a procedural transgression. The matter was further aggravated when the archbishop had a master of the university, John called Žídek (on account of his Jewish origin), pastor at Chvojnov, imprisoned for having written him an extremely daring letter calling him to account for his conduct and demanding Zbyněk's amendment.[84] The university protested, recounting on this occasion the former injustices suffered by it at the archbishop's hands. The king now, on the holy day (April 28), when the imperial and royal insignia were being displayed to a large crowd of people on the New Town square, issued an order commanding the stoppage of payments to the canons of St. Vitus and the All Saints and other priests of the cathedral, as well as to the pastors of the churches in Prague. He gave as his reason that they had spread lies about the realm. The king's officials, as well as the councilors of all three towns of Prague, were appointed executors of the order. The archbishop, who had taken refuge at Roudnice, now

[83] Kejř, *Husitský právník*, pp. 52 ff.
[84] Novotný, *Korespondence*, No. 167.

excommunicated them (May 2, 1411) .[85] The king personally rode to the castle of Hradčany and ordered the sequestration of the cathedral treasures, which were then transferred to his castle of Karlštejn. He retaliated further by ordering a visitation of all ecclesiastical establishments in the whole country, including the monasteries. The populace also took part in the anti-ecclesiastical measures and plundered and burned parsonages, dragged the priests and their concubines naked to pillories, threw them into rivers, and expelled them from the cities.[86]

When the country Diet assembled, it approved all the measures taken by the king, thus censuring the archbishop himself. By this time Zbyněk was so determined to exercise all his ecclesiastical powers that, being instigated to it by his advisers, he pronounced (June 20) an interdict over Prague and its environs for two miles around. The terrible weapon, normally stopping all church services and ministrations such as baptisms, weddings, funerals, and granting of all sacraments, failed of effect. The king simply forbade its observance. Those priests and prelates who had defied his order were deprived of their positions, which were then filled by such as were obedient to his will. The canons of St. Vitus fled and their places were taken by others. This obviously hopeless struggle continued to be waged by the archbishop for only two weeks. On July 3 he, along with the remaining prelates and priests who remained faithful to him, accepted the arbitration proffered him by the king. On the other hand, Hus along with the university rector, Simon of Tišnov, and Thomas of Lysá, accepted the offer of conciliation to be effected by the royal Council.

The arbitration committee appointed for the purpose consisted of six outstanding members of the Council, to whom were added two emissaries of King Sigismund just then sojourning in Prague—Rudolph, duke of Saxony, and Stibor of Stibořice. Among the members of the commis-

[85] Palacký, *Documenta*, pp. 429-32.
[86] Novotný, *Jan Hus*, I, pp. 478-81; Palacký, *Documenta*, p. 735.

sion were also Wenceslas Králík, patriarch of Antioch, and Conrad of Vechta, bishop of Olomouc. Three days later this august commission signed its verdict, proposing to the archbishop that he submit to the king and stop the ecclesiastical disorders at home; he was to annul the excommunication of Hus and lift the interdict; secure from the pope the cancellation of Hus' citation to personal appearance and the termination of all proceedings against him and all others who were involved in the process. Further, he was to declare that there existed no heresy in the land. In turn, the royal Council promised to secure from the king the release of all those incarcerated, the resumption of all incomes of the clergy, and the restitution of their sequestrated property. The concept of the letter drawn up for Zbyněk contained a statement that he had come to a complete accord with Hus.[87]

As for Hus, he was ordered to submit to the curia, and to write a letter of submission to the pope and the cardinals, humbly professing his faith and asking for suspension of all proceedings against him. He gladly wrote these two letters—to the pope on September 1, to the cardinals during the next few days.[88] In the letter to John XXIII, after professing his orthodoxy in explicit terms, he enumerated the charges against him and made a pertinent reply to them. These accusations included such items as the teaching of remanence, holding that a priest in mortal sin does not consecrate the sacraments, asserting that secular lords should deprive the priests of property and withhold the tithe, declaring that "indulgences are nothing." All these he denied, as well as the further charges that he had advised the killing of priests with the sword, that he had preached some errors and heresy, that he had caused the expulsion of the Germans from the university, and that the Bethlehem Chapel is a private place. He admitted that he had appealed from the charges of Zbyněk that there exist in Bohemia and Moravia "errors and heresies which infected the hearts

[87] Palacký, *Documenta*, pp. 437-40.
[88] Novotný, *Korespondence*, Nos. 31, 32.

of many people," and stated the reasons why he did not obey the summons to personal appearance at the curia. He humbly appealed to the pope to absolve him from the necessity of personal appearance, protesting that he is now "in complete accord with the aforesaid most reverend father in Christ, Lord Zbyněk." He concluded the letter by expressing willingness to submit to the testing of his faith by the university.

In the second letter, written to the college of cardinals, Hus skillfully reminded them that he had acknowledged that body prior to and during the Council of Pisa, while the archbishop still had remained in Pope Gregory's obedience, and had forbidden such transfer of jurisdiction. He therefore prayed them "on bended knees that they might look at him, a poor man, with kindly eyes and by their gracious efforts would free him from the hardship of a personal appearance and the rest of the hardships connected with such appearance." He enclosed with the plea a public testimony to himself by the University of Prague.

Some two weeks later, however, Hus again publicly defended Wyclif, disregarding the effect such an action might have on his judges both at home and abroad. The occasion was the visit to Prague of a member of the English embassy sent by King Henry V to Sigismund of Hungary, John Stokes, a master of Cambridge University. Stokes had declared that anyone who has read or studied Wyclif's books, would sooner or later fall into heresy, no matter how well he were grounded in the faith. Hus challenged him to a public disputation. Stokes replied that he was ready to accept the challenge, but not in Prague; he suggested Paris, Rome, or any other neutral university. He also added that in England Wyclif was regarded as a heretic and his writings were burned. Nevertheless, Hus published his reply,[89] in which he declared that "he, along with the members of our university, has now read those books for twenty and more years." He argued that whenever truth is not defended, it is

---

[89] *Historia et monumenta*, I, pp. 135-38; new edition in Eršil, *Polemica*, pp. 59-70; also Novotný, *Korespondence*, No. 33.

denied. Therefore, if Master Stokes regarded his proposition as true, he "should defend it to death." He further asserted that it was absurd to claim that just because some people in England, France, and Bohemia say that Wyclif is a heretic, it follows that he actually is one. It would then likewise follow that because Turks, Arabs, and Tatars deny that Christ is divine, He is therefore not God. Duke John of Lancaster, King Henry's progenitor, was not a heretic, although he protected Wyclif. A heretic is not one who errs, but he who stubbornly defends an error contrary to the Holy Scriptures. Therefore, it is by no means certain whether Wyclif is a heretic. Furthermore, since "the Oxford university has for the last thirty years read, held, and studied the books of M. John Wyclif . . . therefore in the whole Oxford university there could hardly be found a man who would not be involved in heresy."

Although the concept of the letter to be sent by Zbyněk to the curia, in accordance with the terms imposed on him, had already been drawn up, the archbishop never sent it. He apparently hoped to secure an amelioration of the terms by having an interview with the king. For five weeks he sought an audience with the king, but in vain. At the beginning of September, just as the royal Council intended to call both sides to a hearing to urge that the terms of pacification of July 6 be carried out, Zbyněk left Prague for Litomyšl, the see of the king's stout adversary, Bishop John "the Iron." The latter advised him to refuse the terms imposed upon him and to seek refuge at the court of King Sigismund at Buda. Zbyněk accepted this counsel and wrote Wenceslas a letter (September 5),[90] in which he complained that although he could get no audience with the king, "my adversaries always had a hearing with Your Grace whenever they needed it." He charged that even after the concord had been reached, "other priests openly carried on and preached errors and blasphemies against the Holy Church," undoubtedly meaning thereby Hus. He detailed a number of instances when his jurisdiction had been inter-

[90] Palacký, *Documenta*, pp. 443-46.

fered with and priests and prelates had been despoiled of their property or exiled from the land. Nor had the sequestrated property been restored to some of them. Neither his interdict nor his excommunication had been observed. He protested that to write to the pope as bidden and to annul the excommunication and the interdict as he had promised "were contrary to his soul and honor." Therefore, he had to leave Prague, where he was not safe, and to seek refuge with Sigismund. Nevertheless, he prayed the king to rectify the evils complained of and thus "restore him with his clergy to the ecclesiastical order."

Thereupon, without waiting for the king's answer, Zbyněk continued his journey to the Hungarian court. Sigismund appears to have come to meet him at Bratislava. There, however, Zbyněk suddenly and unexpectedly died on September 28, before he met the king. It is possible that the death was not the result of natural causes. In the Old Czech Annals it is asserted that Zbyněk had been poisoned by his cook. Bartoš also suggests the possibility of the murder of Zbyněk.[91]

Thus the long-drawn-out struggle between the archbishop, Hus, and the king was terminated by the death of the thirty-six-year-old archbishop. The trial at the curia, however, instigated and fomented by Zbyněk even by unworthy means, continued to grind on inexorably toward its fateful end.

[91] Šimek, F., ed., *Staré letopisy české* (Praha, Historický spolek a Společnost Husova musea, 1937), p. 8; also F. M. Bartoš, in R. Říčan and M. Flegl, eds., *Husův sborník* (Praha, Komenského ev. fakulta bohoslovecká, 1966), p. 18.

here was no lack of candidates for the lucrative archiepiscopal see, made vacant by Zbyněk's death. No less than twenty-four eager applicants contended for the coveted position, among them the formidable Bishop John "the Iron." The victor proved to be the king's personal physician and professor of the university physicians' faculty, Dr. Albík of Uničov. He was elected by the chapter in October, and the choice was approved by the pope in the middle of January. The fact that Albík was the highest bidder among the seekers was by no means overlooked. Theologically, he was no better prepared for the duties of the highest ecclesiastical office in the land than Zbyněk had been, although he possessed far higher academic qualifications than his predecessor. He had not studied theology and had not been ordained to priesthood until after his election. He then successively acquired the necessary grades of ordination and consecration. The king was tired of the constant controversy over Wyclifism, and the new archbishop was eager to "let sleeping dogs lie." The trouble was that they were not sleeping.

The legal process at the curia now implicated in its clutches even Hus' principal lawyer, John of Jesenice. Michael de Causis, unable to cope with Jesenic's legal acumen, resorted to the usual maneuver of accusing him of Wyclifism. Jesenic retorted by lodging a charge of defamation against his tricky opponent. Since an older conflict of Jesenic with a certain Simon Burda added to the existing complication, the judge to whom the case was assigned—the auditor Berthold of Wildungen—now dealt with three charges: that of Burda, that between Michael and Jesenic, and Jesenic's countercharge against Michael. The aim of de Causis was to remove Jesenic from the scene altogether, since his conduct of Hus' process was turning out successfully. Michael brought against him cunningly formulated accusations which, in fact, were directed primarily against Hus as a supporter and defender of Wyclifism, but implicated Jesenic, as if by defending Hus, he defended the latter's heresy as well. Auditor Berthold indeed imposed on Jesenic a term within which he had to answer the charges, and forbade him to leave Rome until he had done so. Soon after, in February, 1412, Jesenic's cause suffered a serious setback, insofar as the pope took Hus' case from Zabarella's hands and placed it in the jurisdiction of Cardinal Brancatiis.[1]

The new judge retarded or even prevented any favorable development which might have resulted from Zabarella's just procedure in dealing with Hus' case, by the ingenious means of simply refusing to act in any way whatever. This method allowed all decisions formerly taken against Hus to remain in full force. Jesenic, with the other advocates, was utterly stymied in the face of this refusal to act. All his repeated efforts to have Hus freed from the citation of personal appearance, and consequently from Colonna's excommunication, necessarily failed. In the end Brancatiis, claiming papal command, forbade any further legal steps and even the procurators' appearance before him.[2] Jesenic, wholly committed to Hus' defense, did not obey the cardinal's prohibition and continued to press the case. Thereupon, in March, he was imprisoned. Nevertheless, he succeeded in escaping, by what means we do not know. He took refuge in Bologna, where he peacefully engaged in the study of law at the university, earning thereby his doctor's degree. Michael, who now secured another change of

---

[1] *Ordo procedendi*, in V. Novotný, *M. Jana Husi Korespondence a dokumenty* (Praha, Komise pro vydávání pramenů náboženského hnutí českého, 1920), p. 229. Also Jiří Kejř, *Husitský právník, M. Jan z Jesenic* (Praha, Československá akademie věd, 1965), p. 59, n. 76. He points out that there were two cardinals of that name, older and younger. He suggests that it might have been the younger, Thomas, a relative of the pope, who perhaps could not even read Latin.

[2] *Ordo procedendi*, p. 229; Kejř, *Husitský právník*, p. 60.

judges, alone attended the trial between himself and Jesenic. Under these circumstances, on July 29, 1412, the judge pronounced in Michael's favor and excommunicated Jesenic for non-appearance. The most successful procurator of Hus was thus permanently eliminated from the trial.

The situation was growing increasingly threatening for Hus. Potentially, the most serious aggravation of the development was Pope John's "crusading" bull, which he issued on September 9, 1411.[3] In fact, it was the conflict over this bull of indulgences which proved fatal to Hus: during it he was deserted by most of his former friends, with the exception of a few brave souls such as Jerome of Prague and Jakoubek of Stříbro, and abandoned to his fate by the king. It was occasioned by the fact that Gregory XII, despite his deposition at the Council of Pisa, retained enough supporters still to make himself dangerous. He was aided by King Ladislas of Naples, who took Rome and dislodged Pope John from it; the latter had to seek refuge in Bologna. John, therefore, proclaimed a crusade against him. He ordered all patriarchs, archbishops, bishops and other prelates, on pain of excommunication, "publicly, and in a loud and intelligible voice," to decree Ladislas "excommunicated, perjured, a schismatic, a blasphemer, a relapsed heretic, protector of heretics, guilty of the crime of lèse majesté, a conspirator against us and the Church."[4] Included in this rather fulsome condemnation were "the accomplices adhering to and following him." They, too, were summarily excommunicated and anathematized, incurring thereby punishment and guilt. Even if Ladislas were to be absolved on his deathbed by John or his successor, yet he must be denied ecclesiastical interment forever. The pope thereupon

[3] "Bulla indulgentiarum Pape Joannis XXIII," in *Historia et monumenta Joannis Hus atque Hieronymi Pragensis, confessorum Christi*, 2 vols. (Norimberg, 1715), I, pp. 212-13.

[4] The bull actually does not name Pope Gregory, but since the excommunication of Ladislas' supporters is included, Gregory is included in that category. Also *Výklad modlitby Páně*, in K. J. Erben, ed., *Mistra Jana Husi Sebrané spisy české*, 3 vols. (Praha, B. Tempský, 1865-68), I, p. 342; and J. B. Jeschke, ed., *M. Jan Hus, Postilla* (Praha, Komenského ev. fakulta bohoslovecká, 1952), pp. 22 f., 172-73.

went on to implore, "by the blood shed by the Savior," all emperors, kings, princes both secular, ecclesiastical and monastic, as well as prelates, universities, and individuals of both sexes, to seize the sword "in defense of the Church and us," to exterminate Ladislas and his accomplices. The pope promised "to all truly penitent and confessed," who would take up the cross (i.e., arms) either at their own expense or who would equip and support a soldier for a month, "remission of such of their sins of which they were heartily contrite and which they had confessed [*illam peccatorum suorum, de quibus corde contriti et ore confessi fuerint*]."

Shortly thereafter the pope issued a second bull (December 2),[5] in which he appointed for this task two commissioners for the cities of Salzburg, Prague, and Nuremberg. They were Wenceslas Tiem, a Moravian German, then dean of Passau and a notorious pluralist, and Pax de Fantuciis of Bologna. In this bull the pope condemned by name Angelo Corrario who "dares sacrilegiously to call himself Gregory XII." Ladislas rated a renewed condemnation as the enemy of the Church. John repeated almost verbatim the conditions of his granting the remission of sins, and defined the duties of the indulgence commissioners. He called upon all in authority, both secular and ecclesiastical, to aid the commissioners in all possible manner.

The papal bull, however, did not meet with a ready reception in many countries. In France it was treated with indifference. The same fate awaited it in England. The University of Vienna opposed the promulgation of the bull so strongly that the Austrian duke forbade it to be read in churches.[6]

The commissioner for Prague, Wenceslas Tiem, reached that city on May 22, 1412. He carried with him the pallium

[5] "Alia bulla commissionariis data," in *Historia et monumenta*, I, pp. 213-15.

[6] V. Novotný, *M. Jan Hus, život a dílo*, 2 vols. (Praha, Jan Laichter, 1919-21), II, p. 71.

for the new archbishop, Albík. In addition to Prague, the southern city of Krumlov, the seat of the powerful nobles of Rožmberk, secured for itself an independent privilege to sell the indulgences. The king, the archbishop, and the majority of the university masters did not hesitate to receive Tiem. He even gained King Wenceslas' help in securing the consent of the Polish king to the sale of indulgences in his land. At home, Wenceslas shared in the proceeds of the sale. The commissioner then farmed the indulgences to subordinate sellers, who in turn exploited their opportunities to make as much money as the traffic would bear. Hus characterized the procedure by writing that "the papal legate sold whole deaconries, towns and cities as much as he could, to unworthy clerics living in concubinage or tavern habitues who, furnished with these indulgences, taxed the populace as much as they wished."[7] Tiem also set up at the three principal churches in Prague—the cathedral of St. Vitus, the Týn church, and St. James—large, iron-bound coffers for the safe-keeping of the money thus amassed. This reprehensible hawking of indulgences was indistinguishable from selling forgiveness of sins, penance or no penance. Such simoniacal degradation of the sacrament cried loudly for redress.

Hus could not keep silent in the face of this nefarious traffic in sacred things. He did not oppose indulgences as such, in principle; his denunciation was directed against the sacrilegious manner of their sale and the call to war contained in the bull itself. Nevertheless, he at first limited his censures to his own pulpit. Later he consulted his friends about more far-reaching steps, but met with bitter disappointment in an effort to secure their support. One by one his friends fell away from him until he found himself isolated, almost as if he were a voice crying in the wilderness. The bitterest of these experiences was the parting with his old friend and intimate companion, Stephen Páleč, and with his highly honored teacher, Stanislav of Znojmo. In *Contra Paletz* Hus specifically states that it was

[7] Novotný, *Korespondence*, p. 124.

the sale of indulgences and the erection of the cross [i.e., the crusade] against Christians which first separated me from that doctor. If he would confess the truth, he would admit that he had declared that the formula of absolution, which he had first shown me with his own hands, contains palpable errors . . . To him I said at last and have never conversed with him since: "Páleč is a friend, truth is a friend; and both being friends, it is holy to prefer the truth."[8]

Páleč never denied that he had found the errors, but insisted that they were not in the papal bull, but in the formula of absolution which the commissioners gave the concessioners to be proclaimed as if it were contained in the bull itself. He even forbade to have the formula read in his church, but claimed that he did not on that account "blaspheme" the pontiff's bull.[9] In his De ecclesia, however, Hus wrote that "he heard Páleč say concerning the formula that it had been given him by the papal legates and that it contained palpable errors. Furthermore, that the formula was extracted from the bull and was passed on by the legates and the first commissioners to be promulgated, under papal authority, by the preachers."[10] In his critique of the bull, Hus quotes the formula word for word as follows:

In the formula of absolution given to the papal commissioners, among other matters is inserted this statement: "And also by apostolic authority granted me, I absolve thee from all sins, if you are truly contrite and confess them to God and me. If you cannot personally undertake the project [i.e., of joining in the crusade], but wish to bring a contribution according to your ability in compliance with my and the commissioners' terms in defense and aid of the above-named project, I grant and concede thee the fullest remis-

---

[8] "Contra Paletz," in Historia et monumenta, I, p. 330; new ed. in J. Eršil, ed., Magistri Johannis Hus Polemica (Praha, Academia scientiarum Bohemoslovaca, 1966) , p. 268.

[9] Stephen Páleč, De ecclesia, in Jan Sedlák, M. Jan Hus (Praha, Dědictví sv. Prokopa, 1915) , supplement, pp. 280-81.

[10] S. Harrison Thomson, ed., Magistri Joannis Hus, Tractatus de Ecclesia (Boulder, Colorado, University of Colorado Press, 1956) , p. 135.

sion of all your sins, including punishment and guilt. In the name of the Father, of the Son, and of the Holy Spirit.[11]

Where then does the truth lie? It must be freely admitted that the formula in the explicit version given above is not found in the papal bull. This is an exceedingly puzzling matter, for Hus had the bull before his eyes when he wrote, since he quotes verbatim other excerpts from it. In the present state of our knowledge of the matter we must concede that Páleč was right. He himself spoke only of the formula of absolution. It was Hus who added the further details that the formula had been shown to Páleč by the legates and had been extracted from the bull. On the other hand, even if the formula in its explicit version cannot be found in the bull, its essential assertion is contained there implicitly. There are phrases in it which clearly state that the commissioners and concessioners could, by papal authority, remit sins to buyers on certain conditions. For instance, it is stated that to those who fitly conduct the business, "we commit the granting of remission of sins." Further, after enumerating the pertinent conditions of the sale, the bull declares that "to such who are heartily contrite for their sins and confess them, we grant remission of sins . . . To all who are heartily contrite and confess . . . we grant indulgences and . . . an increase of eternal blessedness." These and other similar expressions leave no doubt that the very purpose of the document was to grant authority to bestow indulgences from sins, including punishment and guilt, to those who join or support the crusade. Why else would the bull have been published? Thus Hus was not wrong in making these specific charges.

Páleč, now Hus' bitterest enemy, possessed a considerable advantage over him. He had received about this time his doctorate and had been elected dean of the theological faculty. He thus became Hus' immediate superior, for Hus was still a candidate for the doctor's degree in that faculty.

Although isolated, with the exception of Jerome of Prague

[11] John Hus, "De indulgentiis sive de cruciata papae Joannis XXIII," in *Historia et monumenta*, I, p. 223; Novotný, *Jan Hus*, II, p. 76.

and Jakoubek of Stříbro, who joined him, Hus undertook
to deliver at the university an extended and severe critique
of the papal bull (June 1412) .[12] He proposed as his theme
the question whether the papal bull could be approved as
conforming to the law of Christ. He divided his subject into
three sections: remission of sins; the subsidy for the war;
and the manner of the sale of indulgences. As for the first,
he asserts that to remit sins is exclusively God's own prerogative. Priests have the power to absolve the penitents only
ministerially, as declaring, under certain strictly limited conditions—namely, that the sinner who repents of his sins,
confesses them, and resolves to sin no more, has God's forgiveness. The penitent must further sincerely resolve henceforth to observe all God's commands. These are the presup-
positions of absolution of all sins. No one can grant remission of sins of his own power and authority, but only declare them to be granted by the grace of God. Nor can the
ministers of God grant indulgences for a certain specified
length of time, or charge money for the absolution.

The second heading under which Hus deals with the
subject is the war. Waging of war is restricted to secular
rulers, and they alone may demand support in the execution of this their duty. Nevertheless, under all conditions
"the art of war is dangerous and difficult."[13] It is subject to
restriction as to the cause, the manner of waging it, and the
aim to be attained by it. As for the first, it must be waged
only in defense of the faith, not for temporal gain. The
manner of conducting it should be moderate. Its ultimate
aim must be love, gaining the enemy and making him a
friend. The popes and clergy should not fight with the material, but only with the spiritual, sword, namely, with
prayers and appeals for concord. The pope should not fight
for temporal dominion or objective. Hus quotes for this
opinion many authorities from the canon law and the Fathers of the Church. The text, "Behold, here are two
swords,"[14] which the Church has usually interpreted as con-

12 *Historia et monumenta*, I, pp. 215-35.
13 *Ibid.*, I, p. 217.          14 Luke 22:38.

ferring upon it the use of both the temporal and spiritual powers, Hus explains in the sense that the Church possesses the spiritual, the seculars the temporal, sword. He then asserts that even though the pope rightfully possesses spiritual authority, he does not always wield it justly; hence, not all his commands are to be obeyed. He quotes the great Old Testament Hebrew scholar, Nicholas of Lyra, to the effect that if the command of anyone in authority contains a manifest falsity or error, it is not to be obeyed. He further cites the provision of the canon law that "whatever command is contrary to the law of God, is not catholic but is heretical,"[15] and as such should not be held. The pope should follow Christ in declaring "My kingdom is not of this world."[16] Instead, however, he seeks temporal advantages which constitute the real aim of the bull of indulgences. Hus states bluntly that the bull is the means of amassing money.

The third section, which deals with the manner of granting indulgences, is the longest. It contains the formula of absolution, the text of which was given above. This formula embodies three errors or evils: first of all, the denial that forgiveness of sins is granted by God freely and should be freely bestowed by His ministers. To demand that the buyer join the crusade or support the war project is wrong, because it posits a requirement beyond the free grant of God's grace. Even more serious, in fact blasphemous, is the assertion that the remission of sins is granted in the pope's or the sellers' own names. It amounts to the presumption of granting the Holy Spirit. Hus writes: "Accordingly, it would be an extreme temerity to say that a sinful man grants the Holy Spirit . . ."[17] Later in his *Postil* Hus expressed it most cogently, if bluntly, by exclaiming: "What a strange thing! They cannot rid themselves of fleas and flies, and yet want to rid others of the torments of hell . . .!"[18] Furthermore, no man's sins can be forgiven unless he repents of

15 "De indulgentiis," p. 220.
16 John 18:36.
17 "De indulgentiis," p. 223.
18 *Postilla*, p. 22.

them. Since the pope cannot know whether or not a man had truly and heartily repented, he cannot grant him on his own authority full remission of sins. Moreover, the bull nowhere mentions the third component part of the doctrine of penance, namely, satisfaction for the sins committed by the restitution for whatever wrong had been done. For another matter, indulgences granted to a foreknown sinner are invalid, for God does not forgive those who do not repent. At all events, God's forgiveness precedes the priest's or the pope's act: they merely declare it but do not grant it. Hus gives an example of a hardened sinner who had committed mortal sins, who upon a pretended confession, having contributed to the crusade, is granted by the pope full remission of sins; thus upon his death he would go directly to heaven. Another man who had lived a righteous life and had committed only venial sins, but had not bought indulgences, upon his death would have to undergo the pains of purgatory. Would that be divine justice?

Lastly, if indulgences are valid for life and death, they could in the end altogether empty purgatory. Also, if the pope had such power, why restrict its exercise only to those who buy indulgences? Why not save all? Hus then turns upon those who justify the indulgence traffic on the ground that the pope cannot err. He declares that such a statement is a blasphemy, for it would ascribe to the pope sinlessness which Christ alone possesses. Not only did popes err, but some of them were heretics. On all these grounds, to oppose the bull is not wrong, when the criticism is motivated by true piety and a regard for truth.[19]

This daring critique of the papal "crusading bull" was eloquently and emphatically supported by Jerome of Prague. Both men were stormily and enthusiastically applauded by the students, who afterward accompanied Jerome to his home in a demonstrative escort. Jerome had intended to go directly to the City Hall to demand an end to

[19] See P. de Vooght, *L'hérésie de Jean Huss* (Louvain, Publications universitaires de Louvain, 1960) , pp. 193-97. He condemns the bull as a "vast undertaking of simoniac swindle" (p. 196) .

the indulgence traffic, but was dissuaded from it by the university rector, Mark of Hradec. Hus issued, shortly thereafter, another denunciation of the pope's bull, which was much shorter than the previous one. It contains nothing essentially new and therefore need not be analyzed here.[20]

These challenges to the archiepiscopal and theological faculty's authority could not be ignored. In fact, Dean Páleč, who had forbidden the disputation to take place, now in behalf of the faculty sent two of its members to Archbishop Albík to demand that any further dispute over the bull be countermanded. Hus was cited to the archiepiscopal palace where he was confronted by Albík and also by the two papal legates who had been sent to Prague in connection with the archbishop's elevation to office. The legates questioned Hus whether he were willing to obey the apostolic mandate. It, of course, never entered their minds to doubt that the term "apostolic" was not identical with "papal." Hus must have thoroughly enjoyed discomfiting them by taking advantage of this confusion of terms. He promptly and with all the readiness in the world replied that he indeed "heartily aspires to fulfill the apostolic mandates." Highly pleased, the legates turned to Albík to say that Hus consented "to obey the mandates of our Lord." Thereupon Hus took delight in enlightening them as to his real meaning:

Lords, understand me. I said that I heartily aspire to fulfill the apostolic mandates and to obey them in everything; but I call apostolic mandates the teaching of Christ's apostles. In as far as the mandates of the Roman pontiff are in harmony with the apostolic mandates and teaching . . . to that degree I am most willing to obey them. But should I find any of them opposed, those will I not obey, even if the fire to burn my body were placed before my eyes.[21]

[20] "Contra bullam papae Joannis XXIII," in *Historia et monumenta*, I, pp. 235-37.

[21] *Contra octo doctores*, in *Historia et monumenta*, I, p. 367; a new edition is that of Eršil, *Polemica*, pp. 375-76. Also Novotný, *Jan Hus*, II, p. 92.

Pleasantries of this sort, indulged in at the expense of papal legates by a mere university master, did not endear him to them or to the archbishop! For in effect Hus declared that he would not obey the pope's "crusading" bull.

We must interrupt the sequence of this fateful development of Hus' affairs in order to glance at some of his other concerns during this period. He wrote several short treatises, partly in response to inquiries and partly from other motives. Their composition belongs to the third quarter of the year 1411 and the early part of 1412. The shortest of all his treatises is entitled *The Five Priestly Offices*.[22] It consists of mere enumeration of priestly duties with supporting biblical texts. Hus places as the first such duty the preaching of the gospel of Jesus Christ. The remaining four consist of praying for the people, administration of the sacraments, study of Scripture, and the example of good works.

As has already been mentioned, Hus was spied upon in his preaching. Two such spies are either definitely known or suspected. The first of these who attended his preaching with that intent was the priest John Protiva; the second, the inquisitor Maurice Rvačka. On the first such occasion Hus recognized Protiva among his hearers and sarcastically taunted him by calling to him to write down his words and carry them to the authorities. It is against the second spy, Maurice Rvačka, that in October 1411, Hus wrote a treatise, *Against a hidden adversary*,[23] in which he subjected to sharp criticism this hidden enemy's censure of his sermon of the previous month. Hus restates, first of all, his critic's charges: that in his preaching he not only aimed to destroy the priesthood, but the law of God as well. Hus was further said to have asserted that Christ, in driving the sellers and buyers from the temple, empowered the secular kings and princes to correct the clergy. This, Rvačka said, was contrary to blessed Gregory's pronouncement that Christ alone is their

---

[22] Joannes Hus, *De quinque officiis sacerdotis*, in *Historia et monumenta*, I, p. 191.

[23] Joannes Hus, *Contra occultum adversarium*, in *Historia et monumenta*, I, pp. 168-79; the new edition in Eršil, *Polemica*, pp. 73-107.

corrector. The adversary further charged that Hus had asserted that the downfall of Jerusalem was principally caused by the vices of the clergy. He even accused Hus of "adulterating the Word of God." And finally, he claimed that although Hus had denounced all priests living in concubinage as committing mortal sin, he had not included in his condemnation priests disobedient to their ecclesiastical superiors.

Hus felt keenly the charge that his preaching "destroyed the law of God." He insisted in his reply[24] that if what Rvačka had declared was true, then Jesus and His apostles, by criticizing the ecclesiastical authorities of their times, destroyed the law of God. Paul denounced Peter for his non-fellowship with the Antiochene gentile converts. Christ wept over Jerusalem that on account of its rulers' sins the city would be destroyed; and Titus and Vespasian actually destroyed it. The priestly sins cause ruin of the people who follow them therein. Christ gave the secular rulers the power to govern their realms according to His laws; therefore, when they punish priestly evildoers, they do so in conformity with the duty laid upon them by God. Emperor Charles used to correct his clergy and did not for that reason destroy God's law. Hus cites the examples of many other kings who ruled their clergy, as did King Wenceslas of Bohemia. To the objection that he castigated the gravely sinning clergy, but exempted the disobedient priests from his censure, he retorts that on the contrary he has insisted that priests obey their superiors in all things lawful. He himself refused to obey only when the order was contrary to a divine command. After this general response, Hus answers each charge separately. This involves him in much repetition but, on the other hand, deals most explicitly and successfully with his accuser's complaints. Novotný expresses his estimate of this treatise by saying that it is "among the most brilliant of Hus' works of this nature."[25]

24 Novotný, *Korespondence*, No. 37, pp. 111-13, as well as in the above-mentioned treatise.
25 Novotný, *Jan Hus*, II, p. 10.

Another man, a certain Master Hašek, otherwise unknown, likewise wrote a sharp critique of the same sermon.[26]
But since Hus never answered him, we need not concern
ourselves with it.

Toward the end of 1411 Hus wrote his friends in Plzeň—
an important city which contained many of his followers—
a letter[27] in which he takes them to task for discord and
quarrels among themselves. He praises their former fervent
zeal for God's cause, but strongly disapproves their aban-
donment of it and their present disunity. After these exhortations to peace and amity, Hus goes on to say that
he had just received a second letter from them, informing
him that some priests had forbidden reading the Scriptures
in the vernacular. We have already dealt with this section
of the letter in treating of Hus' nationalism; suffice it here
to say that he resolutely repudiated any such prohibition
and enjoined his readers to read the Scriptures in whatever
language they could.

Hus' letter further mentions a priest, preaching at the
ordination of a candidate for priesthood, who declared
that a priest in mortal sin is not a servant or a child of the
devil. Next, the preacher declared the ordinand had been
up to that time a son of God; but after the ordination he
would become the father of God and the creator of God's
body. The priest concluded by asserting that the worst priest
is better than the best layman. Hus soundly trounced such
blasphemies. Later, he wrote a Latin treatise where his answers are given in a more extended form.[28] We shall follow
the exposition of this treatise. Hus was not unacquainted
with the exaggerated exaltation of priesthood found in a
very popular book of the time entitled *Stella clericorum.*
In his reply to the first statement, that a priest in mortal
sin is not a servant of the devil, Hus quotes Christ's saying:
"Amen, amen, I say to you that everyone that commits sin

[26] Novotný, *Korespondence,* No. 38, pp. 114-16.

[27] *Ibid.,* No. 35, pp. 104-08.

[28] Joannes Hus, *Contra praedicatorem Plznensem,* in *Historia et
monumenta,* I, pp. 179-85; Novotný, *Jan Hus,* II, pp. 15-16.

is a servant of sin."[29] It follows therefore that such a priest is a servant of the devil. Since the devil is the father of every mortal sin, particularly of lies, everyone who lies is the son of the devil. The priest who preached such a lie is himself the devil's son. The second assertion of the Plzeň preacher, that a priest celebrating the mass is God's father and the creator of God's body, also derives from the *Stella clericorum*. Hus bluntly calls it a lie as well as blasphemy. To create means in fact to make something out of nothing. In this sense God alone is creator. He thus created heaven and earth as well as man. To assert that a priest is the creator of his own Creator is absurd and nonsensical; it is contrary to God's word and to plain common sense. The third state-ment, that the worst priest is better than the best layman, would have as a consequence that Judas (as a disciple of Christ) was better than David. But Christ said of Judas, in speaking to the disciples: "One of you is a devil."[30] Hus writes further that some priests go so far as to declare that the worst priest is better than the Virgin Mary for "she bore Christ only once, while every priest creates him as often and can create Him any time he wishes": he is therefore holier and worthier than she. This insane self-glorification in ele-vating oneself above the Mother of God is sheer blasphemy.

Sometime in November 1411, Hus preached a sermon on the text, "Martha said to Jesus,"[31] which he later expanded into a small pamphlet. Since the text suggested the theme of death, Hus devoted the sermon to the subject of funerals and purgatory.[32] Funerals of the rich at that time were con-ducted with great pomp and a display of wealth. A large number of priests and singers were invited to the house for the wake and the various rites and ceremonies of the most

[29] John 8:34.
[30] John 6:70.
[31] "Dixit Martha ad Jesum," in *Historia et monumenta*, II, pp. 76-84. The text is in John 11:21.
[32] J. Huisinga, in his *The Waning of the Middle Ages* (London, Edward Arnold & Co., 1924), p. 41, also describes this custom of elaborate funerals as being common in Western Europe. For that mat-ter, I myself remember it from my childhood, for it survived in central Europe even then.

splendid kind. The dirges were long; the church bells rang loudly; the funeral procession was an ostentatious display of wealth; the masses were numerous. After the funeral, the participants and the clergy were entertained at a sumptuous feast accompanied by a drinking bout wherein no trace of sorrow for the deceased could be discerned. Hus then describes the haggling with the parish priest for the customary masses to be said for thirty days. This custom Hus regards as unseemly as well as simoniacal, for it amounts to selling a sacrament for money. He eloquently and indignantly denounces all these practices, not only as a waste of money but as a display of pride rather than of pious sorrow, or a reminder of every man's mortality.

This theme naturally leads to a consideration of purgatory. Hus does not repudiate the doctrine of purgatory as such, but only its abuse. Although he admits that masses are an aid in shortening the length of the suffering of the soul in purgatory, they cannot be said for all indiscriminately; for those who died in sinless state do not need them, while those who departed impenitent in mortal sins are past all human help. It is only the middle class, those who died in venial sins and are expiating them in purgatory, who can be truly aided by the prayers of those still living. Hus sharply and decisively repudiates the statement falsely ascribed to St. Gregory that at every mass at least one soul is released from purgatory. He brands it a lie derived from the *Stella clericorum*. It is remarkable that Hus still adheres to the doctrine of purgatory despite his repeated assertion that only Scriptural doctrine is binding on Christians, and although he knows and admits that the purgatory tenet was not taught by Christ or His apostles nor derived from any book of the canonical Scripture, but is found solely in the apocryphal II Maccabees.[33] Nevertheless, he taught that "it is safer to live well, than to expect release after death by the aid of others."

Although Hus himself, then, did not repudiate the doctrine of purgatory, another contemporary of his, the radical

---

[33] II Maccabees 12:43-45.

Nicholas of Dresden, in his *De purgatorio*, did come to that conclusion; he even quoted copiously from Hus' sermon in support of his opinion.

The last two of Hus' treatises we wish to mention are *The Three Uncertainties* and the related *Concerning Believing*.[34] Hus had many adherents in the important Moravian city of Olomouc, the seat of the bishopric. An unknown supporter of his in that city sent him a request for comments on three doubts he apparently entertained: whether one should believe in the pope; whether a man who did not confess to a priest at the time of his death could be saved; and whether any doctors taught that some of those in Pharaoh's army drowned in the Red Sea, or some of those submerged in Sodom, were among the saved. Hus answered the first question negatively. He had recently replied similarly in his comments on Lombard's *Sentences* as to whether one should believe in the Church. He recounts his favorite theory about believing: it is one thing to believe something in the same sense that we believe about God whom we do not see; it is another to believe in a thing, as we believe that Scripture is true; and it is still another thing to believe as we trust and love God supremely. Christ said of this last kind of belief: "I say unto you that whoever believes in me has life eternal."[35] No one else, whether the pope or the Church, or anything else, is to be believed in this way save God alone.

The second query Hus answers by saying that what is essential in confession is a sincere sorrow for sin and a heartfelt desire for divine forgiveness. God forgives a contrite sinner, even though he had no chance to confess orally to a priest. Hus cites several Scriptural examples of this type of confession, among them that of the publican in the temple who beat his breast, saying: "O God, have mercy on me, a sinner."[36] Christ declared him to be justified.

---

[34] *De tribus dubiis*, in *Historia et monumenta*, I, pp. 208-10; *De credere, ibid.*, pp. 210-12.

[35] John 6:40.

[36] Luke 18:13. This example again illustrates Hus' preference for sober, religiously responsible, emphases in theological discussion as against mere speculative predilection and inordinate curiosity.

As for the third typically medieval, fancifully theoretical, question, Hus answers it in a practical and positive manner. He asserts that the time for repentance is offered to man throughout his life and to the very end. Therefore, it is unsafe for anyone, unless he has a Scriptural proof or a private revelation to the contrary, to say that any particular man is eternally damned. Hus himself resolutely held to this principle in respect of Wyclif, in refusing to consent to those who arbitrarily declared him to be among the damned.

This short treatise, *The Three Uncertainties*, aroused his doughty foe, Prior Stephen of the Carthusian monastery of Dolany in Moravia. The prior attacked him in his polemical *Antihussus*.[37] Either at the same time or later another determined opponent, the Benedictine monk John of Holešov, joined the fray by opposing the first question of Hus' *De tribus dubiis* by a treatise *An credi possit in papam*.[38] Having learned of Stephen's attack, Hus wrote to the monks of Dolany a letter defending himself against their prior's invectives.[39] He earnestly implores them, for their own salvation and not for his own justification, not to believe that he has held any error contrary to Scripture. He would not do so even if an angel from heaven, not only Wyclif, came down and taught otherwise than Christ and the apostles did. He repeats the excuses given a number of times elsewhere as to why he found it impossible to obey the cardinal's citation to the curia. Finally, he addresses the prior himself, reminding him of Christ's admonition: "Judge not and ye will not be judged."[40]

In the short pamphlet *De credere* Hus expands the argument in question treated in the previous treatise (*De tribus dubiis*) and applies it primarily to the faith in God. He re-

---

[37] Stephen had previously written the treatise *Antiwyclefus*; besides *Antihussus*, he later published *Liber epistolaris ad Hussitas, Dialogus volatilis inter Aucam et Passerem*. Pez, *Thesaurus anecdotorum novissimus*, IV, pp. 149-706.

[38] Jan Sedlák, ed., *An credi possit in papam*, in *Hlídka* (Brno, 1911); De Vooght, *Hussiana*, pp. 116-22. I have commented on the treatise in *John Hus' Concept of the Church*, pp. 151-57.

[39] Novotný, *Korespondence*, No. 41, pp. 120-21.

[40] Matt. 7:1.

peats almost verbatim his exposition of the theme in the *Super IV Sententiarum*. Suffice to say that only his third definition, wherein saving faith in God is defined as combining belief with love of God, adhering to Him and indwelling in Him, is the true faith.[41] By this kind of faith one does not believe in the Church, or the saints, or the Virgin Mary, but in God and Christ alone. As for the pope, we are to believe that he is the immediate vicar of Christ and the supreme priest only if he follows the Lord Jesus Christ; as such, he has authority to absolve and excommunicate, to grant indulgences, and all other things belonging to the power of the keys.

Finally, passing on to the exposition of the seven chapters of the First Corinthians,[42] we find him following the usual pattern of collecting for the purpose a large number of authoritative comments by outstanding Fathers, such as Augustine, Gregory, Ambrose, Cyprian, Bernard, and even Wyclif, whom he calls "Doctor evangelicus."[43] Above all, his work is replete with Scriptural quotations. He also depends for his exposition on the recognized biblical authority of Nicholas of Lyra and on the glosses. His aim, like the aim of all medieval learning, is not to present his own views, but to confirm, and conform to, the generally held views of Scriptural and patristic authority. Innovations, viewed with suspicion in all ages, were particularly frowned upon in the Middle Ages. The word had a sinister aura, suggesting not merely nonconformity, but even rebellion. From that point of view it is highly instructive to compare the exegetical and homiletical practice of Hus' time, as evidenced by the examples under consideration, with the New Testament studies today. Hus does not attempt to present the historical or religious background of the situation in Corinth; he does not place the events described in the first seven chapters of I Corinthians *in situ*; instead, he collects authoritative comments from a large number of

[41] *De credere*, p. 211.

[42] *Explicatio M. Joannis Hus in Septem Priora capita Primae Epistolae S. Pauli ad Corinthos*, in *Historia et monumenta*, II, pp. 131-65.

[43] *Ibid.*, p. 152.

sources, explaining each phrase, sentence, and sometimes every word of the text. No true historical conception of the subject studied could be gained by such a procedure. The fault, however, is not Hus' but that of the system as such. Even so Hus was able to propound ideas which, at the time of their presentation, went unchallenged, but which later were branded as heretical by Stanislav of Znojmo and Stephen Páleč. Thus, for instance, in commenting on the verse, "For no other foundation can one lay than that which is laid, which is Christ Jesus,"[44] Hus rejects the dogma that the Church is founded on Peter. He asserts, on the contrary, that it is based on Peter's confession that Christ is the son of the living God.[45] Even so, he bolsters his assertion by a citation of the same interpretation made by St. Augustine.

The *Quodlibet* held in January 1412 was under the management of Michael of Malenice, known as Čížek. It dealt largely with philosophical themes. Jerome of Prague took part in it, but his address is not extant. The exception to the predominance of the philosophical character of the academic tournament was the subject of Jakoubek of Stříbro, who chose to discuss whether it can be clearly proved from Scripture that the Antichrist would personally appear "at the end of time." He utilized for this purpose, even verbally, both Milič's and Janov's well-known anticipations of the Antichrist and asserted that "the end of time" is at hand because of the Schism of the Church. The Antichrist, therefore, has come. Indeed, he is the present Pope John XXIII. Jakoubek did not name him, but the inference was unmistakable.[46] This declaration caused a sensation which made the *Quodlibet* one of the most memorable.

Stanislav wrote a treatise, *De Antichristo*, against Jakoubek's position. He tried to prove that Scriptural references could not be applied to the popes, for they were not *total* adversaries of Christ. Nor have the prophesied signs

---

[44] I Cor. 3:11.
[45] *Explicatio*, p. 145.
[46] Novotný, *Jan Hus*, II, pp. 43-45; De Vooght, *L'hérésie*, p. 181; Sedlák, *Studie a texty*, III, pp. 25-29.

of the coming of the Antichrist been fulfilled as yet. This is the first work by Stanislav clearly indicative of his break with Hus and his party. Jakoubek answered it in his sermon "For my ways are not your ways."[47]

Another member of the extreme left of the reform party, the German Nicholas of Dresden, also aroused considerable resentment with a publication in which he attacked the pope. He had been forced to flee from Dresden on account of his radical views; in Prague he taught a German school at "The Black Rose." He published a treatise entitled *Tabulae veteris et novi coloris*, in which in nine dyptichs he contrasted an ancient scene (the old color) with a contemporary one (the new).[48] For instance, the first tableau depicted the pope riding his horse in all his pomp as a secular prince, while Christ was shown in his poverty and humility, having no place to lay his thorn-crowned head, bearing his cross. In the next three dyptichs the poverty of Peter and the apostles was contrasted with the wealth and pride of the prelates; the gentleness of Christ with the harsh rule of the pope; and the canon law opposed to the gospel. In the fifth tableau the simony and immorality of the prelates was castigated. The last picture portrayed the pope as the Antichrist arrayed in all his splendid regalia, displaying his power derived from the Donation of Constantine. Later, Nicholas expanded the scope of this treatise in his *Consuetudo et ritus*, and also in *Dialogus de purgatorio*.

Let us now return to our consideration of the proceedings against Hus undertaken by the dean of the theological faculty. Having so far failed to stop the protests against the sale of indulgences, Páleč, in the name of the faculty, pub-

---

[47] Jakoubek of Stříbro, "Sermones ad clerum," in Sedlák, *Studie a texty*, III, pp. 38-74.

[48] Howard Kaminsky et al., eds. and transls., Master Nicholas of Dresden, *The Old Color and the New* (Philadelphia, Transactions of the American Philosophical Society, new series, vol. 55, pt. 1, 1965) ; also his *A History of the Hussite Revolution* (Berkeley and Los Angeles, University of California Press, 1967) , pp. 40-48; F. M. Bartoš, *Husitství a cizina* (Praha, Čin, 1931) , pp. 142-53; De Vooght, *L'hérésie*, pp. 181-82.

lished a remonstrance against Hus, intended to secure action in non-academic quarters, particularly from the king.[49] It charged Hus with having declared at the recently held *Quodlibet* (January 1412) that the time of the Antichrist is near and that the pope is the Antichrist, whom he would resist. That statement had been made, as we know, by Jakoubek of Stříbro, not Hus. The theological faculty could not but know it; hence, they deliberately lied. They further charged that despite the prohibition of the king, Hus had preached against the "crusading" bull and indulgences and thus had contradicted the king's express order. Furthermore, they stated that Hus had preached at various places, including schools, and that he had publicly defamed the members of the faculty before the people. The faculty, therefore, forbade all their bachelors to attend any and all such meetings. Finally, they professed, for their own part, to "believe simply as our fathers had believed and as Christendom for hundreds of years has held and believed, that the pope can and does grant full remission of all sins . . .; we also believe that the pope may call upon Christ's faithful, whenever necessary, to demand from them temporal aid in defence of the city of Rome and of the Church . . ."

To this proclamation Hus made an ironical reply to the effect that the king should establish an academic prison, if he wished to enforce his will. That, too, was a remark not strictly calculated to endear him to the king, whose aid, after all, he desperately needed. But Hus was not a "diplomatic" person.[50]

Although the protest of the theological faculty was not addressed to the king explicitly, he actually undertook to act upon it. He was, moreover, incensed at the popular opposition to the sale of indulgences which often took ridiculing or violent forms. Jerome of Prague in particular publicly denounced the indulgences, declaring that they were not to be believed and were worthless. He even boxed the ears of a Minorite friar who had insulted him and would

[49] Palacký, *Documenta*, pp. 448-50.
[50] *Ibid.*, pp. 450-51; De Vooght, *L'hérésie*, p. 193.

have punished the friar even more severely, had not a member of the royal Council restrained him.[51] Even one of the king's favorites, Voksa of Valdštejn, had taken a prominent part in these public demonstrations. He had organized a procession, in which a student, dressed as a prostitute, with bared breasts, and hung about with pretended papal bulls, offered the indulgences by imitating the sellers' enticing sales-talk, to the huge exhilaration of the beholders. The mock parade wound its way among the jeering crowds to the New Town square. There the "bulls" were burned. The king could not tolerate such public demonstrations against the papal bulls: he issued a strict order that no one oppose the indulgences or sing disparaging songs about them.[52]

Moreover, Wenceslas, who was then staying at his castle of Žebrák, called representatives of the two warring camps to the castle (July 10). Before they appeared there, Páleč demanded of Hus and Jakoubek the written texts of the speeches delivered at the recent *Quodlibet* dealing with indulgences. Jakoubek complied with the request, having first taken the precaution of notarizing the text of his *questio*. Hus, however, refused to submit his speech, on the ground that it had been delivered publicly and was therefore public property. This indeed furnished Páleč with the welcome opportunity of accusing Hus of academic disobedience, which he promptly seized upon. He now wrote, undoubtedly with Stanislav's aid, as Hus supposed, a treatise pompously entitled *Tractatus gloriosus*,[53] presumably representing the views of the whole faculty. He complained in it of Hus' disobedience. To this Hus replied at the Žebrák meeting that he was willing to produce the text of his disputation and defend it to the death by fire, provided all the doctors bound themselves, in case they failed to prove any error or heresy therein, to suffer the same penalty.[54] Shocked at this request, the doctors, after a con-

---

[51] Novotný, *Jan Hus*, II, p. 104.  [52] *Ibid.*, II, pp. 105-07.

[53] J. Loserth, ed., "Beiträge zur Geschichte der husitischen Bewegung, IV" in *Archiv für Oesterreichische Geschichte* (Wien, 1889), Vol. 75, pp. 333-39. See my analysis of it in *John Hus' Concept of the Church*, pp. 157-71.

[54] *Contra octo doctores*, in *Historia et monumenta*, I, p. 366.

sultation, offered one of their numbers to undertake the obligation in behalf of all. This Hus refused: since all of them accused him, let all share the responsibility. In this impasse the royal Council advised the parties rather lamely: "Come to a good concord with one another!" We would like to know how the strife was settled, but are left in suspense.

The royal Council in charge of the conference consisted of ecclesiastical and lay dignitaries, but did not include Hus' friends at court. Páleč's party included two of Hus' enemies of long standing, John Eliášův and Andrew of Brod, who had desired condemnation of Wyclif even at the time when Stanislav of Znojmo and Stephen Páleč were leaders of the extreme Wyclif faction among the reformists. The latter two, although already alienated from that party, had not yet made a clean break with it. Now they were faced with the decision of declaring themselves out-and-out opponents of Wyclif. Thereupon, they took the plunge: along with all theological representatives, they not only condemned anew Wyclif's forty-five articles—seven of which they branded as heretical—but added seven new ones, framed to deal with the present circumstances.[55]

Briefly stated, these added articles were as follows: (1) Anyone who thinks of the sacraments and the keys of the Church otherwise than the holy Roman Church does is a heretic. (2) Anyone who says that these are the days of the Antichrist's reign, who has come in accordance with the faith of the Church, of the Holy Scriptures, and the holy doctors in the end of the age, holds an evident error. (3) To assert that the constitutions of the holy doctors and the laudable customs of the Church are not to be held, because they are not contained in the Bible, is an error. (4) To say that the relics and bones of the saints and their vestments are not to be venerated by Christ's faithful is an error. (5) To assert that priests do not absolve from sins nor remit sins

---

[55] Palacký, *Documenta*, pp. 451-56. This text is reprinted in *John Hus' Concept of the Church*, Appendix I. See also De Vooght, *L'hérésie*, pp. 200-201.

in the sacrament of penance, but merely announce the absolution of the penitent, is an error. (6) Whoever asserts that the pope cannot, in necessity, call upon Christ's faithful, requesting them for temporal aid in the defense of the Apostolic See, the status of the Roman Church and of the city of Rome, and grant remission of sins to the truly penitent who are contrite and confess their sins, is in error. (7) It is affirmed that the mandate of our lord king and civil magistrates that no one clamor against the preachers of indulgences and the papal bulls, is and has been just, reasonable, and holy.[56] The decisions of the theological faculty were accepted by the royal Council and proclaimed as having the king's approval.

While these things were transpiring at Žebrák, a bloody event occurred at Prague which gave the revolt its first martyrs. Three young men, Martin, John, and Stašek, who had loudly protested the sale of indulgences at the three principal churches—St. Vitus cathedral, the Týn church, and St. James—were seized and put in jail in the Old Town Hall. The next day the councilors called together the inhabitants to the square to witness their punishment. Fearing its cruel severity, Hus, accompanied by some masters, bachelors, and students, arrived early in the morning and asked for an interview with the councilors. He pleaded with them for a moderate punishment of the young men, declaring that he himself had been the chief protester against the indulgences. The councilors promised to deal leniently with the young men; but as soon as Hus, along with many of the assembled crowd, had left, they ordered them to be beheaded, not at the usual place of execution, for they feared the remaining crowd, but nearer the Town Hall (July 11). The people, hearing the fearful news, quickly reassembled in immense numbers, and taking up the three dead bodies, carried them, in a procession headed by young John of Jičín, to the Bethlehem Chapel. It was almost a religious procession, the people singing "Isti sunt martyres." The bodies were then buried in the chapel with reverent

---

[56] Thereafter these seven articles were referred to as six in number; either No. 7 was omitted or was incorporated into No. 6.

ceremonies; Hus sang the martyrs' mass over them. The chapel was filled to overflowing by people who regarded the young men as veritable martyrs of the reform. Hus at first did not mention the event in his sermons, so as not to increase the public indignation; but two weeks later he did praise the young men for their courage in defending the truth, and exhorted the congregation to follow their example.[57] At the Council of Constance, both Hus and Jerome were charged with having proclaimed the young men "saints"—an act which the Holy See alone has the right to exercise.

The aroused populace, however, could not be easily pacified. They besieged the Town Hall and threatened the councilors with punishment. Many of the populace were seized and imprisoned, which excited the crowd still more. The uprising lasted several days. Finally the frightened councilors appealed to the king. Wenceslas, whose temper was a tinderbox easily ignited by any defiance of his will, was seized with one of his paroxysms of rage. He shouted that even if a thousand rose up against his authority, they would suffer the same fate as the three young men.[58]

Furthermore, the king ordered another step in the matter of pacification of the two theological camps and their differences over the indulgences. He called a meeting of the university and clergy for July 16 at the Old Town Hall. It was presided over by Wenceslas Králík, titular patriarch of Antioch, and Conrad of Vechta, bishop of Olomouc. All the members of the theological faculty were present with the exception of Matthew of Zbraslav.[59] Hus was absent.[60] The university was headed by its rector, Mark of Hradec. The

---

[57] Novotný, *Jan Hus*, II, pp. 116-19; for an eyewitness account of the event, see František Šimek, ed., *Staré letopisy české* (Praha, Historický spolek a Společnost Husova musea, 1937), pp. 10-11.

[58] Matthew Spinka, ed. and transl., *John Hus at the Council of Constance* (New York and London, Columbia University Press, 1965), pp. 219-20.

[59] Sedlák, *Studie a texty*, I, pp. 38 ff.; also *Postilla*, p. 97, where Hus specifically names Páleč, Stanislav, John Eliášův, Andrew of Brod, George Bor, and Simon as approving the action of the prelates.

[60] Bartoš, *Čechy v době Husově*, p. 358, mentions this circumstance; also Sedlák, *Studie a texty*, I, p. 42.

inquisitor, Bishop Nicholas of Nezero, after delivering a speech about the evil repute of Bohemia because of rumors of heresy, then read the decrees of Žebrák. On the basis of these he announced that anyone daring to defend Wyclif's theses or to attack indulgences was to be exiled from the country. All university disputations about Wyclif were likewise forbidden. The bishop then demanded that all those present give consent to these decisions. Mark of Hradec was then asked to speak for himself personally, since he was known to be a prominent member of the reform party. He bravely declared that some of the forty-five articles could be understood in an acceptable sense rather than in the sense ascribed to them by the theological faculty. Those that could not be so understood he rejected. His stand was shared by Procopius of Plzeň, Friedrich Epinge of Dresden, and a few others; but the majority of the university masters, including the dean of the faculty of arts, Brixi of Žatec, dared not oppose the demand. The members of the theological faculty, of course, made their assent in high glee.

Although the above description is based on the record of a notary, which the theological faculty ordered to be made, it is not complete. In later controversies between Hus and Páleč, other details are mentioned. Thus, for instance, it is asserted that it was declared at the meeting that "whoever does not obey the pontiff's order shall die!" Páleč did not deny the statement; but he explained that it was based on the divine command given in Deuteronomy 17:9, commanding that in matters of serious controversy involving death, recourse should be made "to priests and Levites," which he interpreted to mean popes and cardinals.[61]

Before the meeting was concluded, Mark of Hradec requested the members of the university to meet in a separate convocation in Charles College. It was attended generally, with the exception of the theological faculty, whose members claimed to be afraid of being roughly mishandled.

[61] The text of the notarized record is in Sedlák, *Studie a texty*, I, pp. 55-65; the controversy with Páleč in Sedlák, ed., *Antihus*, in *Hlidka* (1912), pp. 10 and 12.

Later, when Hus wrote his *Postil*, he stated that they had no Scriptural proof for their position, and therefore refused to attend.[62] This meeting, then, despite the prohibition adopted the day before, discussed the forty-five theses anew, and declared some of them to be defensible "in their acceptable sense."

It was now incumbent on the reform leaders to prove that some of the Wyclif articles were defensible. Toward the end of July 1412, a few masters—among them Hus, who had in the meantime returned to Prague—undertook to do so in spite of the royal prohibition. The disputation dealt with eight articles, of which Hus chose six.[63] None of them dealt with the pope or his powers. Hus delivered three separate lectures at the *Carolinum*, at the first of which he dealt with articles 13 and 14. He argued that those who ceased preaching or hearing the Word of God on account of unjust excommunication, are themselves excommunicated; and that it is lawful for a deacon or priest to preach without the episcopal or papal permission. As for the first, Hus asserts that preaching is a divine command and the principal duty of the priest. He does not say that authorities can never licitly stop preaching, but only that they should not be obeyed when they order its cessation unjustly. He handles the second prohibition similarly; the command of Christ to preach is of greater authority than human permission. The priest, having been once ordained to his office, needs no special permission to preach, since that is his principal task. Hus is aware that canon law forbids preaching without episcopal permission, but interprets it as applying to the absence of proper ordination. It would, therefore, appear that he does not uphold indiscriminate lay preaching.

Hus was perhaps followed by Friedrich Epinge, bachelor of canon law, who defended Wyclif's article 11, that no prelate should excommunicate anyone of whom he does not

[62] *Postilla*, p. 75.

[63] The text of these six disputations is found in *Historia et monumenta*, I, pp. 139-67; see my *John Hus' Concept of the Church*, pp. 122-26, for more extended comments.

know that he had first been excommunicated by God.[64] Thereupon Hus' stout companion in the reform struggle, Jakoubek of Stříbro, undertook to defend article 32, stating that to endow clergy is against the law of Christ, and article 33, that Pope Sylvester and Emperor Constantine erred in endowing the Church.[65]

A few days later Hus lectured on two other articles (16, 18), namely, that secular lords may at will deprive habitually delinquent priests of their temporalities; and that tithes are not obligatory, but merely alms. Hus' dealing with the first of these propositions well illustrates what he means by holding to Wyclif's articles only "in their acceptable sense." He completely omits the second clause of article 17, which adds that lay people may correct the lords at will. Thus he implicitly admits that he does not agree with the sentiment expressed in that clause. It is a pity that he does not say so outright. Such is, however, his invariable technique; he explicitly upholds Wyclif's position only when he regards it as not contrary to his understanding of sound gospel teaching, while he passes in silence over items with which he disagrees. He cites examples from the Old and New Testaments to prove the proposition that secular rulers have exercised jurisdiction and punished evildoers even of the priestly class. Christ taught his disciples to obey rulers and to render unto Caesar what is Caesar's. Hus argues that King Wenceslas would not be truly king over his own territories, had he not the right to rule the clergy. For that matter, the anti-reformist party sought the aid of the king whenever it suited their purpose in attacking their opponents.

The same tacit omission of part of Wyclif's next proposition (18) characterizes Hus' dealing with that question. He limits his discussion to the first clause, "tithes are mere alms," deleting the remainder of the sentence, "and parishioners may withhold them at will on account of the sins

[64] The text is in S. Harrison Thomson, ed., *Mag. Johannis Hus, Tractatus responsivus* (Princeton, Princeton University Press, 1927), pp. 72-133.
[65] *Ibid.*, pp. 28-53.

of the prelates." He thus does not demand the abolition of all tithes, but only their forcible imposition by both the ecclesiastical and the civil authorities. He claims that they were originally voluntary offerings and insists that such is their proper character even at present. He draws therefrom the conclusion that clerics are not owners, but merely custodians, of the wealth bestowed upon them for their frugal support and the relief of the poor.

It must be remembered that tithes constituted a very heavy burden against which the peasants sometimes violently revolted. For in addition to the regular tithe, the Church imposed the death duty, on the theory that the regular tithe had not always been paid. This tax was often abused, as when the greedy priest took as his share the best piece of furniture, or a head of cattle, or another valuable chattel.[66]

In the third session Hus defended articles (15 and 4) stating that no one is civil lord, prelate, or bishop while he is in mortal sin; and that a bishop in mortal sin does not transubstantiate or baptize. These were, of course, the most radical tenets of Wyclif's entire body of doctrine, for they undermined the whole power structure of the Roman Church both in secular and in spiritual aspects. In dealing with these dangerous theses, Hus does not so much interpret them in their acceptable sense as, by radical insertions of a qualifying clause, change their meaning. Nowhere is the difference between Wyclif and Hus so patently apparent as in these instances. He introduces modifiers "worthily and justly" into the sentences so that they read: None is worthily and justly civil lord, etc., and that a bishop or priest does not worthily ordain, transubstantiate, or baptize. There certainly can be no objection to the propositions so modified. But they no longer represent Wyclif's thought; they are essentially different in Hus' transformation—one can almost say, subversion—of the original meaning. The change even raises a question as to the legitimacy of such a transforma-

<hr>

[66] James Westfall Thompson and Edgar N. Johnson, *An Introduction to Medieval Europe, 300-1500* (New York, W. W. Norton & Co., Inc., 1937), p. 670.

tion and forcibly suggests the unwisdom of Hus' exposing himself to the charge of Wyclif's defense. Perhaps the best that can be said about the procedure is that Hus, in searching how Wyclif's articles could be understood in an acceptable sense—for he and his party were convinced that the forty-five articles did not represent his authentic teaching—overstated his case in the opposite direction. At least, it should be clear that he differed from Wyclif to an essential degree and that even those articles he chose to defend he interpreted in a sense not only divergent from that ascribed to them by his enemies, but even inconsistent with Wyclif's own intention.

Such an excellent opportunity to attack Hus was not to be overlooked. It was seized by Stanislav of Znojmo, who preached, at the Týn church on August 28, a violent sermon against five of Wyclif's theses, three of which had been defended by Hus. He completely disregarded Hus' restrictions and reinterpretations and denounced them as if Hus held them in the sense ascribed to them by Stanislav himself or the other members of the theological faculty. In particular he vehemently excoriated the right of secular rulers to alienate ecclesiastical property for any cause whatsoever, or to subject the Church to secular jurisdiction. Church property is God's property; to tamper with it is sacrilege. The same stricture applies to tithes, which belong, as of divine and human right, to the clergy outright. To regard them as voluntary offerings is to fly in the face of divine command.[67]

Páleč did not allow himself to remain behind his esteemed senior. He preached, on September 4, a sermon vigorously denouncing Hus' defense of Wyclif, likewise without the slightest regard to the latter's careful delimitation of his subject. All pretense of friendship was gone by this time. He rode roughshod over his erstwhile friend's opinions, which presumably he formerly had shared. He declared that no article of Wyclif was capable of being interpreted

[67] Jan Sedlák, ed., "Mgri. Stanislai de Znoyma Sermo contra 5 articulos Wiclef," *Hlídka* (Brno, 1911), pp. 49-60. See my comments in *John Hus' Concept of the Church*, pp. 132-33.

in an acceptable sense, for "none of them is catholic, but they are all either heretical, erroneous, or scandalous . . ."[68]

Since Hus, because of his continued defense of Wyclif and defiance of the indulgences, was deserted by his former friends and out of the king's favor, Michael de Causis succeeded in renewing Hus' trial at the curia. The process, which had been held in abeyance by Cardinal Brancatiis, was transferred in July 1412 to the jurisdiction of Cardinal Peter degli Stephaneschi. Michael seized this opportunity of securing his eagerly sought goal of having Hus finally condemned. He found a comrade-in-arms in this proceeding in Dr. Maurice Rvačka, who had sought to accomplish the same end in Prague. The latter was just then attending the Roman Council held in 1412-13. The two men joined forces and presented the cardinal with yet another charge against Hus. The cardinal acted quickly and declared Hus under major excommunication for non-obedience of the summons to appear before the curia, although not for heresy. Should he not appear before him in twenty days, or should he ignore the summons for twelve days thereafter, an interdict would be pronounced over Prague or any other place where he might reside. From the day of promulgation of this sentence, all faithful were forbidden to communicate with him "in food, drink, greeting, discourse, buying and selling, conversation, shelter, or in any other way. In any place where he might seek shelter, all church services and ministrations must be stopped and remain suspended for three days after his departure. Should he die, he must not be buried; or should he be buried, his body must be exhumed."[69]

The sentence was announced in Prague by Cardinal John, called Lisbonensis, sent by the pope for this very purpose. It was solemnly promulgated at the synodical meeting on October 18. Its proclamation was accompanied by the usual ceremonies: the ringing of bells, lighting and extinguishing

[68] Jan Sedlák, ed., "Mgri. Stephani de Páleč Sermo contra aliquos articulos Wiklef," *Hlídka* (Brno, 1911) , pp. 63-81; also my *John Hus' Concept of the Church*, pp. 133-35.

[69] Novotný, *Korespondence*, pp. 125-28.

of candles, elevating of the cross, and throwing of stones in the direction of the excommunicate's dwelling. These ceremonies incited crowds to loud protests.

Hus, who probably had heard of the sentence prior to its publication, now took a step wholly unknown to canon law: since any further appeal to the pope was obviously useless, he now appealed to God and Christ, "the most just judge who knows, protects, judges, declares, and rewards without fail the just cause of every man."[70] This almost unprecedented step (Hus cites two other previous examples of it) was an open declaration of Hus' final break with the papacy and the curia. In his view, no justice could be found in Rome. Although legally the act was a revolt against ecclesiastical jurisdiction, morally it could be regarded as a courageous protest against ecclesiastical injustice. John of Jesenice knew well that the appeal would be interpreted later as an act of rebellion, as it actually was. For since Hus appealed to Christ after the sentence of excommunication had been passed on him, his action had a "clearly provocative" character.[71]

Since Hus continued to preach, the major excommunication notwithstanding, this defiant action called forth from the pope an order (probably in August) that the Bethlehem Chapel be pulled down. It reached Prague toward the end of September. This authorization afforded the German parishioners of the neighboring church of Sts. Philip and James an opportunity to attack the hated Bethlehem Chapel. Under the leadership of Bernard Chotek, they stormed the building in an armed attack during a worship service, but were repulsed. Thereupon, the councilors of the Old Town called a meeting of both Czechs and Germans to consider how the chapel could be pulled down. The Germans were for its destruction and gained for it even one Czech, John the dove-seller; but when he propounded the

---

[70] Palacký, *Documenta*, pp. 464-66; Novotný, *Korespondence*, No. 46, pp. 129-33. A translation of the text is found in my *John Hus at the Council of Constance*, pp. 237-40.

[71] Jiří Kejř, "Právo a právní prameny v Husově díle," in *Husův sborník*, p. 87.

suggestion to the rest of the Czechs, the majority of them rejected it. Hus, who described the scene in his *Postil*, indignantly exclaimed: "Observe the audacity of the Germans! They would not be permitted to pull down their neighbor's oven or stable without the king's permission, and they would dare to attempt to destroy God's church!"[72]

Moreover, other violent measures were resorted to against those who continued to protest against ecclesiastical abuses. Hus recalls in his exile that the priests of the cathedral seized such would-be exhorters and beat them in the sanctuary itself, and then dragging them into their residential quarters, ordered them scourged. A similar disturbance occurred at the church of St. Mary of the Snow in New Town and in other monasteries.[73]

Twenty days after the promulgation of the sentence having passed, the interdict was imposed on Prague and its environs. Hus was confronted with the excruciatingly painful decision of whether to remain at his post, in accordance with his recently defended thesis that whoever ceased to preach on account of an unjust excommunication is himself an excommunicate. He was troubled because of Christ's saying that a good shepherd stays with his sheep in time of danger, while a hireling flees. On the other hand Christ said: "When they persecute you in one city, flee to another."[74] Moreover, he dreaded to have his people deprived of all spiritual ministrations by the interdict imposed on his account. "For the Antichrist has no stronger net than the stopping of the divine service, to which priests resort according to their will whenever they so desire."[75] In this dilemma he consulted his two assistants at the Bethlehem Chapel, Nicholas of Miličín and Martin of Volyně. We do not have his co-pastors' reply, but it appears to have

[72] *Postilla*, pp. 131-34. My translation is found in *John Hus at the Council of Constance*, pp. 242-46. See also Hus' letter to the Praguers, written from exile in November 1412, Novotný, *Korespondence*, p. 145.

[73] Novotný, *Korespondence*, p. 143.

[74] Matt. 10:23. Hus' doubts about leaving Prague are well described in *Postilla*, pp. 195-96.

[75] *Ibid.*, p. 196.

been in favor of his leaving Prague. Moreover, the king, fearing an outbreak of further disorders, ordered him to leave.[76] When the nobles in southern Bohemia offered him refuge, Hus decided for the exile. Nevertheless, he intended, whenever opportunity occurred, to visit Bethlehem secretly "to strengthen Christ's sheep." He also intended to preach wherever he happened to reside.

The very same month in which Hus left Prague, the news reached the city (October 16) that the pope had concluded peace with King Ladislas four months before! What an ironic denouement to Hus' tragic struggle against papal indulgences, which more than any other event sealed his fate!

[76] Bartoš, *Čechy v době Husově*, p. 363.

pon leaving Prague on October 15, 1412, Hus remained in the vicinity, although we do not know his exact whereabouts. In fact, from the beginning of January 1413 until Easter, he secretly visited the city from time to time. He himself informs us that even though the officials knew he was in Prague, they did not impose the interdict if he did not preach. "But when I preached once, they immediately stopped the services, for it was hard for them to hear the Word of God."[1]

According to another passage, he preached several times and on each occasion the services were suspended.[2] These visits were therefore furtive and intermittent. He also preached outside of Prague.

Before his first visit to Prague, he wrote from an unknown place several letters to his flock at Bethlehem and to the university masters.[3] One would have expected him to be discouraged and in low spirits, if not in despair. On the contrary, it is he who in these letters encourages others. He has not lost heart in what to others might have appeared as a losing, hopeless battle. To the university masters he appeals for the defense of the Bethlehem Chapel, which, as has already been mentioned, his enemies intended to destroy.[4] He further pleads with them in behalf of the land and the people who are being attacked "by the Antichrist." Nevertheless, he assures them that the adversary is chained and will do them no permanent harm. "Behold, he has at-

[1] J. B. Jeschke, ed., *Mistr Jan Hus, Postilla* (Prague, Komenského ev. fakulta bohoslovecká, 1952), p. 231.
[2] *Ibid.*, p. 195; also Paul de Vooght, *L'hérésie de Jean Huss* (Louvain, Publications universitaires de Louvain, 1960), p. 231.
[3] V. Novotný, ed., *M. Jana Husi Korespondence a dokumenty* (Praha, Komise pro vydávání pramenů náboženského hnutí českého, 1920), Nos. 48, 49, 50, 53, 55.
[4] *Ibid.*, No. 48.

tacked me for several years but so far has not, I believe, harmed a single hair of mine." Let them, therefore, stand in the faith "to the end."

In several other letters written to Praguers[5] he appeals to them in pregnant language to remain faithful in the truth they have found. He mentions that "many out of fear have already left [the truth], fearing more a miserable man than the Almighty God." Apparently, his enemies had already applied methods calculated to counter, by all available means, Hus' influence upon his hearers. He again mentions in a letter that efforts are being made to destroy the Bethlehem Chapel. In another letter he encourages the people by writing that for one preacher the officials silenced —Hus himself—"twelve others have arisen. . . . Instead of the infirm and weak goose, truth gave Prague many falcons and eagles."

He also wrote to his old friend and benefactor, Christian of Prachatice, then the university rector.[6] Christian had written Hus a consoling letter, exhorting him to patience, for "all who wish to live piously in Christ Jesus must suffer persecution." Hus gratefully received this well-meant exhortation. In his reply, he assures his friend that persecution does not discourage him and professes his determination to live piously, no matter what the Antichrist may do to make him suffer for it. He repeats his intention to fight against the Behemoth, whom he identifies with the pope and his masters, doctors, and lawyers who "by a false name of sanctity cover the beast's ugliness."

Hus also made an appeal to the supreme court of the land, which met on December 14 for a three-day session, pleading with the assembled nobles for protection and restoration of permission to preach.[7]

I am grieved that I cannot preach the Word of God, because I have no desire to have the divine services stopped and the people distressed. Consider, dear lords, even if I

[5] *Ibid.*, Nos. 49, 49*, 50, 53, 55.
[6] *Ibid.*, No. 52.
[7] *Ibid.*, No. 54.

were entirely guilty, whether they should restrain the people of God from the praise of the Lord God and grieve them by such excommunications and cessations of divine services.

He calls upon the assembled lords to stop such abuses, "so that the Word of God would have freedom." He offers to defend himself "before all masters, prelates, and Your Graces, gladly to hear their accusations of myself and to answer them and suffer the verdict, as befits a poor priest . . ." He also hopes that the king and queen, to whom perhaps he also wrote, will come to his aid.

Nor did Hus appeal to the supreme court in vain. The nobles, with the active cooperation of the king, who once again suffered himself to interfere in Hus' behalf, actually undertook one more effort to settle the affair. King Wenceslas, undoubtedly under the pressure and advice of Hus' friends at the court, issued, on January 3, 1413, an order convoking a special general synod of the clergy, to meet at Český Brod for "the extirpation of heresy." Bishop Conrad of Vechta, who had recently purchased the archiepiscopal office from Albík of Uničov, and acted as its administrator, was ordered, along with Bishop John "the Iron" of Litomyšl, to carry out the royal decree.[8] Conrad was not installed as archbishop until July 17, 1413. He issued the call for the meeting. Perhaps later, as an afterthought, the king requested the university to present its opinion as to the best means of terminating the struggle between the two parties. This actually had the effect of subverting the original plan of the clerical synod, which was to act unilaterally as a judge and not as a mere arbiter in the matter. Under the altered conditions, the synod was confronted with the university's opinion, which actually represented Hus' own conditions presented in the university's name. For this reason it appears that Bishop John of Litomyšl refused to take part in the proceedings. Conrad of Vechta thus found himself entrusted with the task of alone carrying out the

[8] F. Palacký, ed., *Documenta Mag. Joannis Hus* (Praha, F. Tempsky, 1869), pp. 472-74.

royal will, which aimed at pacification. That was all to the good of Hus' cause.

Instead of meeting at Český Brod on February 2, the synod was held, perhaps for the convenience of the university, at the archiepiscopal palace in the Small Side four days later. Both parties to the struggle were well prepared to defend their cause. Principal speakers for the prelatical party were Stanislav of Znojmo and Stephen Páleč. Contrary to the king's intention, that party came not to seek an accommodation and peace but to gain a clear-cut victory over their opponents. Throughout the negotiations, they showed themselves intransigent toward any concessions or compromise, by which means alone a peaceful solution could be obtained. At first, they proposed as the basis of negotiations *Confessio doctorum contra Hus.*[9] The document once again condemned Wyclif's forty-five articles, asserting that Hus actually upheld them and was therefore justly condemned and placed under the interdict by the curia. The interdict then was by right imposed upon Prague. In other words, the party fully approved Hus' condemnation pronounced by Cardinal Peter degli Stephaneschi. Since such a summary verdict was obviously unacceptable to Hus' party, Stanislav and Páleč, in the name of all the doctors of theology, reworked this document into a new form entitled *Consilium doctorum facultatis theologiae studii Pragensis.*[10] This formulation of the basis of the controversy, sometimes referred to as the "three truths," remained henceforth the principal text defended and assailed in the long-drawn-out subsequent controversies. As such, it is of primary importance.[11]

Summarized briefly, it asserts that the Czech clergy (meaning the prelatical party), along with the entire Christendom, adheres to all the rites and ceremonies of the Roman Church. This includes the conviction that the pope

[9] Jan Sedlák, ed., *Několik textů z doby husitské* in *Hlídka* (Brno, 1911), I, pp. 48-49.

[10] Palacký, *Documenta*, pp. 475-80.

[11] For an almost full translation of the document, see my *John Hus' Concept of the Church* (Princeton, Princeton University Press, 1966), pp. 142-44.

and the cardinals constitute the body of that Church. Their function is to define the faith of the entire Church and to exercise jurisdiction in it by correcting all abuses. There exists no substitute for them. The document makes the complaint that "certain clergy" (meaning the party of Hus) in Bohemia declare that the condemnation of Wyclif's forty-five articles is iniquitous and unjust, and refuse to acknowledge them as false.

The second cause for dissension is the acceptance, on the part of the Czech clergy, of all decisions of the Apostolic See in matters of faith. "Certain clergy," however, desire to have the holy Scriptures as the sole judge in such matters. Furthermore, they interpret the Scriptures according to their own understanding, and not as the Church teaches.

The third reason for dissension is that the Czech clergy hold it to be an apostolic doctrine that all Christians must render obedience to the Apostolic See and the prelates "in all things whatsoever," where no good is prohibited and no evil prescribed. "Certain clergy," however, inculcate disobedience to the papal, episcopal, and priestly authority.

The *Consilium* then asserts that the gravest punishment should be imposed on anyone who should hold any view contrary to that of the Roman Church. Anyone found adhering to Wyclifite views should be declared an enemy of the Church, the king, and the kingdom. Furthermore, the doctors reaffirm that none of the forty-five articles is catholic but all are either heretical, erroneous, or scandalous. They conclude that it is not for the Prague clergy to judge whether Hus' condemnation is just or unjust.

Before the synod met, Hus had presented it with his demands. Although the document is undated, it is clear from its contents that it had been submitted prior to its first meeting. From some unknown place where he then resided, Hus wrote his *Conditiones concordiae.*[12] He summarized his demands in nine propositions, and requested that the pacification concluded between Archbishop Zbyněk and himself (July 6, 1411) by the arbitrators appointed by the king

[12] Palacký, *Documenta*, pp. 491-92.

169

be taken as the basis of the present negotiations. The Bohemian kingdom should retain all its laws, liberties, and customs as other kingdoms possess them, as far as ecclesiastical matters are concerned. In other words, the king is to have the right to pronounce upon the judgments of the Apostolic See. Hus further demands that he himself, whom Zbyněk charged with no crime, be invited into the synodical meeting; if anyone there wishes to charge him with error or heresy, let him do so with the understanding that he is subject to the same punishment, if he fails to prove his charge, as Hus himself if he be proved guilty. If no one rises against him, let the king and the bishops announce it publicly that Hus is willing to defend his cause; if anyone wishes to accuse him of anything, let him report himself in the archiepiscopal palace. If no one appears to do so, let those who had reported to the pope that Bohemia and Moravia were infected with heresy be called to prove it. If they fail, let them be punished. The archbishop should then order that no one should be called a heretic and the interdict should be lifted. The king should collect subsidy from the clergy to send an embassy to the curia to inform it that no heresy exists in the country.

Jakoubek of Stříbro also came to Hus' defense.[13] He was entrusted with this task by the university. It is uncertain whether his *Consilium* was actually presented to the synod.[14] However, his suggestions were abstractly theological and not suitable for practical dealing with the problem involved.

Another friend who came to Hus' defense (October 10, 1411) was the then rector of the university, Simon of Tišnov. He testified to the activity of Hus as aiming "to the benefit of the Church and the well-being of his fellowman."[15] He declared that Hus spent many years in such

[13] *Ibid.*, pp. 493-94.

[14] Jiří Kejř, *Husitský právnik, M. Jan z Jesenice* (Praha, Československá akademie věd, 1965), p. 76. F. M. Bartoš expresses the opinion that it was presented to the synod; *Čechy v době Husově* (Praha, Jan Laichter, 1947), p. 363, n. 3.

[15] This pronouncement is not found in Palacký's *Documenta*. F. M. Bartoš published it in an article, "Neznámý projev rektora Karlovy university na obranu Husovu," in *Jihočeský sborník historický*, VII (1934), pp. 84-86.

activity at the university in lecturing, and preaching on the commemorative occasions and at synodical meetings, as well as to the people. He never taught nor held any error, but proved his doctrine from the Holy Scriptures, and by the doctors.

The principal reply to the proposals of the evangelical party, as the reformers now called themselves, was made by the doughty Bishop John "the Iron" of Litomyšl. Since he was not present at the synod, he had to be informed of the proceedings by someone who did attend it. His informant was the inveterate enemy of all reforms, Dr. George of Brod, a member of the faculty of theology. The bishop, himself an outstanding adversary of the evangelical party, repudiated, in his letter sent to Bishop Conrad on February 10, 1413, Hus' *Conditiones*. He dealt with each of the nine paragraphs separately, and particularly urged that Hus be deprived of all opportunities to preach in the Bethlehem Chapel. His books should be condemned as erroneous and their circulation be stopped. Hus' request that the pacification of July 1411 be taken as the basis of negotiations was scornfully rejected and the suggestion that a subsidy be taken from the clergy for an embassy to the curia summarily repudiated. The bishop even suggested basic changes in the university organization, urging that a vice-chancellor be elected who would exercise disciplinary powers. All preaching by Hus' party must be forbidden.[16]

After receiving and debating these two proposals, the work of the synod came to an end (February 19). But the parties continued to wrangle in behalf of their respective positions.

Thereafter, Hus again returned to Prague, keeping himself in seclusion at the Bethlehem Chapel. A little before his return he had completed (on February 2, as he expressly stated) his militant treatise *On Simony*,[17] dealing aggres-

[16] Novotný, *M. Jan Hus, život a dílo*, 2 vols. (Praha, Jan Laichter, 1919-21), II, pp. 252-53.

[17] My translation of the treatise is found in *Advocates of Reform, The Library of Christian Classics* (Philadelphia, The Westminster Press, 1953), XIV, pp. 196-278; for an analytical summary of its contents, see my *John Hus' Concept of the Church*, pp. 308-17.

sively with that most burning question of the times. This cancer infested and was consuming not only the body of the Church but the body politic as well. Hus utilized for his own work Wyclif's similar treatise, *De simonia*. Hus' selections, however, are limited to about one-eighth of Wyclif's text. Moreover, Hus' version is written in pungent, popular language—a pleasant contrast to Wyclif's academic, stilted treatment. Its scope also was greatly enlarged by the inclusion of treatment of the parish clergy and the academic circles. He urges as a remedy the voluntary poverty of the clergy; but he does not go all the way with Spiritual Franciscans in advocating no possessions at all. He urges that the clergy be satisfied with adequate provisions for their necessities.

During the time of his secret residence at the Bethlehem Chapel, Hus also worked on and finished the treatise *De sex erroribus*.[18] Later he expanded it into a Czech version entitled *O šesti bludich*. Hus even had the Latin text inscribed on one of the walls of the Bethlehem Chapel.

Since the synodical meeting of February 6 failed to bring about the pacification of the warring factions, the whole problem was remanded, by Bishop Conrad, to the royal court, with a hearty sigh of relief on the bishop's part. The attempt to solve the problem was renewed in April, when the king named a four-member royal commission. Among the members were two well-disposed and friendly men, Christian of Prachatice, then rector of the university, and Zdeněk of Labouň. The other two members were Dr. Albík of Uničov, the former archbishop, and Jacob of Dubá, the dean of Vyšehrad. The composition of the commission was thus unusually favorable to Hus, for Christian had been from the beginning of Hus' career in Prague his fatherly benefactor, while both he and Zdeněk belonged to the evangelical party. Of the other two, Jacob of Dubá was a member of the crown Council and inclined to trim his sails in ac-

[18] Bohumil Ryba, *Betlemské texty* (Praha, Orbis, 1951). A short summary of its contents is found in my *John Hus at the Council of Constance* (New York and London, Columbia University Press, 1965), pp. 60-61.

cordance with the direction in which the wind was blow-
ing. In this instance, it was favorable to Hus. The Commission was to examine anew the proposals made at the synod.

Since the *Consilium* of the doctors now became generally
known, it was promptly attacked by the members of the
university in two documents. The first of these was written
by Hus himself somewhere outside of Prague. It bears the
title *Contra falsa consilia doctorum*[19] and constitutes the
second half of a similar, even more thoroughly grounded,
rebuttal written by John of Jesenice in the name of the university masters.[20] The latter document is entitled *Replicatio
magistrorum Pragensium contra conditiones concordiae a
facultate theologica latas.* Jesenic, as doctor of both laws,
based his arguments on the *Decretals*, the *Sexts*, and the
*Clementines.* He refuted the charges of the doctors one by
one. He rejected their assertions that "certain clergy" were
heretical because they did not hold what the Roman Church
held, and all the rest of the charges. Kejř regards this polemic of Jesenic as the most effective rebuttal of the doctors'
*Consilium*, exceeding in its calm reasonableness even Hus'
own arguments. He ranks only Hus' *Contra Stanislaum* and
*Contra Paletz* as more effective.[21]

The four-member Commission met in April prior to
Easter (which fell on April 23) in the parsonage of rector
Christian of Prachatice and held a two-day conference with
the parties. The theologians were represented by Stephen
Páleč, Stanislav of Znojmo, Peter of Znojmo, and John
Eliášův. Against them stood Jakoubek of Stříbro, Simon of
Tišnov, John of Jesenice, and one other unnamed master.
It was Jesenic who seemed to have been chosen as their
spokesman. Even prior to this meeting, Christian of Pracha-
tice had written Hus, who had withdrawn from Prague.[22]
Before the negotiations between the two parties began, both
groups had to pledge in advance, as was the custom, that

19 Palacký, *Documenta*, pp. 499-501.
20 *Ibid.*, pp. 495-99. A fairly full treatment of these two documents
is found in *John Hus' Concept of the Church*, pp. 177-93.
21 Kejř, *Husitský právník*, p. 79.
22 Novotný, *Korespondence*, No. 56.

they would abide by the final decision of the Commission. Should they refuse to submit to its ruling, they would be heavily fined and exiled from the country. The theologians were at first loath to make such a potentially dangerous promise; but since without it no further transactions were possible, they, in the end, reluctantly yielded.

Thereupon, the theologians, who had reworked their February *Consilium* without essentially changing its substance, presented their new document, the *Conditiones concordiae*.[23] In it they demanded that their adversaries solemnly forswear Wyclif's forty-five articles, and further, that they accept all the rites and ceremonies of the Roman Church. They must also swear that Wyclif's doctrine concerning the seven sacraments is false; and further, that no one at the university hold or teach the forty-five articles. If anyone should be apprehended among the students or laymen doing so, he must be punished. They likewise specified that Hus be stopped from preaching and remain outside Prague until he secured absolution of the curia from his excommunication.

Jesenic, speaking for the party of Hus, demanded once more that the basis of negotiations be the pacification made by the royal arbitration commission between Archbishop Zbyněk and the university in July 1411. He also persisted in rejecting the outright condemnation of the forty-five articles. When, however, a reconciling formula, suggested by Jacob of Dubá, that both parties declare their submission to the holy Roman Church in all matters touching the catholic faith, was proposed to them, to the astonishment of their opponents, they consented to it. The doctors were also willing to accept the general pronouncement, provided that the term "the holy Roman Church" be qualified by the explanation that it is the church which consists of Pope John XXIII as the head and the cardinals as the body. Jesenic accepted even this formula in behalf of his party, although he added to the phrase that all should obey the Church "as

---

[23] Palacký, *Documenta*, pp. 486-88; for Páleč's later description of the meeting, *ibid.*, pp. 507-10.

every good and faithful Christian should." The royal Commission was gratified by this show of accommodation on the part of the evangelicals. The doctors, however, regarded the ambiguous clause with understandable suspicion as being capable of misunderstanding or misinterpretation. They could not accept it, for they thought that it contained a loophole, nullifying their demand for unconditional obedience of the Church authorities. Nevertheless, since they had already consented to the formula in its original form, they feared that the royal Commission might possibly regard their refusal as a breach of promise. In the end, they decided to accept the ambiguous formula, each party interpreting it in its own way. Nevertheless, when the four doctors were required to write a letter to the curia stating that peace between the two parties had been re-established, they refused. They were, thereupon, subjected to the penalty agreed on between them and the Commission at the beginning of the proceedings—a fine and exile from the country. The four theological professors fled from Prague, and the king later deprived them of their benefices and their chairs at the university, and sentenced them to exile. Stanislav and Peter of Znojmo, along with John Eliášův, found refuge in Moravia; Stephen Páleč was protected at the court of Bishop John of Litomyšl. Thus, most unexpectedly, Hus and his party emerged victorious from this difficult combat, which at first seemed to have been weighted against them. The theological faculty, bereft of four of its leading members, was so badly crippled by this blow that it continued for some years greatly weakened and, with the outbreak of the Hussite wars, foundered altogether.

Christian of Prachatice corresponded with Hus throughout the negotiations and thereafter. Since Christian's term of office as rector of the university expired on April 25, and Hus in his two extant letters (one was lost) addressed him as rector, the correspondence must have been held prior to that date.[24] In the first of these letters Hus declares that he does not believe the conflict between the two parties

---

[24] Novotný, *Korespondence*, Nos. 58, 60.

can be settled by the proposals of the theological faculty's *Consilium*. He particularly protests against the formula that the pope with his cardinals constitute the Roman Church and that God cannot give the Church other successors [to Peter] than these. "If they stated that God cannot give his Church worse successors than the pope with his cardinals, their statement would possess more likelihood."[25]

In the next letter Christian again inquires of Hus whether he would be willing to accept the proposition that the pope is the head of the Church and the cardinals its body, and to "accept all judgments and determinations of the holy Roman Church." Hus replies that the above-mentioned formula is "a veritable snake in the grass"; for it asserts that the pope and the cardinals constitute the *whole* Roman Church and would have to be obeyed in everything. That obligation would hold even if "Satan incarnate with twelve of his proudest devils sat in Peter's seat!" All they should decide upon would then have to be held as of the faith, a dogma. He points out that nowhere in the *Consilium* is it asserted that Christ is the head of the Church. Since the curia has declared that he, Hus, is obstinate in his excommunication, and thus a heretic, if what the doctors demand were accepted by him, he would thereby consent to the verdict. He recites other decisions against him and his fellow-reformers which would have to be accepted and obeyed as just. He concludes that if the Roman Church is identical with the pope and the cardinals, it then is not the catholic and apostolic Church, for no part of the Church constitutes the whole body. He would be willing to accept the doctors' formula, if they held that all Christians, adhering to the faith of Christ, constitute the Roman Church of which Christ alone is the head. "I acknowledge that the pope is the vicar of Christ in the Roman Church, but do not hold it as an article of faith." For if the pope is of the predestinate and follows Christ in his life, then he is the head of the Church he governs (i.e., the Roman Church). If he is not, he is Antichrist. Finally, he declares:

25 *Ibid.*, p. 163.

Whatever the holy Roman Church or the pope with the cardinals decrees and commands to be held and done in accordance with the law of Christ, that I wish humbly, as a faithful Christian, to esteem and accept with veneration. Not, however, whatever the pope and cardinals define and command in general [that is, without Scriptural basis].

The four-member Commission, having reported its inconclusive negotiations to the king, was bidden to continue its efforts. This was the point in the whole development in the struggle when the fortunes of the evangelical party were the brightest and most promising. The most formidable opponents were now in exile, and the remaining members of the theological faculty had no stomach to risk dangers similar to those of their colleagues.

About the middle of June, the Commission undertook again to proceed with its onerous task. When finally some members of the theological faculty consented to take part in the negotiations on some basis of compromise not clearly defined, Christian announced this new development to Hus. It was now that Hus himself, in his uncompromisingly stringent rectitude and devotion to truth, made all further negotiations impossible. In a letter packed with emotion —the so-called *Responsio finalis*—he answered his old benefactor, resolutely rejecting all compromise:[26]

With the help of the Lord Christ, I will not accept the counsel of the theological faculty, even if I should stand before the fire prepared for me. I hope that death will sooner remove me or those two renegades from the truth [i.e., Stanislav and Páleč] either to heaven or to hell, than that I agree with their opinions. . . . Páleč calls us Wyclifites, as if we had deviated from Christianity. Stanislav calls us infidels, perfidious, insane, and scurrilous clergy. All such slanders I would have ignored, had they not strengthened the Anti-

---

26 Novotný, *Korespondence*, No. 63. Novotný lists it as having been sent to Hus' friend, John Cardinal of Rejnštejn (and Kejř agrees with him in *Husitský právník*, p. 82, no. 40). Nevertheless, I follow the judgment of Bartoš, who still ascribes it as being addressed to Christian. See *Čechy v době Husově*, p. 368.

christ in his wrath. I hope, however, with God's grace to oppose them until I am consumed by fire. . . . It is better to die well than to live wickedly. One should not sin in order to avoid the punishment of death. Truth conquers all things.

By this heroic but self-defeating pronouncement Hus burned all bridges behind him. This act put an end to the royal intervention. By hazarding the king's favor, Hus lost thereby the last possible chance of securing his effective support for the quashing of the curial excommunication. Henceforth, Wenceslas never again consented to come to his aid or to raise a finger in his behalf.[27] By this act of Hus, Jesenic's legal devices proved altogether futile, or at most their execution was rendered immensely more difficult.

Nevertheless, Jesenic did what he could at this critical juncture. About this time he published anonymously glosses on the papal bull announcing the results of the Roman Council held during 1412-13. On February 10, 1413, this obscure and thinly attended Council had condemned Wyclif's works as "full of errors, heresies, and inexactitudes." They were publicly burned in front of St. Peter's basilica. When the bull reached Prague, it was either ridiculed or ignored. Jesenic, however, attacked it savagely.[28] He excoriated the nepotism of the pope and derided the statement that the works of Wyclif had been examined by "certain venerable brethren" by remarking that some of them, hinting at the pope's nephews, hardly knew Latin and could with difficulty stumble through [syllabicare] Wyclif's extensive writings. Moreover, how could anyone read the voluminous works of the English scholar in four days?

Hus now definitely left Prague, tired and exhausted, and took up his residence in southern Bohemia at the small and obscure castle of Kozí[29] near Sezimovo Ústí. He perhaps had found refuge there before. This small and exceedingly

---

[27] Bartoš, *Čechy v době Husově*, p. 369.

[28] Palacký, *Documenta*, pp. 467-71, where both the text of the bull and Jesenic's glosses are given. At the Council of Constance, Hus was accused of having written the glosses.

[29] J. Švehla, *Kozí* (Tábor, 1920).

modest stronghold, surrounded by a wall and a moat, had
for its living quarters only one room in the tower. It appears that Hus lived there along with the whole family of
the owners, Ctibor and John of Kozí.[30] It is a marvel that,
under these crowded conditions, he could produce a remarkably large number of books and smaller treatises, both Latin
and Czech; for he wrote most of the works of this period
there. After all, for the preparation of his polemical and
other works he needed a considerable number of source ma-
terials and other aids, which we know he used. How could
he concentrate sufficiently on this exacting and exhaustive
task in a room occupied by perhaps a large family of his
hosts? Altogether, when one realizes the physical discomfort
under which he was forced to work, one wonders at his accomplishment. Luther at Wartburg was incomparably better accommodated; and yet Hus spent almost two years at
Kozí. Not only did he write most of his Czech works at Kozí
—no mean literary feat in itself. He also had to engage for a
year or longer in an incessant and acrimonious contest with
his opponents who, although also in exile, continued to attack him savagely.

Besides his literary activity, he engaged in preaching, both
in the castles of the wide, surrounding territory and under
the open sky. He himself refers to these preaching journeys
in the *Postil*: "I preach in cities, castles, fields and forests."
He regrets that contrary to his Savior's example, he rides
out to such preaching places, instead of walking, as Jesus
had done.[31] Kozí itself, the ruins of which are still standing,
was located in deep woods. The country round about, which
was poor and sparsely settled, before regular parishes were
established, had been spiritually cared for by monk-her-
mits, called "black fathers." They used in their services the
Slavic rite understood by the common people. Thus the
populace was ready to receive sermons in the vernacular
when delivered by such an eloquent and powerful preacher

[30] T. Č. Zelinka, "Kozí Hrádek vstoupil do dějin," in *Kostnické
Jiskry*, October 23, 1962.
[31] *Postilla*, pp. 306, 372.

as Hus. Moreover, since the beginning of the fourteenth century, the region had been colonized by the German settlers from Austria, mostly Waldensians. They soon coalesced with the native population, whom they zealously sought to bring to their own religious views. Whole villages became Waldensian. Thus the ground was spiritually prepared for Hus' preaching. He ranged surprisingly far and wide into the territory, and immense crowds came to hear him.[32] It was this region so evangelized by Hus that later became the chief recruiting ground for the armies of Žižka and the community of Tábor. Furthermore, we have another way of gauging the success of Hus' work: when after the martyr's death the Czech nobility rose in revolt against this tragic deed, on one occasion 452 members of the nobility and the lower gentry of both Bohemia and Moravia sent a protest to the Council, appending their seals to the document. This spirited protest is still extant. Almost one-fourth of the signers have been traced to the regions covered by Hus' preaching activity. It is obvious that he was highly successful in his efforts.

In this period Hus was, as we have noted, remarkably busy with his pen. His opponents, immediately after the February 6 synodical meeting, or even before, occupied themselves with polemical works. Among them were John of Holešov,[33] Andrew of Brod,[34] Stephen of Dolany,[35] and the "Anonymous":[36] these treatises Hus did not answer. He concentrated on replying to the extensive writings of Stanislav of Znojmo, Stephen Páleč, and the eight doctors of the

[32] T. Č. Zelinka, "Přátelé Husovi v Bechyňském kraji," in Rudolf Říčan and Michael Flegl, eds., Husův sborník (Praha, Komenského ev. fakulta bohoslovecká, 1966), pp. 103-10.

[33] A full account of his treatise, An credi possit in papam, is found in my John Hus' Concept of the Church, pp. 151-57.

[34] Andrew of Brod, Contra objectus Hussonitarum, in Archiv für Oesterreichische Geschichte (Wien, 1889), LXXV, pp. 342-44.

[35] B. Pez, ed., Stephen of Dolany's Dialogus volatilis inter aucam et passerem adversus Hussum, in Thesaurus anecdotorum novissimus, 6 vols. (Augsburg, 1721-29), IV, pp. 431-502.

[36] An analysis of this treatise is found in my John Hus' Concept of the Church, pp. 247-51.

theological faculty who were his chief accusers at the
Žebrák meeting in 1412.[37] Since these were the principal
polemical treatises of his most outstanding opponents, we
shall limit our consideration to them, and also incorporate
into them briefly Hus' rebuttal.

Stanislav of Znojmo wrote two works against Hus:
*Tractatus de Romana ecclesia*[38] and *Alma et venerabilis*
. . .[39] His basic proposition, endlessly and tiresomely reiterat-
ed was, that before Christ's ascension to heaven, He constituted His Church as the mystico-ecclesiastical *compositum*,
of which Peter was the head and the apostles the body. It
passed into history as the Roman Church composed of
the pope and the cardinals. This mystico-ecclesiastical body
possesses the sole authority and power to decide disputes
about the right faith and the supreme jurisdiction over the
entire Church on earth. No other such body exists. Thus
the papacy is a juridical corporation. This mystico-ecclesiastical *compositum* is the Church in its real essence. The
bearers of the office of papacy and the cardinalate come and
go, but the formal essence [*formale esse*] of the Church remains. They, being human, may err; the Church in its essence is infallible.

*Alma et venerabilis* . . . , the second of Stanislav's treatises,
is a reply to Jesenic's and Hus' *Replicatio*. Stanislav repeats
the "three truths" of the *Consilium*, and that all Wyclif's
forty-five articles are "either heretical, erroneous, or scandalous"; further, that all must obey their ecclesiastical superiors in all things whatsoever, provided such commands
are neither purely evil nor opposed to anything good. How
the faithful can discern what the correct command is
Stanislav does not say. Nevertheless, this formula obviously
imposes upon them the duty of judging their superiors' demands. In respect of the requirement of the evangelical

---

[37] *Ibid.*; for Stanislav, Chapter VI, pp. 172-208; for Páleč, pp. 209-47;
*Contra octo doctores*, pp. 158-71.

[38] J. Sedlák, ed., *Stanislav of Znojmo's Tractatus de Romana ecclesia*,
in *Hlídka* (Brno, 1911), pp. 85-95.

[39] J. Loserth, ed., *Stanislav of Znojmo's Alma et venerabilis* . . . in
*Archiv*, LXXV, pp. 75-127 (in reprint).

party that all papal and Church pronouncements agree with the Scriptures, Stanislav bluntly affirms that all decrees of the Roman Church are "consonant with the sacred Scripture. . . . The omnipotent Christ knows and is entirely able to prevent . . . that no part of its visible rule in whole or part become unfit or disordered by heresy . . ."[40] To Hus' objection in the *Replicatio* that a foreknown pope cannot be the head of the Church, Stanislav replies that Hus fails to make a correct distinction between the person and the office of the pope. The office does not depend on the holder's moral qualities.

Hus made a fuller and more adequate rebuttal of Stanislav's treatise in his *Contra Stanislaum*.[41] It does not cover the entire treatise; for one thing, he did not have its whole text, and secondly, he did not choose to answer all he had. He had answered some of the arguments in his *De Ecclesia* and did not wish to repeat himself.

First of all, he bravely comes to the defense of Wyclif's articles; not that he accepts or approves them all but because some are defensible "in their right sense" (i.e., not in the interpretation given them by Stanislav). He reminds Stanislav of his former excessive admiration of Wyclif, including even Wyclif's doctrine of remanence. He then dissects his former teacher's definition of the concept of the Church, and opposes to it the only true mystical corpus of the Church universal composed of Christ as the head and the predestinate as the body. He challenges Stanislav to prove that the pope and the cardinals are of the *corpus mysticum*; in order to do that, he would have to demonstrate that Pope John XXIII and his cardinals are of the predestinate—an impossible demand! On the contrary, the popes by their luxury, pride, and self-exaltation have shown themselves to be vicars of Caesars rather than of Christ. Nor

40 *Ibid.*, p. 93.
41 "Responsio Joannis Hus ad scripta M. Stanislai," in *Historia et monumenta Joannis Hus atque Hieronymi Pragensis, confessorum Christi*, 2 vols. (Norimberg, 1715), I, pp. 331-65. Newly edited by J. Eršil, *Magistri Johannis Hus, Polemica* (Praha, Academia scientiarum Bohemoslovaca, 1966), pp. 273-367.

does the catholic faith require that the faithful believe that Alexander V, John XXIII, and Gregory XII "are or have been true successors and manifest vicars of Peter."[42]

Hus also denies that plenitude of power is restricted to the pope: equal power had been granted by Christ to all the apostles. The power of the keys was given to the entire Church, not to Peter alone. This power is *spiritual*, not temporal. Peter was distinguished above all other apostles by the qualities of his character, by his greater love and firmer faith. Only such qualities make the pope a *veritable* holder of his office, not a legitimate election alone. To Hus, only the *veritable* pope is a true pope, even though a legitimate pope holds his office *de facto*.

Of great importance is Hus' federal concept of the Church temporal. The pope, even though properly qualified, rules only over his own Roman Church, which constitutes only part of the whole. Besides the pope, there exist other legitimate heads of churches outside the limits of the Roman patriarchate. All particular churches, Roman included, together constitute Christendom. The pope's claim to universal jurisdiction is, therefore, unfounded and falsely claimed. Moreover, it contradicts the actual situation prevailing in Christendom. To be sure, the true Church, the invisible mystical body of Christ, is only one. But it has Christ alone for its head, and the predestinate belonging to all the particular churches as its body. The unity of the ecumenical Church is spiritual, not organizational or juridical.

Páleč was Hus' other most formidable adversary. He wrote no less than four treatises against Hus (five, if we include the *Tractatus gloriosus*, ostensibly written by Páleč on behalf of the whole theological faculty).[43] Essentially, his position was the same as that of Stanislav, but he discussed subjects which Stanislav did not touch upon. We shall emphasize these items in our short survey. In the first of his

42 *Contra Stanislaum*, p. 338.
43 I have treated his views fairly extensively in my *John Hus' Concept of the Church*, pp. 209-46.

treatises, *De aequivocatione nominis ecclesia*,[44] he gives six definitions of the word "Church." Nevertheless, his "working" definition is the one Stanislav employed so assiduously, namely, that consisting of the pope and the cardinals. The only remarkable thing in this connection is Páleč's assertion that the Church catholic does not possess the juridical and administrative functions that the Roman Church has. These functions are exercised solely by the pope and the cardinals. Accordingly, the Church catholic is, in this regard, subordinated to the Roman Church. What then is the real significance of the Church catholic, or does it have any?

Hus completed and published his *De ecclesia* in May 1413. It is generally regarded, and quite properly, as his major work, expressing his mature concept of the Church in the fullest and most systematic manner.[45] The first ten chapters had been written before Hus received the text of the *Consilium*. The remainder of the book is a reply to that document. Hus gives a detailed account of his views on the subject that remained essentially unchanged throughout his mature life, even though in less developed form. To a great extent he clothes his formulation in Wyclif's language; the latest estimate of his dependence upon the English scholar amounts to 23 per cent.[46]

As we have pointed out in several other connections, Hus defines the Church as the totality of the predestinate, past, present, and future, on earth and in heaven. This is Christ's mystical body, of which He alone is the head. Thus the Church is one in Him, for the bond of predestination binds all the elect, no matter to which of the particular churches they belong. Nevertheless, the predestinate in the Church

[44] J. Sedlák, ed., *Stephen Páleč's De aequivocatione nominis ecclesia*, in *Hlídka* (Brno, 1911), pp. 99-106 (in reprint).

[45] An extensive analysis of this work is found in my *John Hus' Concept of the Church*, pp. 252-89. The Latin text was edited by S. Harrison Thomson, *Magistri Johannis Hus, Tractatus de Ecclesia* (Boulder, Colorado, University of Colorado Press, 1956). A recent Czech translation was made by F. M. Dobiáš and Amedeo Molnár, *Mistr Jan Hus, O církvi* (Praha, Československá akademie věd, 1965).

[46] F. M. Dobiáš, "Jubileum Husova spisu o církvi," *Kostnické Jiskry*, October 31, 1963.

militant are mixed with the foreknown. These latter are not predestinated by God to eternal damnation; God desires all men to be saved. Yet, because He had endowed His human creatures with free will, they may choose to reject His grace and to follow their own selfish will. They are, therefore, damned by their own choice, by rejecting God's saving grace. Thus they are *in* the Church, but not *of* the Church. Ultimately, as Christ taught in the parable of wheat and tares, they will be plucked from the Church militant at the Day of Judgment. The identity of the predestinate cannot be known with absolute certainty; the only criterion is "By their fruits ye shall know them." Yet some who appear to be of the predestinate may not persevere to the end, may not attain to the "faith formed by love," and thus fail to complete the course. Others who may appear to live wickedly for the time being may ultimately prove their election. Hus was persistently accused, particularly at the Council of Constance, of denying the very existence of the Church militant, by asserting that the Church is only one, composed only of the predestinate. This was a willful perversion of his clearly and frequently expounded views.

Hus then goes on to explore the delicate question whether the Roman Church may be equated with the Church catholic. Since the Roman Church is said to consist of the pope and the cardinals, this definition deprives the rest of its members—the hierarchs, clergy, and laymen—of sharing in it. Such a concept makes it woefully, fantastically incomplete, for it then consists of some thirteen members! Moreover, there exist along with the Roman Church the Eastern Orthodox and other churches. It is clear, therefore, that the Roman Church cannot be identified with the Church catholic and apostolic.[47]

In commenting on the fulcral text of Matt. 16:16-19, presumably asserting that the Church is founded on Peter, Hus insists that it is Peter's confession that Christ is the Son of the living God that is the foundation stone on which the

[47] *De ecclesia*, p. 44.

Church is built. The Church catholic is the mystical body of Christ, and "in that sense, it is an article of faith."[48]

Among the deductions from the assertion that the Church is founded on faith in Christ, Hus stresses the duality of faith: the unformed, possessed by the wicked and even the demons, and "the faith formed by love." It is only the latter that saves.[49] Thus faith alone is not enough; it must be built up throughout one's life by good deeds until finally it culminates in the total, all-absorbing love of God.

Hus asserts that the necessary truths of Christianity are contained in Scripture. Whatever is beyond or contrary to it is to be rejected. The popes, as Peter's successors, should manifest their worthiness for the office by possessing the same spiritual qualifications he had.

The tenth chapter of *De ecclesia* deals with the authority granted by Christ to his vicars. It is restricted to spiritual power, to the administration of the sacraments. This power is shared by every priest. It is not temporal or coercive; that power belongs to the civil government. Toward the end of this chapter Hus, who had by that time received the text of the *Consilium*, begins his spirited reply to it. Since we have already been introduced to this document and its contents, we need not present a summary of it here again. It will be dealt with in connection with Páleč's reply to the whole treatise of Hus.

Páleč's response is couched in a treatise bearing the same name, *De ecclesia*.[50] As against Hus' position that the real Church, the mystical body of Christ, consists only of the predestinate, who with the foreknown compose the Church militant, Páleč recognizes three churches: he acknowledges the Church composed of the predestinate and the foreknown as Hus does, but in addition he regards the Church militant and the Roman Church as worthy of the name of Church as well. The difference between the two men is thus essentially

---

[48] *Ibid.*, p. 45.
[49] *Ibid.*, p. 53.
[50] J. Sedlák, *M. Jan Hus* (Praha, Dědictví sv. Prokopa, 1915), presents excerpts from this treatise in the Supplement, pp. 202-304.

terminological. Nevertheless, on this flimsy, insubstantial ground Páleč charges Hus with having denied the very existence of the latter two bodies. It is this confusion in the usage of the different concepts and in nomenclature that had tragic consequences for Hus; for it persisted not only to the Council of Constance, where it played a prominent part in his condemnation, but in the literature dealing with this subject down to the present.

Páleč furthermore differs radically from Hus in the matter of the primacy of the headship of the Church. For Hus, Christ alone is the head of the Church catholic. The pope, if he is predestinate, is the head of the Roman Church alone. Páleč acknowledges that Christ is the *caput supremum*; but He had appointed Peter as His vicar, who in turn was succeeded in this office by the pope. The Church is thus built on *both* Christ and Peter, although in different senses. Moreover, it was not on account of his character, but simply because of Christ's arbitrary appointment, that Peter was chosen as vicar. The Church, then, is a juridical body, ruled by the pope and the cardinals. Submission to the pope is necessary to salvation. He is thus essential and necessary to the Church, for, without him, it would not be what Christ desired it to be. All the ecclesiastical power of the rest of the hierarchs and clergy is derived from him. The Roman Church so constituted is infallible "in judgment and decisions which they [the pope and the cardinals] have passed on to the faithful in all matters whatsoever. . . ."[51] These decisions have, on many occasions, exceeded the literal precepts of the Scriptures.

Hus asserted in *De ecclesia* that priests do not forgive sins of their own power in administering the sacrament of penance, but act only ministerially, on behalf of God. Páleč denies these views altogether. The sacraments are valid of themselves—*de opere operato*—if the proper formula of consecration or dispensation is used. The priest acts in his own power, conferred on him at his ordination, in God's stead.

Páleč further launched a vitriolic attack upon the univer-

[51] *Ibid.*, p. 228.

sity masters for their reply to the *Concilium*, which he entitled *Replicatio contra Quidamistas*.[52] Later, he wrote his *Antihus*.[53] Hus responded to both of these in his *Contra Paletz*.[54] The treatises of the two former friends, now radically and irreconcilably estranged, are replete with repetitions of their former arguments, employed here in a more violent form. Páleč descends to personal abuse, calling Hus a *baccalarius deformatus*, instead of *formatus*. He charges that Hus and his whole party have denied the faith professed by all Christians, and have brought shame and dishonor upon the kingdom of Bohemia by refusing to hold the "three truths" comprising the Christian faith.

How then dare you profess yourself a sincere Christian, not deviating from the faith . . . ? For on the forementioned three truths the whole Christian religion depends. . . . If you opened the blinded eyes of your mind, you would find yourself with your master Wyclif the most dangerous assailants of the Christian faith and religion.[55]

One remembers that Páleč himself, after he had arrived at Constance and had learned of the temper of the Council and the probable fate of John XXIII, quickly changed his mind as to the absolute necessity of submitting to the pope's jurisdiction! If only the fathers of the Council had known of Páleč's lavish profession of loyalty to John XXIII and of his violent denunciation of Hus because he did not share his views!

On Hus' part, his language is likewise more unrestrained than ever before. Throughout the treatise he calls Páleč "the Fictor" (a deceiver or liar). He refers to his arguments as "all this mud [*brodium*] in which there is not a glimmer of Scriptural proof."[56] He indignantly denies the aspersion of heresy by declaring:

[52] J. Loserth, ed., *Stephen Páleč's Replicatio contra Quidamistas*, in *Archiv*, LXXV, pp. 344-61.

[53] J. Sedlák, ed., *Antihus* in *Hlídka* (1913).

[54] *Responsio Mag. Joannis Hus ad scripta M. Stephani Paletz*, *Historia et monumenta*, I, pp. 318-31. A new edition in Eršil, *Polemica*, pp. 235-69.

[55] *Antihus*, pp. 79-80.          [56] *Contra Paletz*, p. 323.

I trust that by God's grace I am a sincere Christian, not deviating from the faith. I would rather suffer the dire punishment of death than to put forth anything contrary to the faith or to transgress the commands of the Lord Jesus Christ. . . . Hence I wish that the Fictor would show me today one precept of sacred Scripture that I do not hold.[57]

About the middle of 1413 Hus at last found time to reply to Páleč's and Stanislav's *Tractatus gloriosus*, written in the name of the eight doctors of the theological faculty, by his extensive treatise *Contra octo doctores*.[58] Most of the arguments are already familiar from Hus' other writings. What perhaps may be further emphasized is his demand that the doctors prove their case from Scripture. They replied that they could not; but that the Church has, by its traditions, gone beyond the Scriptural text, and that their position was validated thereby. They accused Hus of belonging to "the Armenian sect," which presumably refuses all but Scriptural authority. Not only does Hus uphold this kind of principle, they said, but he interprets Scripture according to his own understanding, rather than submitting to the Church's *magisterium*. To this accusation Hus responded that in harmony with many Fathers, he regards the Scriptures as supremely authoritative in all matters of faith. As for himself, he "desires to hold, believe, and assert whatever is contained in them (i.e., the Scriptures) as long as I have breath in me."[59] He does not interpret them arbitrarily, "out of his own head," but by tradition as summarized in the Apostles', Nicene, and the Athanasian Creeds, the principal doctors, especially those of the first five centuries, the ecumenical councils, and the decrees of the Church.

We may include at this point Hus' dealing with Scripture in his *Postil*. He there stresses again his exclusive dependence on the Word of God, declaring: "Finally, I rest with the conviction that every word of Christ is true; and what I do

[57] *Ibid.*, p. 325.

[58] In *Historia et monumenta*, I, pp. 366-407. New edition by Eršil, *Polemica*, pp. 371-488. I have summarized the treatise in my *John Hus' Concept of the Church*, pp. 158-71.

[59] *Historia et monumenta*, I, p. 369.

189

not understand, I commit to His grace in the hope, that I shall understand it after my death." Hus denounces those priests and doctors who resent it when ordinary lay Christians defend themselves with Scriptural proofs. They immediately cry against such lay folk: "He is one of them, a Wyclifite! He does not obey the holy Church, meaning thereby that he does not do what they wish."[60]

Nevertheless, although one has no doubt of Hus' sincerity in thus regarding Scripture as the sole criterion of the Christian faith, he was too much a child of his age to realize that some tenets of his own were unscriptural. He held, for instance, a firm belief in the Virgin Mary and her resurrection and ascension to heaven; in the saints; in purgatory (although he knew the flimsy basis for it) ; in transubstantiation and the three-fold holy orders. He simply did not test these doctrines rigorously enough to find that they were not contained in Scripture, but were developed in tradition during the intervening ages.

Such, then, in brief outline, were the principal controversies which kept both his opponents and Hus extremely busy during the action-crammed years 1413-14. In addition to these polemics, Hus engaged in writing in Czech an amazing number of treatises and pamphlets for the use of his non-academic adherents—the shoemakers, tailors and scribes—as Páleč scornfully called them; these we shall take up in the next chapter.

In the middle of July 1414, Hus accepted the invitation of Lord Henry Lefl of Lažany, the chamberlain of King Wenceslas and the leading member of the royal Council, to live at his castle of Krakovec. He had been forced to leave Kozí in the Spring, and found new refuge in the nearby Sezimovo Ústí. But he did not feel secure there. Therefore, he gladly accepted the offer of his stout supporter, Lord Henry, to go to Krakovec. Lord Henry had bought this magnificent castle only four years before. In comparison with Kozí, or even with other castles built chiefly for defense, this establishment was intended for commodious and even

---

[60] *Postilla*, pp. 86, 111.

luxurious residence. It was located in western Bohemia, not far from Karlštejn. Krakovec had twenty-six chambers, besides a magnificent great hall and a sumptuously decorated chapel. Hus continued to preach in the neighborhood under the open skies, and great crowds from near and far come to hear the famed preacher. He spent only some four months at Krakovec, most of the time preparing for the forthcoming Council of Constance, which he promised to attend.

# The Principal Czech
# Writings of Hus

**M**edieval life in all its aspects was inextricably interwoven with religious sentiment. This religious thought and feeling constantly tended toward externalism, ceremonialism, and particularly sacramentalism. Men were often occupied with observances of outward forms of religion and the practice of formal external acts without inner meaning or spiritual content and significance. Sacraments were regarded as magical means of salvation rather than as the outward signs of inner grace. They were also commonly confused with *sacramentalia,* no essential difference being made between them. Reformers protested vainly against the enormous proliferation of church festivals of all sorts and the ever-increasing number of holy days.[1] They urged that the splendor of the church services, the increase of images and their worship rather than veneration, the pilgrimages, the excesssive worship of saints and the Virgin Mary, should be restricted. All kinds of superstitions abounded. Even when people attended the services, they were usually occupied in passive observance of the external acts, such as crossing themselves with fingers dipped in holy water, and kissing the images of their favorite saints or of the Virgin. They gaped at the dramatic priestly ministrations, the splendid vestments of the clergy, and the gorgeous ceremonies. They rarely communed and, if they did, they regarded partaking of the host "as if they conferred a benefit on Christ."[2] Holy days were occasions for violent drinking bouts and debauchery in general. Pilgrimages were looked upon as a lark and an opportunity for immoral behavior.

[1] J. Huizinga, *The Waning of the Middle Ages* (London, Edward Arnold & Co., 1924) , p. 138.
[2] *Ibid.,* p. 144.

Thomas à Kempis remarked that those who often partici-
pated in them "rarely became saints."[3] Among the princes
and the wealthy patricians, as well as churches and monasteries, collection of the relics of saints was a rage, and the
pilgrimages to the places where particularly famous relics
were exhibited became a chief source of revenue. Huizinga
cites the example of the French King Charles VI who, in
1392, distributed the ribs of his ancestor, St. Louis: D'Ailly
and the dukes of Berry and Burgundy received one each.[4]

These practices were to be found not only in France, England, and the Netherlands, but in Bohemia as well. The
Czech moral reformers before Hus, Milič of Kroměříž and
Matthew of Janov, strenuously inveighed against them. Hus
himself sought to combat these and other evils and to call
men to inner piety. His literary activity in exile, directed
particularly to the common people, aimed at inculcating
principles of moral reformation and spiritual religion.

Since the common people were not, and could not be, acquainted with Hus' Latin works, he did not hesitate to
repeat in the vernacular what he had formerly written in
Latin. We shall, however, endeavor to keep repetition to
the minimum, by referring the reader to the previous works.
Furthermore, since his aim was to instruct the people in the
most basic elements of the Christian faith, no great novelty
of content or form can be expected. Yet it is essential that
these creedal views of Hus be considered, if for no other
reason than the importance with which he himself regarded
them. They undoubtedly had a strong impact upon the
populace, and it was perpetuated in the movements which
later constituted the carriers of the Czech reformation. The
organized armies of the Praguers, Taborites (although these
were influenced greatly by Wyclif), Orebites and later
Orphans constituted the chief strength of popular reform
which succeeded in dominating the whole country. The
academic leadership of the university gradually dwindled
into a conservative and relatively weaker force or petered

3 *Ibid.*, p. 145.
4 *Ibid.*, p. 151.

out altogether. It would, therefore, be a serious error to underestimate the value and effect which these elementary Czech treatises exerted upon future events.

Even prior to his exile Hus wrote such small works as *The Nine Golden Theses* [*Devět kusův zlatých*] (1409-10), a translation from the Latin popular particularly in the Netherlands; *The Three-stranded Cord* [*Provázek třípramenný*] (1412); and *The Mirror of a Sinner* [*Zrcadlo člověka hříšného*] (1412). In exile at Kozí Hrádek he continued to produce similar small treatises aimed at edification of the common people, among which *The Daughter* [*Dcerka*] is outstanding. Its rightful title, *How to Know the Right Way to Salvation*, indicates its theme. Nevertheless, it goes generally under the shorter title, because every chapter begins with the exhortation "Hear, O daughter!"[5] It was intended for the pious women living in the vicinity of the Bethlehem Chapel, the daughter of Thomas of Štítné among them. The book exhorted them to self-knowledge, to the consciousness of the misery of the present life, to the struggle with the three principal enemies—the body, the world, and the devil—to repentance, the final judgment, and the supreme love of God. This treatise is one of the best and most eloquent directories to devotional life, worthy of being classed along with Gerard Groote's *Following of Christ*, or Thomas à Kempis' *Imitation of Christ*, which is based on Groote's work, or François de Sales' *Introduction to the Devout Life*. Furthermore, the Czech version of the earlier Latin text of *De sex erroribus* [*O šesti bludich*] was completed there on June 21, 1413. *The Kernel of Christian Doctrine* [*Jádro učení křesťanského*], finished at Sezimovo Ústí on June 26, 1414, was intended for catechetical instruction. As such it contains a brief explanation of Christian doctrine. *Books against the Cookmaster* [*Knížky proti kuchmistrovi*] were written shortly after. They represent a polemic against an unnamed priest-cook, who

[5] This and the following treatises are published in K. J. Erben, ed., *Mistra Jana Husi Sebrané spisy české*, 3 vols. (Praha, B. Tempský, 1865), III.

194

called Hus "worse than the devil," because he, having appealed to the pope, ignored the summons to personal appearance at the curia. In self-defense, Hus challenges the cook-master to prove his charge, and accuses him in turn of abandoning his proper calling, that of a priest, for a lucrative secular career. The cook is also acting contrary to Christ's command that we judge not that we may not be judged.

Hus' teaching may be derived from his chief Czech works more systematically than from his Latin writings, for those works, although they too contained many polemical references, were not constrained to limit themselves to the answering of the charges of his opponents. We shall therefore analyze briefly five of his principal works, particularly the three *Expositions* (of Faith, the Decalogue, and the Lord's Prayer), which constitute its basis.[6] These *Expositions* were completed about November 10, 1412. They were intended to teach the common people what to believe, how to keep God's commandments, and how to pray; the three things necessary to salvation. They were necessarily written in simple, popular language appropriate to the instruction of technically unlearned believers.

Before undertaking the extended consideration of the *Expositions*, we shall deal with the other two major Czech works of Hus, *The Treatise on Simony* [*O svatokupectví*][7] and the *Postil* [*Postilla*].[8] In these works Hus follows his customary practice of drawing upon a large number of eminent doctors of the Church, including Wyclif. Nevertheless, since his own work was specifically intended for popular instruction, he avoids Wyclif's scholastic abstruseness. Above all, one must consider not merely what Hus accepted from Wyclif, but particularly what he left out.

6 *Ibid.*, I: *Výklad víry* [*Exposition of the Faith*], pp. 1-52; *Výklad desatera* [*Exposition of the Decalogue*], pp. 52-288; and *Výklad modlitby Páně* [*Exposition of the Lord's Prayer*], pp. 288-358.

7 V. Novotný, ed., *O svatokupectví* (Praha, O. Otto, 1907). My translation in *Advocates of Reform, Library of Christian Classics* (Philadelphia, The Westminster Press, 1953), XIV, pp. 196-278.

8 J. B. Jeschke, ed., *Mistr Jan Hus, Postilla* (Praha, Komenského ev. fakulta bohoslovecká, 1952).

*Simony* was written between the end of 1412 and February 2, 1413. As the title indicates, it dealt with the corrosive evil of the time which permeated all life of the period. Novotný characterizes the treatise as "the most daring and sharpest of Hus' works."[9] It reflects Wyclif's *De simonia*; but since it is couched in the language of the people, and describes the situation prevailing largely in Bohemia, it must be pronounced as essentially independent of Wyclif.

Hus defines simony as heresy, to which prelates, including the pope, are preeminently prone. The pope commits simony when he strives to secure the highest office in the Church on account of its power, dignity, or wealth. Likewise is he a simoniac when he appoints anyone to ecclesiastical office for a payment, particularly when the appointee is unworthy or unqualified for it, or simply because he is the highest bidder. As an illustration of such practices Hus cites the case of the Prague archbishopric, for which a large number of men contended and which was awarded to the highest bidder. Nor has the pope ever appointed a bishop without exacting a heavy payment from him.[10] Hus includes papal indulgences among simoniacal practices.

In the next place, Hus writes of episcopal simony. It consists of very much the same abuses of office as that of the pope, but on a lower level. Bishops may be guilty of simony not only by requiring payment for priestly ordinations and consecration of churches and altars, but also by buying their own consecration. Hus held that as in the early Church, no one was considered fit to exercise power who strove for it. It was the established custom for members chosen for episcopacy to declare: "Noli episcopari"—and some of them actually meant it!

Hus then considers monastic simony: monks may be

---

[9] Novotný, *O svatokupectví*, p. xvii.

[10] Another papal abuse consisted of appointing more than one man for the same office, and needlessly multiplying ecclesiastical offices in order to have more places to sell. The revenue derived from such nefarious practices was enormous. See James Westfall Thompson and Edgar N. Johnson, *An Introduction to Medieval Europe, 300-1500* (New York, W. W. Norton & Co., Inc., 1937), p. 972.

guilty of it if they secure entrance into the Order by means of a payment, or by seeking higher dignities or a comfortable life, instead of spiritual discipline. He bewails the cupidity of monks, their notorious wealth, luxury, gluttony, and life of ease.

As for priests, they commit simony by paying for their ordination, and then charging fees for their sacramental ministrations. They even refuse to bury the dead until they are paid for the service. Moreover, they exercise pressure upon the old to name them beneficiaries in their wills. Hus further denounces them for wasting the money thus acquired upon their concubines, and upbraids bishops for allowing such loose clerical conduct and even taking money for permitting it.

Lay people may commit simony as well. This is particularly true of the princes and lords who control advowsons, i.e., the rights to present candidates for priestly benefices. Any improper appointment to such a benefice, motivated by less than the highest good of the people, is an abuse and simony. Advowson is not private property but a spiritual office.[11] It is not to be sold or misused. If the owner alienates the revenue to his own use, he has committed a theft.

As for the *Postil*, completed at Kozí on October 27, 1413, it comprises sermons for a year. Essentially, it is a reworking of the Latin *Postil* of 1410-11, the so-called *Sermones in Bethlehem*.[12] Hus, however, expanded the text by many autobiographical recollections and polemical references. Thus the character of the *Postil* is both defensive and offensive. Bartoš writes that it comprises Hus' "reform program in its final form and maturity."[13] Comments on these two works, *Simony* and *Postil*, will be integrated into the

11 It was generally regarded as property and was granted, sold, or divided like any other property. See Thompson and Johnson, *Medieval Europe*, p. 666.

12 V. Flajšhans, ed., *Mag. Io. Hus, Sermones in Bethlehem, 1410-11*. 5 vols. (Praha, Královská česká společnost nauk, 1938-42) .

13 *Postilla*, p. 8.

commentary of the *Expositions*, to afford the reader a survey of Hus' theological thought.

Let us now consider Hus' *Exposition of the Faith*, which consists of a commentary on the Apostles' Creed. Novotný regards it as "the most significant" work of Hus.[14] Hus assumes, along with his whole age, that the Creed was composed by the apostles immediately after Christ's ascension to heaven, each of them composing one clause of the document. He defines faith as fundamental to the entire spiritual life of Christians, without which no other virtue can take root and develop. Faith consists in believing in the invisible verities, and as such it exceeds human reason. Nevertheless, by itself faith is not enough; it must ultimately be fulfilled in love. Without love, faith is dead. No other foundation of faith can be laid than that which has been laid by Jesus Christ. As has been noted previously, Hus was fond of distinguishing between three aspects or degrees of faith: one is "believing God," which he explains as meaning that what God has declared is true; but even the wicked have that degree of faith. In the second place, "to accept God" implies belief in His existence; but even the wicked so believe. It is only the third sense, "to believe *in* God," which constitutes the true and saving faith. It necessarily involves "adhering to Him and being incorporated in Him," and thus constituting the transforming spiritual process.[15] Accordingly, we should not believe *in* the pope, or *in* Peter, or even *in* the Virgin Mary or the saints. We should believe the pope when he speaks the truth and observes the law of God. If, however, his life contradicts that of Jesus Christ, he is the Antichrist. Hus writes that priests frighten the people by telling them that the pope "rules the whole world and can do whatever he wishes."[16] The doctors further assert that he cannot err and no one can say to him "what doest thou?" Nevertheless, even the pope is a sinner, liable to error as all men are; if he lives well and perseveres

[14] V. Novotný, *M. Jan Hus, život a dílo*, 2 vols. (Praha, Jan Laichter, 1919-21), II, p. 198.
[15] *Výklad víry*, p. 7.
[16] *Ibid.*, p. 8.

in the good to the end, he will be saved; if he lives wickedly, he will be damned.

In the *Postil* Hus further condemns the pope's pride and the adulation offered him by the cardinals and all petitioners. He denounces the custom of kneeling before him and kissing his golden slippers. He confesses that when in his youth "I did not know the Scriptures well and the life of my Savior, I thought it well done; but now I know by His gift that the practice is veritable blasphemy against Christ and rejection of His Word and following."[17] Hus also lashes out against the persecution of those who preach against the adulation of the pope and against observing his commands more than those of Christ. He writes that "in Bohemia and Moravia, in Meissen and England as well as elsewhere, severe persecution exists for that reason, as I myself am aware of: for they murder, torture, and condemn faithful priests. Nor can one expect relief from Rome, for there is the summit of all Antichrist's wickedness: of pride, miserliness, adultery, hypocrisy and simony."[18]

To return now to the Creed. God is Spirit, whom no man has ever seen with his bodily eyes. He is immortal, eternal, and unchangeable. He has created heaven and earth and all that there is; for He alone is Creator.[19] In the *Postil* Hus repeats the assertion that to create is to make something out of nothing. Only God can do that.[20] This eternal God has revealed Himself as Trinity in unity. Hus also bears witness to the existence of the triune God revealed to men as Father, Son and Holy Spirit. These three "persons" are equal to each other in being, power, wisdom and goodness. They are not three gods but one Godhead.[21] The reward of thus believing is life eternal. To be a son of God is worthier by far than to be a pope or the king of the world.

The second clause of the Apostles' Creed asserts faith in Jesus Christ as the unique Son of God. It teaches that He possesses a twofold nature, for He is both the true God and

[17] *Postilla*, p. 147.   [18] *Ibid.*, p. 21.   [19] *Výklad víry*, p. 13.
[20] *Postilla*, p. 411.
[21] *Ibid.*, pp. 211, 237, 254.

true man. Hus explains the name Jesus as signifying Savior, for all who live in grace will be saved by Him. The term Christ means "anointed," because Christ possesses the Holy Spirit in the supreme degree. If we do not follow Christ, we are but false Christians.

The third clause of the Creed asserts that Jesus was begotten of the Holy Spirit and was born of the Virgin Mary. He could not accomplish his work of salvation on earth in his divine nature alone, and therefore assumed the human nature as well. No one has ministered to sinners so faithfully as He. This is followed by the clause: suffered under Pontius Pilate. Jesus died the shameful death on the cross to save us from eternal death.

Hus has an unusual comment in regard to the clause, "He descended into hell." He advances the curious theory that there are four "hells": the first and the deepest is that of the damned, where everlasting suffering prevails; the second is that of unbaptized or uncircumcised children, where there is no suffering; the third is purgatory, where souls are purged of the still unexpiated sins; and the fourth is the limbo, where there is no suffering, for it is the abode of the "holy fathers," presumably of the Old Testament.[22] It is the fourth to which Christ descended and from which He led all the saints. Since then, no one has entered it; thus it has remained untenanted. Some say that Christ also entered purgatory and led some of the inmates out, whose expiation He deemed completed. But in his usual sober view, Hus declared that "he does not assent to it."

The next two clauses assert that on the third day Christ rose from the dead, and after the resurrection, ascended into heaven. There He sits at the right hand of God Almighty. Hus comments that the latter assertion should not be understood as if God the Father and the glorified Christ had a material body. God, being Spirit, does not have a body. It means that in the spiritual sense Christ abides in the power of God that fills "all heaven and earth and the hearts of the saints."

22 *Výklad víry*, p. 18.

The eighth clause asserts that Christ shall come again to judge the quick and the dead. Hus comments that on the Day of Judgment Christ will descend to earth in the same way as He had ascended to heaven. The description of the dread Judgment follows Christ's own picture drawn in Matt. 24:31-46. All people will then be divided into the righteous on the right hand and the wicked on the left. The former will be rewarded with the kingdom of heaven, while the latter will be punished by eternal fire. The just judge will reward each man according to his deeds: "the clever will not talk himself out, the powerful will not escape by force, the rich will not buy himself out. . . . He [the judge] will not regard the papacy, kingdom, wisdom, beauty or wealth, but only the faithful observance of His commands, in order to apportion to each according to his deserts."[23] It must be admitted that in describing the horrors of hell, Hus shared with his contemporaries a very material conception of it—far from Dante's vision of the *Divine Comedy*!

The next clause avows belief in the Holy Spirit. Hus teaches that the Holy Spirit is the third person of the Godhead, but not a third god. There is only one Lord, the Creator, the eternal God. The Holy Spirit proceeds from the Father and the Son; this is, of course, the *Filioque* clause of the Western version of the Niceno-Constantinopolitan Creed, which differs from the original version by the addition of the phrase "and the Son." It is still held by Western Christendom. Hus further explains that the dove which descended upon Jesus in baptism and the tongues of fire which appeared on the apostles at Pentecost, were not the Spirit Himself, but only His signs. For these objects are created things of which the Spirit is the Creator. The Spirit departs from the heart of man in mortal sin, although minor sin does not force Him to leave the sinner.

The clause that follows asserts that the holy Church is our mother in the supreme sense. It has existed from Adam and shall exist to the last man. Although there is a basic distinc-

23 *Ibid.*, p. 21.

201

tion between the predestinate and the foreknown members, the first group forming the communion of saints and the second the community of the wicked, yet both form one visible Church.[24] Christ alone is the head of the predestinate, who constitute His mystical body. This body of Christ comprises all those already in heaven—the Church triumphant; those who are now living—the Church militant; and those who are now in purgatory—the Church dormient. They will all ultimately, on the Judgment Day, become one Church "without spot or wrinkle."

The next clause asserts the communion of saints and the forgiveness of sins. Hus expatiates at length on forgiveness of sins. He again emphasizes that it is God and Christ alone who forgive sins; priests only declare such forgiveness ministerially. He denounces as blasphemous the claim of priests to forgive sins directly, of their own power, whenever and wherever they want. Particularly does he excoriate the practice of some priests of demanding money for such "forgiveness," asserting that penitence is its only necessary condition.[25] He also explains the text in John 20:22-23, spoken by Christ to all disciples, "Receive ye the Holy Spirit; whosesoever sins ye remit, they are remitted unto them; and whosesoever sins ye retain, they are retained." Further, the verse in Matt. 16:19, spoken only to Peter, "I will give unto thee the keys of the kingdom of heaven; and whatsoever thou shalt bind on earth, shall be bound in heaven; and whatsoever thou shalt loose on earth shall be loosed in heaven." He comments on these sayings by again referring the initial action to God Himself: the priests of the Church are only the instruments whom God uses for that purpose. Hus illustrates this concept by a man chopping wood: it is his hands and the ax which he employs as instruments of the action, and yet the intention originates in the man's mind.[26]

[24] The same is asserted in *Postil*, p. 79.

[25] *Postilla*, p. 172.

[26] A strikingly similar sentiment about forgiveness is expressed in "The Parson's Tale" in Geoffrey Chaucer's *Canterbury Tales* (transl. by J. U. Nicholson, New York, Garden City Publishing Co., Inc., 1934),

The twelfth clause asserts belief in the resurrection of the body and the life eternal. To this last clause Hus devotes more space than to any previous one. As for the resurrection, he asserts that all men, both the predestinate and the foreknown, will rise on the Last Day in their bodies and souls. The only exceptions are those who have already risen from the dead, Jesus Christ and his Mother. Every other person will receive judgment according to his deserts. Since Christ rose from the dead, no Christian need doubt resurrection. We need not, therefore, feel too great a sorrow at the death of our friends or loved ones. Nor do we need to fear death overmuch. Furthermore, this faith, he says, disposes of the error of the transmigration of souls, such as the Patarines of Bosnia entertain. The physical body of the predestinate will be transformed into the glorified body, incorruptible and immortal. The life eternal consists of knowing and enjoying God by reason and seeing Christ and all the fellow-saints. The foreknown will depart into eternal damnation.

Some time later Hus abstracted the *Exposition of the Faith* into a shorter form, which bears the title *The Lesser Exposition.*[27]

Then follows the *Exposition of the Decalogue*, which forms the longest of the three treatises, being almost twice as long as the other two combined. After a long introduction, enumerating the reasons, both spiritual and material, for observing the commandments of the Lord, Hus sums up the Decalogue in Christ's words: love of God and love of man. Of the former, the Decalogue deals in three commands; of the latter, in seven. This division follows, of course, the custom still received by the Roman and the Lutheran churches, originally adopted by Augustine.

In explaining the first commandment, "Thou shalt have no other gods before me," Hus points out that since God is the supreme good, all men should love Him above all other,

---

pp. 542-65. But when we realize that the parson was a Lollard, this coincidence becomes easily understandable.

[27] *Výklad víry*, pp. 44-52.

lesser goods. It also forbids all pictures and likenesses of heavenly objects to which men would pray; for that is idolatry. For whatever man loves most is his god. Thus considered, the greater part of the total number of Christians are idolaters.

Why then should there be pictures at all? Hus answers that they serve as the bible to the illiterate and unlearned. As such, they are as useful to the populace as books are to scholars. Of course, men must not take pictures for the things or persons depicted, and pray to and worship them as if they were divine. Only God is to be worshipped. Hus warns against observing church services and ceremonies only outwardly—as do the debased who gape at pictures, the vestments of the clergy, and the chalices, and delight in the sound of bells, the organ, and the chanting—without an inner adoration and prayers to God. People today, he says, indulge in sentiment and feeling rather than in reason and spirit. Hus also denounces the painting of secular subjects— the battles of Troy instead of the apostles, and of nude women rather than of saints. Likewise, he condemns veneration of relics, particularly their exhibition for the purpose of collecting revenue. He recounts what he himself heard in a sermon preached in a church in New Town. Three devils went to a festival: one to close the hearts against repentance, another to prevent prayers, and the third to close people's purses. The third, the preacher declared, is the worst.[28] In a passage in the *Postil*, Hus severely castigates bishops, priests, and particularly canons, who go through the service hurriedly so they can repair the sooner to the grogshops, to dances, and to lewdness.[29]

The second commandment forbids the taking of the name of God in vain. Every Christian has assumed Christ's name in baptism. If he does not follow Christ, he bears His name in vain. He also takes it in vain when he fails to

[28] *Výklad desatera*, p. 80.
[29] *Postilla*, p. 42. These same disorders prevailing in England are described in shocking detail in Thompson and Johnson, *Medieval Europe*, p. 665.

persevere in the way of salvation to the end. In speech men take God's name in vain when they employ it casually or habitually, for they must render an account of every such empty word on the Day of Judgment.

Secondly, we use God's name in vain when in prayer we employ it thoughtlessly, or when we are in mortal sin. As Christ said: "This people draw unto me with their mouth and honor me with their lips; but their heart is far from me."[30] We also take God's name in vain in careless oaths. For in an oath we call upon God Himself for a witness. Even when men swear otherwise than by God, it still implies that God is invoked. Of course, when men intentionally swear falsely, they call God to witness a lie or deceit. Our Lord taught us not to swear at all, but that our assertion should be limited to yea, yea, nay, nay.[31]

In view of Christ's explicit words, therefore, should one swear at all? Hus answers that swearing is good when affirming innocence, truth, right and obedience, such as in swearing fealty on the part of lords and knights. He remarks in passing that the German settlers in Bohemia should take such oath to the king; "but that will happen when a snake warms itself on ice!"[32] Further, the marriage vow is good as well as the oath taken by priests at ordination.

Should every oath be kept? Again Hus makes a distinction: a wrong promise should not be kept. For instance, when Herod was tricked by his promise to Salome to give her the head of John the Baptist, it was wrong for him to keep it.[33]

The third commandment enjoins "remember the Sabbath Day to keep it holy." Hus first undertakes to explain why Christians do not observe the seventh day, Sabbath, but rather the first day, Sunday. He stresses the figurative character of Saturday as the day of the Lord's rest, and argues that Jesus' rest in the grave and the resurrection represent

[30] Matt. 15:8.
[31] Matt. 5:33-37.
[32] *Výklad desatera*, p. 100.
[33] Very similar sentiments are expressed in Chaucer's *Canterbury Tales*, pp. 582-83.

the rest prefigured in the Sabbath. His resurrection is also the "first-fruits" of our own resurrection and eternal rest. He offers a number of other arguments for the transposition of the Sabbath rest to Sunday, but they are founded on arbitrary dating of events in the Lord's life, and therefore are not convincing.[34]

There is to be no manual work on Sunday. Hus particularly specifies agricultural labor and craftsmanship as prohibited. Priestly ministrations are not regarded as "work" in the proscribed sense. But the real observance of Sunday consists in worship of God, cultivation of piety and, last of all, care for the body. No fast is ever held on Sunday. Committing sin on that day is its principal desecration. The commonest of such sins are drunkenness, loose language, obscenity, carnal sins, jousting, playing chess and other games, dancing, selling and buying, and worldly amusements. His was a "puritanical" notion of Sunday! He bewails his participation in the feasts held by the burghers and the university masters, in which he suffered spiritual harm. Refraining from sin is "the most useful, most needful, and perfect observance of Sunday."

Passing now to the second "table of the law," we begin with the fourth commandment, enjoining "Honor thy father and thy mother, that thy days may be long in the land which the Lord thy God giveth thee." Hus first explains that by the term "father" are meant not only the natural parents, but also the spiritual fathers, such as the priest who brought the child to the knowledge of God. The honor to parents is to be shown by deed, heart, and language. Children should obey their parents in all rightful commands, but not in any sinful request. Since God forbids sin and He is the supreme Lord and Father, obedience to Him takes precedence over any other command. We should further obey even wicked parents and lords when they order anything good, but should refuse obedience to all evil, no mat-

[34] *Výklad desatera*, p. 129. Hus speaks of Sunday as the "eighth" day, instead of the first.

ter by whom enjoined. For Christ said: "Whoever loves father or mother more than me, is not worthy of me."[35]

The reward for honoring parents is long life. Hus denounces the contemporary priests who divert for their own benefit children's gifts intended for their parents. He scores lawyers and bishops who demand that their decisions be observed more assiduously than God's commands. The secular lords act similarly regarding their legal pronouncements. On the other hand, the spiritual father who sincerely cares for the welfare of his flock should be honored more than the natural parents. The same applies to the spiritual mother of Christians, the Church.

The fifth commandment enjoins: "Thou shalt not kill." Hus adds to the phrase the qualifier "lawlessly" or "unjustly." One may kill by thought, word, or deed. Anyone who hates another man is already his murderer; for hatred leads to the act of murder. It is proper and right to hate a man's sin but to love the sinner. God Himself acts in such a manner. In fact, he is a true friend of a man who chastises him for his wrongdoing. Conversely, he who condones sins of another for his own advantage is his and God's enemy. Hating a man's sins, we should admonish the sinner three times to desist from his unrighteousness; if he pays no heed, we should cease to have communion with him, but not kill him. Hus repeats this sentiment in the *Postil* as well.[36] He also denounces the prevailing custom of the judges and lords of taking a graduated money payment for killing a man: for a peasant five, for a townsman ten, for a squire forty, and for a noble fifty *kopas*. Does not God esteem a pious peasant more than a wicked squire?[37] A sentiment like this cuts clear across the surviving notions of the worth of the different classes of society; it is on such grounds that communists of today regard Hus as a social

[35] Matt. 10:37.

[36] *Postilla*, p. 77.

[37] *Ibid.*, p. 311. It is remarkable to note that very similar sentiments about homicide were expressed at length by the parson in Chaucer's *Canterbury Tales*, pp. 579-81.

revolutionary. Hus, however, based his conviction on the grounds of divine justice. God alone, who created man's soul and joined it with his body, disposes rightfully of his life. Nor are murderers only those who actually commit the deed; those who incite it by counsel and urging are equally guilty.

There are, however, cases of legitimate and just killings, namely, by lawful decree, in self-defense, and by involuntary accident. Hus warns judges against prejudice or spite in sentencing men to death. However, he counsels knights and gentry rather to suffer injustice than to take life, even in self-defense. They should seek an accommodation with their adversaries and fight only when all peaceful means fail. Christ gave us the example of rather suffering unjust death than of self-defense. Nothing could be farther from the dominant notions of knightly honor which prevailed generally at the time than this encouragement to offer "the other cheek!"

Although the lords and knights by their very profession exist for the purpose of redressing injustice and wrong, yet fighting, Hus says, is a very dubious means of bringing about justice. Combat should be resorted to only for the defense of the faith and truth and not for worldly goods, fame, or revenge.[38] Nor should the nobles seek out inoffensive pagans and wantonly fight them on the pretense of defending the faith. Hus set up an almost impossible criterion of love which alone is to be the motive in waging war. He judges war by comparing it clause by clause with Paul's "hymn to love" in I Cor. 13, and naturally finds war incompatible with it. Such a comparison descends from the sublime not so much to the ridiculous as to the well-nigh impossible. Perhaps the ideal was set so high in order to tame the "ferocious and passionate" soul of the Middle Ages, to overcome the surviving pagan mores![39]

Does the above argument mean that no Christian should

[38] *Výklad desatera*, pp. 160 ff.
[39] See J. Huizinga, *The Waning of the Middle Ages* (London, Edward Arnold & Co., 1924), p. 94.

engage in combat? Or to put it another way, is Hus a pacifist? Not at all! Fighting in good causes is the duty of the
seculars of the noble class. Kings, princes, lords and
knights should fight against sin, the devil, the world, and
the enemies of the Church. Although Hus still stresses the
strict limitations under which seculars are placed, yet on the
whole he cites Paul's injunctions regarding the duties of
rulers detailed in Romans 13:1-4. He repeats these injunctions in the *Postil*, where he asserts that the secular lords
possess the sword in order to force their subjects to the
good life.[40] But the ecclesiastics, popes, bishops, and priests
should not fight with the sword at all, except by spiritual
weapons such as prayer and all other means of combating
the devil, the world, and one's own wrongful will. Hus
acknowledges that the pope engages in war and grants the
bishops freedom to do likewise; but in this regard the pope
does not do well. Christ commanded Peter, who had drawn
his sword to defend his Master in the garden of Gethsem-
ane, to desist and to sheathe his sword.

Hus further explains the common teaching of the time
that the Church possesses two swords, the material and the
spiritual, by saying that it is only the spiritual sword that the
Church should employ in its behalf, while the material
sword is used by the rulers for the Church's defense. Perhaps
reminiscing about his own early journey in King Wenceslas'
entourage, Hus exclaims: "Go to the Rhine, and you will
find there bishops wearing breastplates, trappings, swords,
pikes, shields, and accoutrements."[41] Such warlike trappings
obviously are out of place on a bishop! To the objection
that a priest, when attacked by an enemy, has the right to
defend himself by force, Hus replies that he should rather
suffer death, praying for his enemy, as the Lord did when
He prayed for those who crucified him: "Father, forgive
them, for they know not what they do!"[42]

The sixth commandment forbids adultery and fornication. Sexual indulgence and perversion were rife at the time

---

[40] *Postilla*, p. 283.  [41] *Výklad desatera*, p. 175.
[42] Luke 23:34.

and, contrary to some modern standards, were still regarded as vices. In the catalogue of sexual offenses Hus calls a spade a spade, and he includes in their prohibition not only the sexual act itself, but lewd thoughts as well. The latter are sinful when permitted to occupy the mind; but when they are repressed by an act of will, they do not constitute sin. Man's will is sufficiently free to withstand the temptation, which in itself is not sin. "No one shall be judged saved or damned except on the basis of good or evil will."[43] Hus recalls the Czech proverb that free will is both paradise and hell. He describes the various kinds of adultery and all other sexual perversions at length and in great detail, as befits the widely prevalent evil.

As for lawful marriage, Hus follows the contemporary theological opinion that its principal aims are producing progeny, mutual obligation, and avoidance of adultery. These objectives alone make it legitimate; for even marriage may be grossly abused.[44] The indispensable condition of marriage is free consent of both parties, without which no marriage is valid. Hus also subordinates women to men on the hoary ground that it was Eve who tempted Adam to disobey the divine prohibition of eating from the forbidden tree.[45]

The seventh commandment forbids stealing. Hus defines it as comprising stealing, robbing, taking goods by force, nonpayment of debts, simony, usury, and business deceit. All stealing consists not only of the act, but also of an inordinate desire leading to it. Hus expounds as his own Wyclif's theory that since God is the supreme sovereign who gave men all they possess on condition of their faithfully rendering Him service, the man in mortal sin robs God of His due, and thus loses the right to his possessions. This applies to the emperor, kings, princes, as well as to all men who hold any property whatever. The rulers also commit

[43] *Výklad desatera*, p. 191.
[44] *Ibid.*, pp. 196 ff.; see also *Postilla*, pp. 50 ff.
[45] A detailed discussion of this subject, very similar to that expounded by Hus, is found in *Canterbury Tales*, pp. 604-11.

theft by excessive taxation of the poor. Among the merchants usury, which is forbidden by Scripture, is rife. Therefore, "good men loan to the poor asking no other reward than the love of God and of neighbor."[46]

The priestly class is all too often guilty of simony. It is theft of a particularly despicable and grave nature, for it is trafficking in holy things. We have already considered Hus' treatise on simony, and need not repeat its arguments again.

As for the eighth commandment, "Thou shalt not bear false witness against thy neighbor," Hus teaches that to do so is mortal sin. If the false witness harms the neighbor's property, it is a grave sin; if it besmirches his honor, it is even graver; if it threatens his life, it is the gravest. The sin of the tongue consists of talk against God, speech against oneself, and slander against one's neighbor. There also exists the sin of silence, when one refrains from defense of truth and right. Blasphemy is the sin of speaking against God. Hus confesses that "when as yet I had no understanding of it, I often felt distressed at the death of a good man"; but he has learned since to submit to God's will. "Since then I do not concern myself about the future, how it shall be, believing that whatever God is pleased to cause, will come to pass."[47] As for speaking against one's neighbor, it consists of slander, false witness, or conspiracy of silence against him. The gravest slander is calling an innocent man a heretic. The slander by a priest, whose voice should declare the Word of God, is particularly reprehensible. To harm a neighbor by keeping silent when he is unjustly accused is likewise abominable. Not to defend truth is to be a traitor to it. To refuse to stand against Christ's enemies is to be unworthy of Him. Hus also rejects the assertion that the lower clergy and particularly laymen have no right to judge or punish their ecclesiastical superiors when the latter commit wrong. He affirms the same duty in the *Postil*, where he illustrates it by a driver of a wagon guiding it so

46 *Výklad desatera*, p. 217.
47 *Ibid.*, p. 227.

carelessly as to endanger the safety of the passengers; he should be admonished for their sake.[48] He further argues that a peasant or a woman in grace are greater in the sight of God than a bishop in mortal sin.

Another sin of the tongue is flattery or adulation, particularly when it is practiced for one's profit (in Czech, the word *pochlebenství*—flattery—is formed on the root *chléb*—bread). Hus bewails the great number of such flatterers who seek secular or ecclesiastical dignities: "one wishes to become a pope, another an archbishop, or an ecclesiastical official, or a priest, or a monk."[49] Christ does not want such followers, but only those who would follow Him for His own sake.

The ninth commandment forbids coveting a neighbor's house or wife. Hus recalls Paul's saying that the root of all evil is an evil desire.[50] No one sins mortally except he who turns his will from the highest good, God, to some lesser good. Hus then considers the second clause of the commandment, which forbids coveting a neighbor's wife. He repeats essentially what he wrote about the fifth commandment. He testifies that he knew many priests who lived with concubines or who even committed incest with their own sisters.

The tenth commandment prohibits coveting a neighbor's goods. Hus utilizes it for stressing his favorite doctrine of voluntary poverty on the example of Christ. Every faithful Christian should do as Christ had done, especially priests, for whom sufficiency of food and clothing should be enough. He denies that the wealth and pomp of the Church are necessary for its success.

All these divine commandments should be observed for the love of God, not out of fear of punishment; nevertheless, their willful transgression brings about eternal punishment in tortures that exceed all imagination. He graphically illustrates the eternity of such punishment as follows: "If

[48] *Postilla*, p. 136.
[49] *Výklad desatera*, p. 259.
[50] I Tim. 6:10.

the whole world were filled up to heavens with poppy seed or sand . . . and after a thousand of thousand years one grain were removed, even so man would gladly await cessation of torture according to the number of the seeds, for the end would come some time; but in eternity which has no end, how could relief come to the damned?"[51]

Thereupon follows the *Exposition of the Lord's Prayer.* Hus prefaces the exposition proper by an explanation of what prayer is. He defines it as "the pious lifting of one's mind to God."[52] The mind has "two wings" whereby it is lifted to God: the knowledge of one's dire need and of God's mercy. No one can, in his own strength, fulfill the commandment, "Thou shalt love the Lord thy God with all thy heart, all thy soul, and all thy mind."[53] By God's mercy, however, every man can be brought out of his impotent misery. He should, therefore, fear nothing but sin, knowing that "All things work for the good of those who love God."[54]

As for the place where one should pray, Hus names, first of all, the sanctuary. It is the house of prayer. All worship there should be conducive to prayer. Hus denounces the irreverent or actually offensive priestly behavior: priests conduct their services negligently, mechanically, hurrying through the antiphonal responses without waiting for each other's completing of his part. "What does it profit when we howl like puppies in a sack, not understanding what we howl? Having our minds in the street or in a pub, while our bodies are in the church?"[55] After citing the abuses of church worship, Hus expresses the opinion that these malpractices are a sign of the imminent coming of the Day of Judgment, in accordance with Christ's prophecy of "the abomination of

51 *Výklad desatera,* p. 285.
52 *Ibid.,* p. 391.
53 Matt. 22:37.
54 Rom. 8:28.
55 *Výklad modlitby Páně,* p. 300. Similar abuses practiced in England are condemned by the bishop of Exeter. See Thompson and Johnson, *Medieval Europe,* p. 665.

desolation standing where it ought not."[56] He pleads that worshippers should do nothing in churches but what is to the praise of God: engaging in prayer, in contemplation of God, in listening to His word, singing, and confessing one's sins.[57]

But prayer is not restricted to the sanctuary. Christ teaches, "When thou prayest, enter into thy chamber and when thou hast shut the door, pray to the Father. . . ."[58] For as Chrysostom said, "The holy place does not make a man holy, but a holy man makes the place holy."[59]

As for the time for praying, Hus advises holy days and above all Sundays; but again praying is not restricted to these times. One should pray always. Prayer is useless unless it comes from the heart. "The tongue works in vain if the heart does not pray."[60]

But why should we pray? Surely, the Lord knows our needs without our telling Him about them. The answer is that God does not need our prayers, but we do. Nor does the man praying for something always get it. For one reason, he may not be worthy, or he prays for an unworthy or an unnecessary thing. Furthermore, the man whose prayer is unanswered may need to pray more earnestly and persistently. Hus humbly confesses that he never did anything quite adequately in God's service.

Hus then comments on the text of the Lord's Prayer itself. The first petition, "Our Father who art in heaven," asserts that God is the Creator and Sustainer of the universe, whose majesty exceeds all imagination. He is our Father and we are His children. If an emperor or a king were to acknowledge a poor peasant as his son, how deeply grateful would the poor man be! God is above all comparison in dignity and power, and yet Christ teaches us to call Him our Father! The common fatherhood of God places all men—popes and kings as well as their poorest subjects—

[56] Mark 13:14.
[57] This passage is repeated in *Postilla*, p. 346.
[58] Matt. 6:6.
[59] *Výklad modlitby Páně*, p. 304.
[60] *Ibid.*, p. 306.

on equality. This is the clear implication of the word "our." No one may claim Him more than another: we do not pray to "My Father," but to "Our Father." Moreover, the petition places God in heaven. This phrase does not mean that God dwells only in heaven and not on earth, for His presence and might pervade the whole universe.

The petition "Hallowed be thy name" implies that this sanctifying action should transform us. God himself cannot be holier than He is. It is we who must strive not to sully His name by our sins. Hence we pray: "Hallowed be Thy name that, having pure hearts, we may praise Thee forever."[61]

The next clause states, "Thy kingdom come." God's kingdom is in heaven, where He alone reigns; or it may denote the company of the elect, in whose hearts He reigns; or it signifies Christ Himself. Christ has been present in the world by His incarnation and in His abiding presence since His ascension. He will come again at the Judgment Day. In praying that God's kingdom may come, we pray that He would complete the number of the elect that they all, living and dead, may enjoy the eternal bliss with Him.

The petition "Thy will be done on earth as it is in heaven" signifies that we should conform to God's will in all we do. God's will shall be done in any event, whether we pray for it or not. But a sinner may repudiate God's will and prefer doing his own. The righteous man, therefore, prays that he would desire and actually do what God wills.

In the next petition, "Give us this day our daily bread," Hus distinguishes three kinds of bread: the natural bread for our bodies, the Word of God for our souls, and the bread of the life eternal. In the first sense the term "bread" comprises all bodily needs: food, clothing, and shelter. The second kind of bread was referred to by Christ in His temptation when He answered the tempter: "Man shall not live by bread alone, but by every word which proceeds from the mouth of God."[62] That bread we need more than the ma-

[61] *Ibid.*, p. 322.
[62] Matt. 4:4.

terial bread, for the soul is more important than the body. The bread of the life eternal is the sacrament of the body of Christ,[63] of which Augustine said: "What the eyes see is bread; but what faith requires for instruction is the bread which is the body of God." This is what the Gospel of Matthew calls "the non-material bread" as against Luke who speaks of "daily bread."[64] Hus teaches that although participation in the communion of the sacrament is normally obligatory, one may, if necessary, commune by faith. As Augustine wrote: "Believe and thou hast eaten."[65]

This petition is followed by the clause, "Forgive us our debts as we forgive our debtors." Hus explains the term "debts" by substituting for it "sins" or "guilt." Mortal sin destroys God's grace in the soul, thus rendering it dead. In the *Postil* he adds that by mortal sin one loses the likeness of God, in which he was created, although he is not bereft of the image of God. Accordingly, he ceases to be in the likeness of the Trinity, which he would have retained, had he not sinned mortally.[66] Basing his comment on the parable of the king who forgave his servant an enormous debt, while the servant refused to do the same in regard to an insignificant sum owed him by his fellow-servant,[67] Hus concludes that God will not forgive the many of our sins, if we refuse to forgive the few trespasses committed by our neighbors against us.

The next petition pleads: "Lead us not into temptation." God "tempts" the saints to strengthen their virtue, while the devil tempts men to lead them into sin. Even Christ was tempted by the devil. Temptation itself, as has been said before, is not sin; consenting to it is. When a good man refuses consent to temptation, he is strengthened in his righteous disposition. One should, therefore, rejoice when he is tempted, provided he overcomes the attack.

---

[63] Matt. 6:11. Hus uses the term *chléb nadpodstatný*; the Vulgate term is *panem nostrum supersubstantialem.*
[64] Luke 11:3.
[65] *Výklad modlitby Páně*, p. 332.
[66] *Postilla*, p. 255.
[67] Matt. 18:23-35.

Without a struggle there is no victory. Sin has its source in the heart and the will.

In connection with the last petition, "But deliver us from evil, Amen," Hus alludes to St. Bernard,[68] who enumerates three steps of the freedom of the soul: the will is free from necessary consent to evil; freedom from mortal sin here on earth; freedom of the redeemed in heaven from all sin. It is possible for us on earth to gain the first two stages of freedom, but not the third. Our enemies are the world, the flesh, and the devil. We pray to be victorious over them.

Such, then, is the teaching of Hus' principal Czech treatises. He combats the external, mechanical piety of the time by opposing to it the piety of the heart and the spirit. As has already been pointed out, his reformatory endeavors remind one of similar attempts elsewhere to revive real piety, such as that of the Brethren of the Common Life and the regular canons of the Congregation of Windesheim in the Netherlands.

Hus indeed shares many of the notions and sentiments of his day; this is understandable, and, in fact, it could not be otherwise. More important are the instances where he emancipated himself from the prevailing opinions of his age. A simple comparison of his views with the tenor of his age, an age depicted in masterly fashion in such a book as Huizinga's *The Waning of the Middle Ages*, suffices to make one aware of Hus' advanced position. Even omitting his forward-looking theological views, which have been previously summarized, one may point to the social opinions which set Hus off from his times.[69] His obvious and oft-expressed sympathy with the common people, oppressed and exploited by both secular and ecclesiastical superiors, is itself a revolutionary phenomenon. He was motivated by considerations of justice, not of class consciousness, and stressed moral and truly religious means for rectifying these unjust

[68] Hus probably here alludes to Bernard's *The Steps of Humility*, transl. by George B. Burch (Cambridge, Mass., Harvard University Press, 1942), or his *On the Love of God*, transl. by T. L. Connolly (Kentucky, Abbey of the Gethsemani, 1943).

[69] See, for instance, my *John Hus' Concept of the Church*, pp. 386-90.

conditions, not the use of force. He sought spiritual transformation of men, not merely a change in their economic or political conditions. The revolutionary movements that followed, such as the Hussite Wars and the emergence of the Utraquist Church, wrought a basic change in his land in ways that Hus would not always have wished or wholly approved, but that nevertheless realized at least a minimum of his reforms.

## Chapter VIII

## At the Council of
## Constance, I

The Council of Pisa, which was convened in 1409 to end the Great Schism by deposing the two existing popes, Gregory XII and Benedict XIII, did what it intended to do. After getting rid of the two obstinate old men, the Council thereupon elected the new pope, Alexander V (1409-10). But the deposed popes did not stay deposed, so that the net result of the Council was an aggravation of the Schism, since there were then three popes who divided the West among them. As Cardinal d'Ailly characterized the situation, the Church passed from *dualitas infamis* to *trinitas non benedicta, sed ab omnibus maledicta.*[1] Alexander died less than a year after he became pope and was succeeded by John XXIII. The only remedy for the abnormal situation seemed to be the convoking of another Council, which would deal with the fantastic state of affairs in a lasting manner.

To King Sigismund of Hungary, who was elected as King of the Romans on July 11, 1411, it seemed a splendid opportunity to gain prestige as the restorer of peace to the Church. This he sought to accomplish by convoking another Council. Pope John, who had already held an undistinguished and ill-attended Council of Rome (1412-13), was less than enthusiastic about the suggestion. However, since Pope John's Council did not deal with the Schism, and, though prorogued to reassemble three months later, did not meet, Sigismund now urged the reluctant pope to fulfil his promise and to call the Council so that a new assembly of Christendom could deal primarily with the termination of the ill-fated Schism. As John had had to seek

[1] A. Franzen and W. Müller, eds., *Das Konzil von Konstanz* (Freiburg, Basel, Wien, Herder, 1964), p. 41.

refuge in Bologna when King Ladislas of Naples, supporter of the deposed Gregory XII, again invaded Rome (June 1413), he urgently needed the help of Sigismund, and was not free to withstand his wishes. In the end John agreed to call the Council to Constance, the place preferred by Sigismund. The king feared too large an attendance of John's Italian partisans if the Council were called to an Italian city. Constance, an imperial city, was located in Swabia, almost on the Swiss border and north of the Alps. Without waiting for the pope's express consent, Sigismund announced the meeting of the Council on October 31, 1413.[2] The edict promised that the king would "do all in our power to keep each and every person at the Council in entire safety and liberty . . ." The pope announced his consent to the Council the next day.[3] The bull of convocation, however, was not published until December 9,[4] and specified November 1, 1414, as the date of the Council's opening.

King Wenceslas heartily approved his younger brother's zeal for terminating the disastrous state of the Church. He was willing to cooperate, for he was eager to clear the good name of his kingdom from the continual aspersion of heresy. For that reason he wished to induce Hus to attend the Council, which, among other tasks, was to deal with the elimination of heresy.

Sigismund was equally eager to secure Hus' voluntary attendance, for he wished to have the charges brought against Hus cleared up. Two Czech knights, John of Chlum and Wenceslas of Dubá, had been serving in his campaign in Friuli and were returning home in the Spring of 1414; as they are referred to as the king's councilors and familiars,[5] they must have held positions of some influence with Sigismund. The king entrusted John of Chlum with a mes-

[2] Louise R. Loomis, transl., *The Council of Constance; the Unification of the Church*, ed. by John H. Mundy and Kennerly M. Woody (New York and London, Columbia University Press, 1961), pp. 70-71.

[3] *Ibid.*, pp. 72-75.

[4] *Ibid.*, pp. 75-78.

[5] Matthew Spinka, ed. and transl., *John Hus at the Council of Constance* (New York and London, Columbia University Press, 1965), p. 89.

sage to Hus. Perhaps in the middle of April, John of Chlum offered Hus, in the king's name, a safe-conduct if he would accept the invitation to attend the Council. Hus journeyed to Prague to consult with his friends, but was detected there and caused quite a commotion. His friends advised him against the dangerous venture and at first he refused the offer, fearing an attempt at entrapment once he left the protection of his friend, Ctibor of Kozí. In fact, he feared that he might be put to death, as he intimated in his *Books against the Cook-master.*[6]

Thereupon, a much wider net was spread for Hus, extending to the highest Church authority—the pope. On April 30, at the request of Bishop John of Litomyšl, the pope issued an authorization empowering the bishop to begin an attack on the Prague archbishop, Conrad of Vechta, the bishop of Olomouc, Wenceslas Králík, and the inquisitor, Bishop Nicholas of Nezero, to force them to carry out the terms of the interdict pronounced upon Hus. If they procrastinated any longer, they themselves were to suffer severe punishment. Furthermore, the University of Paris joined in these proceedings, initiated by the chancellor, John Gerson. Later, a formidable threat was launched against the king himself: he was ordered by the pope to clear the country of heresy, which meant in the first place dealing with Hus. Wenceslas was threatened with dire consequences involving the whole land unless he promptly acceded to the request. This implied perhaps a crusade against Bohemia.

Wenceslas could not ignore a threat so ominous. Nevertheless, in his accustomed lethargy, he did not undertake to deal with the matter personally, but turned it over to his principal adviser, Lord Henry Lefl of Lažany. In order to make the task of negotiating easier for himself, that nobleman invited Hus, as has already been mentioned, to his castle of Krakovec. Furthermore, he took steps to secure con-

[6] Bartoš interprets thus Hus' remark: "It will happen when the pope's emissaries shall seize me and take me before him . . ." K. J. Erben, ed., *Mistra Jana Husi Sebrané spisy české*, 3 vols. (Praha, B. Tempský, 1866), III, p. 253.

cessions from King Sigismund. Lord Henry was in a position to do so because he had also been entrusted with the task of dealing with Sigismund's request that he be crowned king of the Romans, a dignity to which he had been elected three years previously. At that time, since Wenceslas still claimed that office in which he had been confirmed by the Council of Pisa, the two royal brothers agreed that Sigismund was to be permitted to hold the kingship, provided he was not crowned during Wenceslas' lifetime. Sigismund now asked that the condition be annulled and that a coronation ceremony take place, since it was necessary that he preside over the Council as the king of the Romans.

Under these circumstances, Lord Henry now secured from Sigismund terms for Hus much more favorable than those previously offered: the king was willing to grant Hus the so-called court safe-conduct, assuring safe passage to and from the Council no matter what the decision of that august body might be. In addition, the king promised Hus armed protection on the way. In exchange for this greatly amplified pledge, Lord Henry promised Sigismund Wenceslas' consent to the coronation—a promise which he obtained.[7]

It was difficult for Hus not to accept this greatly improved offer. For one thing, since he had lost all hope of obtaining justice at the papal court, by consenting to the invitation he might perhaps fare better at the Council. Moreover, Lord Henry undoubtedly informed Hus of the papal threat hanging over the whole country on his account. Nevertheless, Hus appears still to have entertained fears of possible, if not inevitable, mortal danger. At this juncture his close friend, Jerome of Prague, visited him at Krakovec and urged him to accept the offer. Jerome even promised to come to his aid, should the need arise.[8] Furthermore, when Sigismund's

[7] F. M. Bartoš, "Na obranu M. Jana proti jeho obránci," in M. Kaňák, ed., *Hus stále živý* (Praha, Blahoslav, 1965), pp. 110-11; also his "Král Zikmund, Václav IV. a M. J Hus v r. 1414," *Věstnik české akademie*, 53 (1944), pp. 19-26.

[8] F. Šmahel, *Jeronȳm Pražskȳ* (Praha, Svobodné Slovo, 1966), pp. 152-53. But in Constance Hus recalled that Jerome had said: "If I go

emissary, Lord Mikeš Divoký of Jemniště, came to Wenceslas's court to conclude the agreement about his master's coronation, he confirmed the promises Lord Henry had made in Sigismund's name. With inducements seemingly so great and the knowledge of the danger to the country so immense, Hus could hesitate no longer. On September 1, he wrote Sigismund a letter declaring that he was ready, on the conditions confirmed by the king's emissary, to attend the Council.[9] He specified that he expected to be allowed "to profess publicly the faith I hold," but made no explicit mention of the free return from the Council in case his defense proved unsuccessful. At most, one may read such implication into the phrase that he hoped the king would "bring the trial to a laudable end." However, he did state that he was consoled "by what the noble and courageous lord . . . Your Majesty's messenger, told me." Since this promise included the assurance that he would be free, under any circumstances, to return home, this should have sufficed to pass for a binding pledge of a king.

Nevertheless, even here there exists a discrepancy, or perhaps a contradiction, in the report of Mikeš' assurances. In one of the letters written by Hus from Constance, he mentions that Mikeš told him in the presence of John of Jesenice: "Master, you may take it for certain that you will be condemned."[10] Hus adds that Mikeš obviously knew his master's faithlessness and trickery. This illustrates dramatically the difference between Mikeš' official message and his private opinion!

The anti-reformist clergy in Bohemia during this time was by no means idle. The king had apparently put pressure on the archbishop to adopt measures which would satisfy the demands of the pope and Paris University. Conrad thereupon called a special meeting of the synod, which met

---

to the Council, I suppose I shall not return." V. Novotný, ed., *M. Jana Husi Korespondence a dokumenty* (Praha, Komise pro vydávání pramenů náboženského hnutí českého, 1920), No. 126.

[9] Spinka, *John Hus at the Council of Constance*, No. 5, pp. 247-48.

[10] *Ibid.*, No. 14, p. 259.

early in August. It dealt with "king's business," perhaps that of imposing a voluntary contribution for defraying the expenses to be incurred in sending a delegation to Constance, to be headed by Bishop John of Litomyšl.[11] This purpose of the meeting was affirmed in a sermon preached in memory of Hus and Jerome some time after the outbreak of the Hussite wars, in which an anonymous preacher asserted that the clergy had "extorted from the people" 53,000 Florentine gulden in order to secure at Constance the burning of Hus.[12]

At the castle of Krakovec Hus was busily engaged in preparing for the journey. In this task he was greatly aided by his legal adviser, John of Jesenice, who because of the excommunication imposed on him in Rome, could not accompany Hus to the Council. According to Kejř, Jesenic was convinced that the case was hopeless even before Hus embarked on the journey;[13] an opinion shared by Bartoš. Kejř cites the letters of farewell written by Hus to his friends:[14] the so-called "Last Will," left to Martin of Volyně and the letter addressed to "all faithful Czechs." There is no doubt that Hus realized the gravity and danger of the projected journey, and considered it possible that he would not return. Under such circumstances it was only prudent to make his last will, to be opened only in the event of his death. In the second letter he specifically mentions the possibility of death: "Perhaps you will not see me in Prague before my death; if the Almighty God will be pleased to return me, we shall meet so much more gladly; and of course when we meet each other in the heavenly joy."[15] These letters do not express Hus' certainty of death, but only the possibility, and a hope of return. After all, he did not altogether distrust Sigismund's promised

[11] *Ibid.*, p. 94.
[12] "Sermo de martyribus Bohemis," in V. Novotný, ed., *Fontes rerum Bohemicarum* (Praha, Nadání Františka Palackého, 1932), VIII, p. 371; also Jiří Heremita, *Život M. Jana Husi*, in *ibid.*, p. 379.
[13] Jiří Kejř, *Husitský právník, M. Jan z Jesenice* (Praha, Československá akademie věd, 1965), p. 86.
[14] Novotný, *Korespondence*, Nos. 86-87.
[15] *Ibid.*, p. 208.

safe-conduct, of which he had been assured by his powerful friend, Lord Henry Lefl. Perhaps he should have been
more reserved about the promises, for Sigismund was notorious for his treachery. Had he been certain of the flimsi-
ness of the king's promise, Hus could have refused to go to
Constance, as he had when first invited. All these considerations seem to indicate that Hus was indeed aware of the
danger involved in the journey but that he still entertained
a hope of return, whatever the result of the Council proceedings. He expressed this hope a number of times in his
letters from Constance.

If Jesenic could not go to Constance, he at least carefully
drilled his friend in what to do and how to act when subjected to examination. Jesenic knew that a condemned
heretic could not be shielded before ecclesiastical authorities
even by a royal safe-conduct. Hence, Hus had to be able to
prove that he had never been officially declared a heretic.
Even the excommunication imposed on him by Cardinal
Peter degli Stephaneschi was not for heresy but for contumacy on account of his non-appearance. Nor had he been
convicted of heresy at home, even though he had been accused of it often enough. Hus therefore challenged, by public notices posted at many places, anyone who wished to
accuse him of heresy to declare it and stand up to prove it.
If his accuser failed legally to do so, he would be subject
to the same penalty Hus would incur if convicted. He also
offered to appear before the archbishop at the forthcoming
synodical meeting (which was to be held the next day) and
to debate with anyone who would challenge his orthodoxy.
He declared further that he intended to defend himself
before the general Council as well.[16] He informed the king,
the queen, and the royal Council of this intention but received no answer from them. The next day, Jesenic went to
the archiepiscopal court where the synod was being held
and sought admittance to it, in order to deliver the message; when denied entrance, he secured a notarized
testimony of the fact. Nevertheless, when Jesenic applied to

[16] Spinka, *John Hus at the Council of Constance*, pp. 91-92, 94.

the inquisitor, Bishop Nicholas of Nezero, for a certificate of Hus' doctrinal soundness, he promptly received it. Furthermore, when the plenary session of the nobles of Bohemia, attended by Archbishop Conrad of Vechta, was held, to Hus' request that they inquire of Conrad whether he knew of any heresy of Hus, the archbishop answered negatively. He even testified to it in a personal letter. Three prominent nobles, favorable to Hus, added to the archbishop's testimony their own request to Sigismund that he secure for Hus a public hearing at the Council. Finally, in order to guard against the common German charge that Hus was principally instrumental in the expulsion of the German masters from Prague, a friend of his secured from the then rector of the university an official copy of the decree of Kutná Hora, and a copy of the university protest against the burning of Wyclif's books.[17]

Hus, hopefully anticipating that he would be allowed to address the Council publicly, prepared—in an astonishing excess of optimism—a sermon, De pace, and a short exposition, De sufficientia legis Christi. If any proof were needed that he had confidence in Sigismund's promises, these two speeches should furnish it.[18]

Jesenic also realized that Hus must be well versed in the proceedings of his trial, both at the curia and at home, in order to be able to challenge any misstatement or misinterpretation of his position which might be brought against him. He, therefore, drew up for Hus' use a brief résumé of the whole process, called the Ordo procedendi. This invaluable statement of the sequence of events is of immense help in our reconstruction of the proceedings involved.[19]

Another attempt to assure Hus' security at the Council was made in preparing a treatise concerning the relation

[17] Kejř, Husitský právník, p. 87.

[18] "De pace" in Historia et monumenta, I, pp. 60-71. "De sufficientia," ibid., pp. 55-60. A Czech translation of "De pace" by F. M. Dobiáš and A. Molnár was recently published (Praha, Kalich, 1963).

[19] Novotný, Korespondence, No. 101, pp. 225-34. He argues that Hus finished Jesenic's preliminary concept.

of the papal and the imperial power, addressed directly to King Sigismund. It was originally attributed to an unknown Czech canon lawyer, tentatively identified with Jesenic, but this theory was recently abandoned. A new theory, propounded by Bartoš, designates John Cardinal of Rejnštejn as the most probable author of the treatise.[20] Rejnštejn was not only a close friend of Hus and a distinguished canon lawyer but was the official representative of the University of Prague to the Council, to which he traveled in Hus' company. As such, he could address the king not only in his own name, but with the implied authority of the university behind him. The document was most likely written in Prague and taken along to the Council, to be presented there to Sigismund. It consisted of carefully selected legal, biblical, and historical precedents of cases where kings exercised authority over ecclesiastics, including popes, and as such indicated the most painstaking and time-consuming preparation.

The author of the treatise begins his argument by asserting the superiority of the natural law over all other legal enactments, both secular and ecclesiastical. Sigismund is exhorted to exercise this authority in presiding over the Council of Constance, in order to secure far-reaching reforms. That the royal power is of sacred character, superior to the ecclesiastical, is proved by many examples showing how kings dominated Jewish high-priests and Christian bishops and popes. These historical facts suffice, in the author's opinion, to prove the claim made for the secular superiority, and lead to the daring suggestion that since the popes have rescinded many previous papal pronouncements, Sigismund has the right to rescind the "Donation of Constantine," on the ground that what one emperor had granted another could annul. For that matter, the "Donation," asserts the author of the treatise, has brought moral decay into the

20 This theory is discussed extensively in F. M. Bartoš' unpublished essay, "Reformní program vyslance Karlovy university pro koncil kostnický" (1967), in which he identifies the author as John Cardinal of Rejnštejn. (Dr. Bartoš very kindly sent me a carbon copy of this essay, for which I take this opportunity to thank him.)

Church and has been the cause of many wars even to the present: The bishops have no right to carry and use the sword, for Christ ordered Peter to sheathe his sword. Hence, it is not fitting that the pope should bestow the sword upon the emperor in the coronation ceremony, or should claim kingdoms in fief, or Italy as patrimony of Peter. Finally, the author of the treatise exhorts Sigismund to prohibit and exterminate simony according to the laws of Justinian, confirmed by Pope Paschal. He concludes by entreating Sigismund to accept the treatise and to carry out its recommendations for the good of the Church. It is not certain, however, that John Cardinal ever delivered the document to the king after Sigismund arrived in Constance.

Thus prepared for every eventuality that he or Jesenic could foresee, Hus started on the journey from Krakovec to Constance on October 11, 1414, without the promised safe-conduct. He was accompanied by two knights assigned for his protection, John of Chlum and Wenceslas of Dubá, the former of whom had originally delivered to him Sigismund's invitation. John of Chlum had engaged as his secretary a young bachelor of arts, Hus' former student, Peter of Mladoňovice, who wrote a detailed *Relatio* of the events in Constance.[21] This invaluable eyewitness account is the only description of the trial written by a friendly, although dependable, witness. Without it, we would have only fragmentary and, on the whole biased, official records and scattered notices of the trial by several members or observers at the Council. In the entourage was also a representative of the University of Prague, Hus' friend, John Cardinal of Rejnštejn. Although Peter does not mention him, another bachelor of arts, Oldřich of Znojmo, appears to have been in the company.[22] A few servants completed the

[21] "Petri de Mladoniowicz Relatio de Magistro Johanne Hus," in V. Novotný, ed., *Fontes rerum Bohemicarum* VIII, pp. 25-120; my translation of the entire work in *John Hus at the Council of Constance*, pp. 89-234.

[22] F. M. Bartoš, *Husitská revoluce II: Vláda bratrstev a její pád, 1426-37* (Praha, Československá akademie věd, 1966), p. 130.

party. They traveled by several wagons while Hus rode his own horse.

Before Hus left Krakovec, he left behind the two letters previously mentioned: the "Last Will," addressed to Martin of Volyně, and the letter to his parishioners.[23] The first is a deeply moving expression of Hus' concern for the spiritual and temporal welfare of his former pupil; the greater part of it is taken up with exhortation of Martin, whom he had known all his life, as to his conduct as priest. Hus earnestly warns him to preserve chastity and gives him fatherly advice on how to behave should he be appointed to a benefice. He even warns Martin against ostentation in dress and begs him not to follow his own early example "in any levity that you have seen in me." Hus entrusts to him his two nephews and gives direction how to distribute among his young student-famuli either some money or his gowns. The other letter is also an exhortation addressed to his hearers, entreating them to stand firm in his teaching. He expresses hope that God will grant him "the wisdom and bravery of the Holy Spirit to remain steadfast, so that they would not be able to swerve him to the wrong side." He informs his parishioners that among his enemies "the worst are my countrymen." This letter was falsified in Constance by the insertion of the phrase that if he "should abjure, understand that I do it only orally, without consenting to it in my heart."

The journey through Germany resembled a triumphal procession. Although he had left without the promised safe-conduct, nowhere was he molested, nor were church services stopped on his account anywhere along the route. One would have supposed that the allegations of heresy would have been spread by his enemies throughout Germany. Yet, wherever he stopped he was received in a friendly manner by the local clergy and the municipal officials. Hus had even posted written notices inviting anyone who wished to do so to confer with him. Peter reported him as having said:

[23] Novotný, *Korespondence*, Nos. 86-87; my translation in *John Hus at the Council of Constance*, pp. 95-98.

"I never rode with the donned hood, but openly with un-covered face."[24] Nor was this only in smaller places, where it could be assumed that Hus was not known. In Nurem-berg, for instance, where the streets were filled with eager crowds, when it became known that Hus' party was to arrive, the pastor of the principal church, Albert Fleisch-mann of St. Sebald, found no fault with Hus' answers to his questions. Hus concluded his letter, in which he narrated this story, with the sentence: "You should know that as yet I have not been aware of any enemy."[25] At the small village of Biberach John of Chlum argued on Hus' behalf so zeal-ously that his interlocutors thought him to be a learned doctor. He was jokingly nicknamed by his friends (including Hus) as the "Biberach doctor." What had become of the rumors of Hus' heresy or of his already being excommuni-cated and under an interdict? Why was he not seized, when he had no safe conduct?

At Nuremberg, Wenceslas of Dubá left the party to go to Aachen, where Sigismund was to be crowned the king of the Romans. He was to bring Hus, rather belatedly, the promised safe-conduct. The rest of the company continued on to Constance, not to double up on their tracks need-lessly and to save expenses. This was a mistake which at the time no one seemed to have perceived. Had Hus gone to join Sigismund's entourage, he would not have entered Constance until Christmas night and in the king's com-pany, instead of early in November and alone; perhaps he would thus have avoided being taken prisoner. However, this is by no means certain. The Council, as the events were to show, was determined to treat Hus as an already con-demned rebel, whom no safe-conduct could shield.

Under these circumstances, Hus reached Constance on November 3. Two days later, Lord Wenceslas brought him the safe-conduct, which had been issued by the royal official, Canon Michael of Přestanov, at Speyer, on October 18, a week after Hus had left Krakovec. Instead of a safe-conduct plain-

24 Spinka, *John Hus at the Council of Constance*, p. 99.
25 *Ibid.*, p. 100.

ly stating the conditions agreed upon by Hus and Mikeš Divoký, Sigismund's envoy, and Lord Henry Lefl, who represented King Wenceslas, the document issued to Hus was a mere pass.[26] Nothing in it specifically guaranteed to Hus the privilege of presenting his case freely before the Council, or his return home under any eventualities, even if the Council decreed an unfavorable judgment. Since it was delivered to Hus only after he had reached Constance and, moreover, during Sigismund's absence from the city, no protest on Hus' part could be made. In fact, we hear of no such protest even later. Hus and his friends treat the pass as if it were a safe-conduct embodying the agreed-upon conditions.

Hus and his guardians, along with Peter of Mladoňovice, found lodgings in a house belonging to "the good widow Fida," in St. Paul's street, which is now called *Hussen-strasse*.[27] The house still stands, designated by a memorial plaque with Hus' bas-relief.

Pope John had entered Constance a week earlier (October 28). On his way, when crossing the Arlberg, his carriage overturned and he was pinned beneath it in the snow. When his retinue, after rescuing him, anxiously inquired whether he was hurt, he peevishly exploded: "Here I lie in the devil's name!" When nearing Constance, he remarked: "That's how they catch foxes!"[28] Before entering the city, he stayed overnight in the monastery of Kreuzlingen, just outside the gates of the city. He was accompanied by nine cardinals, many bishops, and an entourage of about 600 retainers. Next morning, Sunday, he entered the city with great pomp, under a golden canopy given him by the citizens of Constance. He was met by all the prelates of the city and the surrounding towns, canons of the cathedral, all the clergy of the city, and an immense crowd of people. In advance of the papal procession were nine white horses, eight of which carried boxes of apparel and other papal be-

26 *Ibid.*, pp. 89-90, where the text is given.

27 For an excellent map of Constance, identifying the various places mentioned in the narrative, see Loomis, *The Council of Constance*, facing p. 88.

28 *Ibid.*, pp. 88-89.

231

longings, while the ninth was saddled with a monstrance containing the sacred host. The cardinals, clad in red mantles and hoods, wore their wide-brimmed red hats. The procession went to the cathedral where a solemn *Te Deum* was sung. Thereupon the pope was accommodated in the episcopal palace next to the cathedral.

The day after Hus and his guardians arrived in the city, Henry of Lacembok and John of Chlum went to the pope to announce that they had safely brought Hus to Constance, and asked for his protection.[29] Pope John assured them that Hus would remain unmolested "even if he had murdered my own brother!" A week after his arrival, however, Hus was visited by a distinguished delegation sent by the pope, consisting of the auditor of the sacred apostolic palace (almost certainly Berthold of Wildungen), the Bishop of Constance,[30] and a town official, Conrad Helye. They announced to him that after a stormy discussion between the pope and the cardinals, it was decided to suspend the interdict and Hus' sentence of excommunication (so that religious ministrations would not be stopped in the city on his account). He was free to visit the city whenever and wherever he wished, including the churches. Nevertheless, he was requested not to attend high masses, in order to avoid giving offense to the worshippers. Nothing was said in the letter, in which this information was conveyed by John Cardinal Rejnštejn to the friends at home, about Hus' being prohibited from preaching or celebrating the mass, as some writers allege.[31] Rejnštejn, however, does mention that the authorities feared Hus' preaching. An absurd rumor circulated in the town that he was to preach in one of the Constance churches and "would give a ducat to everyone present." Hus never preached, although he celebrated the mass

29 Palacký, *Documenta*, p. 246.

30 *Ibid.*, pp. 79-80; my translation in *John Hus at the Council of Constance*, pp. 104-06. I there remark (n. 64) that the bishop, Otto III of Hachberg-Sausenberg, was not in Constance at the time. He was probably represented by his vicar, John Tenger. See Richental's description of the visit in Loomis, *The Council of Constance*, pp. 129-30.

31 It is so stated in C.-J. Hefele and H. Leclercq, *Histoire des conciles* (Paris, Letouzey et Ané, 1916), VII/I, pp. 164-65.

at his lodgings every day. In a postscript to the letter, apparently written by Hus himself, he jocosely remarks: "The Goose [meaning himself] is not yet cooked and is not afraid of being cooked." How mistaken he was!

The Council sessions were opened on November 16 in the cathedral, the pope presiding. Cardinal Francesco Zabarella of Florence then read the convocation decree. After the mass, the pope delivered a sermon on the text, "Speak the truth,"[32] exhorting the members to zeal in seeking the Church's peace. This meeting was thinly attended as most delegates had not yet arrived. Among the earliest were those from England and France. The eminent members of the French contingent were Cardinal Peter d'Ailly, who later became, along with his pupil, John Gerson, chancellor of the University of Paris, the principal judge of Hus, and John Mauroux, titular patriarch of Antioch. Altogether, on the opening day, there were assembled sixteen cardinals and thirty-two prelates, mostly Italian.

Despite papal assurances to the contrary, Hus' freedom was soon curtailed. Shortly after Stephen Páleč arrived, he joined Michael de Causis and the two immediately set to work. Stanislav of Znojmo did not reach Constance, for he had died at what is now Jindřichův Hradec in Bohemia. Hus' two enemies drew up a list of charges, most of which, they said, were abstracted from *De ecclesia*.[33] They accused Hus of having taught, preached, and held remanence; that a priest in mortal sin does not transubstantiate; that the Church does not consist of the pope, his cardinals, prelates, and the clergy subordinate to them; that Constantine erred in endowing the Church and that the Church should not possess property; that an ordained priest or deacon cannot be forbidden to preach; and other such accusations. Michael then "scurried around among the principal cardinals, archbishops, bishops, and other prelates,"[34]

---

[32] Zechariah 8:16.

[33] Palacký, *Documenta*, pp. 194-96. The articles bear the title "First Articles against M. J. Hus by Michael de Causis presented to Pope John XXIII."

[34] Spinka, *John Hus at the Council of Constance*, p. 101.

distributing among them copies of these charges and urging them to procure Hus' arrest.

Their endeavors finally bore fruit when, in less than a month after Hus' arrival, he was treacherously lured away from his lodgings and arrested. On November 28, the emissary who had been sent to Sigismund's court to ask for the king's consent to Hus' arrest, returned, bringing back Sigismund's permission; along with him came the king's envoys. Thereupon, a delegation consisting of two bishops, those of Trent and Augsburg, a lawyer, Dr. Ottobono, the burgomaster of Constance, and a knight, promptly visited Hus.[35] He was just then dining. The distinguished visitors told John of Chlum that they had been sent, at the pope's command, to invite Hus to an interview with the cardinals. The doughty knight, distrusting the fine speech of his visitors, warned them to do nothing which would contravene his master's safe-conduct. The bishops assured him that they came "for the sake of peace." Thereupon, Hus spoke up and signified his willingness to go to meet the cardinals, even though he had come to the city not for that but to meet the whole Council. In the meantime, however, the city guards had surrounded the house, obviously intending to take Hus by force, if he refused to go voluntarily. His landlady, Fida, comprehended the situation better than he: she answered his farewell in tears, knowing that she would see him no more.

Hus, accompanied by John of Chlum, was then led to the palace occupied by the pope, where the cardinals awaited him. They asked him about the errors and heresies which he, according to the rumor, had disseminated throughout Bohemia. He denied the accusation. After some inconsequential remarks, they left him in the custody of the guards. While waiting, he was accosted by a Franciscan friar who professed to be a simple and unlearned person. The friar asked him whether he believed that after the consecration,

---

[35] The papal notary, Cerretano, expressly recorded in his *Journal* that it was by the order of the pope and "the envoys of the king" that Hus was arrested. Loomis, *The Council of Constance*, p. 469; also Bartoš, *Čechy v době Husově*, p. 392.

the host remains bread. Hus replied, "I do not hold it." The friar, astonished, repeated his query three times; Hus denied it every time. It was then that John of Chlum interfered, roughly chiding the friar for his persistence in asking the same question. When Hus, after being further subtly interrogated, perceived that he was dealing with merely pretended ignorance, and accused the friar of double dealing, the latter left. The guards then informed him that the visitor was Dr. Andreas Didacus de Moxena, a distinguished Spanish theologian, sent by the cardinals to catch Hus in some heretical pronouncement. The cardinals were all convinced that Hus held the Wyclifite heresy of remanence; and the easiest way of convicting him was to induce him to profess it.

Toward evening, John of Chlum was told to leave, while Hus was ordered to remain. Chlum flared up in hot anger and stormed into the pope's presence. Without any circumlocution, he charged the pope with breaking his promise to protect Hus against molestation. The pope then appealed to the cardinals to bear witness that he did not order Hus' arrest. Afterward, when he was alone with Chlum, he claimed that the cardinals insisted on the arrest and that he "had to receive him as prisoner."[36] After his escape from Constance, Pope John admitted that he gave the order for Hus' arrest.

Thus Hus found himself a prisoner and remained one throughout his stay in Constance. After eight days during which he was kept in a precentor's house—the pope would not have him spend even a single night in the palace—[37] he was removed to a horrible hole of a cell in the Dominican monastery on the island off the shore. (The place is now a luxurious hotel—the Insel Hotel—the best in town.) He lay there from December 6, 1414 to March 24, 1415. Under the terrible conditions he had to endure, he fell dangerously ill. The pope sent his own physician to prison; on urgent request of the Czech and Polish nobles friendly to Hus,

---

[36] Spinka, *John Hus at the Council of Constance*, p. 116.
[37] Cerretano's *Journal*, in Loomis, *The Council of Constance*, p. 469.

he was then transferred, on January 9, to a better location in the tower. A little earlier John of Chlum succeeded in bribing the jailers to allow correspondence to pass between Hus and his friends.

The Council thereupon appointed a panel of three judges, consisting of John of Rupercissa, patriarch of Constantinople; Bishop Bernard of Città di Castello; and John of Bořenice, bishop of Lubus.[38] This commission examined Hus on December 6 as to his adherence to Wyclif's forty-five articles, confidently expecting to convict him of heresy on that ground. It must be remembered that these articles, along with Wyclif's books, had been condemned as heretical in the Spring of 1413 at the Council of Rome. Any adherence to them, therefore, constituted an *ipso facto* conviction of heresy. Hus at first refused to answer at all, on the ground that he came to the Council to present his own views, not to deal with those of Wyclif. He regarded his imprisonment as illegal. When threatened that his refusal might be construed as a confession of guilt, he yielded. The commissioners must have been rudely shaken in their preconceived assumption of Hus' guilt when he replied that he did not hold and never held thirty-three of them, while the remaining twelve might have a correct sense. This implied, of course, that in their present form they did not possess a correct sense. This failure to obtain an easy conviction of Hus then led the commission to produce a number of hostile witnesses, whom they brought into his prison at the time when Hus was dangerously ill.[39]

John of Chlum vigorously protested, on December 15 and again on December 24, against Hus' arrest by affixing proclamations at various public places, including the door of the cathedral. He also informed Sigismund of this breach of his safe-conduct. The king thereupon sent emissaries to Constance with the demand that Hus be released from

[38] The papal notary, Cerretano, lists twelve members of this commission in his *Journal* whose names do not correspond to those given above. Loomis, *The Council of Constance*, pp. 469-70.

[39] The list of the witnesses is given in my *John Hus at the Council of Constance*, pp. 117-18.

prison. He threatened, if his orders were ignored, to force open the prison door.[40] Nevertheless, the doors of the prison remained shut, and the king's threat did not materialize. Of course, if the king had consented to Hus' imprisonment in the first place, all his storming about the accomplished fact was but mere shamming. He ordered, however, that nothing of importance be done until his arrival.

Sigismund, having been crowned king of the Romans at Aachen, arrived at Überlingen with a splendid retinue on Christmas night. The next day he entered Constance and assisted the pope, in the office of deacon, in the grand mass which was then celebrated. Thereupon, he seated himself on the throne prepared for him in the cathedral.

More than a year later (March 21, 1416) Sigismund wrote the Czech estates[41] that he had intervened in Hus' behalf and had violent scenes with the pope and the cardinals. He affirmed that several times he had left the papal court in anger, and once even had left the city altogether. All in vain. The Council protested against his interference in their conduct of the work entrusted to them and threatened to suspend all action, unless he desisted. In the end he capitulated. On January 1, 1415, he consented to allow the Council to deal with Hus as it would. His safe-conduct thus proved to be another worthless piece of paper, and the royal promises were repudiated. In fact, as Cerretano informs us, Sigismund urged that "the case of John Hus and other minor problems ought not to interfere with the reform of the Church and of the Empire, which was the principal object for which the Council had been convened."[42]

Thereupon, the trial of Hus was resumed within a few

[40] Hefele and Leclercq, Histoire des conciles, VII/I, p. 179. The story is strongly suspect, for we know that Sigismund later tried to justify his faithless conduct, and was not particular as to the means he used.

[41] Ibid., p. 180; Palacký, Documenta, No. 95.

[42] Loomis, The Council of Constance, p. 476. In fact, the king's claim that he had left the city in protest against Hus' imprisonment is equally false. The only evidence of his two-day absence was recorded, for June 24, by Cardinal Fillastre; but it was on account of the dilatory proceedings against Duke John of Burgundy for his murder of Duke Louis of Orleans in 1407. Ibid., p. 249.

days. By subjecting him to a legal process, the Council made clear that it was continuing the trial which he had undergone in Rome and in which he had been condemned. From the legal point of view, this was almost certain to lead to the same result, as Hus' lawyer, John of Jesenice, fully realized when he learned of it. Thus Hus' original intention, to come to the Council to present his own views for its information, was already nullified. Hus had not been cited to the Council, but came voluntarily: This point was vital to his case. But by being subjected to a continuation of the previous trial, his case was lost at the very start. However, after protesting the procedure, Hus of necessity submitted to what he regarded as unavoidable.

He was then presented with forty-two articles newly formulated by Páleč.[43] In a letter written by Hus to his friends on January 3, he complained: "Almost the whole last night I wrote responses to the articles formulated by Páleč. He labors directly for my condemnation."[44] The articles were allegedly extracted from Hus' *De ecclesia*. Since we are familiar with the contents of that book, there is no need to recount the charges in detail. Hus branded as a lie Páleč's charge, presumably based on Hus' declaration in a sermon, that even if he were forced to recant Wyclif's articles, he would do so with his tongue but not his heart.[45] Actually, this charge was based on the falsified letter which Hus had left for his people before he started on his journey to Constance.[46] Even more absurd was the charge that upon his arrival in the city Hus wrote home that the pope and the cardinals had received him with honor. We know how honorably they received Hus when they had enticed him to leave his lodgings to speak with the cardinals! Did not his judges know it as well?

The next day John of Chlum wrote Hus that Sigismund had secured from the Council a firm promise to allow him

---

43 Palacký, *Documenta*, No. 9, pp. 204-24, where they are presented with Hus' replies.

44 Spinka, *John Hus at the Council of Constance*, No. 7, p. 249.

45 Palacký, *Documenta*, pp. 223-24, paragraphs 41-42.

46 Spinka, *John Hus at the Council of Constance*, pp. 96-98.

a public hearing.[47] This was undoubtedly the Council's reward to the king for abandoning Hus to their mercies. Chlum encouraged Hus to stand firm for his truth and "not retreat from it on account of any fear of the loss of miserable life." Is this a mere enheartening phrase, or did Chlum know of some definite threat to Hus' life? Hus himself answered Chlum the same day[48] to the effect that he could not anticipate the questions he would be asked. He informed the Council that he would answer "in due academic form," and perhaps would deliver a sermon, if he should be allowed to do so. His friends, particularly Jesenic, had been greatly disturbed on account of the examinations to which Hus had been subjected, for Jesenic realized that to allow the case to be treated as a continuation of the previous trial would be fatal. Whether or not Hus understood the matter in that sense, he now pleaded with his friends not to be disquieted, that no other means had seemed at hand. He told then of some scenes with his examiners: Patriarch Rupescissa insisted that Hus had 70,000 florins, and Michael de Causis added caustically, "What has become of the bag full of florins? How much money do the barons of Bohemia owe you?" Although Hus did not say so, is it possible that the judges were hinting at a willingness to be bribed? In a letter written to Peter of Mladoňovice, Hus actually makes a definite mention of a demand made on him by the commissioners to pay two thousand ducats "for expenses"; otherwise he would not be granted a hearing.[49]

It is a pity that our sources do not give us specific information as to whether or not the sum was paid. There are only slight hints that perhaps John of Chlum and John Cardinal of Rejnštejn did pay it. Hus, who had to borrow money for the journey from his friends, probably was not able to spare such a large sum. In the two letters written to Chlum about the same time and on March 5,[50] Hus writes definitely about

[47] *Ibid.*, No. 8, p. 252.

[48] *Ibid.*, No. 9, pp. 252-54.

[49] Novotný, *Korespondence*, No. 110, pp. 244-45; it is dated (by the editor) "after January 19."

[50] *Ibid.*, Nos. 111, 114.

the hearing he obviously expects. He asks his protector to arrange that he be placed near the king, so that the latter could hear well what he had to say. He also requests that the king be asked not to allow him—Hus—to be returned to prison after the speech. This indicates a high degree of confidence or even expectation that his declaration to the Council would be successful. In the second letter, he refers to his friend, John Cardinal of Rejnštejn, of whom he said that "he had expenses with us." Admittedly, this is a most indefinite statement; the "expenses" could have been incurred for a great many other things than the paying of the two thousand ducats demanded by the judges. Nevertheless, the sudden access of confidence that he would be heard and perhaps freed, together with the mention of "expenses" incurred for some unknown reason, suggest that perhaps the sum demanded was paid.

The letter of March 5 addressed to John of Chlum[51] contains other interesting items. Hus again mentions the matter of expense, as he did in the previous letter: "Do not vex yourself because the expenses are great; economize as much as you can. If God will liberate the goose [i.e. Hus] from prison, He will cause you to cease your regret over those expenses." Again, Hus expresses a hope to be freed from the prison on account of the "expenses," which seemed to have been shared by Chlum along with Rejnštejn. This would strengthen the supposition that the requested sum had been paid.

Moreover, Hus writes that he was touched to tears when Christian of Prachatice unexpectedly visited him in prison. Christian had come to Constance as a member of the royal embassy, perhaps to find out whether the time was propitious for requesting from the Council a permission for granting communion in both kinds to lay people.[52] There existed at home considerable agitation for this reform, which was held to be essential, because St. Paul and Christ com-

[51] *Ibid.*, No. 114.
[52] At least, this is Bartoš' guess at the purpose of Christian's visit.

manded it. Hus had been asked about it, and had even written a treatise about it soon after he came to Constance.[53] He approved the practice in principle, but advised that the Council be petitioned to permit it. Christian perhaps came to feel out the attitude of the Council toward such a radical reform. Michael de Causis, however, instigated the authorities to arrest him. After a rigorous examination, he was conditionally released, but secretly left the city.

Another matter touched upon in the letter concerned the twenty articles,[54] in which John Gerson charged Hus with heresy and error. During the previous year Archbishop Conrad had submitted to Gerson some extracts from Hus' *De ecclesia* for his opinion. The Parisian theologian condemned them in the harshest terms. Having had these charges approved by the Sorbonne, Gerson arrived at Constance on February 25, 1415, bringing them along. They formed then, along with Páleč's articles, further basis of accusation. On the same day or later Hus wrote to Mladoňovic:

O that God would grant me time to write against the lies of the chancellor of Paris, who so daringly and unjustly, before such a large multitude, was not ashamed to declare an almost complete untruth! Perhaps God will forestall my writing either by my or his death and so will decide everything better than I could have written![55]

In that same letter Hus mentions that he had again suffered excruciating pains with gall-stones, which he never had before, and with severe vomiting and fever. The attack was so serious that the guards feared he would die and led him out of the prison. It was on this occasion that Páleč greeted him before the commissioners with the brutal remark that "since the birth of Christ no more dangerous heretic has arisen, save Wyclif!" He further declared that all who had attended his preaching were infected with

---

[53] *Utrum expediat laicis fidelibus sumere sanguinem Christi sub specie vini,* in *Historia et monumenta Joannis Hus atque Hieronymi Pragensis, confessorum Christi* (Norimberg, 1715), I, pp. 52-54.

[54] *Ibid.,* I, pp. 29-30.

[55] Novotný, *Korespondence,* No. 118, p. 256.

Hus' heresy, namely remanence. This is the second time that Hus fell dangerously ill: on January 9 he had been transferred, on account of illness, to a better room in the Dominican monastery; but even so he again became ill.

About the middle of February, Bishop Nicholas of Nezero, the Prague inquisitor, who had given Hus a splendid clearance as to his orthodoxy, came to Constance as a member of the royal embassy. He was promptly seized and subjected to a harsh examination for having granted Hus so favorable a testimony. Because he had remarked in that document that he had "supped with Hus," he was derisively dubbed "supped-with-the-devil." He would have been severely punished had he not ingratiated himself with his judge, Cardinal d'Ailly, by testifying that Hus had not come to Constance of his free will, as he claimed, but had been forced to do so by the king. Bishop Nicholas was thereupon freed, and wisely concluded that Constance was no place for an honest inquisitor. He promptly left for Prague.

In the meantime, an organized movement, comprising the nobility of Bohemia and Moravia, had been waging a campaign protesting Hus' imprisonment and Sigismund's non-observance of his safe-conduct. As we have mentioned, Hus had appealed, even before his departure for Constance, to the Czech nobles gathered at Diet, and three of the most notable among them had actually addressed a letter to Sigismund, requesting him to secure for Hus a free hearing at the Council. They also inquired of Archbishop Conrad whether he knew of any heresy of Hus, to which he gave a negative answer.

In January 1415, at a meeting of the Moravian nobles held at Meziříčí, a vigorous letter of protest was adopted and sent to Sigismund, which he received at the latest by February 13. They requested him to secure Hus' release from prison and a public hearing, "For otherwise there might result harm to Your Grace and the whole Bohemian crown ..." The letter was signed personally by ten nobles.[56]

---

[56] The text of the letter is found in Spinka, *John Hus at the Council of Constance*, pp. 153-54. The case for Jesenic's authorship is argued by Kejř in his *Husitský právník*, pp. 140-46.

Kejř raises the question as to who was responsible for composing these and five subsequent letters sent to Sigismund or the Council in the course of time. They are quite similar in the recounting of events and in the biblical and other arguments. He comes to the conclusion that it is more than probable that it was John of Jesenice who, although absent from Constance, continued Hus' defense by these means. The nobles—Czech, Moravian, or even Polish—as we shall see later, turned to him as their legal adviser, knowing of his previous services in Hus' cause.

In the meantime, a most important event took place in the conduct of the Council, which had far-reaching consequences. For, despite the fact that the Council had opened its sessions early in November, it was not yet definitely organized. What business was accomplished was voted upon individually by the members of the Council. This method overwhelmingly favored the large Italian contingent brought along by Pope John. He was also well supplied with large sums of money and a plentiful number of appointments and reservations with which to buy any northern prelates who might prove to be for sale. In this way he hoped to secure a safe majority of the delegates who would support his candidacy as the pope selected from among the three claimants. His name was actually proposed in the session of December 7 by the Italian contingent.[57] Only the plea of the English delegate, Thomas Polton, that the Council await the arrival of the full English contingent, prevented the vote from being taken. The request of King Sigismund, that nothing of importance be done before his arrival, also helped to prevent the vote.

All this time John's conduct of the Council grew ever more arbitrary: he denied freedom of speech to the cardinals, even to such an outstanding one as Cardinal d'Ailly, bishop of Cambrai. This led to an increasing resentment against him. A rash of proposals aimed at his deposition soon appeared. One advocated the deposition of all three popes, particularly John, who was declared "the worst of the three,

---

[57] Louise R. Loomis, "The Organization by Nations at Constance," *Church History* (December 1932), p. 194.

a shedder of innocent blood, a Judas who sells God's service for gold and plunders the German Church."[58] The sessions of the Council were postponed several times, awaiting a fuller representation. When on January 21 the English, numbering twenty-seven and led by Robert Hallam, bishop of Salisbury, appeared, they and the Germans soon worked in comparative harmony. Nevertheless, the English were numerically the smallest delegation, having only three bishops among them. After the Italians, the French were the most numerous. Furthermore, Pope John created over fifty new prelates *in camera*.

It was, therefore, obvious that as long as the voting was by heads, there was no hope of deposing John and thereby solving the Schism in a way acceptable to all nations. By February 7 it was decided by the French, English, and German delegations that the voting was to be by nations, not by individuals.[59] Each nation as a whole then was to cast one vote, whereby the vast majority of the Italians, who possessed about as many members as the three other nations put together, were reduced to one, on equality with the rest. The cardinals did not join in this proposal, although they did not oppose it, either. The new arrangement reduced them to an anomalous position of constituting a body separate from the voting nations and without a vote of their own. Yet they realized that this *de facto* solution was the only one which offered a possibility of ending the Schism acceptable to all nations.

Pope John's schemes for dominating the Council by sheer numbers of his subordinate and suborned members was thus effectively countermanded. Any show of force on his part would only make things worse. He decided, therefore, to appear willing to cooperate with the Council, which thus freed itself from his overweening authority. To be sure, he protested against the abolition of the *de jure* method of voting, whereby the smallest delegation— the English—had

[58] *Ibid.*, p. 197.
[59] *Ibid.*, pp. 201-02; E. Delaruelle et al., *L'Eglise au temps du Grand Schisme et de la crise conciliaire, 1378-1449*, 2 vols. (Bloud & Gay, 1962-64), pp. 174-76.

as much weight in deciding matters as the largest, the Italian. When protests proved vain, he offered a vaguely worded promise to resign, after his rivals had done likewise, and had Cardinal Zabarella read it before the Council. The three nations requested a more definite statement. Thereupon, John worked out a slightly more satisfactory formula, which, however, was still not acceptable. The three nations then composed a formula of their own, which Sigismund presented to the general session. With the exception of the Italian, all other members approved it. Seeing the inevitable defeat, John, in the session of March 2, solemnly accepted it, and promised to abdicate, provided his two rivals did likewise. A great jubilation ensued, during which the *Te Deum* was sung and Sigismund, throwing himself before the pope, kissed his foot.[60]

The seeming victory of the Council over the pope was, however, of short duration. During the night of March 21, after secretly securing the armed protection of Duke Frederick of Austria, John fled, disguised as a workman, and reached Schaffhausen in safety. There he summoned the cardinals to his side with the intention of making the continuance of the Council impossible.

The pope's flight at first produced consternation at the Council; for its meeting could not be held *de jure* without the pope. Legally, therefore, the Council faced the possibility of dissolution without accomplishing any of its declared objectives: the termination of the Schism, the uprooting of heresy, and the reformation of the Church "in head and members." However, courageous voices were raised counseling radical measures, the continuance of the Council *de facto*, as the Council of Pisa had conducted its affairs despite the opposition of both popes then existing. Sigismund declared himself ready to proceed with the meetings. John Gerson preached a sermon in the name of the French

---

[60] Loomis, "Organization of Nations at Constance," pp. 205-06; see the formula of abdication in Hefele and Leclercq, *Histoire des conciles*, VII/I, p. 189; see also Cardinal Fillastre's *Diary*, in Loomis, *The Council of Constance*, pp. 218-19.

deputation, advocating that the Council continue its work without the pope. In fact, he urged that the Council proclaim itself superior to the pope. Cardinal Zabarella declared that since the Council had been convoked regularly, the flight of the pope changed nothing.[61] Dietrich of Niem clamored for John's deposition.

As for Hus, he was left in prison untended by his guards, who had followed the pope. He feared that he would have nothing to eat. In a pitiful letter written to John of Chlum[62] Hus implored him to appeal to the king to send his own guards to take over the service at the prison, "or that he free me from the prison this evening." He urged Chlum to come to see him for a talk as to what should be done, since the bishop of Constance and the cardinals declared that they "wished to have nothing to do with him." We do not know whether Chlum delivered the message to Sigismund; but the latter, instead of doing what Hus had asked for, turned the keys of the prison over to the bishop of Constance, Otto III of Hachberg, although at this crisis he could have freed Hus. The bishop the same night promptly ordered Hus transferred by boat, under the guard of 170 armed soldiers, to his own castle of Gottlieben, some miles north on the Rhine. There he was imprisoned in the upper story of an airy tower and kept in bonds during the day and chained by one hand to the wall during the night. He stayed there practically incommunicado from March 24 to June 3. With the exception of one or two letters, we have no correspondence from his pen during this period; thus, for over three months there exists almost a blank in our information about him.

Another remarkable event occurred on April 4 when Jerome of Prague secretly entered the gate of Constance, obviously in fulfillment of his promise to come to Hus' aid. Hus had warned him in his letters against such a rash and foolhardy undertaking, but the impetuous Jerome did not

[61] Delaruelle, *L'Eglise*, pp. 177, 179.
[62] Novotný, *Korespondence*, No. 121, p. 258.

heed him. Hus' friends at Constance were not only astonished but alarmed. They knew that Jerome risked the danger of being instantly apprehended, if his presence in the
city became known and his place of concealment discovered. They urged him, therefore, to leave immediately. He
obeyed and removed to nearby Überlingen. During the next
three days he wrote a number of protests against Hus' arrest, and the king's breach of his safe-conduct, which his
friends posted on the doors of churches and the cardinals'
residences. The audacious challenge was, of course, useless.
To Jerome's request for a safe-conduct, the king answered
that he had trouble enough with Hus' protection, while
the Council was willing to grant him permission to come
but not to leave.[63] He secured from the Czech lords confirmation that he had made the request. Having done
what he could in redeeming his promise to Hus, Jerome
secretly left. He reached the Bohemian border where he
was apprehended and imprisoned at Sulzbach. He was returned to Constance in chains and promptly imprisoned.[64]
When brought for examination before the Council, Jerome
was threatened with burning. He replied: "If you want my
death, may God's will be done." Bishop Hallam of Salisbury thereupon responded: "No, Jerome, for it is written,
'I desire not the death of a sinner, but that he repent and
live.' "[65] In his letter of June 7, Hus remarked: "I should
like to know how the bearded Jerome is, who refused to
listen to the counsel of his friends!"[66]

In the meantime, the Council proceeded with its reorgani-
zation. On April 6 it actually issued its decree *Sacrosancta*,
boldly declaring that it was "lawfully assembled in the
Holy Spirit . . . [and] possesses its powers directly from
Christ. All persons of whatever rank or dignity, even a
pope, are bound to obey it in all matters pertaining to faith

[63] "Vita Magistri Hieronymi pro Christi nomine Constantinse exusti,"
in V. Novotný, ed., *Fontes rerum Bohemicarum*, p. 353.
[64] Šmahel, *Jeroným Pražský*, pp. 154-57.
[65] Novotný, *Fontes rerum Bohemicarum*, p. 356.
[66] Novotný, *Korespondence*, No. 125, pp. 262-63.

and the end of Schism and the general reformation of the said Church in head and members."[67]

Thereupon, the members proceeded to implement the first objective, the termination of the Schism. Pope John was accused of a long list of crimes and malfeasance in office, totaling seventy-two charges.[68] In the end, this number was reduced to fifty-four. He was seized at Breisach on the Rhine, tried and deposed on May 29, and then imprisoned at the castle of Gottlieben. Pope Gregory XII, an old man of 89, through his delegation headed by John Dominici, cardinal of Ragusa, and Duke Charles of Rimini, offered to resign on condition that the Council agree to be convoked by him and thus "legitimized." It is remarkable that the Council accepted this astonishing proposal of an already deposed pope, for it thereby acknowledged its illegitimacy as convoked by John XXIII. In this way Gregory was recognized as the legitimate pope, whereupon he resigned on July 4. Consequently, the legitimate line of the popes is traced through Gregory, while the names of the other two popes were deleted altogether. Thus the best of modern popes, John XXIII, could assume that name as if the previous pope of that name had never existed.

Pope Benedict XIII resisted all efforts to induce him to resign. Sigismund undertook a journey to Narbonne with the view to talk him over, but in vain. Benedict was then abandoned to his fate by Spain and Portugal, and died at Peñiscola in Spain. He was deposed by the Council on July 26, 1417, claiming to the end to be the only true pope.

Since the papally appointed commission for Hus' trial lost its jurisdiction with the pope's flight, a new commission was appointed on April 6. After some changes this body was dominated by Cardinal d'Ailly, John Gerson, and Cardinal Zabarella. They all were prejudiced against Hus, considering him an already condemned heretic, although Zabarella was less biased than the other two. This is a remark-

---

[67] The text is published in my *John Hus at the Council of Constance*, p. 65.
[68] Hefele and Leclercq, *Histoire des conciles*, VII/I, pp. 234-39.

able fact, for in many of their opinions they really agreed with Hus, had they taken the trouble to learn his real views. Unfortunately, they were content to accept the calumnies of Hus' enemies for truth. Gerson, for instance, was, with the exception of Dietrich of Niem, the strongest and most consistent critic of the papacy as an institution. On May 19 he preached a sermon which was regarded as "a commentary on the decree of superiority of the Council" over the pope.[69] In the later decree *Frequens*, of which he was the principal author, the papacy was reduced to the status of constitutional monarchy subjected to the periodic sessions of the Council. He held that the Council could be convoked, under certain conditions, without the consent of the pope, or even contrary to his express prohibition. In these and many other opinions he actually agreed with Hus' milder strictures of the papacy. Gerson, however, because of his refusal to credit Hus' protestations of the charges of which he was not guilty, became an accomplice in Hus' judicial murder. De Vooght declares that Gerson was an authoritarian by nature, "a born papalist."[70]

Cardinal d'Ailly, who in his younger years was quite radical in his views,[71] moderated his opinions considerably after Pope John granted him the red hat (1411). Under the circumstances confronting him at Constance, he changed his mind as to the Council's "infallibility." He also developed a sense of solidarity with the cardinal college in conformity with the corporate interests of that body. Like Gerson, he refused to believe that Hus' protestations represented his real opinions and continued as a nominalist to believe that Hus must be a remanentist.

De Vooght adds to these two men—Hus' principal judges,

[69] Paul de Vooght, "Jean Huss et ses juges," in *Das Konzil von Konstanz*, p. 167.

[70] *Ibid.*, p. 171. A sketch of Gerson's life is found in my *John Hus at the Council of Constance*, pp. 17-19.

[71] Francis Oakley, *The Political Thought of Pierre d'Ailly* (New Haven and London, Yale University Press, 1964), pp. 22-33; also Irwin W. Raymond, transl., "D'Ailly's Epistola diaboli Leviathan," in *Church History*, XXII (1953), pp. 181 ff.; also my *John Hus at the Council of Constance*, pp. 13-17.

whose opinions proved decisive in condemning him as a heretic—the papal secretary, Dietrich of Niem, who was the most radical of them all. De Vooght pronounces his views as "typically Wyclifite."[72] Dietrich identified the true Church with the Church apostolic, not papal. Christ alone is the head of the Church, just as Hus never tired of declaring. Yet Dietrich was most intemperate, even raging, against the Czechs, whom he called "unworthy of the name of Christians" and "rascally." Hus was the chief heretic and his *De ecclesia* was as inimical to the catholic faith as was the Koran of "the damned Mohamed."[73]

Despite this increasingly threatening attitude of the Council to Hus, there were apparently rumors circulating as far as Aragon that Sigismund intended to free him. Perhaps they were much belated reports of the king's supposedly stormy defense of his safe-conduct after arriving in Constance on Christmas, 1414. At any rate, King Ferdinand of Aragon, perhaps incited to it by Dr. Didachus de Moxena, the "simple friar" who had attempted to snare Hus in an incriminating remark, wrote Sigismund two letters, replete in Biblical quotations and pious exhortations, imploring him "not to release that wicked man that he might not persuade the people, nor that his false heresies be publicly heard, but that he be immediately punished . . ."[74]

Ferdinand need not have been apprehensive. About a week after he had written the letters (there is no mention when they were received), the Council undertook to deal with Wyclif and his books.[75] To be sure, he had been condemned two years before at the Council of Rome and his books had been burned in front of the basilica of St. Peter. That Council, however, had been so thinly attended that it was thought proper to deal with the subject again. The examination included the forty-five articles. There was no doubt what the result would be, and the condemnation

[72] De Vooght, "Jean Huss et ses juges," p. 172.
[73] *Ibid.*, p. 173.
[74] Spinka, *John Hus at the Council of Constance*, pp. 155-57. Both letters are dated April 28, 1415.
[75] Hefele and Leclercq, *Histoire des conciles*, VII/I, pp. 223 ff.

caused no surprise to anyone. Thus the judgment formerly passed by regional and university authorities now received conciliar approval, binding on all. Henceforth, to convict anyone of Wyclifism was an *ipso facto* conviction of heresy. For that reason Hus' judges worked hard to prove valid the charge of Wyclifism against him.

If these actions were potentially highly dangerous to Hus, his friends now exerted themselves even harder to come to his defense. They were represented by the Czech, Moravian, and Polish nobles, either meeting at home or in attendance at Constance. The earliest of these is the letter of protest and of pleading sent by the nobles of Moravia assembled at Brno on May 8, 1415.[76] It is addressed to Sigismund and pleads that Hus "be freed from the cruel prison and receive a public hearing, instead of being so surreptitiously and erroneously slandered, contrary to right, justice, and the safe-conducts."

A similar letter was written by the nobles of Bohemia, assembled in Prague on May 12.[77] The letters are so similar in their content that Kejř's suggestion spoken of previously, that all the protests of the Czech, Moravian and other nobles were written by the same man, John of Jesenice, finds strong support. They emphasize that after the pope's flight, Hus could have been freed by Sigismund. Unless the king liberates him, "there would result, on account of such illegal and unjust imprisonment of a just man, first of all a great injury to Your Grace, and likewise to the entire Bohemian nation."

Whether these letters had any effect upon Sigismund we do not know: but neither do we have any indication that he raised a finger to comply with the requests. Of more effect was the petition of the Czech and Polish nobles actually present in Constance, which was submitted to the deputies of the Council on May 13.[78] If this view of the events

---

[76] Spinka, *John Hus at the Council of Constance*, pp. 158-59.

[77] *Ibid.*, pp. 159-62; also Kejř, *Husitský právnik*, pp. 141-50.

[78] *Ibid.*, pp. 123-26. It was formerly thought that Peter of Mladoňovice composed this document; but Kejř argues vigorously for Jesenic's authorship. See his *Husitský právnik*, p. 142.

so quickly following each other is correct, it would bear witness to the close contact between the Czech and Moravian nobles and the Council. The petition is a long, legally worded document, written most probably by John of Jesenice and sent to Constance. After reciting the familiar story of the seizure of Hus despite his safe-conduct, the lords demanded that he receive a public hearing "in order that he might publicly render account of his faith." They warned that there was danger in delay, hinting at Hus' deteriorated physical condition. Furthermore, they complained that "certain traducers and enemies of the honor and fame of the . . . illustrious kingdom of Bohemia" had informed some members of the Council that "the sacrament of the most precious blood of the Lord is being carried about Bohemia in bottles and that cobblers are now hearing confessions and administering the most holy body of the Lord to others." The lords besought the members of the Council not to believe "such false detractors, for these perverse defamers of the said kingdom tell lies."

When the second paragraph of this petition, dealing with the sacramental abuses in Bohemia, was read, Bishop John of Litomyšl, the only Czech bishop present, rose up and demanded that he be given an opportunity to answer these charges. He was granted the permission for May 16.

On that day the bishop's answer was read by his official.[79] He not only confirmed the report concerning the "Wyclifites," but proudly asserted that "to uproot this sect I have labored along with other prelates, doctors, masters, and countless other Catholics . . . to defend Christ's faith." He professed to have done so "not to disgrace the kingdom itself . . . but rather for the honor of the kingdom . . .; for the followers of this sect in many cities, villages, and places of that kingdom, laymen of both sexes, commune in both kinds of bread and wine and persistently teach that this is the way communion must be administered." He furthermore adduced a case when a certain woman had snatched the host from the hands of a priest and administered the communion

---

[79] *Ibid.*, pp. 127-29.

to herself and others. He appealed to the Council to investigate these occurrences and "provide a fitting remedy for it." He repudiated as calumny the aspersion of the nobles that he and his party were "defamers, traducers, and false and iniquitous enemies of that kingdom of Bohemia," but turned the charges on the nobles themselves.

The petition of the Czech and Polish nobles was orally responded to by Bishop Gerard de Puy of Carcassonne, but the text of his speech is not extant. It may, however, be reconstructed from the reply made to it by the petitioning nobles on May 18.[80] The nobles denied that they were ill-informed on certain points. One of these was that Hus had received the safe-conduct fifteen days after his arrest. The nobles replied that one of their number, John of Chlum, on the very day Hus had been arrested, told the pope, when he inquired about it, that Hus had the safe-conduct and that the cardinals present heard it. Lord John afterward showed the document to "counts, bishops, knights, squires, and the notable citizens of this city of Constance," and called upon them for confirmation of his statement. He also appealed for support of all those who had been in King Sigismund's presence when the safe-conduct had been granted.

Furthermore, the objection that Hus had been condemned for non-appearance at the curia, and thereafter remained excommunicated for five years without troubling himself about its annulment, but continued to preach even in Constance, the lords likewise denied. They professed to know nothing about the citation except by rumor. They urged, however, that Hus had sent his procurators who had presented his reasonable excuses for his non-appearance. These legal representatives were, however, imprisoned. As for continuing to preach after being excommunicated, he had done so under appeal. As for his preaching in Constance, the nobles cited John of Chlum's positive testimony that Hus had "not taken a single step outside the house in this city to the day and hour of his arrest." The nobles concluded by thanking the members of the Council for

[80] *Ibid.*, pp. 129-33.

having "favorably responded" to the request for a speedy trial of Hus.

The Czech nobles (without the Polish group) then answered on May 31 the statement of Bishop John of Litomyšl[81] as follows: They declared that they did not believe what Bishop John had said about the communion in both kinds being practiced in Bohemia. They demanded that a more convincing proof be first brought forth by him. If such a proof were produced, the lords pledged themselves to "devote their powers . . . to mitigate and eradicate" the practice. They furthermore did not accept the bishop's statement that he had reported the practice "for the honor and protection of the forementioned kingdom." They asserted on the contrary that "he has shown himself as doing or having done otherwise." If he could prove that he did it for reasons alleged, they were willing "to labor for the same end by their counsels and aid." To his charge that not he but they were the defamers of the kingdom, the nobles angrily retorted that he had slandered them. "Were it not for his episcopal dignity, they would retort more harshly to his accusation . . ." They asserted that their own and their forefathers' reputation was well known, while "they have heard nothing of the sort about his own progenitors and forefathers." Finally, they replied to the bishop's request for their names "that he might know whom to answer," that they indeed were willing to give him not only their own but their forefathers' names. "They did not ask for his name, knowing well who his progenitors were"—an obvious reference to the bishop's illegitimate birth.

This slugging match between the Council, Bishop John, and the Czech and Polish nobles being over, another protest of the Moravian nobles was read to the deputies.[82] The nobles testified that Hus was orthodox in his public professions, citing the text of one of them, and that the charges against him were made in a biased form. They demanded that he be "fairly heard by learned men so that he could

81 *Ibid.*, pp. 133-36.
82 *Ibid.*, pp. 136-41.

freely state his own views"; and they offered guarantee for his person if he were released from prison until his presence at the trial was required. To this demand John Mauroux, the patriarch of Antioch, replied on behalf of the deputies of the Council.[83] He asserted that the truth of the matter as to whether the accusers or Hus were right would become evident during the trial. He gave the same answer to the charge that the articles accusing Hus had been falsified. Concerning the guarantee, he replied that "if a thousand such guarantors were offered, it is against the conscience of them, the deputies, to surrender such a man into the hands of the guarantors; for under no circumstances is he to be trusted." This was then a condemnation of Hus even before the trial began—an eloquent indication of the mind of the Council. Finally, Mauroux declared that Hus was to receive a public hearing on June 5 and that the deputies "were willing to deal kindly with him."

During all these protests and the Council's replies to them, Hus was visited only once by his judge, Cardinal d'Ailly (May 18). The cardinal brought with him eight representatives of the Council, two from each nation. D'Ailly obviously hoped that the promised public hearing and the trial of Hus might be obviated, if Hus could at last be induced to recant. The severe conditions to which Hus had been subjected at Gottlieben were aimed at softening the prisoner and making him more amenable to the wishes of the Council. Hus, however, refused both the blandishments and the threats, and insisted on being granted a free hearing before the whole Council. He promised to submit to its decisions, if he were proved wrong on the basis of Scripture. The delegation returned to Constance disappointed.

The controversy with Bishop John of Litomyšl brought to the attention of the Council the matter of communion in both elements of bread and wine. The abuses which he cited might or might not have actually occurred; we have no evidence one way or the other. The fact, however, re-

[83] *Ibid.*, pp. 141-42.

mains that in some churches in Prague clerical members of the evangelical party had made a beginning of such communion. Among them were Nicholas of Dresden, Christian of Prachatice, and above all Jakoubek of Stříbro. It appears that the agitation for granting the cup to the laity originated in the report which Jerome of Prague, who had visited Poland and Lithuania in 1413, had brought back to Prague. In the latter country he attended, to the scandal of the Roman Catholic clergy, services in Orthodox churches, where he observed the granting of the cup to the laity. When he returned and told his friends about it, his report caused a sensation among them. Jakoubek was particularly impressed. He began to study the question on the basis of historical sources, particularly of Gratian's *Decretum*. He found that the communion had been administered in both elements up to some two centuries before.

Jakoubek, in his zeal for the restoration of the primitive Church order, brought the discussion of this important matter to the forum of the university. There is no record of the procedure;[84] nevertheless, Andrew of Brod, a member of the theological faculty, had attempted previously to dispute Jakoubek's arguments, but failed. Now he kept his peace. Either then or previously, Jakoubek communicated with Hus at Krakovec, asking for his opinion. Hus approved the granting of the cup to the laity in principle, but counseled a delay in actual practice. Jakoubek promised to wait. However, when Hus left for Constance Jakoubek, in his zeal for doing what was right, actually began the practice along with a few other friends. There is uncertainty as to the priority. It is most likely that Jakoubek began the practice on October 28, along with some of his friends.[85] Be that as it may, the initiation of the granting of the cup to the laity during the Hussite Wars became so closely identified with the cause of reform that the very banners of the Hussite

[84] F. M. Bartoš deals with this whole subject in "Velké výročí české reformace," *Kostnické Jiskry*, 1964, No. 37.

[85] The sequence of the introduction of the communion in both elements is found in T. Č. Zelinka, "Martin a Michal," in *Kostnické Jiskry*, 1964, No. 37.

armies bore the emblem of the cup in red in a black field. In the Utraquist Church, the communion *sub utraque specie* constituted the principal difference between its sacramental ministrations and those of the Catholic Church.

To return to the fate of the newly established practice as it concerned Hus at the Council of Constance. Even prior to his imprisonment, he wrote a treatise dealing with the subject, as has already been mentioned. Nevertheless, his friends at home had requested John of Chlum that he ask for Hus' opinion. He answered on January 4, 1415[86] that he had no more to say than he had written in the above-mentioned treatise, except that "the gospels and Paul's epistle definitely state so and that the early Church observed the practice." Now, when the matter was brought to the attention of the Council by Bishop John, it was referred to a commission of theologians, and on June 15 the decision was reached: the communion *sub utraque specie* was prohibited to the lay people and infants except under certain conditions, as being against the laudable custom of the Church. For it is to be believed that the whole body of Christ is contained in either of the elements. All ecclesiastical authorities are commanded, under pain of excommunication, to punish those who should transgress this order.[87] Hus, writing to Havlík, implored him not to oppose the granting of the cup and added: "Now the Council, giving 'custom' as the reason, has condemned the lay participation in the cup as error. Whoever would practice it, unless he recover his senses, shall be punished as a heretic. Alas! now malice condemns Christ's institution as an error!"[88]

[86] Novotný *Korespondence*, No. 106, pp. 239-41. The title of the treatise is "Utrum expediat laicis fidelibus sumere sanguinem Christi sub specie vini."

[87] Hefele and Leclercq, *Histoire des conciles*, VII/I, pp. 284-87, where the official text is published.

[88] Novotný, *Korespondence*, No. 141, pp. 294-95.

Chapter IX

At the Council of
Constance II

At last the long-awaited day (June 5) arrived
when Hus was to be granted a public hearing! Two days
before, he had been transferred from the castle of Gottlieben
to the prison in the Franciscan monastery, located near St.
Stephen's church. It was in the refectory of the monastery
that his examinations were held. At first the session was
conducted in Hus' absence. The articles, allegedly drawn
from his books and the testimonies of witnesses, were read,
followed by the garbled version of the letter he had left behind before starting on his journey to Constance. Thus,
despite the solemn promises made by both Sigismund and
the Council that Hus was to be given a free hearing, it
turned out that he was to be judged in his absence and
brought into the session only to hear the sentence! Fortunately, in some unexplained way a retainer of John of
Chlum was present at the meeting, and hastened to inform
Peter of Mladoňovice, who in turn alerted John of Chlum
and Wenceslas of Dubá. They immediately sought out the
king and told him of the proceedings which were being carried out in Hus' absence. Sigismund, undoubtedly much an-
noyed, sent his courtiers, Louis of the Palatinate and Frederick, burgrave of Nuremberg, to the Council, forbidding
it to proceed without Hus. Whatever decisions they had already arrived at were to be reported to him in writing.

John of Chlum and Wenceslas of Dubá also requested
the two princes to take to the Council three of Hus' books—
*De ecclesia, Contra Stanislaum,* and *Contra Paletz*— in order
to prove that the articles against Hus had been falsely abstracted. Quite properly, the princes required that the Council, after examining the books, return them to the nobles.

Hus was thereupon brought into the assembly, since he

258

was imprisoned in the same monastery. His friends, the two Czech lords and Peter, were not admitted. When shown the books, Hus inspected them and acknowledged them as his, adding that he was ready to amend whatever was proved to have been stated erroneously. Thereupon, the examination proceeded. But so many members shouted at him at the same time that he was not able to answer amidst the confusion. His friends, who apparently stood outside the refectory or behind the door, heard the commotion but could not distinguish the words. Despite that, Peter reported that Hus turned hither and yon in a vain effort to answer the shouts. When he tried to explain his own version of the accusations which ascribed a wrong sense to him, the members of the Council would not let him speak but shouted: "Leave off your sophistry and say 'Yes' or 'No.' "[1] When he remained silent, concluding that it was useless to answer the dismal clamor, they immediately interpreted this as an admission of error. Finally, the presiding officers, seeing the impossibility of conducting an examination under such disorderly circumstances, adjourned the session to June 7. We are not told why they did not establish order in the proceedings.

On his way back to prison, Hus passed by his friends who, instead of encouraging him to steadfastness, were themselves encouraged by him. When he said to them: "Do not fear for me!" they answered that they did not fear, and he responded, "I know well, I know well!"

We have additional information about the events of June 5 from Hus' own report, written the same day and sent to his friends in Constance.[2] He states joyfully that two articles brought against him were already eliminated. Peter, who could not know this since he was not admitted to the session, does not record it. We cannot, therefore, be certain which articles Hus refers to. He mentions how the members shouted at him "like the Jews had done to Jesus." But surpris-

[1] The whole scene, as described by Peter, is found in Matthew Spinka, ed. and transl., *John Hus at the Council of Constance* (New York and London, Columbia University Press, 1965), pp. 165-66.
[2] *Ibid.*, No. 10, pp. 254-55.

ingly, he chides his friends for offering to the two princes, besides the books mentioned by Peter, his *Against a Hidden Adversary*.[3] For some reason he supposed that they had offered the Council this treatise along with the others. It is rather puzzling why Hus wanted this treatise, written probably against Maurice Rvačka, the inquisitor, withheld from the Council. His judges could get much the same material from the works submitted. When his friends assured him that they had not offered it, he expressed his satisfaction that "the hidden remained hidden." He was glad that the princes had stipulated that the books be returned; for some members, particularly Michael de Causis, had shouted the demand that they be burned. He further sadly remarked that he had not a single friend among the members except "Pater," a term often used for John Cardinal of Rejnštejn, and a Polish doctor, most probably Dr. Paul Włodkowicz, dean of the faculty of theology at the University of Cracow. He had known the Pole in Prague, when he was a student there.[4] Hus further mentions that the presidents of the Council did not allow him to discuss his concept of the Church. "If only I could be granted a hearing that I might reply to the arguments of those who wish to impugn the articles stated in the treatises!" he sighed. "I imagine that many who now shout would turn dumb!" That, however, was exactly what, throughout the examinations, he was not allowed to do. It was against established principles for the Council to argue with a condemned heretic. Hus was compelled to reply to cunningly devised and distorted charges of matters he did not teach, and was never permitted to state freely what he did hold and teach.

On June 7 there occurred an almost complete eclipse of the sun. An hour after, Hus was again brought into the refectory of the Franciscan monastery, where his examina-

[3] *Contra occultum adversarium*, in *Historia et monumenta Joannis Hus atque Hieronymi Pragensis, confessorum Christi*, 2 vols. (Norimberg, 1715), I, pp. 168-79.

[4] F. M. Bartoš, "Veliké dílo protihusitské polemiky," in *Jihočeský sborník historický*, XIII (1940), p. 16, where he identified the two friends of Hus at the Council with the two above-mentioned persons.

tion was held under the chairmanship of Cardinal d'Ailly. This time King Sigismund was present, and the two Czech nobles with Peter came in along with his entourage. The king, however, arrived late, after the proceedings had begun. Accordingly, Peter could not from his own knowledge describe the examination completed prior to the time he arrived.[5] The proceeding then dealt with the testimony of witnesses, both in Prague and in Constance. They were not mentioned by name, but only by their titles. Hus was again charged with holding remanence, to which he replied that he had protested only against an incorrect definition of the eucharist by Archbishop Zbyněk by explaining its correct, orthodox understanding. In this claim he was wholly right. But that was not enough for Cardinal d'Ailly: somebody the night before had suggested to him to convict Hus of remanence on the basis of philosophical realism. Such philosophical problems were not a proper subject for a strictly theological examination, although they might have been suitable enough for an academic disputation. Hus replied by reaffirming the dogma of transubstantiation, no matter what the logical consequences of the Wyclifite realism might be. Several Englishmen could not resist entering the fray, but were ignominiously refuted by Hus. Thereupon John Stokes of the University of Cambridge, with whom Hus had had an exchange of arguments over Wyclif in Prague some time before, spoke up asserting that he had seen on that visit a treatise ascribed to Hus that taught remanence. Hus flatly called this a lie.

The attempt to convict Hus of remanence, however, was not abandoned even then. Much testimony was brought forth against him that apparently early in his ministry, even prior to his ordination, he had defended that doctrine. Cardinal Zabarella then pointed out that "well-nigh twenty witnesses" affirmed the charge, and inquired what he, Hus,

---

[5] The whole proceeding is described in my *John Hus at the Council of Constance*, pp. 167-81, and is recounted in considerable detail in my *John Hus' Concept of the Church* (Princeton, Princeton University Press, 1966) , pp. 360-65.

had to say to it. When Hus solemnly called upon God and his conscience that he had never preached the tenet nor had it ever entered his heart, Cardinal d'Ailly sternly declared: "We cannot judge according to your conscience, but according to what has been proved . . . and some things you have confessed . . . We must believe them." He further reproved Hus for having suspected even Stephen Páleč of unfairness and bias, and above all, for having similarly accused John Gerson "than whom surely no more renowned doctor could be found in all Christendom!" If any proof of d'Ailly's prejudice against Hus were needed, it is supplied in this angry outburst of his. After all, the commission of which he himself was the head had rejected as unfounded twenty-three of the thirty-four articles selected by Páleč. Moreover, if we recall the former trumped-up charges in Páleč's polemics against Hus—which the Council did not know—we have even more concrete evidence of the sheer fatuity and naïveté of d'Ailly's judgment that Páleč was more than lenient in his treatment of Hus. As for Gerson, his ignorance of Hus' real position was so great that he actually identified Hus' views with those of Wyclif, without examining them. So much for his theological "renown"!

Hus was further accused of objecting to the condemnation of Wyclif's forty-five articles. He replied that he did not consent to the doctors' verdict that *all* the articles were "heretical, erroneous, or scandalous." He was further inaccurately accused of having written that a priest in mortal sin did not validly administer the sacraments. He corrected the charge by pointing out that his book said that the priest does not administer them *worthily*, although validly; and by looking up the passage, the judges had to admit that he was right. Páleč also joined the testimony concerning the forty-five articles of Wyclif, claiming that Hus adhered to them. Hus replied frankly and plainly that he did not obstinately adhere to any of them, but that he wished to hear what Scriptural proofs there existed for their condemnation.

Of course, the accusers did not fail to bring against Hus

the charge that he had publicly expressed the wish that his soul might be where Wyclif's was. Hus admitted having said that twelve years before, when he did not know Wyclif's theological works, which were not then available in Bohemia. Further, he declared that he knew of no ground in Scripture or revelation for asserting positively whether Wyclif were saved or damned; but that he hoped he was saved. He again explicitly affirmed that he defended no known error of Wyclif.

His accusers further objected that he had appealed to God and Christ when his appeal to the pope proved futile. Hus resolutely defended the appeal as the most effective method of proceeding when all other means failed—a remark which caused much laughter.

To the charge that he was chiefly responsible for the "expulsion of the German masters," he replied by recounting the actual historical sequence of events. He singled out in the audience the former German dean of the faculty of arts at Prague University, Albert Warentrapp, for confirmation of his account. Instead of Warentrapp, however, it was King Wenceslas' diplomatic representative, Dr. John Náz, a Prague German, who requested to be heard. He then recounted his version of the scene between the king and Hus with Jerome, wherein Wenceslas threatened to burn them. Páleč promptly rose and mendaciously asserted that four doctors of the theological faculty—Stanislav and Peter of Znojmo, John Eliášův, and Stephen Páleč himself—had been exiled from the country "on his [Hus'] account and order." This was a barefaced lie; they suffered the punishment for refusing to accept the decision of the royal commission investigating the charges against Hus, after they had consented to abide by such final verdict.

As a parting shot, D'Ailly then charged that Hus, despite his repeated claims that he had come to Constance unconstrained and freely, had in fact been compelled to do so by the king. It will be remembered that this was based on the forced confession of Bishop Nicholas of Nezero. Hus stoutly reaffirmed his assertion that he had come freely and that neither Sigismund nor Wenceslas could have forced him to come. This was then confirmed by John of Chlum, who said that he himself would have been willing to protect Hus "whether it would have pleased or displeased anyone."

Thereupon, Cardinal d'Ailly spoke in a seemingly fatherly mien, advising Hus to submit to the Council. He assured him that "the Council would deal mercifully with you." Sigismund also added his word to that of the cardinal. Apparently speaking to the previously made statement that he had given Hus his safe-conduct fifteen days after his arrest, the king asserted that it was not true: he had granted him the document even before Hus started on his journey. This, of course, was a mistake on Sigismund's part; the safe-conduct was issued to Hus while he was already on the way, and delivered to him two days after he had reached Constance. It may be, however, that Sigismund meant that he had given Hus a binding *promise* of the safe-conduct before he left Bohemia, which, of course,. was true. Sigismund then added that the protection afforded Hus included his free public hearing by the Council. Then he went on to say, although he surely must have known better, that the members of the Council "have given you a public, peaceable, and honest hearing here." He should have blushed when he uttered such a manifest falsehood, but Sigismund's prevarications were notorious. Sigismund then counseled Hus to accept the cardinal's fatherly admonition "to hold nothing obstinately . . . and to offer yourself wholly to the mercy of the sacred Council." In case he refused, the king assured him that he was not willing to defend any heresy. In fact, in such a case "I myself would kindle [the fire] to burn" you!

Thereupon, after other charges against Hus had been made, he was led back in chains to prison.

In a letter written the same day,[6] Hus expressed his gratefulness to John of Chlum for the manly defense he

6 My translation in *John Hus at the Council of Constance*, pp. 255-56.

had offered at the Council in Hus' behalf. He also rejoiced that he was receiving better food during these trial days; nevertheless, he again mentioned suffering with the toothache. His only reference to the process at the Council was that he supposed "there would be greater discipline and decency."

The next day, Wednesday, June 8, Hus was again brought into the refectory of the Franciscan monastery, where the trial was held. King Sigismund presided along with the judges, among whom Cardinal d'Ailly was preeminent. Again the king arrived late and with him the Czech nobles with Peter, so that the tenth article was read at the time they came. The procedure was based on the thirty-nine articles abstracted from Hus' *De ecclesia, Contra Paletz*, and *Contra Stanislaum*. They were compared with the text of Hus' own books, d'Ailly remarking in some instances that the text of the book was worse than that of the abstracted articles. In reality, the changes thus observed by d'Ailly tended to subvert Hus' real meaning. The largest number, twenty-six, were drawn from *De ecclesia*, while the remaining thirteen were divided between the other two treatises in the proportion of seven to six.[7]

The first eight articles dealt with the concept of the Church: it is the totality of the predestinate, no member of which falls away from it because he is bound to it by predestinating love; even those predestinate not at present in grace are actually members of it, while the foreknown are never of its membership. This totality of the predestinate constitutes the holy Church universal. Mladoňovic, who cited the actual text from Hus' own copy, pointed out the inaccuracies of these accusations. The Council fathers interpreted the presumably incriminating charges in the sense that none other but the Church of the predestinate exists, i.e., that Hus denied the very existence of the Church militant. As we know from our previous acquaintance with his teaching, he consistently asserted that the Church militant exists, but is composed of both the predestinate and the fore-

[7] *Ibid.,* pp. 183-201.

known. The latter will be separated from the former only in the Day of Judgment, so that the Church triumphant will then indeed comprise only the predestinate.

Then followed articles 9-17, dealing with the pope and the cardinals. Since Mladoňovic arrived when article 10 was read, he was henceforth able to report Hus' own comments along with the pertinent text of *De ecclesia*. The articles stated that Apostle Peter was not the principal head of the holy catholic Church. Hus, of course, did assert it, for Christ alone was such a head. The next article asserted that the pope is Christ's vicar in the Church militant only if he follows Christ and His virtues. If he does not so follow Christ, he is "the messenger of Antichrist and an adversary of Peter." The next charge stated that all simoniacs were condemned as faithless, wrongly regarding the sacraments and all the rest of the Church's ministration; this article does not specifically mention the pope, but since he too may be simoniac, he is thus included. To this Hus added that such people lack faith formed by love; hence their faith is dead, and in that sense they are "faithless."

The next article came closer to an attack on the papacy: it asserted that the papal dignity and preeminence were conferred on the pope by the Caesars. Hus amplified the charge by stating that the temporal power and government were bestowed on Pope Sylvester by Emperor Constantine, while the spiritual office originated from Christ. By ignoring this important distinction, the Council distorted Hus' meaning. Cardinal d'Ailly, perhaps feeling the force of the argument, tried to impute an error to Hus' formulation by remarking that it was the Council of Nicaea rather than Emperor Constantine which passed the decree endowing the Church. Anyone knowing the history of the Council of Nicaea is aware that the cardinal was wrong. To d'Ailly's further query why Hus ascribed the grant to Constantine, the latter replied: "Because of the Donation [of Constantine]." Article 16 further adds that Hus taught that it was on account of the Donation that the pope was called "the most holy." The text of *De ecclesia* confirms that sentence, but adds that if the pope "follows Christ in humility, gentleness, patience and labor from the great bond of love, then he is holy." In other treatises Hus was accustomed to make a distinction between a *worthy* pope, possessing, besides the legitimate election, also the necessary character qualifications, and the pope merely legitimately elected.

Articles 13 to 15 assert that Hus taught that no one can know without revelation whether he or another is actually the head of a particular Church, nor should it be believed that every pontiff is the head of a particular Church; for that depends on whether or not he is of the predestinate. If he is not, then he is not even a member of the Church, not to speak of being its head. For the power of such a foreknown pope is "frustrated" as to merit . . . [but] not as far as the office is concerned." He was asked where this explanation is found in the book, and he referred them to the second chapter of *Contra Paletz*.

Article 17 dealt with the cardinals, asserting the necessity of the same "following of Christ" for them as was demanded of the pope. Cardinal d'Ailly naturally took umbrage at this demand and sharply reprimanded Hus for not "observing moderation"; there was no need, he said, to preach such things to the people, since the cardinals were not present. Hus replied that his sermons were attended by priests and learned men and that he spoke of the cardinals to warn his hearers what to guard against. This did not satisfy the cardinal: he harshly declared that Hus did wrong and was "destroying the status of the Church."

The remaining charges were of miscellaneous character. Hus was accused of teaching that a heretic should not be punished by death, but only censured. Hus commented that he had insisted that a heretic should first be instructed from the Scriptures, and only if he had not been willing to desist should he be punished, "even corporeally." He did not specifically say that the heretic should be put to death—for he formerly had objected to the capital punishment for heresy. But the Council lector continued to read the text to the effect that Hus had stated that the Jews who had surrendered Jesus to Pilate had greater sin than Pilate himself. This aroused the Council fathers to a fury, for after all they themselves were engaged in proceedings which would certainly lead to Hus' death for heresy. When Hus confirmed the words of the text, they rightly applied it to the Prague doctors' verdict rather than to the Jews.

The next charge stated that "secular nobles should compel priests to observe the law of Christ." The text did not actually mention priests. This was followed by an accusation that "ecclesiastical obedience is the invention of the priests beyond the express command of Scripture." In this form it was indeed objectionable. The text, however, merely defined the different meanings of the term "obedience": namely, spiritual (i.e., Scriptural), secular (according to civil law), and ecclesiastical (according to ordinances passed by the Church). Thus the charge distorted Hus' sense.

Article 21 stated that if an excommunicate appealed to Christ, he was protected in the highest degree. This wording is not in *De ecclesia*. There Hus explains that when his appeal to the curia proved futile, he at last, as the final resort, appealed to Christ "Who is superior to any pope whatsoever." This was a sore point with the Council, which regarded itself as the supreme arbiter in all matters, even to the submission of the popes to itself. D'Ailly, therefore, ironically inquired whether Hus thought himself above St. Paul, who appealed to Caesar, not Christ. Hus aptly replied that if someone of those present appealed to Caesar, he would be condemned as a heretic, for the Council alone claimed that prerogative. Moreover, Paul, in appealing to Caesar, was obeying Christ, who had bidden him to do so. He, too, appealed to Christ only as the final instance, and continued to perform his ministerial duties under appeal. Cardinal Zabarella ordered his notary to record this statement, as if it were of special importance.

The next article asserted that "if a man is wicked, whatever he does, he does wickedly." The text explained that by wickedness was meant mortal sin; so that a man in mortal sin can do no righteous act in the eyes of God. D'Ailly then quoted the Scriptural saying that we all sin. Hus objected that this referred to venial sins, which did not deprive man of his virtuous status.

It was, thereupon, affirmed that Hus taught that a good priest ought to preach despite "pretended excommunication." The text stressed preaching as the first duty of priests and quoted Augustine's condemnation of those "who are damnedly silent." Hus added the comment that he spoke of a "pretended," i.e., unjust, excommunication.

The next article again stressed that a priest, once he accepted the priestly office, should carry out its duties, an alleged excommunication notwithstanding. This was followed by a statement that ecclesiastical censures were devised by the clergy for the purpose of dominating the laity. The statement as such was not in the book, anymore than the next, asserting that an interdict should not be imposed on the people for the sake of one person so punished. These two articles represent the substance of the matter treated in the last chapters of *De ecclesia*. Hus supported the argument by commenting that neither Christ nor Paul imposed penalties for the persecution they suffered, but commanded their followers to pray for their tormentors.

Thereupon, there followed charges drawn from the treatise *Contra Paletz*.[8] The first of these accusations again affirmed that a pope, bishop, or prelate in mortal sin was not pope, bishop, or prelate. As has already been mentioned, Hus modified such a statement by the saving adjective "a worthy pope," and so on, even though by reason of a legitimate election he was a *de facto* holder of the office. Hus added that the distinction applied to kings as well, illustrating it by God's rejection of Saul for disobeying His command. This, of course, caused a sensation. Sigismund had then been speaking through a window with princes Louis and Frederick, and thus missed the remark. He was saying that there never existed a greater heretic than Hus. The prelates shouted that he be called and ordered Hus to repeat the statement. The king, upon hearing it, remarked: "John

8 *Ibid.*, pp. 201-09.

Hus, no one lives without sin." D'Ailly could not forego the opportunity of adding a word prejudicial to Hus (after all, the king did not need it, since he had just declared Hus to be the greatest heretic!), by commenting that it was not enough for Hus to despise the spiritual order, he must wish to overthrow the secular as well. Páleč poured oil on the fire by a dubious disquisition about the sanctity of kings. Moreover, he emphasized the distinction between the office of the pope and his personal character. "Thus it is proved that someone may be a true pope, king, or bishop although he is not a true Christian." Hus replied by reminding them of the example of Pope John, "now called Baldassarre Cossa," to prove his point that even a legitimately elected pope need not necessarily be a *veritable* pope. Sigismund responded that the Council indeed declared John a true pope, but deposed him for his "notorious crimes," thus joining Páleč in his assertion that a "true" pope may be a criminal! But even this declaration of the king did not hold for very long: in order to secure Pope Gregory's resignation, as has already been noted, the Council on July 4 acknowledged him as the true pope, despite his deposition by the Council of Pisa in 1409. The "legalities" of papal legitimacy were not very long-lasting!

The second charge brought against Hus was that predestination was the bond linking each member of the Church to Christ. We have dealt with this matter previously and need not repeat it.

The third and fourth articles have also been dealt with previously: they state that a foreknown pope or prelate is not a head of a particular Church, for as such they are not even members of the body of the predestinate. Hus commented, as he did before, that such a pope is not the head "worthily," but only *ex officio*. A certain monk in a splendid gown fatuously warned the Council not to be deceived by Hus; he claimed that he had explained the distinction to Hus a short time ago, and that Hus was now repeating it as his own. Hus made short shrift of him: "Have you not heard that they [the distinctions] are in my book and were recently read here?"

The next two charges, that the pope should not be called the most holy and that even if the pope were elected legally, but lives contrary to Christ, he is not a *veritable* pope, have already been dealt with. Hus commented further that Judas had been chosen by Christ himself, and yet "did not ascend through Christ" into the sheepfold. Páleč again cried out that such reasoning was fatuous. Hus defended his view further by stressing that anyone securing an ecclesiastical office simoniacally, for the ease and profit to be enjoyed therein, has not entered "through Christ."

The final charge dealt with Hus' non-condemnation of Wyclif's articles on the ground that all were indiscriminately pronounced "heretical, erroneous, or scandalous." When censured by d'Ailly that he had promised not to defend Wyclif's errors, Hus once more repeated that he did not wish "to defend either Wyclif's or anyone else's errors," but only asked for Scriptural proof for their condemnation.

The third group of charges were drawn from Hus' *Contra Stanislaum*.[9] Articles 1-3 and 5 repeated largely what has already been stated about the distinction between a *veritable* and only a legitimately elected pope, and that a foreknown pope is not the head of the Church of God. The Church militant might remain for a time without a pope, as the existing situation proved. In fact, as articles 4 and 6 stated, Christ could rule His Church better without "such monstrous heads," as it had been ruled by the apostles and faithful priests. Thus the papal office was not necessary to the Church, although, on the other hand, Hus did not object to the Roman Church being ruled by a *veritable* pope.

Although the examination of the thirty-nine charges was thus concluded, the Council had other questions to ask of Hus.[10] Then Cardinal d'Ailly addressed him in a seemingly kind and fatherly tone as follows:

Master John! behold, two ways are placed before you, of which choose one! Either you throw yourself entirely and totally on the grace and into the hands of the Council, that whatever the Council shall dictate to you, therewith you

9 *Ibid.*, pp. 209-13.
10 *Ibid.*, pp. 213-23.

271

shall be content. And the Council, out of reverence for the lord king of the Romans here and his brother, the king of Bohemia, and for your own good, will deal kindly and humanely with you. Or, if you still wish to hold and defend some articles of the forementioned, and if you desire still another hearing, it shall be granted you.

But he warned Hus not to involve himself in greater errors, if he chose the latter course.

D'Ailly did not specify what the second of the "two ways" placed before Hus was. He did not state what would happen if Hus submitted. Would he be freed and allowed to return home? Actually, the choice was not between submitting to the Council and having another hearing, but between it and death. That, however, was not mentioned by the cardinal. Hus, after earnestly assuring his chief judge that he did not intend to hold anything obstinately, but "would humbly submit to the instruction of the Council," only prayed that he be allowed a hearing for explaining his own views. His plea was met with shouts of disapproval. Thereupon, d'Ailly spoke again, but in a very different tone. He acted as if Hus had already submitted to the Council and proceeded to announce to him the decision of "well-nigh sixty doctors." Was the preceding scene a sham and a comedy? What became of the promise to give Hus another chance? From the cardinal's precipitous action it was apparent that the verdict had been held in readiness all the time, and would have been the same no matter what Hus said further. Therefore, without more ado, d'Ailly declared to Hus, on behalf of the Council, that he must acknowledge the errors contained in the articles which he held; that he must recant them and swear to all eternity never to preach and teach them again; that he must revoke them publicly; and lastly, that he must hold and preach their opposite.

In the face of these four demands, Hus begged "for God's sake" not to be forced "to lie and abjure" by recanting articles he had never held. Those he did hold he was willing to abjure, if instructed from Scripture that they were wrong.

272

Then ensued an argument as to the meaning of the term "to abjure": Hus insisted that it meant to revoke what one has held. Others shouted that it did not. The king then interfered, asking why Hus should not recant all the articles testified against him by the witnesses. He professed willingness to abjure whether or not he had ever held a thing. One could well believe him; in fact, he was already notorious for his perverse and dishonest dealings. Hus' conscience, however, would not allow him such a loose exegesis of the term "to abjure."

The wrangling continued until finally Cardinal Zabarella intervened: he promised that Hus would be given "a sufficiently qualified formula of those articles," in which form "he ought to abjure them." Thereupon, the king resumed his word, and stated clearly what the real choice between the "two ways" spoken of by d'Ailly was: if you defend the errors, the Council will know what to do with you! Again Hus begged to be granted a hearing (after all, d'Ailly had offered it to him). To this piteous plea the king retorted: you are old enough to understand; either you revoke all the errors—here he recapitulated the four conditions —or "the Council will surely proceed against you according to its laws."

Once more Hus assured the Council that he was willing to submit, if properly instructed. One priest shouted a warning against allowing Hus to revoke, insisting that he would not observe the revocation. All Hus' protests as to his sincerity were in vain. Then Páleč rose and wished to read a list of nine articles of Wyclif which, he said, Hus had defended, and challenged him to surrender the written text of it or he would surrender his copy. Hus told him to surrender it.

The scene, so moving and important for Hus' future, now entered upon another series of charges. He was accused of having written the scurrilous glosses on the pope's crusading bull in 1411. He denied on the ground that he had never even seen them until they were shown to him in the Dominican prison. When they demanded whether he knew

273

who wrote them, he admitted that he had heard it as a
rumor that Jerome of Prague did. The notary recorded it as
if Hus had reported Jerome's authorship as a fact. Later,
he wished Jerome to be told the real circumstances. They
further reopened the inquiry about Hus' "sanctifying" the
three young men beheaded for denouncing the indulgences.
The English also protested against the falsified letter purporting to be from Oxford University, commending Wyclif's life and doctrine.

Particularly reprehensible was the action of Páleč, who
now testified, as if Hus had already been sentenced, that in
proceeding against him "I did not do it from any malicious
zeal or personal hatred—God is my witness—but solely for
the reason that I should be true to my oath that I had
taken" as a doctor of theology. Michael de Causis professed
the same noble motive. It seems that the depravity of
these "principal enemies" of Hus reached, in these declara-
tions, its lowest depth.

Thereupon, Bishop Wallenrode conducted Hus back to
prison. On the way back, John of Chlum awaited him and
showed his sympathy for Hus by extending his hand to
him.

The king and some members of the Council, presumably
the judges, remained in the refectory for a further word.
The two Czech nobles and Peter of Mladoňovice also stayed
behind without being detected. They overheard Sigismund's private conference with the cardinals. He told them
that he regarded Hus as convicted of heresy on many counts
and urged that if he did not recant, he should be burned.
He furthermore insisted that even if Hus recanted, he
would not believe him. Let Hus, therefore, be restrained
from any kind of preaching. Moreover, King Wenceslas
and the Polish king, as well as other rulers and princes,
should be informed of the action taken by the Council in
order that the errors already spread in their lands be eradicated root and branch. Also, Jerome of Prague (for the
moment he could not recall his name) should be dealt the

same severities as Hus. Sigismund thus at last freely showed his colors, although he did not know that he was being overheard. The story of his treachery was later heralded throughout the lands of the Bohemian crown. When his brother, Wenceslas, died (1419), Sigismund, the heir apparent, was denied the Bohemian throne principally because of his betrayal of Hus and his determination to eradicate "heresy" from the land.

The next day Hus wrote a letter to his friends in Constance in which he expressed his deep appreciation of the gesture of John of Chlum in shaking his hand—"to me, a wretched, despised heretic, bound in chains and cursed by almost all."[11] On June 10 he wrote to John of Chlum, reminding him of Sigismund's and the Council's promise to give him a brief statement which he was then to answer, and asking the Czech noble to secure the cooperation of all other nobles in requesting it. He declared that he preferred to be burned rather than to be surreptitiously silenced, "in order that all Christendom might know what I said in the end."[12] He begged John to remain in Constance to the end, so that he would witness his death. He apparently expected to be called before the Council again the next day to be there condemned to death, for he asked to be informed if that was its intention. He was also painfully concerned as to the repayment of those who had loaned him money, and expressed the hope that the richer would reimburse the poorer. In view of the expected verdict the next day, he also wrote to his friends in Bohemia,[13] exhorting them to faithfulness in the service of God, to a grateful recognition of the lords, both Czech and Polish, who stood by him and defended him before the Council. He asked them to pray for King Wenceslas and his queen, and even for King Sigismund. In deep sorrow he wrote that "the Czechs, our

---

[11] Novotný, *Korespondence*, No. 126, pp. 263-66.

[12] *Ibid.*, No. 128; my translation in *John Hus at the Council of Constance*, No. 12, pp. 256-57.

[13] *Ibid.*, No. 129; my translation, No. 13, pp. 257-59.

fiercest enemies," abandoned both him and Jerome into the power of other enemies; but with exemplary Christian charity he implored, "I beseech you that you pray for them." There was no bitterness in his heart, no recrimination, only love and forgiveness.

His expectation of death proved, for the time being, premature. What caused him to expect it, when he had been promised another hearing before the Council, our sources do not reveal. At any rate, on June 13 he wrote to his friends in Constance,[14] again requesting that the nobles put pressure on the king to grant him the promised hearing: "His shame will be great if he disregards his word." That by this time he mistrusted the king is evident from the remark that "his word is about as reliable as his safe-conduct . . . If at least he had said, 'I gave him a safe-conduct; if therefore he would not submit to the decision of the Council, I will send him back to the king of Bohemia with your sentence and testimonies, so that he . . . would judge him.' " It is obvious that his friends had no opportunity to inform Hus that they had overheard Sigismund advise the cardinals *not* to send him back, if there ever existed any such intention on their part.

Three days later, Hus wrote to his faithful pupil, Martin of Volyně, with whom he had left his "Last Will" upon his departure for Constance, exhorting him again to a virtuous life, repeating partly what he had written in the above-mentioned letter (which presumably Martin had not yet opened). He sent greetings to his friends, "my dear brothers in Christ, the cobblers, tailors, and scribes." He bid Martin pay those from whom he had borrowed, as much as he could: "if for God's sake and love for me they wish to forego [the debt], God will repay them more."

Finally, on June 18, Hus received the final formulation of the charges against him, reduced from thirty-nine to thirty counts. Eleven of the old charges were dropped, among them the most perverted, but two new ones were added. The text of the retained articles was only slightly

---

[14] *Ibid.*, No. 131; my translation, No. 14, pp. 259-60.

modified, essentially nothing in them being changed.[15] At any rate the Council had felt constrained to revise the articles once more, this time in the final form. Nevertheless, Hus was not given another public hearing after all, despite the promises of both Sigismund and d'Ailly, but was requested to answer the articles in writing. He labored at that task for two days. His comments, inserted interlinearly in the text, differed in no essential manner from those he had given several times before. On June 20 he wrote to his friends in Constance, sending them a copy of the final charges and his comments for their information.[16] He remarked that he could not write more extensively because of the lack of time and paper, as well as on account of the danger, the nature of which he did not specify. He knew that the crisis was at hand: "It now remains either to recant and abjure and undergo an appalling penance, or that I be burned."

There is no necessity to comment extensively on the final charges, for I have done so previously.[17] Suffice it to say that with one exception, Hus declared them to be erroneously formulated and his sense in them misinterpreted. They did not correctly represent his own views, but rather the perverted version of them ascribed to him by his enemies. The Council, therefore, did not condemn what Hus actually believed and taught, but what, despite all his efforts to explain his tenets to the Council, that body refused to consider and credit. This is not to argue that the final thirty articles did not represent tenets subject to condemnation by the then current standards of orthodoxy; it only asserts that Hus did not hold them in the sense in which they were formulated and understood by the Council. For that reason, his condemnation was unjust; the Roman Church by right should consider itself under obligation to correct the an-

---

[15] Palacký, *Documenta*, pp. 225-34; the Latin text is reprinted (with Hus' annotations) in Appendix II in my *John Hus' Concept of the Church*; my translation of the text in *John Hus at the Council of Constance*, No. 15, pp. 260-68.

[16] Novotný, *Korespondence*, No. 133, pp. 279-80.

[17] *John Hus' Concept of the Church*, pp. 370-74.

cient wrong. Even Cardinal Beran, the archbishop of Prague, told the Second Vatican Council so in no uncertain terms. So far, that Church has been unready or unwilling to acknowledge the wrong or to take action to remedy it.

Hus' expectation of an imminent verdict again proved premature. For some reason, the Council hesitated to act as Hus anticipated, but instead contemplated measures of inducing him to recant. It would have preferred to secure renunciation of his views instead of a verdict of death, perhaps because such a course on his part would effectually discredit him in the eyes of his followers at home; it would thus contribute toward the extirpation of the "heretical" movement there. That course would prove more advantageous, from the Council's point of view, than Hus' death, which would stiffen the opposition on the part of Hus' friends at home. Probably for these, or other similar reasons, the Council now determined to try a seemingly kindly, friendly approach to the end of securing Hus' recantation, realizing, somewhat belatedly, that more flies are caught on sugar than on vinegar. In fact, someone, probably Michael de Causis, as Bartoš asserts, fearful that the Council might commute the death sentence to that of life imprisonment, as the current law specified in case of recanted heretics, wrote a letter to the judges protesting such an action.[18] The writer pleaded with the judges not to decide the matter by themselves, but to refer the verdict to the whole Council, apparently in the expectation that that body was more likely to impose the death penalty. He also mentioned that his fears were based on the fact that the judges actually sent a member of the Council, referred to only as "Pater," for the purpose of winning Hus' consent to abjuring.

Such, indeed, was the case. The unknown "Father" lost no time in approaching Hus with the above-mentioned proposition. He did so by means of a letter, to which was enclosed "the short formula" promised Hus on June 8.

[18] F. M. Bartoš, "Z posledního zápasu o M. Jana," in *Jihočeský sborník historický*, XVII (1948), pp. 57-60; also Novotný, *Jan Hus*, II, pp. 446-47.

The formula stated ambiguously[19] that "as to all the points of which I am accused, I submit humbly to the ordering, definition, and correction of the holy general Council, and accept all abjurations, retractions, penance, and other measures that the holy Council" may impose.

On June 20 Hus answered this winsomely written letter[20] by thanking the "Pater" for the "kind and fatherly grace." He, however, declared that he dare not submit to the Council on the basis of this formula, lest he condemn many truths he holds and thus commit perjury. He should thereby scandalize many people who heard him preach. He quoted Old Testament examples to bolster his refusal and concluded that by avoiding momentary punishment he would incur an eternal damnation.

The prelate who had undertaken the task of "softening" Hus did not feel discouraged by this reply. Had he succeeded, he would undoubtedly have earned the Council's gratitude, even though at the cost of the greatest disservice to Hus. The latter, however, was well aware of this aspect of the "Pater's" undertaking. The prelate immediately answered,[21] addressing Hus as his "dearest and most beloved brother," assuring him that the responsibility for "condemning the truth" would not fall on Hus but on the Council. The "Father's" moral sensitivity could not have been very keen! He advised Hus not to depend on his own judgment, but to heed the superior wisdom of the Council. Likewise in the matter of perjury: even if he did perjure himself, the guilt would redound on those who had exacted it. The same sophistry was employed concerning heresy, which would cease the moment Hus would stop being obstinate about it! He then insisted that Hus, as an intelligent man, would "not retreat from the truth but yield to the truth . . . You will not cause

[19] Hefele and Leclercq, *Histoire des conciles*, VII/I, p. 299; also Novotný, *Korespondence*, No. 135, p. 281.

[20] Novotný, *Korespondence*, No. 136, pp. 281-83; my translation in *John Hus at the Council of Constance*, No. 16, pp. 269-70. Bartoš identifies the "Pater" with John Cardinal of Rejnštejn. *Čechy v době Husově*, p. 438.

[21] *Ibid.*, No. 137, pp. 283-84; my translation, No. 17, p. 270.

offense but edification." If this prelate represented a fair sample of the membership of the Council, no wonder that Hus was condemned! What a contrast this unashamed urging of perjury affords with the Czech reformer's tender and exacting conscience!

Hus promptly answered the conciliar envoy,[22] not so much responding to his arguments as recounting what the submission to the Council would involve. He concluded with the exclamation how he, who had before his eyes so many examples of courageous resistance to evil, "could fall into the many lies and perjury and give offense to many sons of God? Be it far, far from me!"

In still another letter[23] addressed to his friends in Constance, Hus informed them of the continuous and persistent efforts of many people to induce him to abjure his views; nevertheless, none could answer his objection as to what they would do if they knew that they never held what they were asked to recant. Some claimed that to abjure meant a mere denial of the charges, whether or not he held them. Hus replied: "Very well! I will swear that I have never preached, held, or asserted those attested errors," and will never preach them. Thereupon, they immediately drew back. Others adduced examples of "holy obedience" from the *Patericon*. An Englishman advised him to recant on the ground that in England all masters recanted at the archbishop's order. Even Páleč urged him to abjure without being ashamed of it. Hus countered by pointing out that it was "a greater shame to be condemned and burned than to recant. In what way, therefore, do I fear shame?" He also inquired of Páleč what he would do if he were certain that he was not guilty of the errors ascribed to him. Páleč evasively replied: "That is difficult."[24] A few days later, writing to friends, Hus recounted still another attempt to sway him. A certain doctor insisted that whatever he did in submitting to the Council would be good. He added that if the

22 *Ibid.*, No. 138, pp. 285-86; my translation, No. 18, pp. 270-71.
23 *Ibid.*, No. 143, pp. 296-99; my translation, No. 21, pp. 275-76.
24 *Ibid.*, No. 145; my translation, No. 23, pp. 277-78.

Council declared that he had only one eye, although he had two, he should consent to it! Hus retorted that even if the whole world asserted that, he would not agree![25] What could one expect of a Council which had among its members "doctors" of this kind!

It was perhaps then that the Master-general of the Dominican Order, Leonard Statii de Datis, turned to Hus with the inquiry whether, since the pope is the head of the Church, he should not be obeyed unconditionally in all matters of faith. Hus answered that the Master-general was perhaps not motivated by ignorance, but rather instructed by the Council to catch him in some error. His reply was that the Church has only one head, Jesus Christ, who must be obeyed unconditionally.[26]

On June 22 Hus informed his friends that he had asked the commissioners to assign him Páleč or someone else as confessor. No other act displays his spirit of Christian forgiveness more poignantly than this act. He asked for Páleč expressly on the ground that he was his "principal adversary." However, a monk was assigned to him for that purpose, to whom Hus confessed. Páleč, nevertheless, visited him. The scene that followed is deeply moving.[27] Hus asked Páleč's forgiveness for calling him "Fictor and a pointer dog." Nevertheless, he could not forego mentioning that at one hearing Páleč had declared, "This man does not fear God." Páleč denied it; Hus insisted that he had said it. There were other harsh sayings recalled from the time of the polemics and the legal process, but in the end both men wept.

Michael de Causis also visited the prison several times, although he did not enter Hus' cell. He conversed with the jailers, commenting that with the help of God "we shall soon burn that heretic on whose account I have already spent much money." He even secured an order that no one be permitted to come to the door of Hus' prison, not even the jail-

[25] *Ibid.*, No. 150; my translation, No. 26, pp. 284-85.
[26] Novotný, *Korespondence*, No. 142, pp. 295-96.
[27] *John Hus at the Council of Constance*, p. 276.

ers' wives. He thus wished to deprive the hated Hus of his last solace—his friends' letters—as Hus himself states.[28]

In a letter the day before, on June 21, to his noble protectors and his friends in Constance,[29] Hus candidly and in the most outright manner condemned the conduct of the Council. The prelates call themselves vicars of Christ and of His apostles and proclaim that they are the holy Church which cannot err. Yet, they erred in adoring John XXIII "on bended knee, kissing his feet, and calling him most holy, although they knew that he was a base murderer, a sodomite, a simoniac, and a heretic." Hus recalled the adulation heaped on the pope by Stanislav and Páleč, which was proved utterly misapplied by the condemnation of the pope by the Council itself. He further charged the Council with erring in wrongly abstracting the articles from his books. Finally, he repudiated as madness the Council's condemnation of the chalice in communion, thereby branding as "an error the act of Christ along with the acts of His apostles and other saints." He exclaimed: "O Saint Paul! You have said to all the faithful: 'Whenever you eat this bread and drink this cup, you proclaim the Lord's death until He comes,' i.e., until the Day of Judgment. And behold! it is said here that the custom of the Roman Church is opposed to it!"

He informed his friends as his final decision to "refuse to confess as erroneous the articles which have been truthfully abstracted, and to abjure the articles ascribed to me by false witnesses." He restated his understanding of the term "abjure," as he had done before the Council.

Writing still another letter to his friends in Bohemia,[30] Hus mentioned the condemnation of his books. The Council had voted to burn his books on June 23. At first Hus

---

[28] Novotný, *Korespondence*, No. 145, pp. 299-302.

[29] *Ibid.*, Nos. 139, 139*, and 140. The first letter is in Latin and is followed (139*) by its Czech translation (pp. 286-92); the second letter (No. 140) is also in Latin (pp. 292-94). My translation of 139 and 140 is numbered in *John Hus at the Council of Constance* as 19 and 20 (pp. 271-74).

[30] *Ibid.*, No. 147; my translation No. 24 (pp. 280-83).

understood that all his works were thus condemned. As soon as he had written the letter indignantly protesting against this act (June 24), he in some way was apprised that only the treatises surrendered to the Council were involved. But on June 26 he learned definitely to his deep chagrin that the first information was correct, and all his works had been condemned. He thereupon wrote to his friends in Bohemia, pointing out that with the exception of a few Czechs, the "Italians, French, English, Spaniards, and others" could not read his Czech writings, even if they had them.

Hus was now awaiting his death almost daily. Writing his friends in Bohemia (June 27),[31] he mentioned that he had "many reasons for the strong supposition . . . as if I were to die tomorrow." Nevertheless, there again occurred a postponement. The same day he wrote a farewell letter to his colleagues at the university, exhorting them to mutual love, concord, and the honor of God, remembering that he "ever sought the advancement of the university to the honor of God." He also pleaded for unity among the Czech masters, reminding them of his grief over their discords and excesses. He declared that he had not revoked a single article, unless the Council proved its falsity from Scripture. He signed himself as "expecting tomorrow a terrible death." He implored them to love Bethlehem and to appoint Havlík as his successor. Actually, it was Jakoubek of Stříbro who soon after became the preacher at Bethlehem.

To Peter of Mladoňovice[32] he wrote in the most affectionate terms, declaring that "there is not enough money with which I should like to recompense for your most fervent, most firm, and most faithful love which you have for the truth, and for your services and consolations which you have shown me in my tribulations." Hus instructed him to dispose of his books as he had written to Master Martin, and to choose any of Wyclif's books for his own use. He was still

[31] *Ibid.*, No. 156; the letter is in Czech; my translation, No. 29, pp. 288-89.
[32] *Ibid.*, No. 160; my translation is No. 31, pp. 290-91.

worried about the financial losses incurred by his friends on his account, and asked Peter to request his rich friends, the mintmaster Peter Zmrzlík of Svojšín and his wife, to pay the debt to John of Chlum. This noble was also to receive the horse and wagon (in which presumably Hus had come to Constance), if they were still available.

Then on July 1 Hus made his final declaration to the Council.[33] Since this document is of great importance for the exact terms of Hus' decision, it is recorded in full:

I, John Hus, in hope a priest of Jesus Christ, fearing to offend God and to fall into perjury, am not willing to recant all or any of the articles produced against me in the testimonies of false witnesses. For God is my witness that I neither preached, asserted, nor defended them, as they said that I had defended, preached, and asserted them, etc.

Furthermore, concerning the articles drawn from my books, at least those drawn correctly, I declare, that if any of them contain a false sense, that sense I repudiate. But fearing to offend against the truth and to speak against the opinions of the saints, I am not willing to recant any of them. If it were possible that my voice could now be heard in the whole world, as at the Day of Judgment every lie and all my sins shall be revealed, I would most gladly recant before all the world every falsehood and every error I ever have thought of saying or have said.

This I say and write freely and voluntarily. Written with my own hand on the first day of July.

The final demand for recantation, apparently made by Zabarella, was presented to Hus on July 5, when he was called before his judges. He was to recant all the articles he acknowledged to be in his books and the testimonies of witnesses which he did not deny. As for the testimonies which he denied, he was required to swear that he did not hold them and to promise that he would believe concerning them what the Church teaches. Hus answered by referring to his declaration of July 1 and repeating it in a briefer

---

[33] *Ibid.*, No. 162; my translation, No. 32, p. 292.

form. Zabarella's terms were indeed the extreme concession the Council was willing to grant Hus; even so, he could not accept them, because they still demanded what he could not in conscience admit. He wrote on the same day a letter addressed to the entire world, in which he recounts some of the scenes from the trial on June 8, and once more professes his innocence.[34]

On that same day (July 5) in the evening, John of Chlum and Wenceslas of Dubá, along with four bishops, visited Hus in prison to give him the last opportunity to recant. John of Chlum, then, speaking for himself as well as for his companion, addressed Hus with an urgent appeal to change his mind, if he felt guilty of any of those things charged against him. "But if, indeed, you do not feel guilty of those things charged against you, follow the dictates of your conscience. Under no circumstances do anything against your conscience . . ."[35] Hus, with tears in his eyes, answered the faithful friend that if he knew of having held anything erroneous, he would recant. He said further that he had even desired to be instructed from the Scriptures, if he were wrong, when he would have most willingly recanted. One of the bishops sneeringly inquired whether Hus wished to be wiser than the whole Council. Hus replied again with a request "for the least one of the Council" to instruct him. To that the bishops responded, "See, how obstinate he is in his heresy!"

On the next day, July 6, Hus was taken by Archbishop Wallenrode into the cathedral where the general session of the Council was held. Cardinal John Brogli of Ostia presided, while King Sigismund in full regalia occupied his throne. In the middle of the nave a table was placed on which the priestly garments were arranged for the purpose of defrocking him. A sermon was preached by Bishop Jacob Balardi Arrigoni of Lodi on the text "That the body of sin be destroyed,"[36] incidentally wrenching the

---

[34] *Ibid.*, Nos. 163 and 165; my translation, Nos. 33-34, pp. 292-94.
[35] Spinka, *John Hus at the Council of Constance*, p. 224.
[36] Rom. 6:6.

text violently from its real meaning. Thereupon, after Henry of Piro, the procurator, read the prescribed formula, requesting the continuance of the trial, Berthold of Wildungen, the papal auditor, first read partially 260 articles of Wyclif, and then reviewed the whole trial of Hus, concluding with the final thirty charges against him. While he read them, Hus loudly protested. Cardinal d'Ailly sharply commanded him to keep still, that he would later answer all the charges together. When Hus objected that he could not reflect on them all, and again attempted to comment on the reading, Cardinal Zabarella angrily stopped him with "Be silent now. We have heard you enough already!" Nevertheless, when the lector stated that Hus had declared himself to be the fourth person of the Trinity (a monstrously fantastic and wholly unfounded charge!), he could not keep silent and demanded that the name of the mendacious slanderer be revealed. Even now he was rebuffed with the curt reply that there was no need of it. The guards were ordered to silence him, should he speak again. When charged with appealing to Christ, Hus again protested that he had come to the Council freely, under the safe-conduct of the king, and looked pointedly at Sigismund; the latter blushed.[37] When even then forbidden to speak, he fell to his knees and prayed silently.

After the accusations, including the testimonies of witnesses, were concluded, Anthony, bishop of Concordia, read the definitive sentence.[38] In it, Hus was declared to be an obstinate heretic, a disciple of the heresiarch Wyclif, who had taught and preached many errors and heresies condemned previously by the Church. On that account "this sacrosanct Synod of Constance declares and defines that the articles hereafter described are not catholic . . . but many of them are erroneous, others scandalous, others offensive

[37] Novotný, *Jan Hus*, II, p. 456, n. 2.

[38] There were two versions of this document, both given in Sedlák, *Studie a texty*, I, pp. 349 ff. One of these was prepared for use in the event that Hus recanted. He was then to be imprisoned for life. See Novotný, *Jan Hus*, II, p. 447. My translation of the definitive text is given in *John Hus at the Council of Constance*, pp. 295-98.

to pious ears, and many of them are rash and seditious, and several of them are notoriously heretical." Thereupon, the works of Hus, both in Latin, Czech, or any other language, were condemned to be burned, and his teaching eradicated by ecclesiastical authorities. As for Hus himself, the Synod "pronounces, decrees, and declares [him] . . . to have been and still to be a veritable and manifest heretic." It decrees that "he be deposed and degraded from the priestly order," and appointed seven of its members, archbishops and bishops, to carry out the ceremony of degradation. Hus himself was then to be turned over to the secular arm.

Peter of Mladoňovice records[39] that Hus protested vigorously against being called an obstinate heretic, and once again demanded that he be given "a more relevant instruction from the Scriptures." He remonstrated in the same manner against the condemnation of his books and boldly inquired how the Council could include in it his Czech and translated books which they have not even seen. Thereafter, he knelt and prayed, asking that his enemies be forgiven. The "principal clergy" scowled and jeered.

The ceremony of degradation was all that the name implied. The seven high dignitaries ordered Hus to put on the vestments required for the celebration of the mass. Thereupon, after exhorting him once more to recant, he was bidden to mount the table and from there spoke to the assembly, protesting his innocence. He declared mournfully that he feared to abjure "lest I be a liar in the sight of the Lord and also lest I offend my own conscience and the truth of God." He then descended and the bishops proceeded with the ritual. First they took the cup from his hands with the formula of deprivation. He answered that he hoped to drink from the cup the same day in the kingdom of God. Then they disrobed him, pronouncing in each instance an appropriate curse. He responded that he was willing to suffer shame for the name of the Lord. When it came to obliterating his tonsure, the bishops fell into a dispute

[39] My translation in *John Hus at the Council of Constance*, pp. 228-29.

among themselves as to the proper procedure: was it to be shaved with a razor or merely cut with scissors? Finally, they agreed on the latter method, pronouncing at the same time the formula wherewith they turned him over to the secular arm. Nevertheless, before they actually did so, they placed on his head a tall paper crown on which were painted three devils fighting for the possession of a soul. The inscription on it read: "This is a heresiarch." The bishops intoned therewith the final curse: "We commit your soul to the devil!"— as if they had power over Hus' soul and could order the devil to take it! He rejoined: "And I commit it to the most merciful Lord Jesus Christ!" Thereupon, King Sigismund ordered Duke Louis of the Palatinate to receive Hus from the hands of the bishops; the prince, in turn, entrusted him to the care of the executioners.

If one had the notion that this poignant scene would have made a deep impression on those directly involved in it, he would be mistaken. Cardinal Fillastre recorded in his *Diary* for the day that "The same day it [the Council] passed sentence on Master John Hus, who was present, condemned and degraded him for heresy, and delivered him to the secular court." The papal notary, Cerretano, was even more laconic. The entry in his *Journal* reads: "Condemnation of errors of Wyclif and Hus. Sentence and execution of Hus."[40]

When the sad procession, accompanied by "almost all the inhabitants of that city," was passing the cemetery, where his books which could be found in Constance were being burned, Hus smiled. On the way he exhorted the crowd not to believe that he was guilty of heresy.

When they reached the place of execution,[41] he knelt and prayed that God might have mercy on him. The crowd of onlookers was impressed and uttered their amazement at his prayer. Some thought that he should be allowed a con-

[40] Both quotations are found in Loomis, *The Council of Constance*, pp. 256, 499.

[41] It is now inside the city limits, near the municipal gas works, on the *Alten Graben Strasse*. An immense boulder, inscribed with the names of both Hus and Jerome, marks the spot.

fessor, while a priest on horseback objected that as a heretic he should have none. As has already been noted, Hus had previously confessed to a monk in prison.

While he was praying, the crown fell from his head. Some soldiers exclaimed: "Put it on him again, so that he might be burned with the devils, his masters . . ." Hus then rose and said clearly that he was willing to bear most patiently and humbly the dreadful death. They disrobed him down to his shirt and tied him, with his hands behind his back, to the stake. He faced east, to which some bystanders objected; he was then turned west. When bound by the neck to the stake with a rusty chain, he commented with a smile that his Savior had been bound by a heavier chain. Thereupon, the executioners placed wood interspersed with straw about the body up to his chin.

Before the order to apply the torch was given, the imperial marshal, Hoppe of Poppenheim, and Duke Louis approached and once more exhorted Hus to recant to save his life; but even in this supreme moment of decision, Hus remained firm. Thereupon the two men clapped their hands as a signal to the executioner to proceed with his grim task.

When the fire was lit, Hus began to sing: "Christ, Thou Son of the living God, have mercy on us"; and then "Christ, Thou son of the living God, have mercy on me." In the third place he prayed, "Thou, Who art born of Mary the Virgin —" but he did not finish it, for the wind blew the flame into his face. He continued to pray silently, until he died in a short time, "about the time one could quickly recite 'Our Father' two or three times."

When the pyre died down and the ropes were burned, the remains of the body stood erect, hanging by the chain placed at his neck. The executioners pulled down the body with the stake and adding more wood, burned it, breaking the bones and the skull for quicker incineration. When they found the heart, they impaled it on a sharpened stick and took special care to burn it. The clothing also was thrown into the fire at the order of the marshal, who remarked that otherwise the Czechs might venerate it as a relic. He promised the executioners, who otherwise would have divided the garments among themselves, to reimburse them for it. Finally, loading the ashes into carts, the executioners dumped them into the Rhine. The faithful Czechs did not need any relics; they carried the memory of their great champion of truth in their hearts, and still do.[42]

[42] There is another account of the scene of Hus' execution in Ulrich Richental's *Chronicle* (Louise R. Loomis, transl., *The Council of Constance*, pp. 133-34). This self-professed "eyewitness" is, however, generally so unreliable, particularly in matters pertaining to Hus and Jerome, that I hesitate to incorporate his account into that of Peter of Mladoňovice, even though Novotný (*Jan Hus*, II, pp. 458-60) does include it with reservations. Richental, even though he claimed on other occasions to be an eyewitness, recorded events in such a confused, perverted, and even imaginary fashion (for instance, the ridiculous report of Hus' supposed attempt to escape from Constance, pp. 113 ff.), that I have no confidence in his report of Hus' death, even though he seems to have correct knowledge of a few details. He reports, for instance, that the execution took place on July 8, that the procession to the place of execution was accompanied by more than 1,000 armed guards, which number was increased on the way to 3,000, besides all the unarmed crowd. Hus was led to the meadow beyond the bridge on the Gelting Gate, but the mob was so large that they had to pass the bridge in file for fear that it would break. Richental claims that he was asked—he does not say by whom—to accompany Hus. When they came to the pyre, it was he, Richental, who asked him if he wished to confess, to which Hus was supposed to have answered that he would gladly do so. The priest, Ulrich Schorand, who was authorized by the Council and the bishop of Constance for the purpose, then offered to confess him, if he would recant. Hus answered that there was no need, that he was not in mortal sin. Further, Richental says that Hus began to preach to the assembled crowd in German. Thereupon, the executioners quickly tied him to the stake in his gown, having set a stool under his feet. When his body was burned, the crown on his head (on which two, not three, devils were painted) remained, *mirabile dictu*, "still whole"! It could not have been of asbestos, rather than paper, for the executioners are said to have knocked it down and burned it! By what miracle did it happen that Hus' head could be burned but the paper crown did not suffer even a scorching? So much for the account of this truthful "eyewitness"!

## Chapter X

## Epilogue

𝕴t will prove helpful to cast a hasty glance not only at the proceedings of the Council after the death of Hus, but also to follow therewith a brief outline of some consequences of his martyrdom. Although this must necessarily be limited in scope, it will help to make us aware of the permanent influence of Hus upon his nation, and the Christian world, through his effect upon Luther and the German Reformation. This influence actually has continued up to the present and is felt even by contemporary Marxist intellectuals in Czechoslovakia.

The first concern of the Council after disposing of Hus' case was to deal with Jerome of Prague.[1] As has already been narrated, Jerome had been taken prisoner just as he was about to cross the Bohemian border on his return from Constance. Upon being returned in chains to that city and after a preliminary examination, he was imprisoned in a private house. Peter of Mladoňovice soon learned of his whereabouts and secretly approached the house to speak with him through a window. When the guards discovered him, they promptly drove him away. Jerome was thereupon taken to a prison in the tower of St. Paul's cemetery, where his feet were clamped in a high beam and he was suspended with his head down. He remained in that excruciatingly painful position for a number of days, having been fed only on bread and water. He became severely ill and his life was despaired of, whereupon he was transferred to a better cell and received less rigorous treatment. There he remained almost a year, until May 30, 1416.

As with Hus, Jerome's principal accusers were Michael de Causis and Stephen Páleč. But the stormy protests which arose in Bohemia and Moravia over the burning of Hus

---

[1] František Šmahel, *Jeron ým Pražský* (Praha, Svobodné Slovo, 1966) .

warned the fathers of the Council that the situation might become very serious. Some of the leaders realized that to condemn Jerome to the fate suffered by Hus would only add fuel to the already raging flames. They preferred to secure Jerome's recantation rather than his death. His repudiation of Wyclif's and Hus' teaching would not only thoroughly discredit him in the eyes of the Czech reform party, but would tend to weaken the vehemence of their protest against Hus' condemnation. Thus the same maneuver which had been tried when the Council commissioned the "Pater" to secure Hus' recantation was repeated with Jerome.

Of the four-member commission of judges appointed to try Jerome, the two men who undertook the risky business of securing Jerome's recantation were cardinals d'Ailly and Zabarella. Jerome, for that matter, was no Hus when it came to an unequivocal and resolute defense of his basic convictions. He had found himself in similar circumstances many times before, but had escaped condemnation and almost certain death by his stout denial of the charges. The last such occasion had been his arrest in Vienna in 1410. At that time he was accused on the basis of twelve articles, dealing mainly with his defense of Wyclif, Stanislav of Znojmo, Páleč, and Hus. He promised to remain in Vienna until his trial was terminated. However, he left secretly and sent his presiding judge a letter, ironically informing him of his good health and professing to be at his service. He did not recognize his promise to remain in Vienna, he wrote, because it had been forcibly extorted from him. His irate judges then excommunicated him.

There is no doubt (since he later himself admitted it) that Jerome intended to repeat his maneuver as far as the two cardinals were concerned.[2] He insisted that he had never defended Wyclif's overtly heretical articles, but he nevertheless pointed out that many of the condemned theses of Wyclif could not be documented from his writings. As for Hus, he asserted that the final thirty articles likewise were not in harmony with Hus' authentic writings. He demand-

---

[2] *Ibid.*, pp. 116, 169.

ed that the cardinals bring him Hus' treatises so that he could prove it. They did bring the writings, and after reading them, he professed to find for the first time that the condemned articles actually had been correctly abstracted, and that he was convinced of Hus' guilt.

This was a great triumph for the two cardinals. They now demanded that Jerome make his recantation before the whole Council. On September 11, 1415, he was brought before the assembly, where he declared that he agreed with the condemnation of Wyclif's forty-five articles, "whether they originated from him or someone else," and with Hus' thirty articles, although he would not include in this declaration "those holy truths which those men had taught in schools and among the people." He added that he himself never held any error or heresy. This recantation, hemmed about by qualifying phrases, naturally proved unsatisfactory and therefore unacceptable. Since he had already taken the first step toward revocation, he was induced to follow it by another twelve days later. He then declared in writing:

I, Jerome of Prague, master of liberal arts, confess hereby the true catholic faith and condemn all errors, especially those with which I have been hitherto befouled and which were formerly held by John Wyclif and John Hus in their works, treatises, or sermons intended for the clergy and the people; for which they, along with their views and errors, were condemned by this sacred Council of Constance as heretics.[3]

So that there would be no doubt whether Jerome condemned all Wyclif's and Hus' articles, they were read in their entirety. Nevertheless, since Sigismund was absent, the Council postponed the judgment for a later date. Jerome was remanded to prison, although his treatment there was considerably improved.

He was, however, disappointed with the result. He had

[3] *Ibid.*, p. 168. Šmahel remarks: "It is possible to comprehend Jerome's act, but not to defend it; for otherwise we would be guilty of change of values." (p. 170.)

expected to be set free. Moreover, the situation at the Council changed for the worse as far as his case was concerned. Chancellor Gerson made a public declaration that anyone who ever fell into heresy, even though he repented, could no longer be trusted but must henceforth be imprisoned for life. Michael de Causis and Stephen Páleč also redoubled their efforts to secure Jerome's condemnation to death, and were joined in what they considered a pious effort by Dr. John Náz, King Wenceslas' representative. They secured from the Council (February 24, 1416) the appointment of two new commissioners for Jerome's examination. Accused of having been bribed to favor Jerome, Cardinals d'Ailly and Zabarella were either deprived of their function or resigned in disgust.

Subjected to a renewed trial, Jerome refused to answer questions on the ground of derogatory conduct of the proceedings. He declared categorically that he would answer no charges except at a public hearing. Surprisingly, such a hearing was granted him. On May 23, he was brought into the cathedral, which was packed by the members of the Council and the sensation-seeking visitors. Jerome did not disappoint them. He refused to be subjected to interrogation, and insisted on stating his case in his own words. When his request was rejected, he burst out in a torrent of indignation. His words were recorded by the Italian humanist, Poggio Bracciolini, who, although serving as papal secretary, was full of admiration for the learning, eloquence, and courage of the accused.

What iniquity is this! While I have languished for three hundred and fifty days in the most cruel prisons, in stench, squalor, excrements, and chains, lacking all things, you have ever heard my adversaries and slanderers; but me you now refuse to hear even for an hour! Thus when you listened to them for a long time as they tried to persuade you that I am a heretic, an enemy of the faith, and adversary of the clergy, you refuse to afford me any means to defend myself. For you have already in your minds condemned me as an unworthy man, before you could learn what I really am. But you are men, not gods, not immortals, but mortals! You can fall, blunder, be deceived and misled just like other men. It is said that here are gathered the lights of the world and the wisest of men. For that reason you should take care not to do anything rashly, inconsiderately, or unjustly. I know that I am but a little man [*homunculus*] and in danger of losing my life. I am to die; but of that I do not speak. It appears to me unworthy, however, that the wisdom of so many men be aimed at something contrary to right, which would serve to the future ages not so much as a wrong act, but as an example of wrongdoing.[4]

His outburst was greeted with a storm of protests and denunciations. Since the proceedings were time-consuming, the meeting was adjourned for three days.

On the appointed day Jerome was at last allowed to deliver the speech for which he had fought so hard. His defense was long and eloquent, resembling more an impassioned lecture to an academic audience than a vindication at a trial. He reviewed many historic cases of judicial injustice, such as those of Socrates, Plato, and Boethius, as well as Isaiah, Daniel, and Stephen, stressing the injustice committed by religious leaders upon innocent victims. He then recapitulated his own life and work. Finally, he came to his own recent recantation; he boldly confessed that Hus, "whom he knew since his childhood . . . was an honest, humble and sober man, diligent in teaching and writing, a just, faithful and holy preacher; and whatever Master John Hus and Master John Wyclif preached against iniquity, pride, malice, fornication and avarice of the clergy, all that I desire to hold and will hold to death." Thereupon, he repudiated his recantation, which, he said, he had made

---

[4] "Poggii Florentini ad Leonardum Aretinum epistola de M. Hieronymi de Praga supplicio," in V. Novotný, ed., *Fontes rerum Bohemicarum* (Praha, Nadání Františka Palackého, 1932), VIII, pp. 324-26. English translation in James Bruce Ross and Mary M. McLaughlin, *The Portable Renaissance Reader* (New York, The Viking Press, 1960), pp. 616-17. The translation I use is my own.

"for fear of death." He declared that an injustice had been done to Master Hus and that he, Jerome, spoke against him only to please the Council, "for which he is heartily sorry."[5]

Poggio was filled with admiration for Jerome's courageous conduct: "He stood fearless and intrepid, not affrighted of death but desiring it. I would have said that he was a second Cato."[6]

The enraged Council, declaring that Jerome condemned himself, ordered him to be returned to prison, where again his feet, hands, and breast were enchained. He was there visited by Cardinal Zabarella, who tried in vain to change his resolution. Then on May 30 he was brought into the cathedral and again exhorted to withdraw his decision. He declared:

I call my Lord God to witness and testify before you that I hold nothing heretical, but adhere to and believe all the articles of the Christian faith, which the holy Church catholic holds and believes. But I wish not to accede to the condemnation of the formerly mentioned good masters, whom you have unjustly and maliciously condemned, because they taught and wrote what was to your correction and amendment.[7]

Thereupon, he was sentenced to death and the execution was carried out the same day. He was led to the place where Hus had been burned the year before, having been crowned with a tall paper crown on which devils were painted in red. Before he was tied to the stake, he knelt to pray. He prayed and sang while the executioner piled wood and straw about him. When the attempt was made to ignite the pyre behind his back, Jerome called to the executioner to do so before his face: "for if I had feared it, I would not have come here!"[8]

[5] Novotný, *Fontes*, "Peter of Mladoňovice, Vita Magistri Hieronymi," VIII, pp. 361-62; "Poggii . . . epistola," pp. 330-31.

[6] "Poggii . . . epistola," p. 332.

[7] Novotný, *Fontes*, VIII, p. 362.

[8] "Poggii . . . epistola," p. 333.

The enormous boulder which marks the spot where the two Czech martyrs met their death so piously and courageously bears both their names.

If the avowed purpose of the Council of Constance was to eliminate heresy, that purpose failed; for the condemnation and death of Hus and Jerome led to a determined revolt in Bohemia-Moravia against both the Church and Sigismund. Of that we shall speak later. Similarly, the reforms "in head and members," which had been projected by the Council, largely failed of accomplishment. The Germans and the English advocated that they be enacted before the new pope was elected. Their proposal was defeated: it was voted that only five of the reforms be adopted prior to the election, of which the decree *Frequens* was the most important. It ruled that the next Council be held within five years, to be followed by another in seven, and thereafter be convened every ten years. These Councils were to perpetuate the conciliar dominance over the papacy.

On November 11, 1417, the new pope was elected in the person of Cardinal Odo de Colonna, who assumed the name of Martin V (1417-31). The Council at last healed the forty-year-old Schism—the only permanent accomplishment of which it could rightfully boast. The new pope issued, on March 8, 1418, a bull, *Inter cunctas*, which confirmed the acts of the Council. This document incorporated the forty-five articles of Wyclif and the thirty articles of Hus in its condemnation. In this bull Martin forbade an appeal from the pope to the Council, thus contravening the conciliar assumption of its superiority to the papacy. This policy was followed by his successors, who, in the end, succeeded in nullifying the conciliar principle altogether. Pope Pius II in 1461 prohibited, in his bull *Execrabilis*, any appeal at all from the papal jurisdiction. Thus the papacy emerged as the victor. Martin thereupon closed the Council on April 22, before that body even considered, let alone passed, any adequate reforms.

It is interesting to note in this connection the change of mind regarding the legitimacy of the Council of Constance admitted recently by Paul de Vooght. In his *L'hérésie de Jean Huss*[9] he declared that if Hus were a heretic because he had denied the primacy of the Roman pope, the fathers of the Council were even more guilty by proclaiming the dogma of the superiority of the Council over the pope. He now holds that divine right "permits Council to save the Church in cases when heresy, schism, or scandalous life of a pope offer a risk that the Church might be conducted to its ruin."[10] Recently the learned Benedictine also admitted that Hus' judges sent their victim to the stake "for his 'errors' which he partly never recognized as his own and partly refused to consider as heretical unless so proved."[11] Thus he seemed to modify his opinion about Hus' "heresy." Unfortunately, other Roman Catholic historians do not follow him in this moderation, but quote him in a sense wholly condemnatory of Hus.[12]

When the news of the execution of Hus reached Prague, it aroused immense indignation. A meeting of the Czech and Moravian nobles, called to Prague on September 2, adopted and sent a spirited protest against the deed to the Council. Then, under the leadership of Čeněk of Vartenberg, Lacek of Kravaře, and Boček of Poděbrady, 452 of the most prominent lords and knights concluded a treaty, pledging themselves for six years to defend the cause of reform for which Hus had died. They acknowledged the university as the highest authority in matters of faith. This, in effect, made Jakoubek of Stříbro, soon to become the successor of Hus at the Bethlehem Chapel, the leader of the movement.

[9] Paul de Vooght, *L'hérésie de Jean Huss* (Louvain, Publications universitaires de Louvain, 1960), p. 470.
[10] Paul de Vooght, "Jean Huss et ses juges," in A. Franzen and W. Müller, eds., *Das Konzil von Konstanz* (Freiburg, Basel, Wien, Herder, 1964), p. 165.
[11] Paul de Vooght, "Jan Hus in the Era of Vatican II," in Matthew Spinka, ed., *550 Years of Jan Hus' Witness, 1415-1965* (Philadelphia, The United Presbyterian Church in the United States, 1965).
[12] For instance, the references, drawn almost entirely from De Vooght's books but limited to his derogatory passages, in E. Delaruelle et al., *L'Eglise au temps du Grande Schisme et de la crise conciliaire*, 2 vols. (Bloud et Gay, 1962).

The vast majority of the common people enthusiastically supported the leaders.[13]

The Council, which in the meantime made the situation worse by burning Jerome, answered this revolt of the Czechs by summoning the signers of the covenant to Constance for a trial. They, of course, ignored the summons. The Council demanded that action be taken even against the king and the queen. But Sigismund, when urged to take steps against the Czech nobility, refused to act; in fact, he demanded that the action be abandoned. Nevertheless, the Council appointed Bishop John "the Iron" as its legate, whose task was to carry out its behests against Bohemia. On October 29 he published the decrees of Constance in Prague and placed that city under an interdict. However, the bishop, because of his part in the Hus trial, found it impossible to return to his Litomyšl bishopric and was later appointed bishop of Olomouc in Moravia.[14] Even King Wenceslas forbade him to carry out the Council's directives. The same fate was suffered by Stephen Páleč, who, like the bishop, found it inadvisable to return to Bohemia or Moravia, and instead became professor of theology at the University of Cracow, where he remained to his death.

In response to the measures adopted by the Council, the common people rose in a determined effort to introduce the cup into the communion everywhere. This marks the real beginning of the national revolt which convulsed the country for decades thereafter. Armed bands of the populace attacked the Prague monasteries and parsonages, expelling all who refused to administer the communion *sub utraque*. By February 1416 all the churches were in the hands of clergy who were willing to carry out the reform.

Thereupon the revolt spread throughout the country. The vast majority of churches passed to the control of the

[13] Jiří Kejř, *Husitský právník, M. Jan z Jesenice* (Praha, Československá akademie věd, 1965), p. 142. He asserts that the author of the protests was Jesenic.

[14] For a detailed narrative of this and subsequent events, see F. M. Bartoš, *Do čtyř pražských artikulů* (Praha, Blahoslavova společnost, 1940), pp. 19 ff.

reform party which, because it now generally introduced
the granting of the cup in communion, was known as
Calixtine or Utraquist (from *sub utraque specie*). Suffragan
Bishop Herman, brought from Germany, was willing to
consecrate the clergy for the new order of church administration, so that there was no shortage of priests for the
Utraquist churches. He was, however, soon excommunicated
and his services terminated.[15] The university also solemnly
declared itself for the chalice (March 20, 1417). Čeněk of
Vartenberg, the leading noble in the country, was particularly active in spreading the reform.

Soon after assuming office in 1417 Pope Martin V took
steps to stop the spread of the new order in Bohemia. In
February 1418 he formally declared a crusade against the
country and appointed Cardinal John Dominici as his
plenipotentiary for the task.[16] Sigismund also undertook to
comply with the pope's behests, and urged Wenceslas to
do likewise. The vigorous measures undertaken by the
Council were not without effect in Bohemia, particularly
among the high nobility. A reaction set in, supported by
King Wenceslas. The Utraquists suffered severe losses, particularly in the death of some of their most prominent noble
leaders such as Boček of Poděbrady and especially Lacek
of Kravaře, who was vice-regent of Moravia. The royal Council now also supported the king in his opposition to the
Utraquists, only three of its members remaining faithful
to the reform program. The reaction resulted in a fairly
general restoration of the churches to the Catholics, and
early in 1419 Wenceslas issued an order commanding that
all churches be restored to them. Thereupon, the clergy "re-
consecrated" the churches desecrated by the Utraquist
worship. When this royal act produced a popular protest,
however, the king permitted the Utraquist services at three

[15] Bishop Herman had been kidnapped by Čeněk of Vartenberg in
1417 from his home in Mindelheim and was kept at the castle of
Lipnice. F. M. Bartoš, *Husitská revoluce I: Doba Žižkova, 1415-1426*
(Praha, Československá akademie věd, 1965), pp. 38-39.
[16] Bartoš, *Do čtyř pražských artikulů*, p. 31.

Prague churches, the most important of which was the church of St. Mary of the Snow.

Even more serious was the effect on the Utraquists themselves. The University masters were now divided between those who, following Jakoubek, advocated the communion in bread and wine even for children and an increasingly conservative party that opposed not only this practice but many other reforms as well. Among them were even former friends of Hus, such as Simon of Tišnov, John of Jesenice, and Peter of Mladoňovice. The most serious breach developed between the university masters as a whole and the even more radical advocates of ecclesiastical changes, particularly in southern Bohemia, where they developed into the party of Taborites and even outright heretical sects.

This new party grew among the common people because of resentment against the measures taken for the restoration of the Roman type of worship. Immense crowds used to gather for worship at various places on tops of mountains; a crowd estimated at 42,000 gathered at one time at Hradiště near Bechyně. In the end Hradiště was permanently occupied and transformed into an almost impregnable fortress, renamed Tábor. The people were addressed at these meetings by Utraquist preachers and partook of communion in both kinds. The outstanding clerical leaders among the Taborites were Wenceslas Koranda and, among the left-wing Praguers, John Želivský, while the lay leader of the movement was a squire, Nicholas of Hus, owner of a small castle in southern Bohemia. Želivský, a former Premonstratensian monk of Želiv, had come to Prague as early as 1414 and became attached to Jakoubek.[17] However, he soon exceeded his master in radicalism. The crisis was reached when on July 30 Želivský, who served the Utraquist church of St. Mary of the Snow, led a procession headed by a monstrance containing the host to the church of

[17] F. M. Bartoš, "Počátky Jana Želivského v Praze," in *Theologická příloha Křestanské Revue* (1966), pp. 44 ff.; also B. Auštetská, *Jan Želivský jako politik* (Praha, Husovo museum, 1925).

St. Stephen. Finding the doors locked, the crowd proceeded
to break them down. Želivský then preached a fiery sermon
from the pulpit of the church. On their return, the vast
crowd stopped at the New Town Court house and demanded the release of the prisoners who had recently been
jailed there. The councilors not only summarily refused
to admit their representatives, but allowed the procession
to be stoned from within. The enraged multitude forced its
way into the building and threw the councilors out of the
window. The man who took charge of the courthouse was
no less a person than John Žižka, at that time in King
Wenceslas' service.[18] He had now definitely joined the
revolutionaries.

When the king heard of this "defenestration," he was
seized with paroxysms of rage, but his anger was assuaged
by his courtiers. Nevertheless, he fell ill and on August
13, 1419, suffered a fatal stroke. After burial at several different places, his body was permanently interred, in
1423 in the St. Vitus Cathedral, where the queen had
wished to place it from the beginning.

Since Wenceslas was childless, Sigismund was his heir
apparent. But because of his perfidy in the case of Hus and
Jerome, and his treachery in dealing with Wenceslas, he was
hated by the populace. They feared, quite rightly, that he
would insist on a complete restoration of the old ecclesiastical order and would suppress the Utraquist worship altogether. Accordingly, they refused to recognize him as
Wenceslas' successor. This defiant mood was greatly strengthened by Želivský's powerful sermons delivered against the
perfidious king from the pulpit of St. Mary's. He was soon
to dominate the city. Žižka, too, showed himself irreconcilably opposed to Sigismund. The first outbreak of violence occurred under his leadership against the Carthusian
monks of Smíchov, a suburb of Prague, whose monastery
went up in smoke. The monks themselves left unharmed
for another place. The Church of St. Mary of the Pond,

18 Frederick G. Heymann, *John Žižka and the Hussite Revolution*
(Princeton, Princeton University Press, 1955), p. 64.

the Carmelite monastery at St. Mary of the Snow, and the Church of Sts. Philip and James, neighboring the Bethlehem Chapel, were also destroyed. Thereupon, the archbishop imposed an interdict on Prague, but no one paid any attention to it.

The high nobility, under the leadership of Čeněk of Vartenberg, held a Diet at Prague where they agreed on the conditions to be required of Sigismund as the price of recognition. Since the majority still adhered to Utraquism, the demands were largely religious: freedom to preach the Word of God, granting of communion *sub utraque*, guarding the good name of Hus and Jerome from aspersions of heresy, and pacification of the Holy See. This was the beginning of what later developed into the famous "Four Articles of Prague." Such demands were, of course, quite unacceptable to Sigismund. He answered noncommittally, that he would soon come to Prague and talk the matter over with the nobles. In the meantime, he appointed Queen Dowager Sophia as regent and confirmed Čeněk of Vartenberg as the burgrave of Prague. Čeněk actually occupied the royal castle of Hradčany with a force of pro-Sigismund soldiers, many of whom were foreigners. In retaliation, on October 25, 1419, the Prague radicals under Žižka occupied Vyšehrad and later, with Nicholas of Hus, took the Small Side. Čeněk declared war against them as "disturbers of the peace" and in November concluded a truce with the moderate Praguers, by which Vyšehrad was returned to his forces and occupied by them. Prague was then threatened from the south and the east by royal contingents. Žižka and Nicholas left Prague in protest. Žižka went to Plzeň to establish there a new base of operations while Nicholas went east to prepare a similar center at Mount Oreb near Hradec Králové.

In the meantime, Sigismund abandoned his expedition against the Turks and turned against Bohemia-Moravia. He arrived with his forces at Brno in December 1419, but did not dare as yet to declare a crusade against Bohemia. He appointed now as his chief officials Čeněk of Vartenberg as regent, and associated with him Wenceslas of Dubá (the former guardian of Hus in Constance) and Mikeš Divoký of Jemniště, also known to us from his mission to Hus. This new royal regency inaugurated a reactionary rule in Bohemia. In Kutná Hora, on the king's order, some 1,600 Utraquist priests and laymen were flung alive into the abandoned silver mines. Sigismund then proceeded to Vratislav (Wrocław) in Silesia, where at last he openly declared war. The pope also called for a crusade against the heretical Czechs (March 1420).

The radical elements among the people now definitely repudiated Sigismund and prepared for war. Prague, too, resolved to defend its religious freedoms. Žižka, after directing the defense of Plzeň, was forced to surrender it to the royal army. He was allowed a free withdrawal of his forces and intended to retire to Tábor. On the way he was attacked at Sudoměř by a strong contingent of mailed horsemen under the leadership of Mikeš Divoký; although confronted by a greatly superior force, Žižka defeated it. Thereupon, he fortified Tábor, which was situated on a hill, and surrounded on three sides by the river Lužnice, and made it the center of opposition to Sigismund. He became the recognized military leader of its "invincible army," which grew into the strongest unit among the Hussites. The settlers were organized as a brotherhood, a highly unified community with its own municipal, religious, and military orders. The town was a communal organization, each new settler having deposited the money he had received for his property in a large tank placed in the town square. Similar armies were organized by the Praguers under Želivský, by the Orebites under priest Ambrose of Hradec Králové, and by the combined forces of the northwestern cities of Žatec, Louny, and Slaný.

On April 23, 1420, Sigismund left Vratislav and invaded Bohemia. He was headed for Kutná Hora with an army of some 20,000, and was expecting other troops from Hungary. Čeněk of Vartenberg allowed Sigismund to occupy the royal castle of Hradčany. At this dangerous juncture the Prague Utraquists under Želivský decided to call for Žižka's immediate help. He accepted the invitation and with 9,000 men entered Prague on May 20. The Praguers, with the help of the Taborites, then elected new, friendly councilors in both Old and New Towns, and adopted a common religious program, formulated by Jakoubek of Stříbro in the famous Four Prague Articles. The program demanded: (1) that the Word of God be freely preached by Christian priests in the Bohemian kingdom; (2) that the sacrament of the body and blood of Christ be freely ministered in both kinds of bread and wine to all Christians; (3) that priests and monks be deprived of secular power and that they live exemplary lives in accordance with the Scriptures; (4) that all mortal sins be prohibited and punished in each estate by those in authority.[19] Henceforth, this was the program of all Hussite parties, no matter how they differed among themselves in other particulars. The archbishop Conrad of Vechta now himself accepted the Four Articles, thus joining the Utraquists and thenceforth ordaining their candidates for priesthood.

When Sigismund reached Prague, his army had increased to 100,000. This immense host occupied all Small Side and Hradčany and held Vyšehrad. Žižka was joined by other contingents such as those of Žatec-Louny-Slaný, along with the Praguers themselves. In order to protect Prague from the east, he occupied the high ground of Vítkov. There he was attacked by the royalists; however, he not only repulsed their assault, but, along with his allies, inflicted a crushing defeat on them (July 14, 1420) on Špitálské Pole. Thus Prague was saved. In addition, the crusading army was afflicted with an epidemic and lack of supplies. Thereupon, having been hastily crowned as king by Archbishop Conrad in St. Vitus Cathedral (July 28), Sigismund left for Kutná Hora.

Žižka and his Taborites returned to Tábor, while the Praguers laid siege to Vyšehrad. Because of lack of supplies, the defenders agreed to surrender, if aid did not reach them by a certain date. When the king failed to relieve it, the

[19] Bartoš, *Husitská revoluce I*, p. 71. A full discussion of the Four Articles is found in Heymann, *John Žižka*, pp. 148-57.

stronghold was taken by November 1. Among the fallen was Henry Lefl of Lažany, the one-time protector of Hus.

By this time the Hussites were already divided into two religious camps: the Praguers and the Taborites. Each camp further subdivided into three distinct groups. The Praguers differentiated themselves into the conservatives led by Christian of Prachatice, John Příbram, Procopius of Plzeň, and Peter of Mladoňovice; they advocated the retention of much of the old worship as long as it did not contradict the Scriptures. The moderates were headed by Jakoubek of Stříbro, who professed to adhere to the Bible as the supreme rule of faith and life. The radical wing, led by John Želivský, repudiated everything non-Scriptural, and advocated a radically new social order. The Taborites, on the other hand, differed among themselves even more. They drew apart from both the Roman and the Utraquist groups by establishing their own episcopate: they elected, in September 1420, Nicholas of Pelhřimov as their bishop. He was consecrated presbyterially, and in turn ordained their candidates to priesthood. The moderate wing among them was headed by John Jičín, Procopius the Bald, and, among the lay leaders, John Žižka. They stood close to the teaching of Jakoubek. The largest party among them, however, was constituted of resolute Taborites, led by John Němec. In the basically important concept of the Lord's Supper he stood close to Wyclif's idea of remanence, Christ being present in the host sacramentally but not realistically. To this group belonged Bishop Nicholas, who in his treatise *Ad sacramenti eucharistiae in veritate magnificationem*[20] vehemently protested against the adoration of the sacrament as idolatry. The left wing of the Taborites was represented by Wenceslas Koranda of Plzeň and John Čapek, who denied Christ's presence in the eucharist altogether. Čapek also became a fervent chiliast and incited men to war against "the enemies of the Word of God."

[20] F. Hrejsa, *Dějiny křesťanství v Československu*, 4 vols. (Praha, Husova ev. fakulta bohoslovecká, 1947-48), II, p. 146.

The most radical group was made up of "Picarts."[21] Their origin was traceable to the French and Belgian emigrants who came to Bohemia in 1418 to escape persecution at home and who were known as "Picards." Their extreme radicalism led to their expulsion from Tábor and ultimately to their extermination by Žižka. Their leaders were Martin Húska and Peter Kániš. They taught that Christ was not present in the eucharist at all, it being a mere commemoration of his death. A small group of them developed into fanatical Adamites who lived in a state of nudity on a small island near Tábor. They developed pantheistic tendencies, regarding themselves as incapable of sinning.

Aside from these religious parties in Tábor stood Peter Chelčický, who became the spiritual father of the Unity of Brethren.[22] Bartoš identified him with Peter Záhorka, a squire of Záhorčí near Vodňany, born c. 1379-81.[23] He received private, but fair, education under his clerical uncle.

In Prague he became well acquainted with the works of Wyclif, of Thomas of Štítné, of Hus, whose preaching he attended, and particularly with Jakoubek. He copied some of Hus' early works and drew heavily upon them later. When, however, the war against "the enemies of Christ" embodied in Sigismund's armies was imminent, Chelčický, who again visited Prague at the time, denounced even Jakoubek for consenting to it. When Žižka came to the aid of Prague and won the victory at Vítkov (1420), Chelčický, disappointed with what he regarded as a betrayal of Christianity, returned to Chelčice, where he remained for the rest of his life. Thereupon, he determined to advocate by all means possible a purely spiritual, pacifist Christian society built exclusively on Christ's gospel.

[21] F. M. Bartoš, "Pikardi a Picarti," in *Husitství a cizina* (Praha, Čin, 1931), pp. 176-208.

[22] Matthew Spinka, "Peter Chelčický, the Spiritual Father of the Unitas Fratrum," in *Church History* (1943), pp. 271-91.

[23] F. M. Bartoš, "Kdo byl Petr Chelčický," in *Jihočeský sborník historický*, XV (1946), pp. 1-8; "Památce Petra Chelčického," XVI (1947), pp. 1-9.

In his first treatise, *O boji duchovním* [*The Spiritual Combat*] written in 1420-21, he formulated his basic principle that a Christian must engage not in "carnal" but in spiritual combat alone. He concluded in a radical pacifist fashion that all killing, including that of war, is sin. Hence, he repudiated all political power with its inevitable use of force; he regarded the state as a necessary evil, consequent upon man's disobedience of God's law, and the Church, as the realm where alone God's rule, which is peace, should prevail. He thus advocated a radical separation of Church and state.

Society, therefore, should be radically reorganized. Instead of its current division into the priestly, noble, and commoners' estates, he divided it into the worldly society, governed by its unchristian or imperfectly Christian orders, and the Church where only God's will prevails. Therefore, the laws governing the world have no place in the Church. No class distinctions are to be recognized there; the law of love alone is the supreme rule. These views were expressed in Peter's *O trojím lidu* [*The Three Estates*].

The most comprehensive of his works is the large treatise entitled *Síť víry* [*The Net of Faith*].[24] It is an extended commentary on the text in Luke 5:4, "Put out into the deep and let down your nets for a draught." These words spoken by Christ to Peter, Chelčický applied to the Church-state relationship. In the net, signifying the Church, many fish were caught, good and bad. The two largest, which broke the net, were the emperor and the pope. From them "many strong and wicked hordes were born," which tore the net so completely that nothing but sorry shreds remained. This corruption is traced to Constantine's endowment of the Church with secular power and rule. The only remedy is the restoration of the pre-Constantinian condition of the Church. The Church must cut itself off completely from the state, for the Church is founded on the law of love, while the state depends for its very existence on force. The Church

---

[24] E. Smetánka, ed., *Petra Chelčického Síť víry* (Praha, Melantrich, 1929; reprinted Orbis, 1950).

must, therefore, surrender its secular rule, wealth, and privilege; it must repudiate war and every physical compulsion. Christ's realm is not of this world; His disciples are not to rule but to serve. The true Christian submits to the state as an evil necessary for the preservation of unregenerate men, but must not willingly cooperate with it. There is no compulsion by which a man would of necessity become a Christian; that happens only by the free acceptance of God's redeeming grace.

In advocating these views, Peter gathered about him a group of earnest, like-minded men and women who formed a brotherhood bound by no outward organization, but only by love. Although undoubtedly close to his neighbors, the Taborites, Chelčický carried on polemics with them over their views of the communion and their use of force, even though it was used by them in the defense of faith. He likewise came into conflict with the views of the Utraquist archbishop-elect, John of Rokycany, whose moderate mediating position on the relation of his communion to the Roman Church Peter regarded as unbecomingly compromising. His greatest service was the influence he exerted, through Brother Gregory, on the founding of the Unity of Brethren, in which his spirit still lives. He died perhaps in 1460, shortly after Gregory established his "Brethren" at Kunvald.

To return to the main developments in the country. Since it could be expected that Sigismund would again attempt to conquer the country and in the meantime the land was without a governing body, a Diet was held at Čáslav in June 1421, at which the king was declared deposed as unworthy of the Bohemian throne, and negotiations were undertaken to secure someone else in his place. A delegation was sent with the offer to the Polish king Władysław II or the Lithuanian Grand Duke Vitold. Władysław was not willing to accept the Czech crown for himself; but he permitted his nephew, Sigismund Korybut, to accept the offer as Vitold's deputy. Although Sigismund consented to the Four Prague Articles, he strove to bring about peace with the Roman Church. This made him unpopular with the radical elements among the Czechs. Twice he had to leave the country, in 1427 for good.

. The anticipated invasion of the country was soon realized when the second crusade, conducted by the Meissen, Silesian, and other German armies, actually won a victory at Žatec. Žižka did not take part in it. He was already completely blind, for in addition to the loss of one eye suffered previously, he was blinded on the other during the siege of the castle Rábí.

Sigismund also began another invasion of the country from the Moravian border in December 1421, when he approached Kutná Hora. Žižka, now recognized as the commander of all Hussite forces, had occupied that important town earlier in the month. He now left the town, mistrusting the loyalty of the local miners. Thereupon, they admitted Sigismund's armies into the city. Then on January 6, 1422, Žižka attacked the crusaders and won a decisive victory over them. Sigismund left the town in panic; during his retreat he twice attempted to stand up against the pursuing forces, but was disastrously defeated. At the second of these engagements, fought at Německý Brod, a contingent of his army tried to cross the River Sázava on ice, for the bridge was choked with troops; but the ice broke and a large force was drowned. This was Sigismund's "gravest defeat."[25]

In Prague in the meantime the leadership passed in February 1422 into the hands of new councilors, hostile to Želivský. The next month he was invited to the Old Town Hall, presumably for a conference. When he arrived with some companions, he was treacherously seized and immediately beheaded. This act signified the victory of the conservative and even reactionary elements in the city.

Even greater catastrophe overtook the whole Hussite movement when John Žižka, the invincible "warrior of God," died of the plague on October 11, 1424, while besieging Přibyslav on the Moravian border. The two wings of the Taborite-Orebite brotherhood, which most closely co-

---

[25] Heymann, *John Žižka*, chap. 18, pp. 286-306.

operated with each other, now divided into separate groups. The Orebites soon after assumed the name "Orphans," as if their father had died. Their headquarters were at Hradec Králové in eastern Bohemia. The mantle of Žižka as far as the Taborites were concerned fell on priest Procopius the Bald (or Great), while the Orphans were led by Procopius the Less.

In order to prevent further invasions, the united Hussite armies under Procopius the Bald undertook, in 1426, an expedition against Meissen. His armies were confronted at Most by larger forces of Saxons, but he defeated them with great slaughter. The Czech armies were regarded throughout Germany as irresistible, and the fear of invasion increased the dread in which they were held.

In two years another invasion was undertaken, this time under the leadership of Henry, Cardinal Winchester, the legitimized son of John of Gaunt, the onetime protector of Wyclif. The army was confronted by the Hussite forces at Stříbro and retreated to Tachov. There it was turned into a panicky flight which the "English cardinal" tried in vain to stop. Tachov was then occupied by the Czechs.

Henceforth, Hussite invasions of the neighboring territories were ever more frequent. The most devastating was the so-called "magnificent ride" [spanilá jízda], which penetrated deep into German territory northward into Brandenburg and westward as far as Bayreuth and Munich. The forces were largely unopposed and returned with enormous spoils.

Under such conditions, the German princes and Pope Martin V organized still another crusade in which they concentrated all their resources (1431). The pope appointed as its leader the young Cardinal Julian Cesarini. His armies comprised 90,000 infantry and 40,000 horsemen. Awaiting a further contingent of the Austrian Duke Albrecht, the crusaders did not venture far into the country, but on August 1 laid siege to Tachov on the Bavarian border; then they proceeded to nearby Domažlice. The Hussite armies also gathered a considerable force, which, however,

311

amounted to less than one half of the crusading host. This largest and most determined effort permanently to crush the Czech revolt resulted in the most ignominious defeat ever suffered by the crusaders. When the Czech armies were still some four miles off, the roar of their iron-clad wagons and the echo of their choral reached the Germans. The Hussites were singing their famous war hymn which, like Luther's "Ein feste Burg" a century later, gave courage to their armies:

> All ye warriors of God, who fight
> In defense of His law
> Him beseech for succor and might
> To Him most trustfully draw;
> For with Him ye shall ever conquerors be
> For with Him ye shall ever conquerors be!

> Fear not your inveterate foes
> Regard not their great host;
> To God commit your grievous woes
> For Him fight at your post;
> Before your enemies never craven be
> Before your enemies never craven be!

The battle proper was actually never joined. The crusaders, seized with an overpowering panic, precipitously fled toward the Bavarian border. The frantic cardinal tried to stop them, cross in hand; finally, he himself, abandoning his sumptuous tent, fled disguised as a common soldier. Thereafter, he remained in hiding, for his own soldiers would perhaps have cut him to pieces, regarding him as the chief cause of their defeat. When the Hussites reached the camp, all they had to do was to pursue the fleeing hosts, of whom they killed many thousands. Their booty was enormous, including some 3,000 wagons.

This tremendous victory of the Czechs at last convinced even their most determined enemies, Cardinal Cesarini among them, that they could not be defeated by force of arms. Peaceful negotiations had to take the place of violence. Pope Martin had already called another general Council, which was to meet in March 1431 in Basel. He died, however, before the Council opened its sessions, and Eugenius IV was elected in his stead. When the news of the disastrous defeat at Domažlice reached the Council, that body was willing to invite the Hussite representatives for negotiations.

In the meantime, the ecclesiastical situation in Bohemia also changed. Archbishop Conrad, who had served as the head of the Utraquists, died. Receiving an invitation to attend the Council, the Czech leaders met in a Diet in February 1432, and after much dispute accepted it, but insisted, first of all, on certain conditions. They were not ready to be treated as Hus and Jerome had been dealt with by the Council of Constance. The Basel Council was obliged to send its representatives to a meeting at Cheb, held on May 9, where the Czech delegation, consisting of John of Rokycany, Peter Engliš (i.e. Payne), Martin Lupáč, Procopius the Bald, Nicholas of Pelhřimov and Markold of Zbraslavice, met them.[26] There an agreement was reached that the negotiations at the Council were to be conducted on the basis of the law of God, the practice of Christ and the apostles and of the primitive Church, as well as of the councils and doctors based on them.[27] This was the famous "judge of Cheb," whereby the claim of the Council to be supreme in all matters of faith was substantially modified.

In August 1432, the delegates to the Council were chosen at the synod held in Kutná Hora. The most important among the nobles elected was William Kostka of Postupice; of the clergy, John of Rokycany, Peter Engliš, Procopius the Bald, Nicholas of Pelhřimov, Oldřich of Znojmo, and three others were selected. Altogether, there were fifteen delegates. They arrived at Basel on January 4, 1433. The Council, professing to be governed by conciliar principles, was headed by Cardinal Cesarini. He showed himself friendly to the Czech delegation, particularly to Procopius.

26 Frederick G. Heymann, "John Rokycana—Church Reformer between Hus and Luther," in *Church History* (1959), pp. 3-37.

27 F. M. Bartoš, *Husitská revoluce II: Vláda bratrstev a její pád, 1426-1437* (Praha, Československá akademie věd, 1966), p. 112. I follow Bartoš' treatment of the Council of Basel.

On January 10, Rokycana presented the Czech demands for general Church reforms and especially the Four Prague Articles, of which he defended the granting of the cup. Later, the other members of the delegation—Nicholas of Pelhřimov, Oldřich of Znojmo, and Peter Engliš—defended the remaining clauses of the Articles. Their chief opponents, upholding the strict Catholic positions, were the Croatian Dominican, John Stojković of Dubrovník, Cesarini's adviser; the Spaniard John Palomar, the papal auditor and archdeacon of Barcelona; Guy Charlier, a canon of Arras, nephew of the famous chancellor of Paris, Gerson; and a German inquisitor, Henry Kalteisen. They were bent on repudiating the principles of the "judge of Cheb," and on subjecting the Czechs to the rule of the Council. The chief obstacle to any agreement was the demand for the communion *sub utraque*, the *sine qua non* of the Czechs. When after three months of debate, sometimes acrimonious, no agreement could be reached, and the Czechs refused all compromises on the ground that they had no authority to grant them, the Council, as the last means of preventing the delegation from leaving Basel, decided to offer the Czechs, presumably as a great concession, membership in the Council. This suggestion was made by Cardinal Nicholas of Cusa. Acceptance of it would, of course, have deprived the Czechs of the privilege of dealing with the Council as an independent party negotiating on the basis of the previously agreed upon principles, and would have subjected them instead to the Council's ruling. The proposal was indeed a preposterous trickery, and the Czechs promptly and resolutely rejected it. They returned to Prague on April 14.

Thereupon the Council decided to send its embassy to Prague to negotiate directly with those in authority. It was headed by Bishops Philibert of Coutances and Peter Schaumberg of Augsburg, and among its members were the formidable John Palomar and Guy Charlier. The aim of their diplomacy was to sow dissension among the various Czech parties and secure the support of the most conservative among them. The conciliar delegation was received on June 12 at the great aula of the *Carolinum*. Palomar poured out his most captivating eloquence in an effort to sway his audience. He did not hesitate to repeat the offer already rejected in Basel by the Czech delegation; namely, that the Hussites accept the decision of the Council in all things in exchange for membership in the Council. He valiantly battled for this position for some time, although without success. It was only late in June that at last he came out with the concession that the Council might grant the chalice, provided the Utraquists would submit in all other respects.[28] When even this offer proved unacceptable, he asked for a written statement of the Czech demands, promising to present it to the Council. These demands were then formulated by the conservative university masters under four items, the nucleus of the future *Compacts*: that the Word of God be freely preached, subject to the supervision of bishops; that public sins be forbidden and punished by ecclesiastical or civil authorities respectively; that Church properties be used for the common good and the clergy be deprived of rule over secular matters; and that communion in both kinds, as commended by Christ, be declared a useful and saving ordinance. This version did not satisfy other leaders who prepared a formula more to their taste.

Even so the conciliar delegation was in no hurry to leave Prague. Its members utilized their opportunities for secret negotiations with some nobles; together they plotted an attack on the brotherhoods of the Taborites–Orphans, who were resolutely opposed to any radical concessions. Thus the delegation aimed to divide the Hussite forces on the basis of the time-tested theory of *divide et impera*. In the forefront of the nobles' plot was Menhart of Hradec. The beginning of the fateful struggle was the decision of the Hussite leaders, induced by the traitorous Přibík of Klenová, to lay siege to Plzeň, the stronghold of the Catholic party. This venture ended disastrously for the brotherhoods. Although all three Hussite armies were to undertake the task,

28 *Ibid.*, p. 147.

at first the Orphans did not take part in it because they had previously left the country to aid the Poles. John Čapek of Sány, their captain, led a contingent of some 8,000 to Poland where they, along with the Poles, fought the Teutonic Knights. The Czechs for the first time reached the shores of the Baltic Sea, where 200 of them were knighted for their bravery.

In the meantime, the second delegation, led by the conservative John Příbram and Procopius of Plzeň, arrived in Basel. Palomar, who had learned enough during his two months' stay in Prague to know that unless the Council were persuaded to grant the communion in both kinds all efforts to gain victory over the Czechs would be in vain, exerted himself to the utmost to secure that end. It was not an easy task. The prohibition of the chalice, passed by the Council of Constance, stood in the way. The Czech delegates, on the other hand, insisted on their demand for the chalice. Cesarini was convinced of the necessity of granting it, and was ably seconded by Palomar and Nicholas of Cusa. At last, after violent debates, the request of the Czechs was granted, although the opponents of the measure were assured that it was only a temporary expedient. Late in August 1433, the Council voted the measure, but limited it only "to those who would otherwise submit completely to the rules of the Church."[29] This limitation was aimed at the Taborites and the Orphans. When this decision was announced by the Basel delegation to the Diet assembled in Prague, it was received with jubilation by the conservatives; but the representatives of the brotherhoods held out against it until November 30, when they too were persuaded to accept it as a basis for further negotiations.[30] Thereupon, the Diet was disbanded and the Council delegates returned home, highly satisfied with the results obtained.

Upon their return, the Council promptly proceeded with the execution of the plot hatched by Palomar during his long stay in Prague with the Czech nobles willing to cooperate with him in the destruction of the brotherhoods. This

[29] *Ibid.*, p. 158.　　　[30] *Ibid.*, p. 160.

was to be accomplished not by another crusading expedition, but by the Czechs themselves engaging in a fratricidal combat. Toward the end of February 1434, Palomar left for the previously agreed upon place on the Bavarian border, where the Czech nobles awaited him. He came well supplied with money. Thereupon the nobles organized themselves in April into the league of lords, headed by Menhart of Hradec and William Kostka of Postupice. The first objective of their campaign was the relief of Plzeň, taken with the aid of the Táborite captain, Přibík of Klenová. Palomar then went to Austria to secure the help of Albrecht, and from there to Sigismund. By this time Sigismund had at last been crowned emperor in Rome in 1433. Thereupon, the league armies attacked Prague and took the Old Town in May. An armed attack on New Town prevented it from joining the brotherhood forces. These catastrophic events forced the Taborites-Orphans to abandon the siege of Plzeň and come to the aid of Prague.

They now faced the decisive struggle of their long warfare. Procopius the Bald, forgetting his personal grievances suffered recently when he had been deprived of his command and even imprisoned for a short time, once more assumed leadership of the army. He was joined by John Čapek of Sány, who led the Orphans. On May 30, 1434, the two great armies, both composed of Czech troops, confronted each other at the village of Lipany, not far from Kolín. The army of the league of nobles, commanded by Diviš Bořek of Milotínek, had a considerable advantage in numbers. Nevertheless, at first the brotherhood armies seemed to prevail. When their foes feigned a headlong retreat, they were lured to open their defenses made of armored wagons and to rush in pursuit. But the retreat was a ruse; hidden reserves promptly invaded the opened camp, while the retreating troops turned upon their assailants. The Taborite-Orphan forces found themselves between two assaulting forces and were decimated in ferocious carnage. Some 13,000 of them were killed, among them Procopius the Bald. Only John Čapek with a remnant of his contingent escaped toward Kolín. About 1,000 captives were locked in barns, which were set afire. Thus ended the hitherto invincible power of the brotherhoods; those who remained were relatively powerless to offer further effective resistance. It took Czechs to defeat other Czechs in a fratricidal combat.

After this immense victory of the nobles, it was necessary to conclude a permanent religious settlement and unification of the country. A Diet was called to Prague late in June, which was attended by Sigismund's representatives and even by John Čapek, who declared in the name of the surviving brotherhoods his submission to its decisions. A one-year truce with Sigismund was concluded. A delegation was to be sent to Regensburg to negotiate with the emperor. The Utraquist clergy were to hold their own meeting in July.

The conversations with Sigismund were, as usual, devious. The Czechs were willing to accept him as their king, provided he helped to secure from the Council their religious demands. He promised to attempt the task. Thereupon, in October 1435, John of Rokycany was elected archbishop, to be supported by two bishops. But the election was not confirmed either by the pope or by the Council. The Council wished Bishop Philibert to administer the Church, but this the Czechs refused.

When the Council, no longer fearing the Czechs, refused to grant the already promised *Compacts*, Sigismund, desirous at last to ascend the Bohemian throne, issued a written declaration in January 1436 acknowledging this fundamental document; however, he assured the conciliar legates that he did not intend to keep his promise. The Utraquists, taking him at his word, solemnly proclaimed the agreement on April 23, 1436, at the border town of Jihlava, not Prague. They feared that such an act might lead to a disturbance, were it proclaimed in Prague. Thereupon, Sigismund at last, after seventeen years of struggle for the Czech crown, assumed the rule of the country. Finally, the Council also agreed to recognize the *Compacts* and acknowledged the Czechs as reconciled with the Church.

Entering Prague in splendor and assuming the rule of the country, Sigismund promptly showed his true colors: once again he broke his word. He deprived the resolute defenders of Utraquism of the churches and positions of influence. Even Rokycana had to leave the Týn church, the principal Utraquist sanctuary, which was promptly awarded to a conservative cleric. The administration of the Church was taken over by legates appointed by the Council. Rokycana fled to Hradec Králové where he was protected by a powerful noble. This hostile policy provoked a revolt against the king, in the face of which he was forced to flee. He died while retreating from the country on December 9, 1437. The reaction thus begun continued and culminated in the pontificate of Pius II who, in 1462, rescinded the *Compacts* altogether on the ground that they possessed validity only for the generation during whose lifetime they had been granted.

Since Sigismund had no male children, he was succeeded by his son-in-law, Albrecht II of Austria, but not without powerful opposition. His reign lasted only one year; he died in 1439 at the age of forty.

Albrecht was succeeded by his infant son, Ladislav, born after his father's death and therefore known as Posthumous. Since he was an infant, a regent had to be chosen to administer the land during his minority. This important official was chosen in the person of George of Poděbrady,[31] who in 1444, at the age of twenty-four, had become the head of the Utraquist party. Four years later he was elected the governor of the land and was able to regain Prague and to reintroduce Utraquist ecclesiastical dominance. John of Rokycany was reinstated as archbishop-elect, although he was still not recognized as such by the pope. George vainly endeavored to secure his recognition. In 1452 George was reappointed governor, and next year Ladislav was crowned. His reign,

---

[31] O. Odložilík, *The Hussite King, Bohemia in European Affairs, 1440-1471* (New Brunswick, N.J., Rutgers University Press, 1965) ; Frederick G. Heymann, *George of Bohemia, King of Heretics* (Princeton, Princeton University Press, 1965) .

however, lasted only four years. He died in 1457, victim of a plague, just as he was preparing for a wedding with Margaret, the daughter of the French King, Charles VII.

Thereupon, George of Poděbrady continued the regency of the country, to which he had been confirmed by the young king. But the next year (1458) he was elected king and began a brilliant reign which brought the country once more to the peak of influence it had had in the days of Charles IV. Since Rokycana could not officiate at the coronation, not having the pope's authorization, that ceremony was performed by two Hungarian bishops. The oath George took was ambiguous: the pope interpreted it as having implied repudiation of Utraquism, while George insisted throughout his reign on remaining a convinced Utraquist. He brought to the country such power and good repute that plans were set afoot to make him the king of the Romans. But his religious status rendered the plan futile. During the years 1462-64 George initiated a grandiose plan of a League of European Christian rulers united to oppose the threatening power of the Turks. It was also to serve as an arbiter in any disputes among the member princes and states, and to resolve them by peaceable means.[32] This is sometimes referred to as an early "League of Nations." The pope, however, not only remained hostile; in 1466 he even publicly declared George a heretic and as such deprived him of his throne. To carry out the pope's will, King Matthias of Hungary entered upon a warlike expedition against him. George, however, inflicted a crushing defeat on him. Both George and John of Rokycany died in 1471.

Hus' influence by no means ceased with the establishment of Utraquism as the dominant religious communion in Bohemia; it continued in the formation of the Unity of

[32] For the text of this important document, see B. Havránek et al., eds., *Výbor z české literatury husitské doby*, 2 vols. (Praha, Československá akademie věd, 1964), II, pp. 399-408; F. G. Heymann, *International Relations in Mid-fifteenth Century Europe and Their Significance for the Peace Plan of King George* (Praha, Academia, 1966).

Brethren, the purest outgrowth of the Czech Reformation. That communion produced the great leader John Amos Comenius (1592-1670), who attained world fame as the father of modern educational methods and a pioneer of ecumenism. He conserved and greatly developed the spiritual heritage of his Church. Hus' spirit is alive as a spiritual force in his native land to this day. Undefeated by the Council of Constance, he emerges in the sweep of history as the victor in the struggle for a purified, vitally transformed Church.

# Selected Bibliography

## Primary Sources: Works on John Hus

Bartoš, F. M., transl., *Listy Mistra Jana Husi* (Praha, Kostnická Jednota, 1925).

————, ed., *Jiří Heremita, Život, to jest šlechetné obcování ctného svatého kněze, Mistra Jana Husi, kazatele českého* (Praha, Ministerstvo informací, 1947).

Císařová-Kolářová, Anna, ed. and transl., *M. Jan Hus, Betlemské poselství*, 2 vols. (Praha, Jan Laichter, 1947).

Dobiáš, F. M., and Molnár, A., transls., *Husova výzbroj do Kostnice* (Praha, Kalich, 1965). Contains "Řeč o míru," "O postačitelnosti Kristova zákona," "Řeč o víře," and "Prohlášení o článcích Pálčových."

————, transl., *Mistr Jan Hus, O církvi* (Praha, Československá akademie věd, 1965).

Erben, K. J., ed., *Mistra Jana Husi Sebrané spisy české z nejstarších pramenů*, 3 vols. (Praha, B. Tempský, 1865-68).

Eršil, Jaroslav, ed., *Magistri Johannis Hus, Polemica* (Praha, Academia scientiarum Bohemoslovaca, 1966). Contains "De libris hereticorum legendis," "Defensio libri de Trinitate," "Contra Johannem Stokes," "Contra occultum adversarium," "Contra cruciatam," "Defensio articulorum Wyclif," "Contra Paletz," "Contra Stanislaum," and "Contra octo doctores."

Fiala, Zdeněk, transl., *Petra z Mladoňovic Zpráva o Mistru Janu Husovi v Kostnici* (Praha, Universita Karlova, 1965).

Flajšhans, V., ed. and transl., *Listy Husovy* (Praha, J. Otto, n.d.).

————, ed. and transl., *M. Jan Hus, Obrany*, 2 vols. (Praha, J. Otto, 1916).

————, ed., *Spisy M. Jana Husi*, 8 vols. (Praha, Jaroslav Bursík and J. R. Vilímek, 1903-07). I. Expositio decalogi; II. De corpore Christi; III. De sanguine Christi; IV-VI. Super IV sententiarum; VII-VIII. Sermones de sanctis.

————, ed., *O mučenicích českých knihy patery* (Praha, 1917).

————, ed., *Mag. Io. Hus, Sermones in Bethlehem, 1410-11*, 5 vols. (Praha, Královská česká společnost nauk, 1938-42).

*Historia et monumenta Joannis Hus atque Hieronymi Pragensis, confessorum Christi*, 2 vols. (Norimberg, 1558; new edition, Norimberg, J. Montanus et U. Neuber, 1715).

Jeschke, J. B., ed., *Mistr Jan Hus, Postilla* (Praha, Komenského ev. fakulta bohoslovecká, 1952).

Loserth, J., ed., *Stephen Páleč's, Tractatus gloriosus*, in "Beiträge zur Geschichte der husitischen Bewegung, IV," *Archiv für Oesterreichische Geschichte* (Wien, 1889), LXXV, pp. 333-39.

Mareš, B., transl., *Listy Husovy*, 2nd ed. (Praha, "Samostatnost," 1901).

Novotný, V., ed., *Jan Hus, O svatokupectví* (Praha, J. Otto, 1907).

————, ed., *M. Jana Husi Korespondence a dokumenty* (Praha, Komise pro vydávání pramenů náboženského hnutí českého, 1920).

Novotný, V., ed., *Fontes rerum Bohemicarum* (Praha, Nadání Františka Palackého, 1932), VIII. Contains "Petri de Mladoniowicz, Relatio de Magistro Johanne Hus," and many other pertinent documents.

Palacký, František, ed., *Documenta Mag. Johannis Hus* (Praha, F. Tempsky, 1869).

Ryba, B., ed., *Magistri Johannis Hus, Quodlibet* (Praha, Orbis, 1948).

———, *Nový Hus* (Praha, Jednota českých filologů, 1948).

———, ed. and transl., *Sto listů M. Jana Husi* (Praha, Jan Laichter, 1949).

———, *Betlemské texty* (Praha, Orbis, 1951).

Schaff, David S., transl., *John Hus, The Church* (New York, Charles Scribner's Sons, 1915).

Schmidtová, Anežka, ed., *Johannes Hus, Positiones, recommendationes, sermones* (Praha, Státní pedagogické nakladatelství, 1958).

———*Magistri Johannis Hus, Sermones de tempore qui Collecta dicuntur* (Praha, Academia scientiarum Bohemoslovenica, 1959).

Sedlák, Jan, Articles from *Hlídka*, vols. 28-30 (Brno, 1911-13). Contains treatises of Stanislav of Znojmo, "Sermo contra 5 articulos Wiclef"; "Tractatus de Romana ecclesia"; and Stephen Páleč's "Sermo contra aliquos articulos Wiclef"; "De aequivocatione nominis ecclesiae"; "Antihus"; and "Několik textů z doby husitské."

———, *M. Jan Hus* (Praha, Dědictví sv. Prokopa, 1915). The Supplement contains Páleč's "Tractatus de ecclesia, partes selectae."

———, *Studie a texty k náboženským dějinám českým*, 4 vols. (Olomouc, Matice Cyrilometodějská, 1914-25). Contains many texts of Hus' smaller treatises, among them "Hic tractatus est contra Huss hereticum et contra eius tractatus, quem 'de ecclesia' appellavit."

Šimek, F., ed., *Mistr Jan Hus, Česká kázání sváteční* (Praha, Blahoslav, n.d.).

Spinka, Matthew, ed. and transl., "Hus on Simony," in *Advocates of Reform, Library of Christian Classics* (Philadelphia, The Westminster Press, 1953), XIV, pp. 199-278.

———, transl., "Peter of Mladoňovice, An Account of the Trial and Condemnation of Master John Hus at Constance," and "John Hus, Letters from Constance," in *John Hus at the Council of Constance* (New York and London, Columbia University Press, 1965), pp. 89-298.

Stein, Evžen, ed. and transl., *M. Jan Hus jako universitní rektor a profesor* (Praha, Jan Laichter, 1948).

Svoboda, M., and Flajšhans, V., eds. and transls., *Mistra Jana Husi Sebrané spisy*, 6 vols. (Praha, Jaroslav Bursík and J. R. Vilímek, 1904- n.d.).

Thomson, S. Harrison, ed., *Magistri Johannis Hus, Tractatus de Ecclesia* (Boulder, Colorado, University of Colorado Press, 1956).

Workman, H. B., and Pope, R. M., transls., *The Letters of John Hus* (London, Hodder and Stoughton, 1904).

Žilka, F., ed., *Mistra Jana Husi Vybrané spisy*, 2 vols. (Jilemnice, n.d.).

SELECTED BIBLIOGRAPHY

## PRIMARY WORKS ON CONCILIARISM, HUSSITICA, AND UNITAS FRATRUM

Blahoslav, Jan, *Pochodně zažžená*, ed. by Pavel Váša (Praha, Jan Laichter, 1949).

Breck, Allen duP., *Johannis Wyclyf, Tractatus de Trinitate* (Boulder, Colorado, University of Colorado Press, 1962).

Cameron, James Kerr, "Conciliarism in Theory and Practice, 1378-1418," 2 vols. An unpublished doctoral dissertation at the Hartford Seminary Foundation, Hartford, Conn., 1953. Selections published in Matthew Spinka, ed., *Advocates of Reform*.

Comenius, John A., *De rerum humanarum Emendatione Consultatio catholica*, 2 vols. (Praha, Academia scientiarum Bohemoslovaca, 1966). Contains the seven pansophic works—Panegersia, Panaugia, Pansophia, Pampaedia, Panglottia, Panorthosia, Pannuthesia, and Lexicon reale pansophicum—published for the first time.

Finke, Heinrich, et al., eds., *Acta concilii Constantiensis*, 4 vols. (Münster, Regensburg, 1896-1928).

———, *Forschungen und Quellen zur Geschichte des Konstanzer Konzil* (Paderborn, Schöningh, 1889).

Friedberg, E., ed., *Corpus juris canonici*, 2 vols. (Leipzig, Tauchnitz, 1879). Vol. I comprises Gratian's *Decretum*.

Gerson, John, "De auctoritate concilii," ed. by Z. Rüger, *Revue d'Histoire Ecclesiastique* (Louvain, 1953), pp. 775-95.

Hardt, Hermann van der, ed., *Magni universalis Constantiensis concilii tomi VI* (Frankfurt and Leipzig, Gensius, 1697-1700). Completed by a seventh volume of indices by C. Ch. Bohnstedt (Berlin, Henningius, 1742).

Havránek, B., et al., eds., *Výbor z české literatury husitské doby*, 2 vols. (Praha, Československá akademie věd, 1963-64).

Jakoubek ze Stříbra, *Betlemská kázání z roku 1416* (Praha, Blahoslav, 1951).

Kybal, V., ed., *Matthew of Janov's Regulae veteris et novi testamenti* (Innsbruck, Wagner University Press, 1908-13); Odložilík, O., ed. (Praha, Česká akademie věd a umění, 1926).

Loserth, J., ed., *Stephen Páleč's Replicatio contra Quidamistas, Archiv für Oesterreichische Geschichte* (Wien, 1885), LXXV, pp. 344-61.

———, ed., *Stanislav of Znojmo's Alma et venerabilis* . . . , in *Archiv*, LXXV, pp. 75-127.

Ockham, W., *Dialogus de potestate papae et imperatoris* (Torino, Bottega d'Erasmo, 1959).

Pez, B., ed., *Thesaurus anecdotorum novissimus*, 6 vols. (Augsburg, 1721-29). Contains treatises of Stephen of Dolany, "Medulla triciti, seu Antiwickliffus"; "Antihussus"; "Dialogus volatilis inter Aucam et Passerem adversus Hussum"; and "Liber epistolaris ad Hussitas."

Richental, Ulrich von, *Chronik des Constanzer Conzils*, ed. by Michael R. Buck (Hildesheim, 1962).

Schenk, Rudolf, transl., *M. Matěj z Janova, Výbor z pravidel starého a nového zákona* (Praha, Blahoslav, 1954).

Sikes, J. G., et al., eds., *Guillaume Occami Opera politica*, 3 vols. (Manchester, University of Manchester Press, 1940-56).

Šimek, F., ed., *Postilla Jana Rokycany*, 2 vols. (Praha, Česká akademie věd a umění, 1928-29).

————, *Jakoubek ze Stříbra, Výklad na zjeveni sv. Jana* (Praha, 1933).

————, ed., *Staré letopisy české* (Praha, 1937).

Smetánka, E., ed., *Petra Chelčického Siť víry* (Praha, Melantrich, 1929; reprinted, Orbis, 1950).

Thomson, S. Harrison, ed., *Mag. Johannis Hus, Tractatus responsivus* (Princeton, Princeton University Press, 1927).

Tomáš ze Štítného, *Řeči nedělní a sváteční*, ed. by J. Straka (Praha, Česká akademie věd a umění, 1929).

————, *Knížky o hospodářovi, o hospodini, a o čeledi* (Praha, Špalíček, 1929).

## Secondary Works

Auštetská, B., *Jan Želivský jako politik* (Praha, Husovo museum, 1925).

Bartoš, F.M., *Soupis rukopisů Národního Musea v Praze*, 2 vols. (Praha, 1926-27).

————, *Husitství a cizina* (Praha, Čin, 1931).

————, *Po stopách pozůstalosti M. J. Husi* (Praha, Společnost Husova musea, 1939).

————, *Bojovníci a mučedníci* (Praha, Kalich, 1939).

————, *Do čtyř pražských artikulů* (Praha, Blahoslavova společnost, 1940).

————, *Počátky české bible* (Praha, Kalich, 1941).

————, *Co víme o Husovi nového* (Praha, Pokrok, 1946).

————, *Čechy v době Husově, 1378-1415* (Praha, Jan Laichter, 1947).

————, *Knihy a zápasy* (Praha, Husova ev. fakulta bohoslovecká, 1948).

————, *Literární činnost M. Jana Husi* (Praha, Česká akademie věd a umění, 1948).

————, *Světci a kacíři* (Praha, Husova ev. fakulta bohoslovecká, 1949).

————, *Ze zápasů české reformace* (Praha, Kalich, 1959).

————, *Husitská revoluce I. Doba Žižkova, 1415-26; II. Vláda bratrstev a její pád, 1426-37* (Praha, Československá akademie věd, 1965-66).

————, Articles in *Jihočeský sborník historický* (Tábor). Titles in the footnotes of the book.

————, Articles in *Kostnické Jiskry* (Praha). Titles in the footnotes of the book.

————, Articles in *Křesťanská Revue* (Praha). Titles in the footnotes of the book.

Bartoš, F. M., and Spunar, P., *Soupis pramenů k literární činnosti M. Jana Husa a M. Jeronyma Pražského* (Praha, Historický ústav ČSAV, 1965).

Bílek, Jakub, *Jan Augusta v letech samoty, 1548-64* (Praha, Jan Laichter, 1942).

Boehner, Philotheus, *Collected Articles on Ockham* (Bonaventura, N.Y. The Franciscan Press, 1958).

Borecký, F., *Mistr Jakoubek ze Stříbra* (Praha, Kalich, n.d.).

Brock, Peter, *The Political and Social Doctrines of the Unity of Czech Brethren* ('s-Gravenhage, Mouton & Co., 1957).

Chaucer, Geoffrey, *Canterbury Tales*, transl. by J. U. Nicholson (New York, Garden City Publishing Co., Inc., 1934).

Combes, André, *Jean Gerson, commentateur dionysien* (Paris, 1940).

Delaruelle, E., Labande, E.-R., and Ourliac, P., *L'Eglise au temps du Grand Schisme et de la crise conciliaire, 1378-1449*, 2 vols. (Bloud & Gay, 1962-64).

Dress, Walter, *Die Theologie Gersons* (Gütersloh, 1931).

Flajšhans, V., *M. Io. Hus, Quodlibet 1411* (Praha, 1938).

Franzen, A., and Müller, W., eds., *Das Konzil von Konstanz* (Freiburg, Basel, Wien, Herder, 1964).

Goll, J., *Chelčický a Jednota v XV. století*, ed. by K. Krofta (Praha, Historický klub, 1916).

Hefele, C.-J. and Leclercq, H., eds., *Histoire des conciles*, 10 vols. in 20 (Paris, Letouzey et Ané, 1916), VII/I.

Heimpel H., *Dietrich von Niem* (Münster, Regensberg, 1932).

Heyberger, A., *Jean Amos Comenius (Komenský)* (Paris, Honoré Champion, 1928).

Heymann, Frederick G., "John Rokycana—Church Reformer between Hus and Luther," in *Church History* (1959), pp. 3-37.

————, *John Žižka and the Hussite Revolution* (Princeton, Princeton University Press, 1955).

————, *George of Bohemia, King of Heretics* (Princeton, Princeton University Press, 1965).

————, *Poland and Czechoslovakia* (Englewood Cliffs, N.J., Prentice-Hall, Inc., 1966).

Hrejsa, Ferd., *Česká konfesse, její vznik, podstata a dějiny* (Praha, Česká akademie císaře Františka Josefa, 1912).

————, *Dějiny křesťanství v Československu*, 4 vols. (Praha, Husova ev. fakulta bohoslovecká, 1947-48).

Huizinga, J., *The Waning of the Middle Ages* (London, Edward Arnold & Co., 1924).

Jacob, E. F., *Essays in the Conciliar Epoch*, 3rd ed. (Manchester, University of Manchester Press, 1963).

Jarrett, Bede, *The Emperor Charles IV* (New York, Sheed & Ward, Inc., 1935).

Kaminsky, Howard, et al., eds. and transls., *Master Nicholas of Dresden, The Old Color and the New* (Philadelphia, *Transactions of the American Philosophical Society*, new series, vol. 55, pt. 1, 1965).

————, *A History of the Hussite Revolution* (Berkeley and Los Angeles, University of California Press, 1967).

Kaňák, M., ed., *Hus stále živý* (Praha, Blahoslav, 1965).

Kejř, Jiří, *Husitský právník, M. Jan z Jesenice* (Praha, Československá akademie věd, 1965).

Krofta, K., *Čechy do válek husitských* (Praha, Vesmír, 1930).

————, *Francie a české hnutí náboženské* (Praha, Melantrich, n.d.).

————, *Listy z náboženských dějin českých* (Praha, Historický klub, 1936).

Kropáček, P., *Malířství doby husitské* (Praha, Česká akademie věd a umění, 1946).

Kubíček, A., *Betlemská kaple* (Praha, 1953) .

Kybal, V., *Matěj z Janova, jeho život, spisy a učení* (Praha, Královská česká společnost nauk, 1905) .

————, *M. Jan Hus, Učení*, 3 vols. (Praha, Jan Laichter, 1923-31) . See also under Novotný and Kybal.

Lechler, G., *Johann von Wiclif und die Vorgeschichte der Reformation*, 2 vols. (Leipzig, Friedrich Fleischer, 1873) .

Loomis, Louise R., "The Organization by Nations at Constance," in *Church History* (December 1932) , pp. 191 ff.

————, transl., *The Council of Constance; the Unification of the Church*, ed. by John H. Mundy and Kennerly M. Woody (New York and London, Columbia University Press, 1961) .

McGowan, John T., *Pierre d'Ailly and the Council of Constance* (Washington, Catholic University, 1936) .

McNeill, John T., "The Emergence of Conciliarism," in *Medieval and Historical Essays in Honor of James Westfall Thompson* (Chicago, University of Chicago Press, 1938) , pp. 269 ff.

Meller, B., *Studien zur Erkentnislehre des Peter von Ailly* (Freiburg, 1954) .

Míka, A., *Petr Chelčický* (Praha, Svobodné Slovo, 1963) .

Molnár, Amedeo, *Bratr Lukáš, bohoslovec Jednoty* (Praha, Husova ev. fakulta bohoslovecká, 1948) .

————, *Boleslavští Bratří* (Praha, Komenského ev. fakulta bohoslovecká, 1952) .

————, *Dochovaná kázání Jana Želivského z roku 1419* (Praha, Československá akademie věd, 1953) .

Morrall, John B., *Gerson and the Great Schism* (Manchester, University of Manchester, 1960) .

Nejedlý, Zdeněk, *Dějiny husitského zpěvu*, 2 vols. (Praha, Jubilejní fond král. české společnosti nauk, 1911-13) .

Novák, Arne, *Dějiny českého písemnictví* (Praha, Sfinx, 1946) .

Novák, Jan V., *Jan Amos Komenský, jeho život a spisy* (Praha, Dědictví Komenského, 1932) .

Novotný, V., *Náboženské hnutí české v 14. a 15. století* (Praha, J. Otto, n.d.) .

Novotný, V., and Kybal, V., *M. Jan Hus, život a učení*, 5 vols. (Praha, Jan Laichter, 1919-31) . I deal with the work separately: V. Novotný, *Život a dílo*, 2 vols. (1919-21) ; V. Kybal, *Učení*, 3 vols. (1923-31) .

Novotný, V., and Urbánek, R., *Sborník Blahoslavův, 1523-1923* (Přerov, 1923) .

Oakley, Francis, *The Political Thought of Pierre d'Ailly* (New Haven and London, Yale University Press, 1964) .

O. Odložilík, "Two Reformation Leaders of the Unitas Fratrum," in *Church History* (1940) , pp. 253-63.

————, "The Chapel of Bethlehem in Prague," in *Studien zur ältesten Geschichte Osteuropas* (Graz-Köln, Hermann Böhlaus Nachf., 1956) , I, pp. 125-41.

————, *Jan Milič z Kroměříže* (Kroměříž, Kostnická Jednota, 1924) .

————, *M. Štěpán z Kolína* (Praha, Společnost Husova musea, 1924) .

————, *Wyclif and Bohemia* (Praha, 1937) .

————, *The Caroline University, 1348-1948* (Praha, 1948) .

————, *Jan Hus* (Chicago, Národní Jednota Československých Protestantů, 1953) .

————, *The Hussite King, Bohemia in European Affairs, 1440-1471* (New Brunswick, N.J., Rutgers University Press, 1965) .

Palacký, F., *Dějiny husitské*, 2 vols. (Praha, J. G. Kalve, 1850-51) .

Parker, G. H. W., *The Morning Star, Wycliffe and the Dawn of the Reformation* (Grand Rapids, Mich., Wm. B. Eerdmans Publishing Co., 1965) .

Říčan, R., *Dějiny Jednoty bratrské* (Praha, Kalich, 1957) .

Říčan, R., and Flegl, M., eds., *Husův sborník* (Praha, Komenského ev. fakulta bohoslovecká, 1966) .

Schaff, David S., *John Hus, His Life, Teachings and Death after Five Hundred Years* (New York, Charles Scribner's Sons, 1915) .

Schreiber, Johanna, "Devotio moderna in Böhmen," in *Bohemia; Jahrbuch des Collegium Carolinum*, Band 6 (München, Robert Lerche, 1965) , pp. 93-122.

Sedlák, Jan, *M. Jan Hus* (Praha, Dědictví sv. Prokopa, 1915) .

Seton-Watson, R. W., *A History of the Czechs and Slovaks* (London, Hutchinson & Co., Ltd., 1943) .

Šimek, F., *Jan Rokycana* (Praha, Jan Laichter, 1949) .

Souček, Bohuslav, *Česká apokalypsa v husitství* (Českobratrská církev evangelická, 1967) .

Spinka, Matthew, "Paul Kravař and the Lollard-Hussite Relations," in *Church History* (1956) , pp. 16-26.

————, *John Hus and the Czech Reform* (Chicago, University of Chicago Press, 1941; reprinted, Archon Books, Hamden, Conn., 1966) .

————, transl., *John Amos Comenius, The Labyrinth of the World* (Chicago, The National Union of Czechoslovak Protestants in America, 1942) .

————, *John Amos Comenius, That Incomparable Moravian* (Chicago, University of Chicago Press, 1943; reprinted, New York, Russell & Russell, 1967) .

————, ed. and transl., *John Hus at the Council of Constance* (New York and London, Columbia University Press, 1965) .

————, *John Hus' Concept of the Church* (Princeton, Princeton University Press, 1966) .

Šmahel, F., *Jeroným Pražský* (Praha, Svobodné Slovo, 1966) .

————, *Pražské universitní studentstvo v předrevolučním období 1399-1419* (Praha, Academia, 1967) .

Švehla, J., *Kozí* (Tábor, 1920) .

Sylvius, Aeneas, *Historie česká*, ed. by Jiří Vičar (Praha, J. Otto, n.d.) .

Thompson, James Westfall, and Johnson, Edgar N., *An Introduction to Medieval Europe, 300-1500* (New York, W. W. Norton & Co., Inc., 1937) .

Thomson, S. Harrison, *Czechoslovakia in European History* (Princeton, Princeton University Press, 1943) .

Urbánek, R., *Věk Poděbradský*, 4 vols. (Praha, Jan Laichter [I-III]; and Československá akademie věd [IV], 1915-62) .

Valois, Noel, *La France et le Grand Schisme*, 4 vols. (Paris, Picard, 1900-02) .

Vooght, Paul de, *L'hérésie de Jean Huss* (Louvain, Publications universitaires de Louvain, 1960).

——, *Hussiana* (Louvain, Publications universitaires de Louvain, 1960).

Workman, H. B., *John Wyclif*, 2 vols. (Oxford, Clarendon Press, 1926).

Wylie, L. H., *The Council of Constance and the Death of John Hus* (London, 1900).

Zelinka, T. Č., *Husitskou Prahou* (Praha, Blahoslav, 1955).

# Index

Aachen, 7, 237

Abelard, Peter, 57

*Acta in curia Romana Iohannis a Genzenstein*, 10, 11

advowson, 197

Aelius Donatus, Latin grammarian, 24

Agnes of Zhořelec, princess, 89

Albert of Engelschalk, 35

Albertus Magnus, 41

Albík of Uničov, archbishop of Prague, 130, 134, 140, 167, 172

Albrecht II, duke of Austria, 311, 319

Alexander V, pope, 86, 105, 107-108, 110-11, 113, 183, 219

All Saints College, 39

*Alma et venerabilis . . .* (Stanislav of Znojmo), 181

Ambrose, bishop of Milan, 18

Ambrose of Hradec Králové, 304

*An credi possit in papam* (John of Holešov), 147

Andrew of Brod, 71, 95, 105, 153, 180, 256

Anna of Schweidnitz, wife of Charles IV, 7

Anne, wife of King Richard II, 18

"Anonymous," 180

Anthony, bishop of Concordia, 286

Anthony, duke of Brabant, 89-90

Antichrist, 13-15, 17, 48, 101, 149-50, 163, 165-66, 176, 198-99, 266

*Antihus* (Páleč), 188

*Antihussus* (Stephen of Dolany), 147

anti-reformist party's theological position, 151, 153-54

Apostles' Creed, 189, 198-203

Aquinas, Thomas, 19, 36, 38, 57-58, 65

archbishop, 7, 12, 107, 112-13, 212, 223, 233, 287

Aristotle, "the Philosopher," 29, 32, 38, 41-42, 93, 111

"Armenian sect," the, 189

Arrigoni, Jacob Balardi, bishop of Lodi, 285-86

Athanasian Creed, 189

Augustine, bishop of Hippo, 18, 36, 43, 57, 65, 149, 203, 216, 269

Averroès, philosopher, 111

Avignon, 8, 15

Baltic Sea, 316

Bartoš, F. M., 9, 11, 15, 21, 25, 33, 41, 48, 100, 129, 197, 278, 307

Bavaria, 23, 312

Bayreuth, 311

Benedict XIII, pope, 82, 90, 105, 219, 248

Beran, Josef, cardinal, archbishop of Prague, 278

Bernard, bishop of Città di Castello, 236

Bernard of Clairvaux, 18, 217

Berthold of Wildungen, curial auditor, 130-31, 232, 286

Bethlehem Chapel, 20-21, 34, 39, 48-50, 52-53, 73, 75, 78-79, 100, 111, 154-55, 164-65, 171-72, 194, 283, 298, 303; founding and description of, 47-50, 102, 120; preaching in it prohibited, 107; the king protests the prohibition, 115; ordered destroyed, 162-63

Biberach, 230

Biceps, Nicholas, 35, 58

Bitterfeld, Henry, 36

"Black Rose," 33, 83, 150

Blanice, river, 22

Blaník hill, 67

Boček of Poděbrady, a Utraquist leader, 298, 300

Bohemia, 4-6, 10, 15, 82, 106, 180, 188, 193, 199, 221, 264, 282, 297, 299, 303-304; invaded from Meissen, 61-62; Church of, 61, 118

Bologna, city of, 116, 124, 132-33, 220; university of, 5, 115, 131

Bonaventura, 57-58

331